D1046980

THE CATHOLIC LABYRINTH

ALSO BY PETER MCDONOUGH

Passionate Uncertainty: Inside the American Jesuits
(with Eugene C. Bianchi)

The Cultural Dynamics of Democratization in Spain
(with Samuel H. Barnes and Antonio López Pina)

Men Astutely Trained: A History of the Jesuits in the American Century

Power and Ideology in Brazil

The Politics of Population in Brazil
(with Amaury de Souza)

THE CATHOLIC LABYRINTH

Power, Apathy, and a Passion for Reform in the American Church

Peter McDonough

OXFORD
UNIVERSITY PRESS

Oxford University Press is a department of the University of Oxford.
It furthers the University's objective of excellence in research, scholarship,
and education by publishing worldwide.

Oxford New York
Auckland Cape Town Dar es Salaam Hong Kong Karachi
Kuala Lumpur Madrid Melbourne Mexico City Nairobi
New Delhi Shanghai Taipei Toronto

With offices in
Argentina Austria Brazil Chile Czech Republic France Greece
Guatemala Hungary Italy Japan Poland Portugal Singapore
South Korea Switzerland Thailand Turkey Ukraine Vietnam

Published in the United States of America by
Oxford University Press
198 Madison Avenue, New York, NY 10016

Library of Congress Cataloging-in-Publication Data
McDonough, Peter
The Catholic labyrinth : power, apathy, and a passion for reform in the American church /
Peter McDonough.
pages cm
Includes bibliographical references (pages) and index.
ISBN 978-0-19-975118-1
1. Catholic Church—United States—History—21st century. 2. Church renewal—
Catholic Church—History—21st century. 3. Conservatism—Religious aspects—Catholic Church.
4. Catholic Church—Doctrines. I. Title.
BX1406.3.M35 2013
282.73-dc23
2012042894

9 8 7 6 5 4 3 2 1
Printed in the United States of America
on acid-free paper

For Josefina

If the long passage of time gives authority to religious rites, we must keep faith with so many centuries and follow our fathers, who followed their fathers and consequently prospered. Let us imagine that Rome herself is standing here now and addressing these words to you: "Best of emperors... respect the number of years that the dutiful performance of religious rites has brought to me. Let me enjoy the ancient ceremonies, for I do not regret them... Have I been preserved only to be criticized in my old age? I will consider the changes that people think must be instituted, but correction in old age is insulting and too late."

—From a petition by Symmachus, prefect of Rome, to the Emperor Valentinian II in 384 CE asking him to restore a pagan altar, quoted by Valerie M. Warrior, *Roman Religion* (Cambridge: Cambridge University Press, 2006), 128–9.

CONTENTS

ACKNOWLEDGMENTS

Many years ago, when I was in training for the Peace Corps, a psychologist periodically distributed questionnaires for us to fill out. One item read "Do you consider yourself to be a special messenger of God?" After the question had appeared a fourth or fifth time in successive tests, one of my colleagues at last stood up and exclaimed "All right! All right! I admit it. I am a special messenger of God!"

Analysts of religion, however, probably owe more to the help of friends and colleagues than divine inspiration. At Oxford University Press, Cynthia Read, an accomplished Latinist and fisherwoman, guided me toward a completed manuscript. Her skills flowed seamlessly into the editorial craft. Lisbeth Redfield and Sasha Grossman also furnished expert counsel. Patrick Ciano designed the book jacket, bringing it to life out of an iPhoto picture taken during my meanderings in Los Angeles. Michael Durnin provided pitch-perfect copyediting. Abidha Sulaiman and her team at Newgen Knowledge Works in Chennai, India, managed the production of the book with grace and dispatch.

I am grateful to three readers for Oxford—Chris Achen, Mary Jo Bane, and Michelle Dillon—for urging me to keep the contours of the narrative in sight while tracking the ins-and-outs of political advocacy, doctrinal jockeying, and institutional reform in American Catholicism. Peter Dougherty and Fred Appel prodded me to get on with the project in its exploratory stage. Tom McDonough, Don Dewey, Sally Crabb, Alice Lewis, Bill McGovern, Alan Greenberg, and Paul Cohen made suggestions on parts of earlier drafts. Ed Keane gave a thorough reading to the entirety of the manuscript. Lee Silver reintroduced me to the mystery lessons of Latin American fiction that stuck through the composition of the book. Jason Berry sent a list of criticisms and interpretative pointers that stimulated me to improve questionable passages. John DiIulio and the late James Q. Wilson provided feedback on Chapters Three, Four, and Five. All of them should be absolved from any errors of fact in the following pages.

The libraries of Arizona State University and the University of Southern California made it easy for me to access indispensable material. Special thanks go to the scores of people who responded to my questions during the fieldwork, for their generosity in bearing with my inquiries and their patience during the long gestation of writing and revision. I like to think that the book took a decade to complete not only because of my dilatory habits but also because ten years is probably the minimum required to track significant change as it unfolds within Catholicism.

The fieldwork persuaded me of two things that academics do well to keep in mind. First, "respondents," "informants," and "interviewees" are generally shrewder and more insightful than we are. Second, under authoritarian conditions, bravery abounds in strange places.

Catholics of a certain age grow up but never grow out of Catholicism. The debt is always there. "Use your head, Mr. McDonough," Sister Euphemia said, "Don't be such a spineless jellyfish." WAP!

"B-but Sister, 'spineless jellyfish' is a tautology."

"Don't *but* me, young man! Tautology?? What kind of language is that? You're bold as brass!!" WAP! WAP!

My greatest debt is to my wife Josefina and our daughters, Graça and Julia. Husbands are basically makeover projects. "Is that &#X% book finished yet?" It is to Josefina that this book is dedicated, with all my love: *mens protestans in corpore latino*.

Glendale, California
New Year's, 2013

PROLOGUE

A thumbnail sketch of what shapes change and resistance to change in American Catholicism might start with demography, especially with the growth in the Hispanic population, and money, how much of it tends to be concentrated among small numbers of large donors. These elements form a center of gravity, tugging change in the church toward cautious outcomes. They are forces that the church cannot afford to ignore, and they impel changes in services and administration that the church can accept, without endangering doctrinal purity. A third set of actors, various dissenting or advocacy groups, usually plays a minor role in advancing change.

Another force—apathy among Catholics themselves—looks even weaker. Its effect, however, may be greater than that of the first three combined. Partly this is because the power imputed to the concentration of economic resources in Catholicism can be exaggerated. It is true that a handful of benefactors in the United States contribute disproportionately to the Vatican, and that these donors carry weight. The Knights of Columbus, the world's largest Catholic fraternal group, has bankrolled traditionalist causes at a prodigious clip.[1] Yet organizational giving in the American church is spread across relatively small, local, family foundations whose missions can scarcely be thought of as coordinated; their aggregate influence does not reflect a master plan. The absence of conspiracy does not prevent small-time interests from wreaking havoc on progressive sectors of the church, as they do when they denounce liberal candidates for bishoprics and heads of seminaries and universities. But their actions are hard to document, and confusion among them is not uncommon. In positive terms, the conservative portfolio is diversified.[2]

The larger point, however, is that the conservatism of American Catholicism stems as much from a paradox in the culture of the church as from immigration or the machinations of economic potentates. American Catholic opinion favors the liberalization of many features of orthodoxy: the rules governing ordination to the priesthood, regulations about sexual behavior and gender roles, and so on. These attitudes track the upward shift in women's education and employment outside the home and allied transformations in family structure.[3] Yet mass preferences don't count for much, and in any case individual Catholics who disagree with the church's prohibition of "artificial" contraception, for example, don't have to apply collective pressure in order to do as they please.

It would be a mistake, however, to blame the lackadaisical state of dissent among Catholics solely on that perennial culprit, American individualism.[4] The trait is not confined to Catholics, and yet non-Catholics are generally more involved in their congregations and synagogues. Habituation to hierarchy within the church reinforces a culture of individualism all its own. "People who wanted to help their church at a time of crisis were rejected, and the vast majority of clergy and laity sat on their hands," the historian David O'Brien contends, capturing the peculiar mix of exclusion and indifference.[5]

Habits of deference give a wavery tone to dissent, in contrast to the energy required for collective initiatives. This is a plausible adaptation to the near futility—the high cost and low efficacy—of protest and the more assertive types of reform in Catholicism, compared to going one's way and getting on with less divisive business like education and the work of social justice in the church's outreach operations. The upshot looks like a balance of impotence between bishops who exercise scant influence over members who, when they think about it at all, feel they have no voice in church affairs. "We have met the enemy," Pogo said, "and he is us." Apathy is a big if decidedly unsensational part of the story.[6]

But the Great Dearth is far from the whole story. Imagine a contrast—simplified yet serviceable—between American Catholicism before and after Vatican II. Prior to that watershed Council, held from 1962 through 1965, a system of fairly uniform beliefs and relatively decentralized administration prevailed within the church. Most Catholics lived in an enclave culture that offered few options other than submission to the moral authority of the clergy. The community ambience was meticulously curated. On the institutional side, bishops ran their own shows within their separate dioceses.

Then, beginning in the sixties, the cultural homogeneity and organizational autonomy of American Catholicism underwent a sea-change. The sexual revolution opened up choices for men and especially women. At about the same time, the dominance of the bishops over the operations of the church started to slip with the growth of professional criteria in educational and health services. These standards, universal in scope, were designed to supersede local variations.

American Catholicism is not a unitary institution. "The church" is shorthand for a medley of beliefs, devotional practices, and ministries that coexist in doubtful syncopation. The arrangement is plainly unlike the system T. S. Eliot feared, one so perfect that nobody would have to be good. It is not quite a hierarchy of pharaonic regimentation. The outward formalism of Catholicism both expresses and obscures a chambered complexity. The precise expressionism of Alfred Hitchcock, a student of the Jesuits, gets this right.

The current ensemble is more the result of a multitude of individual decisions and pell-mell adaptations than it is of collective demand and purposeful change. Cultural liberation has gone on apace, regardless of both the official proscriptions of the church and organized pressure from Catholics themselves. Similarly, the modernization—critics would say, incipient secularization—of many of the ministries affiliated with the church reflects ad hoc policies driven by financial need more than a grand design, and it has developed apart from the cultural revolution with which it happens to coincide.

Decades of desultory change have culminated in an odd combination of apathy among large sectors of the laity toward the sexual program of the church and anxiety among ecclesiastical leaders about the erosion of their authority over the tangible services—the good works—of American Catholicism. Personal liberation has proceeded along with concern about a loss of institutional control. By the same token, habits of local autonomy, though weakened, persist in the dioceses, and efforts at reform run afoul of turf wars at least as often as they are defeated on ideological grounds.

It is this disjointed cultural and institutional landscape, and the conflicts it engenders, that is the subject of *The Catholic Labyrinth*. The labyrinth is part phantasm, part fact. One is intertwined with the other.

THE CATHOLIC LABYRINTH

INTRODUCTION

The effect differs from the idea of "transcendence" in that it does not preclude psychological credibility and… may coexist with a certain cynicism.[1]

The argument of this book is not that Catholicism changes, the little secret that Garry Wills publicized decades ago.[2] Instead the story concerns how the church changes and by how much, and the direction of change as well. The point of departure is the recognition that Catholicism shifts and stretches along three loosely coupled axes. By way of a first cut, call one facet of the transition cultural, another political, another economic.

Since the 1960s the most familiar change in the church has involved liberation from pointless, often dysfunctional rules and protocols. Reform in this area has been circumscribed and subject to retrenchment. Limbo is gone, as are meatless Fridays. But indulgences from the pains of purgatory are back. So is Latin, here and there. Sexual and reproductive proscriptions have been reaffirmed. Gender apartheid continues to rule the priesthood. Hierarchy, like sexual correctness, is an article of faith. These are markers of Catholic culture. They form the citadel of corporate identity.

A second type of change entails innovations in representation and leadership. This touches on politics as the development of governance structures and mechanisms of accountability that revise though seldom repeal inherited ways of running things. Experiments in lay-clergy collaboration are prominent toward the lower and middle rungs of the system. Parish councils, largely appointive, typify such consultative arrangements. Feistier movements—Voice of the Faithful, an ensemble of liberal Catholics is one—are almost never allowed to meet on church property, and sometimes they run up against difficulties in putting their houses in order.

A third change shades into problem solving and institution building of an ostensibly less political sort. Revenues and performance are the bottom lines. Many church-related activities aim at improving the delivery of services that are already in place, some with impressive records of achievement. Agencies like Catholic Charities and Catholic Relief Services can be included here. Some initiatives are geared to salvaging worthy operations from insolvency. Parochial schools are the prime example. While vision statements remain perennially indispensable, the ground game consists of bargaining over programs, budgets, and human resources. The format is more in the nature of let's-roll-up-our-sleeves committees bent on executing the practical business of the church than debating societies.

Such operations add up nationally. "Discrimination against the Catholic minority and strong leadership from Rome," *The Economist* reports, "encouraged Catholics to create a sort of parallel society in the 19th and 20th centuries, with the result there are now 6,800 Catholic schools (5% of the national total), 630 Catholic hospitals (11%) plus a similar number of smaller health facilities, and 244 colleges and universities... Annual spending by the church and entities owned by the church was around $170 billion in 2010... Catholic institutions employ over one million people... For purposes of secular comparison, in 2010 General Electric's revenue was $150 billion and Walmart employed roughly two million people."[3]

American Catholicism, then, is as much an economic force with political reach as it is an arbiter of sexual morality. Concern with forms of governance inside the church—more or less hierarchical, more or less participatory—is hard to keep up when the difference that such distinctions make to getting things done is unclear and when the wishes of ordinary Catholics about certain personal rights (birth control is the outstanding example) have been tacitly conceded. The command structure is less of an issue than the business model. The bromide that the good works of the church provide challenges, not problems, is partially true. Many operate at some remove from the devotional practices of parish life in which clergy are directly involved. They channel energies toward making-a-difference causes that are achievable in the lifetime of participants. They promote good will. They share in "the corporal works of mercy" familiar to Catholic tradition. The feel-good bonus is appreciable. So is the win-win atmosphere. Such vitality is harder to find elsewhere in Catholicism.

There is a snag, however. While the ministries of the church in education, social services, and health care enjoy widespread approval, the outreach network has come to rely in many instances on public sources of funding. This complicated story reflects a multitude of changes—the drying-up of religious vocations, the professionalization of the ministries, the need to finance increasingly costly operations, among others. The transformation has been traumatic for Catholic elementary and high schools. By and large, unlike the universities and health care facilities, these schools do not fall within legal guidelines for federal and state funding. Efforts to remedy the financial crisis of the schools are a prominent feature of a growing friction over issues involving the separation of church and state and restrictions on government support for religious activities. Clerical and civil jurisdictions once thought to be walled off from one another enter into competition. "Though they enrolled 5.2 million students at the height of the baby boom," Sean Kennedy writes, "Catholic schools in the United States... today have just under 2 million students. This year [2012] marks a particularly striking milestone: the first time that charter schools, nationwide, will enroll more students than Catholic schools."[4]

To say that a lot of what goes on in Catholicism involves sex, power, and money sounds blunt but it is also opaque. When I examine strategies of reform, I will use slightly different language, recasting them in ascending order of difficulty as behavioral, institutional, and cultural features of change. Changing how clerics behave and improving outreach activities is arduous but not impossible. This touches on organizational efficiency, on *performance*. Reconfiguring the governance of the church and the celibate male priesthood at the heart of the institution is a steeper climb; fixing the power structure concerns *fairness*. And reimagining the cultural inner sanctum of the church—beliefs about sexuality, in particular—is a very long shot indeed. It poses an existential threat, one that can counterpose corporate *identity* against personal integrity or conscience.

The continuum escalates from behavior modification to institutional reform to regime change. Efficiency, equity, and identity—these are the touchstones of the struggle for change in Catholicism. It is when two or more of these dimensions are perceived to overlap that the struggle turns truly explosive.

The next two chapters lay out the conceptual roadmap. But there is nothing to keep you from skipping to Chapter Three, where the narrative really begins. Here is a mini-guide to the way ahead. Think of it as you would one of those diagrammatic renderings of the New York subway system. It will get you where you need to go.

For starters, two things impede reform in Catholicism. The plainest obstacle is the opposition of conservative groups—in particular, the appeal of their ideas—to which Chapters Three, Four, and Five are devoted. Another is the passivity of many Catholics-in-the-pews, covered in Chapters Six and Seven. The first strategy involves some raw power. It plays, even more, to popular revulsion at the intemperate '60s.

As for apathy toward reform and the atrophy of associational life in the church, quiet concessions (regarding birth control, most notably) have reinforced an acquiescence among Catholics regarding customs most of them no longer support—the celibacy requirement for the priesthood, for example—but which they feel little incentive to strenuously oppose. Myopia and looking the other way, not to mention enchantment with the hieratic and a longstanding culture of deference, have their uses. American Catholics are not seething with discontent. A set of sketchily diagnosed subclinical disorders, barely distinguishable from apathy or a culture of passivity, appears to be the realistic preliminary assessment. Yawning, like snickering, is impolite and possibly worrisome. But neither has been known to bring down empires.

Two further considerations shape the pace and extent of reform. The ministries, the governance structure, and the sexual teachings of the church exist in some tension. The intricate connections across these semi-insulated domains are mirrored in a division of labor among reformers, who specialize in targeting—albeit with some overlap—behavior, or institutions, or beliefs, and who mount challenges with increasing difficulty as the gradient climbs from actions to organizational renewal to dogma.

Change in one area need not cascade into another. A cartoon that appeared in the 1950s in *Punch*, the now-defunct English periodical, captures some of this mix of lethargy and volatility. A lord is reading *The Times* at a breakfast table set in a cavernous manor house on the family estate. The lady of the manor is sipping tea. "My word!" his lordship, faintly astonished, exclaims, "It says here that the east wing burned down last night!" Catholicism is so big that a disaster here or a crisis there may have only sluggish reverberations elsewhere.

In addition, many American Catholics seem as divided within themselves as they are against one another. The "spiritual but not religious" bloc is sizable, though maybe not a majority. These Catholics probably bolster more than they subvert the resilience of the church. Some are conscience-stricken, others seek their comfort zone. In either case they tend to eschew organized protest. The shadow church makes for customized adaptation. The grumbling has yet to become a formula for collective action.

What causes the church in the United States to move? *Ideas, organizations,* and *personalities* strive for influence in Catholicism. These are my central concerns. They are closer to concrete mechanisms and determined agents than megatrends—Hispanicization, lifestyle shifts, et cetera.[5] Important as they are, such macrofactors smack of change that has everything except courage and purpose; people are simply swept along.

The classification shapes a three-act partitioning of the story. Part Two and most of Part Three focus on *ideas*. Part Four attends to the various advocacy *organizations,* in Chapters Eight through Eleven. (The sequencing of chapters can also be visualized from a slightly different angle, corresponding to the subtitle of the book: Part Two covers "power," Part Three "apathy," and the rest "reform.") Part Five (Chapters Twelve and Thirteen) shifts to the *personalities* behind the ideas and organizations.

As we move from ideas to organizations to personalities, the narrative becomes less schematic. Ideas may be complex and controversial but they are out in the open and relatively transparent. Yet while ideas have a life of their own, it is through organizations and individuals that their consequences unfold. The hitch is that the workings of organizations are clouded in a system like Catholicism that discourages their formation. Individuals and their connections take on importance in a bleak organizational landscape. Actors become "personalities" because of their skill at working behind the scenes.

What is the overall picture? Catholicism in the United States used to imagine itself as a practically self-contained community. This was the insular religion of ethnic enclaves, "the coherent world enveloping Catholic immigrants in the nineteenth and early twentieth century, created by an interlocking and mutually supporting set of church-related institutions, practices, and family life."[6] With assimilation, the Great Chain of Being reaching from family circle to social milieu to all-embracing church came undone.

The rapid erosion of traditional American Catholicism has followed a sequence of thresholds: (a) acceptance of the de facto separation of church and state proclaimed at Vatican II; (b) attenuation of the link between ecclesial authority and ministerial operations, specifically in health care and higher education, that began in the late sixties; and (c) a break in the bond between sexual comportment, gender roles, and church protocols, also initiated in the sixties. The institution no longer has a capacity for or seriously aspires to domination by force, though elbows remain sharp, and clerical control over its material outreach operations has shrunk. This leaves the defense of the church's cultural rationale—the buttressing of moral hegemony, specifically its sexual teachings, sometimes in alliance with outside sympathizers—as a firewall against the dissolution of corporate identity.[7]

So, Catholics are not just at war with one another and within themselves. The church itself faces a secular environment where it feels set upon from all sides. It is the sense of encirclement by externally imposed strictures—the depletion of influence over politics, service operations, and sexual behavior—that helps account for the bishops' tough stance regarding a regulatory context touching on the provision of contraceptives, the ministerial exemption from labor laws on hiring and firing, and the like. The idea is to take back contested ground. Without an institutional presence under the aegis of the hierarchy, the moral stature of the church is thought to be in danger of turning into a ghostly memory; the church is the institutional cornerstone of the good.[8]

Simply put, change in American Catholicism ranges across internal and external zones. At one end is a set of mostly in-house matters concerning the supervision of sexuality and its links with clerical authority. The other extends to the "parallel society" of schools, hospitals, and social services that exist in convoluted legal and financial symbiosis with the larger community. (The big qualifier to any neat dichotomy between the two zones is the abortion controversy.) Conflicts arising from the first cluster of issues are bound up with how the church defines and defends its corporate identity. Tensions surrounding the second group of controversies are murkier but increasingly hard to manage. American Catholicism's infrastructure of ministries has come to depend in varying degrees on outside, often public sources of funding, and this tangled partnership sometimes runs up against strictures built into the political culture of the United States. The relationship between the outreach organizations of the church and American society can be equivocal.[9]

The problem gives rise to a curious symmetry. Rules governing the separation of church and state tend to be as sacrosanct to Americanism, and therefore as difficult to change, as iconic beliefs about priestly celibacy and gender roles are in Catholicism. Principles as well as the power of concrete interests are at stake. People bring up "sacred responsibilities," testily. Paralysis takes hold on both fronts.[10]

The issues, then, span a spectrum. Battles over sexuality and authority make up the proverbial Catholic cluster. These are the staples of frustrated reform in the church, and they are mostly about *fairness*. A second set of issues has to do with improving the management of ministries and diocesan and parish-based services generally. They are about *efficiency* and performance. They tend to be thought of as administrative problems to be handled quietly off-stage.

This view can be less than realistic when significant amounts of money and other resources enter into play. Meat-and-potato matters can also become politicized for other reasons, mutating into a third set of controversies that combine issues of sexual morality and organizational sovereignty. Compared to the first two areas, they have more to do with the external relations of the church than with internal reform. But the dimensions of conflict can overlap and when this happens, seemingly prosaic disputes boil over into battles over institutional *identity*.

The counteroffensive mounted by the bishops against government regulation of the provision of contraceptives in church-affiliated ministries is a good example of polarization on issues assumed to be settled. All of a sudden, it seems, such things have become a bridge too far, a leash too long. The strategy of the bishops has been to frame the campaign as a debate over organizational autonomy or corporate sovereignty more than as a battle about sexual morality and labor policy. This is a dicey gray area where it is extraordinarily difficult to keep existential and business issues apart.[11] As much as the bishops want to assert their corporate power, the ministries find themselves in need of outside funding, public and private. The fusion of threatened privilege, principles in collision, and material constraints heightens the political drama.

Why should we care about any of this? What does it tell us that the tedium of someone else's home movies does not? The Catholic thing is of interest in its own right; it is more than just a MacGuffin for Deeper Thoughts. Yet much is at stake not only for Catholics—in round numbers, Catholics made up 2 percent of the population of the United States in 1800, 13 percent in 1900, and 25 percent in 2010—but for citizens attentive to cultural rupture, continuity, and institutional creativity as well. The trade-offs between efficiency, equity, and identity reach beyond church walls.

Why did I write this book? Because it wasn't there. Books get written for other reasons than to fill an informational vacuum. But the response contains a kernel of truth. At a Georgetown conference on the church a few decades ago, Bryan Hehir commented on a paper I had given, expressing interest in the presentation but wanting to know where the treatment of politics was. Here I have tried to take his suggestion to heart, without neglecting the borderlands of Catholicism that verge on but rarely reach explicitly public expression. A lot of the tension in the church dwells in that hum of implication, almost but not quite beyond hearing.[12]

Rules of thumb lie somewhere between seat-of-the-pants hunches and crisply formulated hypotheses. Five such thoughts underlie the following pages.

First, the efforts of advocacy groups in and around the church are prone to falter. This surmise sets collective action on the part of reformers in realistic perspective, yet it also manages to be both diffuse and deterministic. You can see the institutions crumbling, and pick up the quaking of archetypes, and still understand that the lesions open up opportunities for organizational entrepreneurs. Creative destruction may not be impossible in Catholicism.

On balance, however, the prospects for reform are modest, more like the slow boring of hard boards than the advent of a convulsive transformation. A weirder simile may be just as apropos. The institutional church is a lot like the concrete canoe familiar to students of civil engineering, rich in lessons about durability and flotation. Though not ungraceful, the contrivance is less germane to understanding velocity.

Second, Vatican II was a promulgated revolution. That style of reform, well within the Catholic hierarchical tradition, helps account for the ease with which the emancipatory intentions of the Council have been derailed. The dominant popular response to disappointment with institutional stodginess has been exodus, and the result a kind of restless spectacle, rather than commitment or protest.

Third, however dire the predicament of the church may be, immobilism reflects a fear that commonsensical reforms could be counterproductive, placing the Catholic brand in jeopardy. Hygienic modernism may not be the antidote for obsolescence. Tampering with tradition could make matters worse. "It is the sort of thing," one Jesuit wag quipped, "that gives prudence a bad name." Just as celebrities are people famous for being famous, the venerability of Catholicism gets conflated with being old and staying the same. The fallacy is to reduce the defense of tradition to risk-aversion or an ethic of subservience and wild sacrifice.

Fourth, by the same token, clinging to power in the name of adherence to principle, as if the world would collapse were concessions made, can backfire. Change in Catholicism may be precipitated more by miscalculation from above than mobilization from below.

Finally, *The Catholic Labyrinth* is a long and (judging by the ultra-exfoliated endnotes) suitably winding essay in causal analysis. The purpose is neither to defend nor to indict the church. "Power" and "apathy" take up two-thirds of the subtitle to signal that "a passion for reform" constitutes just one among several positions in American Catholicism—and not an especially homogeneous one at that. My question is why the different strategies emerged in the first place and, second, how they condition the future of the church.

It is easier to focus on one facet—the simultaneous ineptness and arrogance of parts of the hierarchy or the mobilization and varieties of dissent—than to take in the picture whole. In particular, denial about denial is a seductive way of ignoring the casualness with which many Catholics have reacted to the scandals associated with the church. This view relegates indifference to the realm of the unimportant.

But apathy, precisely because it is so extensive, needs to be appreciated in its own right. Otherwise, we miss the point, as if we were to set aside the pauses and silences in a play by Harold Pinter. It is as difficult to overestimate the importance of apathy, of spectacle and spectatorship, in church politics as it is dangerous to underestimate the resources for survival at the disposal of the status quo. Watching the shadows cast by the powerful can be as revealing of their influence as shining a spotlight. Think of the photographs that Weegee made of the crimes and calamities of New York for the city's tabloids during the 1940s and '50s. His attention was on the bystanders and police as often as it was on the evidence of the deed itself. They were the happening.[13]

At a party I attended in Ann Arbor back in the sixties, an episode took place that stuck in my memory. A guest scholar let it be known that she was Catholic. This revelation touched off a tsunami of sympathy among her hosts and colleagues, some of whom were Catholics themselves. "An accomplished woman. In the church. These days. Amazing!" The woman lowered her head, as if she were being observed through the wrong end of a telescope. She screwed her eyes tight in mock defiance and whispered furiously, "Leave me with my oppression, for God's sake!"

In what follows I hope that hints of this ambiguous struggle will emerge. Without it, the humanity of the actors would be lost. "For the drama to deepen," it's been said, "we must see the loneliness of the monster and the cunning of the innocent."[14] It is no small trick to discover the pattern in the carpet, to decipher the rules of the game. Such things are nonobvious in Catholicism. To do this without trivializing the characters as stick figures comes close to the miraculous.

PART ONE

CHAPTER ONE

THE MATRIX OF AMERICAN CATHOLICISM

At 4:30 on the afternoon of December 2, 2006, Thomas E. Golden Jr. stepped to the front of the lecture hall of the Catholic center at Yale, where over 300 guests were assembled for the dedication of the new building. A graduate of the engineering school, class of '51, Golden had donated more than $20 million to the construction. The student center, adjacent to the Saint Thomas More chapel that had been built over half a century earlier, was named after him.[1]

"Now is not the time," Golden began, "to memorialize an old man who has tried in vain to overcome his frailties." He cited the motto of Yale—*lux et veritas*—and he recalled a visit he had made to Rome a few years back, when he had seen inscribed on one of the churches *lux et veritas et historia*—"light and truth and history [or tradition]." Golden talked for another minute or so about "the inexorable bond between faith and reason" and then, because this was Yale and solemn proclamation needed to be salted with drollery, concluded with "Boola boola *vobiscum*!"

More than three years earlier, in March 2003, the Saint Thomas More chapel and the Catholic center at Yale had hosted a conference on "a crisis of a size and scope unprecedented in the American church: The revelations of sexual abuse by priests and the hierarchy's complicity." Some of the organizers of that conference were in attendance now, together with numerous benefactors and well-wishers from other colleges and universities with large numbers of Catholic students.[2]

The afternoon before, to start the festivities, Cathleen Kaveny from the law faculty at Notre Dame had given the annual More House lecture. Her topic was prophecy and casuistry. She contrasted people who declaim as prophets, or true believers, with casuists who take a more dispassionate view of issues like abortion and torture, and she rehearsed the obstacles these styles of discourse pose for civil conversation. The More House series had been launched in 1962 by John Courtney Murray, a Jesuit theologian who was spending a sabbatical in New Haven after being silenced by the Vatican for his then-controversial advocacy of religious tolerance and political pluralism. Now a woman was delivering the talk.[3]

Other women had prominent roles at Yale's Catholic center. One was assistant chaplain. Another was executive director of the chapel. A third, Kerry Alys Robinson, was the director of development, the center's fundraiser-in-chief, and for several months she had been commuting to Washington, where she moonlighted as executive director of the National Leadership Roundtable on Church Management. The Roundtable had been put together in the wake of the sexual abuse scandals as a consortium of about 200 benefactors, bishops, and directors of Catholic ministry associations dedicated to speeding up accountability and the adoption of modern management practices in the church. The ceremonies at Yale coincided with her fortieth birthday and as soon as they were over, Robinson, a mother of two, would assume her job full time.

This is a book about change in American Catholicism in the way that a cubist painting of a guitar is about a guitar. It portrays multiple visions of the church as much as it does the thing itself. There is no reason why the viewpoints should converge on a presiding truth. Still, it is fair to ask what forces underlie the patchwork of changes and push-backs that make up Catholicism in the United States. Since the 1960s the church has undergone at least three upheavals besides the sexual abuse crisis, plus a fourth, less conspicuous change.

First, Vatican II ratified the separation of church and state not merely as a fait accompli but also, with reservations, as an ideal. The turn to religious liberty, freedom of conscience, and political tolerance came as a breakthrough for a church that had long cozied up to dictatorships and flirted with theocratic ambitions.[4] The council marked a watershed in a series of victories for human rights, beginning in modern times with the Atlantic Charter of 1941 and running through the United Nations' Declaration of Human Rights and the decolonization movements of the forties and fifties.[5]

The accomplishments of the council coincided with another sign of the times: an erosion of denominational partitions and sectarian animosities as indelible markers of religious attachment. This development would play out alongside a broadly ecumenical alarm that moral boundaries generally were under assault. But for the moment, optimism reigned.[6]

Second, at around the time Vatican II was finishing its work, Catholics began to experience a distancing of real-life sexual norms and behavior from religious prescriptions. The change swept over traditional ideas about reproductive rights, the role of women, and sexual identity. Catechetical propriety and the conservative habits of ethnic, morally claustral enclaves receded in the face of women's education, the cultural revolution, and the pill.

The timing of the Council and the Supreme Court's decision legalizing the sale of oral contraceptives in 1965 were preternaturally close. Three years after Vatican II completed its work, Pius VI issued *Humanae Vitae*, the decree forbidding artificial birth control. Most American Catholics ignored the encyclical or rejected it outright. The pope never issued another.[7] "When millions of parishioners saw the Church abandoning the Latin Mass and meatless Fridays, but clinging to the contraceptive ban," David Courtwright wrote, "they launched a silent Reformation, remaining Catholics on their own terms."[8]

The onset of a third change can be dated rather precisely too. In October 1965, just two months before the close of the council in Rome, Lyndon Johnson signed the Hart-Cellar Act, opening the United States to vast numbers of immigrants from Asia and Latin America. The legislation altered the American scene as much as celebrated programs of the Great Society like Medicare. Among other things, it reinforced the standing of Catholicism as the largest and ethnically most diverse religion on the continent. White enclaves and their shrunken inner-city parishes became tokens of times gone by. Immigration from outside Europe became the lifeblood of the church in the United States. The popular base of the American church was globalized from within.[9]

Fourth, a massive change got underway in the administration of church-related activities. Largely because of the decline in the number of priests and nuns that accelerated toward the end of the sixties and their replacement by lay people, the outreach ministries of American Catholicism underwent a separation from strict episcopal control. The loosening of clerical dominion has been extensive in higher education and health care, and it is roughly commensurate with the influx of lay personnel to take over positions in teaching, administration, and other services that priests and women religious used to fill.[10]

Bishops can no longer run their dioceses quite so autocratically, like ward bosses, with a frown or a wave of the hand. The classic model of Catholicism that combined uniform doctrine and decentralized administration shows signs of being reversed. Catholics feel freer to pick and choose among moral injunctions—what used to be called "the commandments."[11] At the same time, professionalization, financial accountability, and legal liability have begun to homogenize once-informal modes of delivering services. Here and there parish life has lost some of its mom-and-pop-store flavor, and priestly impunity has begun to crumble.[12]

So, while bishops continue to be hand picked from the top, from Rome, financial pressures that favor administrative regularity and accountability for dioceses and parishes are mounting. This is particularly true for the church's economically strapped network of parochial schools. Simultaneously, fewer Catholics feel obliged to go along with the doctrinal ordinances emanating from Rome or to submit to the reprobation once woven into the social pressure of ethnic ghettoes. Normative restraints have slackened; so has clerical control over some of the institutional operations identified with the church. The professionalization and funding constraints that drove Catholic hospitals and higher education to reform decades ago have been mounting on the parochial schools and many of the parishes themselves.[13]

The result, however, is more like a riptide than a one-way change of course. None of the shifts just listed—an after-the-fact acceptance of the separation of church and state, the loosening of sexual mores (in effect, a near separation of church and sex), the demographic replenishment of American Catholicism from non-European sources, and the growing presence of lay people in its institutional apparatus (a quasi-separation of church, in the traditional sense, and ministries)—can be undone. But the components of the grand transformation don't march in lockstep.

History may be on the side of the separation of church and state and may favor the relaxation of old-time sexual values, and the same may be said for the population and employment shifts that are reshaping American Catholicism.

But it is doubtful whether the latter changes lean as unabashedly to the left as the first two. The new minorities are known more for devotion than dissent, and most lay "workers in the vineyard" are recruited with reliably orthodox credentials. The trends pull at off-angles to one another, like countervailing forces, and the larger dynamic has a strong dose of indeterminacy. The writing on the wall is erratic and blurry.

As the inauguration of the Catholic center in New Haven was getting underway in December of 2006, Roger Mahony, Cardinal of Los Angeles, announced that his archdiocese would pay out $60 million to settle forty-five cases of sexual abuse by priests. About 500 other cases were pending. "There will be more pain," the cardinal told the *Los Angeles Times*. "We will be looking at some lessening of our ministries and services."[14]

The next month, at nine o'clock on Sunday morning, January 7, about a dozen members and sympathizers of SNAP (Survivors Network of those Abused by Priests) assembled on the sidewalk outside Our Lady of the Angels cathedral in downtown Los Angeles. SNAP was organizing vigils in dozens of cities, and Barbara Blaine, a former Catholic Worker, now in her mid-forties and the founder of SNAP, had flown in from Tucson. "We had a vigil there last night in front of a beautiful church," Blaine said, "where they still had all the Christmas decorations with the spotlights on the façade. Our candles made a great visual."

Off on his own, about 20 yards away, toward the corner of Temple and Hill Streets, a thin, almost wraith-like elderly protestor paced back and forth with a "PHONY MAHONY" placard that listed demands in a minuscule handwritten script. He wore a Virgin of Medjugorje T-shirt, and he had taken up his position on the sidewalk with his placard every Sunday for as long as anyone could remember.

The television reporters and cameramen concentrated on Barbara Blaine. A correspondent asked what should be done to prevent abuse. "We are reminded by Elie Wiesel," Blaine said, "that evil that is not remembered repeats itself." One of the spectators demanded that Blaine spell out what should be done. "This abuse has been going on for two millennia," she said.

"That's an attack against the church!" the man shouted, insisting that Blaine was evading the question.

"We are not your enemy," Blaine said, "we are here to talk to the news media." A while later, two smiling gents, one in a Vietnam Marine veteran's cap, had their picture taken with the SNAP vigil keepers, each of whom held a white candle.

This book examines how various groups, made up mostly of lay people, of diverse ideological persuasions and with very uneven resources, have struggled to secure their interests and in some cases tried to reshape the course of American Catholicism. Two of them, the Leadership Roundtable and SNAP, have already been introduced. The actions of these groups unfold in a setting where divergent economic, demographic, and cultural forces are pressing on the church, where the rules are confused or contested, where roles are in flux, where results are frequently hard to assess, and where the right of such groups to exist in the first place is often moot. The signage is awry. The transition feels like crossing a rope bridge at night in a high wind.

With all this by way of background, one thing is important to remember. Some areas in Catholicism are touchier than others, and it is the variable sensitivity of issues that conditions how the groups behave (along with the resources they bring to the struggle and the legal environment surrounding the church). Before describing the actors themselves, a reminder about how the culture of the church shapes their options is in order.[15]

Nowadays, within American Catholicism, questions about the relations between church and state are usually thought to be manageable. The issue typically comes down to the nervous interaction between the two in specific policy areas, not to the goodness or badness of democracy in the abstract. The tumult surrounding public support for church-sponsored services, popularly included under the rubric of "faith-based initiatives," has grown. Yet this turns out to be at least as much about money as constitutional principle. The stakes are often fungible; deals can be struck. It is this plasticity that opens educational issues to negotiation between secular and religious interests.

All the same, certain cases can get very disputatious. How to provide for parochial schools that serve underprivileged children of various faiths has grown into a major dilemma. While support for Catholic education seems widespread, given the crisis in public education, policy mechanisms like vouchers and tax credits remain problematic in view of constitutional traditions regarding the separation of church and state. "Normal" church-state relations can be destabilized.[16]

A second, potentially touchier set of issues bears on social policy. Catholicism has something approaching a consistent body of thought on the subject. It is a doctrine that favors the poor, including the immigrant poor, who comprise a growing number of its constituents worldwide. Still, whatever the written doctrine, the actual preferences of American Catholics on such issues are only weakly predictable from their denominational affiliation.[17]

The tilt in favor of social welfare has a longer tradition, dating at least from the nineteenth century, than does the church's rejection of authoritarian governments—the right-wing variety in particular—which dates mainly from the mid-twentieth. It wasn't until the Christmas message delivered by Pius XII in 1944, when the tide of war had turned against the Axis powers, that the Vatican officially took note of the virtues of democracy. In the end, as far as the intramural politics of the church are concerned, differences over social justice issues do not appear to be significantly more, or less, divisive among ordinary Catholics than they are among members of other denominations. There is certainly no unanimity among Catholics on these matters.[18]

Issues involving sexuality and the role of women in the church are the ones that roil the nonnegotiable core. While even touchier matters—the divinity of Jesus, for example—cut to the doctrinal quick, these have yet to come into play on a wide scale.[19] On the other hand, the occasional woolliness of the church's pronouncements on political pluralism and social policy gives way to explicit prohibitions when sex is on the table.[20]

Three related properties of the church's position on sexuality make this cluster of issues extraordinarily sensitive. First, attitudes toward the subordination of women are conflated with deference toward hierarchy. Disputes over policy—over contraception, divorce, abortion, and so on—are difficult to separate from differences over ecclesiology, the institutional structure of the church. Males vowed to celibacy retain final authority. Positions fuse and harden over the rules governing gender roles, sacerdotal status, and the like. The chain of command is symbol-saturated.[21]

Second, the regulation of sexuality serves as the foundation stone for a vaster edifice of hard-and-fast principles. Behind the one-size-fits-all norm of sexual comportment propagated by the church stands belief in the universality of a moral code. Sex should follow the same rules everywhere; sexual regulations are supposed to be timeless and unchanging. Inflexibility about sexual roles, identities, and practices acts as a bulwark against a larger relativism. The fixity of the sexual value system is emblematic of eternal sureties about the human person. These are the imperishable essence of institutional Catholicism. Flux is impermissible, period.[22]

And yet... the sexual code of the church need not be understood literally, as dogma that is all of a piece, to appreciate that it acts as an objective correlative, a metaphorical bulwark against anxieties related to the erosion of traditional values about gender identity, reproductive behavior, and the role of women. On top of this, while globalization unfetters the here-comes-everybody side of Catholicism, the same process also challenges pretensions to a universal ethical code. The metamorphosis unsettles uniform rules governing sexual behavior and gender dynamics. The church's insistence on the transnational scope and timelessness of these norms is designed to provide a stay against moral vertigo. That gyroscope is sexual certainty.[23]

Third, while they take a virulent form in Catholicism, the patriarchal dispositions of the church are shared with other Abrahamic religions. Their ancestry can be traced back to the onset of agrarian societies more generally. A primal mindset has outlived the social context that nourished it. The imperiled state of sexism is what renders the culture defensive under present conditions. To alter the heritage would be to "go against nature."[24]

The family, along with a gendered hierarchy and division of labor, is to Catholicism what class is to Marxism. But for activities where collectivities larger than the social building blocks of family structures are involved, tolerance of local customs usually prevails. Forms of government and ways of doing business vary, like languages, from country to country. It is this bow to historical and cultural variation that subtends the political suppleness and adaptable social doctrine of Catholicism. No comparable sense of temporal contingency has seeped into the magisterium regarding sex.[25]

In reality the tripartite division between political, socioeconomic, and sexual domains is not hard and fast. Much of Catholic politics can be understood as an effort to bring the spheres closer together. Though the terminology is rarely used anymore, "integralism" and "fusionism" are not entirely dead ideals. Secular programs embedded in church operations, like assistance with reproductive issues, are the flip side of public support for faith-based operations. This is disputed territory, without a self-evident quid pro quo or readily negotiable middle ground. It is no accident that the bishops' efforts to reassert control over Catholic ministries in education and health care center on questions related to sexual behavior or that moves to secure tax credits for parochial schools gather momentum as elementary and secondary education faces financial pressure. The compartmentalization of church and state begins to look insecure once sexual doctrine and money come into play.

"It is politically inconvenient to acknowledge what everyone knows," Alan Greenspan declared in a moment of unwonted lucidity, "that the Iraq war is largely about oil."[26] An analogous truth holds for the role of sex in Catholicism. The nexus between gender and power is what makes the institutional church, the clerical hierarchy at the heart of it, tick. Norms about sexuality and gender roles are woven into the design of Catholicism. Pull one thread—the celibacy requirement for ordination to the priesthood, say—and the fabric of authority unwinds.

This is writing with a blowtorch, but it establishes an essential point. The sex–authority complex is the signature tension of the church. At some remove from but still within its sphere of influence are questions of clerical control over the resources that feed the church's ministries. The slipping constraints exercised by the former, the church's sexual canon, on the latter, its day-to-day outreach, form an important theme of this book. Disputes about sexual morality and reproductive ethics, for example, are prone to become politicized because church-affiliated services have spread beyond the confines of parish life into the secular arena.

But my argument differs from the standard autopsy that points to the Catholic hang-up with sex then ships the corpse off for burial. Questions of sexuality are enormously important in Catholicism not only because they incite strong, frequently obsessive disagreement. They also fuel an intrapsychic civil war. They are capable of fostering an excruciating ambivalence among those on different sides. Some Catholics blithely cherry-pick what they believe; others are uneasily selective about what matters in their faith. Still others can be as tense as tuning forks; they are as conflicted within themselves as they are divided against one another. Who speaks out of conviction? Who shouts down their own doubts? We don't have the figures. This simultaneous divisiveness and ambivalence is probably the most important psychic change that has taken place since the days of fortress Catholicism, when "the church militant" thought of itself as a clan united against external enemies.[27]

Ambivalence may take some of the edge off a confrontational situation. In tandem with the exit option available to disgruntled Catholics, the safety valve of selective adherence and silent dissent, and the entrance of relatively traditional immigrants into the American church, the effect is to slow down reform. These dynamics make the need for change feel less pressing.

Associations that might loosely be termed pressure groups have few options in Catholicism. Either they support the supremacy of male authority or they keep their counsel and go about their business in less neuralgic domains, like good works and managerial improvements, or they migrate to the edges of the church, or they leave altogether.

This said, overwhelming demographic and economic pressure can make distinctions between tractable and less tractable zones in Catholic culture less categorical than they seem.[28] The fate of many of the schools associated with parishes and dioceses has been the most urgent managerial challenge facing the church in the United States, and financial exigencies have generated some of the same power-sharing arrangements between clergy and laity at this level as they did in Catholic higher education from the 1960s on. The inhibitions against organizational problem solving here are more political than theological. Under the American system, in contrast with various models of public support for church schools in the democracies of Europe, Canada, and Australia, measures like vouchers and tax credits for "pervasively religious" parochial schools run up against constitutional provisions regarding the separation of church and state. Parish- and diocesan-run primary schools are still trying to dig themselves out of a hole that Catholic colleges and universities, which qualify for governmental money, overcame decades ago.[29]

The shortage of priests has fostered a similarly desperate situation in the parishes. In this case, however, the problem of human resources and service delivery is as symbolically fraught, entangled in the inheritance of celibacy and male privilege, within the church as are the dilemmas associated with church–state relations within American political culture. One of the unspoken rules of Catholicism is that there is always time for procrastination. But iconic continuity may have to be rethought in the face of the unsustainable, implacable demographics. Boiled down, the future of American Catholicism depends largely on how it handles the plight of its K-12 schools and the dwindling number of priests.[30]

In the culture of Catholicism, then, attitudes toward political, social, and sexual issues can be visualized as composing a set of concentric circles, arranged in roughly increasing intensity as we approach the inner ring. Differences between progressives and conservatives tend to be more sharply defined toward the core and fuzzier toward the periphery. The issues, in other words, lend themselves to distinctive degrees of conflict. They may also be combined in various ways, and this makes for strange bedfellows. Demarcating the ideological profiles of the protagonists that make up the leading actors in this book requires care. They can be arranged along a left–right continuum, but only at the cost of doing some violence to what they are about.

So, for example, most of the intellectuals associated with the conservative periodical *First Things* are categorizable in ideological terms. The magazine has defended Catholic orthodoxy on abortion, homosexuality, and same-sex marriage, even as it has strayed gingerly on issues like economic justice and the Iraq war that occupy the doctrinal outer regions.[31] When, as will happen later in this book, coverage is extended beyond the orbit of *First Things*, the adherence to sexual conventions will loosen up, but the conservative slant of the network should remain recognizable.

Above all, the left–right labeling has to take into account the multidimensionality—political, social-economic, and sexual—of the issues under discussion. Some conservatives and neoconservatives are reluctant to admit to belonging to a club that would have them as members. Perhaps this reflects a supreme elitism or cranky libertarianism. In any case contrariness is a defining quirk of the politically incorrect persona. There are genuine shadings under the conservative rubric that need to be acknowledged.

Compared to *First Things*, the remaining groups—the Survivors Network for those Abused by Priests, the Voice of the Faithful (VOTF), and the National Leadership Roundtable on Church Management—are more liberal, but that pigeonhole also covers a multitude of differences. SNAP bears a family resemblance to movements like MADD (Mothers Against Drunk Driving). It is adamant about pursuing justice for victims of sexual abuse, yet it attacks the behavior of the bishops rather than the hierarchical structure of the church or its doctrinal perspective. SNAP's view is that the clerical establishment is besotted with an incorrigibly backward culture. The system is fundamentally corrupt. Well-intentioned prelates tend to be suspect along with their careerist and dogmatically hidebound brothers. The power and prerogatives of the bishops are to be contained, in the Cold War sense. Indifferent to the doctrine as well as the institutional architecture of the church, SNAP does not style itself as a Catholic or sectarian organization at all. The results it seeks are changes in behavior. Transformations in the structure and teachings of Catholicism, if they occur, are by-products.

The Leadership Roundtable's arsenal doesn't include litigation. Founded in the opening decade of the twenty-first century by Catholic benefactors and philanthropists from Wall Street and Silicon Valley, in reaction to what they perceived as the managerial fumbling of the bishops in concealing sexual abuse and the embezzlement of parish funds, the Roundtable promotes managerial modernization over touchier, possibly more sweeping institutional reform. It tries hard to avoid theological controversy.

Both SNAP and the Roundtable have specific objectives and tangible resources. Much though not all of SNAP's strategy depends on using the legal system, on the possibility of filing suits against dioceses and religious orders, and on gaining traction with the media. The Roundtable's approach is the opposite, one of collaboration rather than confrontation, and it has organizational expertise and access to philanthropic networks to offer. For its part, the coterie around *First Things* and its sympathizers promote an evangelical fervor valued by a church worried about the transmission of its values across generations.

More than these other groups, VOTF styles itself as a reform movement. The organization erupted in 2002 "out of the pews," coalescing around the exposés of sexual abuse and cover-up published by the *Boston Globe*. In contrast to movements put together by political impresarios, the origins of Voice of the Faithful can be traced to a spontaneous flare-up. "You can't build a church out of bullying and broken hearts" was the *cri de coeur* of one member. Participants became giddy with their collective effervescence.[32]

VOTF holds to a belief that change in the church has to follow a grass-roots dynamic, and it has tried to model its internal structure on the open, comparatively populist culture it envisions for a renewed Catholicism. The downside has been disarray. Its overarching goals—"supporting survivors," "supporting priests of integrity," and "promoting structural change"—have been seen as equivocal and partially at odds, its internal politics have been fractious, and its tangible resources are minimal. Unlike SNAP or the Roundtable, VOTF has almost nothing that the hierarchy fears or needs.

While each of the movements, except perhaps for VOTF, has a distinctive set of endowments and a characteristic strategic profile, they have all emerged out of a common historical matrix. Vocations to religious life have fallen, scandals have proliferated, the church is hard up for money, and it is pushed and pulled in various directions. Institutional Catholicism is riddled with stress points.

A quick projection of the story might emphasize how developments in civil society—rising levels of education, social mobility, female engagement in the workforce, and so on—will eventually spill over into the vacancies left by a regime in decline and upend the balance of power between clergy and laity. This is a straight-up version of the demography-is-fate/it's-only-a-matter-of-time argument. The dieback has set in. Patriarchal hierarchy and crony Catholicism are out of joint with the modern era. Like "the debris of a dead but unburied past," as one historian described the Weimar Republic,[33] the clergy-dominated church is supposed to be a spent force. Besides the cultural capital embedded in its traditions, Catholicism has produced impressive amounts of human capital—skilled, disciplined cohorts of lay people whose talents are up to the task of managing the affairs of the church.[34]

But for all the talk in praise of community over rank individualism, Catholicism has a checkered history when it comes to the cultivation of social capital. Voluntary groups capable of guarding their interests, pressing their demands, standing up for themselves, and solving problems in their own right remain an anomaly in a hierarchical church. That needle is very difficult to thread.

The church has spawned an array of movements and voluntary associations. However, most of the *movimienti*—the lay ecclesial movements—that have emerged since Vatican II are devotional organizations with shallow roots in the United States.[35] In addition, the church's own efforts to develop lay organizations in the secular arena have often ended badly in the eyes of the hierarchy. The Christian Democratic parties whose formation the church encouraged in nineteenth-century Europe were rarely as pliable as they were designed to be, and some of them disavowed their allegiance to the hierarchy. In the United States, the bishops disowned the radicalism of the organization that grew out of the "Call to Action" convention they nurtured in conjunction with the 1976 Bicentennial. Another sign of Catholicism's mixed record on social and political capital is the low to middling level of participation in church affairs—the "Catholic deficit"—exhibited by the rank-and-file faithful. The Second Vatican Council itself is partially at fault for stressing ceremonial and theoretical advances while neglecting organizational implementation.[36]

There is a general lesson here. Historically, Catholicism has reconfigured itself through the invention of organizational subunits—activist religious orders, notably the Jesuits, who broke with the monastic tradition, or mixed lay–religious groups, like Opus Dei—rather than by root and branch transformation.[37] The church has tried to channel insurgent energies within its institutional repertoire. The metamorphosis of Catholic health care and higher education from clerical domination to mixed lay–clerical governance, with de facto laicization of professional cadres, is a variation on this pattern. Their missions show continuity with the past; it is their mode of governance that differs from the old clerical monopoly.[38] These are less than revolutionary but more than piecemeal changes.

Where does this incremental arc leave the groups emerging in American Catholicism? From a purely functional standpoint, the celibacy norm for the priesthood has run its course.[39] What's more, in the United States, finances and enrollments in many parishes and church schools are in free fall.[40] These are the crisis points. Bold moves in the first area depend almost entirely on cracks developing higher up in the clerical leadership, beyond whatever pressure lay opinion and lobbying might bring to bear. If there is a predictable next stage in the evolution of the American church, it will involve adapting and spreading the power-sharing experiments introduced in higher education and health care to diocesan and parochial decision-making structures.

As with increases in life expectancy, administrative progress is difficult to argue with in comparison to the alternatives. Managerial reform looks both quiet and sensible. Its potential lies in the cumulative impact of diligent investments and fine-tuned remedies that gather momentum as they proceed, eventually locking in as the new conventional wisdom.[41]

The big question is threefold. First, how steady is the coalition between modernizing benefactors and bishops who, as their status diminishes, may lash out on issues, like women's rights, that they feel threaten their corporate autonomy? There is some affinity of interest but no grand bargain between clerical and lay leaders. Just as some bishops remain wary of "these businessmen telling us what to do," some pillars of the philanthropic community, anxious to put their money where it will do the most good, wonder whether in aligning themselves with one or another klatch of bishops they have bet on the wrong horse.

Second, how viable are bureaucratic improvements as they approach the sacred, cultic spaces of Catholicism, the parishes themselves?

On the supposition that the answers to the first two questions are promising, a third contingency remains: Can the managerial model of reform outpace the numbers simply walking away from the church? Renewed trust is not a straightforward product of enhanced performance. The confidence of benefactors that may accrue from increased accountability on the part of the bishops is not the same as the credibility of doctrine or emotional investment in the culture of the church. The flight of Catholics from the faith of their fathers has so been large (the number of ex-Catholics adds up to the equivalent of the largest denomination in the United States, Catholics themselves) that it might as well as be counted as a fifth megatrend, to be added to the four mentioned earlier.[42] Conceivably, the ship will be more tightly run. How many passengers it will carry is another matter.

We need to be alert to another facile assumption, besides the link attributed between efficiency and the restoration of the credibility of Catholicism. This involves the contrast between redistributive reforms that challenge the nexus between clericalism and sexism, on the one hand, and a meliorism that favors change by pragmatic increments, on the other. The contrast mirrors the dueling priorities of fairness and efficiency in strategies of change.

The comparison is liable to be invidious, pitting a deeper, idealized radicalism against a tepid, cosmetic makeover. It tends to lock into a stereotype of drip-by-drip improvements that ignores not only their cumulative effects but the capacity of nose-to-the-grindstone tactics to redefine the terms of transformation. (Consider "Botts' Dots," the pavement markers designed to make the painted lines separating highway lanes last longer: Adopted around the world, the humble little buttons have had an additional and unexpected safety benefit, alerting motorists when they drift out of their lanes.)[43]

Doctrinal divisions are not matters that most Catholics lose sleep over. A near-sighted parochialism that no longer corresponds to the fluid post-enclave makeup of American Catholicism may be as stubborn an obstacle to reform as ideological recalcitrance. The same inability to abstract beyond immediate local needs—to think strategically—characterizes the dispersion of the church's capital resources, when consolidation could make major reforms economically feasible. Unromantic though they may be, the questions of how to pay for a married clergy, for example, or for decent salaries and benefits for lay workers can no more be kept off the table than differences over symbolic matters. The rival priorities assigned to the growth of resources and the redistribution of roles are as contentious in the church as they are in the secular political arena.

CHAPTER TWO

THE DYNAMICS OF TRADITION

Shortly after John Kennedy was elected president in 1960, the theologian John Courtney Murray appeared on the cover of *Time* magazine. Murray's renown rested on his capacity to persuade Catholics and non-Catholics alike that religious tolerance and political pluralism could be accommodated, and might even be praiseworthy, in the eyes of a tradition, Roman Catholicism, not remarkable for promoting either.

The urbane Murray bore himself with the aplomb of a celebrity intellectual. "He entered a room," a Jesuit colleague recalled, "like an ocean liner."[1] The aura surrounding Murray continued to grow through the Second Vatican Council. His advocacy of "the American proposition," forsaking the anachronistic ideal of a monolithic alliance between church and state, was ratified in the Council's Declaration on Religious Liberty.

The eminence accorded to Murray reflected the high point of the American century in Catholicism. An immigrant church had come of age. Educationally accomplished and economically successful, American Catholics were reaching for intellectual respectability and the highest ranks of political power. Camelot coincided with the beginning of Vatican II.

Then the sixties broke open. John Kennedy was assassinated. By mid-decade, protests against racial segregation and the Vietnam War challenged the social and political order, the cultural revolution and the feminist movement were in full spate, and the gay rights movement was just around the corner. Young people marched in the streets, smoked forbidden substances at university events, and gamboled through the meadows of Woodstock. The sybarites, neurotics, and gurus of Robert Crumb were beginning to appear in underground comics. The Dodgers had already left Brooklyn. Now men started to talk about their feelings. It wasn't pretty. The upheavals derailed Murray's hopes for equable discourse among statesmen-like leaders even before he died of a heart attack in 1967.[2]

Murray's contribution was seminal; it was also ambiguous and incomplete. He loathed "maximalism," "absolutism," and the assorted extremisms that he associated with the over-the-top politics of continental, particularly Spanish and French, reactionaries and their revolutionary antagonists. The Italians could bear watching as well. An intransigent ardor for tradition was nearly as repugnant to Murray as radical talk of strangling the last capitalist with the guts of the last priest. He disdained do-your-own-thing relativism too. Murray was a commanding presence. He looked and sounded like a perfect, plummy English gentleman. Impatient with fools, suave in demeanor, he radiated an inner swagger.

It is not clear when the accommodation that Murray worked out between Catholicism and democracy shifted from détente-like articles of peace—pluralism condoned as a cost of doing business—to a more enthusiastic embrace of democratic procedures.[3] The appeal of Murray's brief in favor of tolerance and pluralism grew out of a conviction that they paid off as a modus vivendi; in the United States, there was no alternative. By dethroning the union of church and state, Vatican II jettisoned an archaic rhetoric that had fueled decades of anti-Catholicism. Now the church could no longer be credibly accused of undermining the republic. Murray succeeded in dialing down "the seemingly endless debate over the 'compatibility' of Catholicism and American democracy."[4] On the other hand, when the danger passed from one of religious contempt for democratic principles to the reverse, one of policy decisions by secular authorities that transgressed core beliefs of the church, how would Catholicism respond?

The pluralist settlement seemed plain enough. Assimilation was a prudential two-way street. The church was not to challenge the sovereignty of the state. That stipulation came directly from the nonestablishment clause of the First Amendment. For its part the state was not to infringe on the business of the church; this derived from the free-exercise clause of the gnomically phrased amendment.[5] Catholicism accepted the rules of the democratic game and the state was to respect the institutional integrity of religion, perhaps even more scrupulously than it would that of any other legally constituted corporate body. These are the "twin tolerations" essential to political comity.[6]

The dilemmas buried here regarding convictions on collision course would erupt when the Supreme Court legalized abortion in 1973. A second problem would emerge as the church's supply of priests and nuns unexpectedly plummeted after Vatican II and the costs of running the church's ministries, especially the primary and secondary schools, soared. The same constitutional principles that sheltered American Catholicism from having reform foisted upon it by public authorities also blocked the parochial educational system from receiving all but minor amounts of federal and state aid.

Another weak spot was that Murray's theology paid more attention to ideas than the power relations surrounding them. His take on reasoned conversation overlooked imbalances between participants and noncombatants. Quiet agenda-setting had a way of excluding all but a clubbable few. Critics of pluralist good manners responded by attacking "elitist democracy."[7]

Still another loose end in Murray's thought was freedom of conscience. Most American Catholics already took the idea of the separation of church and state for granted; the norm was simply nowhere near as controversial as it was for Europeans. But religious tolerance as a collective good also implied individual freedom of conscience, and it was hard to see how this fit with the church's insistence on conformity to doctrinal infallibility.

Murray's thoughts about power within Catholicism were also tantalizingly cryptic. He appears to have been turning over the possibility of applying some of the precepts of pluralism to the church itself. "Gentlemen," Murray intoned on his return from Vatican II, "we have just cleared the decks of certain nineteenth-century business. We have not even begun to deal with the issues of the twentieth century." This, together with a few other offhand remarks and his own experience of having his writings squelched for several years by the

Vatican, suggests that Murray may have been willing to press on with in-house *aggiornamento*.[8]

But the analogy between civil and ecclesial polities was imperfect. The gist of Murray's case regarding church-state relations was that no political system was supreme outside its historical context.[9] His critics claimed the opposite when they praised monarchy and the union of crown and altar as the timeless embodiment of celestial hierarchy. Murray for his part could fall back on the equally venerable notion of "accidentalism." By his account, political regimes are shallow and transient epiphenomena, like Marxian superstructures. This was especially the case when governments were compared to the age-old hierarchies—the abiding subordination of women, for example—embodied in customary family relationships. Politics as a matter of institutional form, of regime type, lay toward the periphery of human concerns.[10]

It was something else, however, to imply that the pillars of authority inside Catholicism, its male-dominated structure of governance, were also historically conditioned.[11] Murray drew back from taking this step. It was politically inopportune. He also sensed that underneath the vigorous clash of doctrinal positions lay barely enunciable questions of sexual identity and gender-based authority. He fretted about "men of diminished manhood, of incomplete virility" whose logical capacities were underdeveloped because, as Aristotle feared, they failed to master their feminine irrationality. Here is Murray at full tilt:

> It is woman who offers man the possibility of headship, of entering into his native inheritance of rule—of realizing himself as head, Logos, the principle of order, which by ordering life rules it. Woman is life, but not Logos, not the principle of order... She is not her own ruler; man is to govern her.[12]

In other words, sexual stratification is at the heart not only of ecclesiastical hierarchy but of traditional social order.

Catholicism, Murray felt, represents a constitutive way of looking at the world. It propagates a gendered slant on things. Political hierarchies are fleeting. Sexual hierarchies are, or should be, ageless. Desire and disorder circle one another like dancers. Saint Augustine, that most sensual of metaphysicians, is often thought to be the genius at the root of this part of the Christian canon.

Nothing better illustrates the tension in Murray's thought than the back-and-forth between the conciliatory ideal—the supreme good of comity—and the adversarial ethos, which he understood as masculine assertiveness. There is the Church Militant, and there is Holy Mother Church. The conflict was not only philosophical, it was erotic. At stake are neither interests nor ideologies alone but personal and communal identities. This is a blessed rage for order in spades. A psychological reversal runs beneath the civil veneer. The subdued panic reflects gynophobia and male hysteria over the crazy lady in the attic of Catholicism.[13]

This tension continues to reverberate in Catholic ideals about religious hierarchy, family life, and cultural harmony, and it resonates in the larger world as well.[14] Certain controversies strike Catholics and many others as peculiarly sensitive. Even when issues appear to involve humdrum concerns, amenable to incremental problem-solving, they veer toward the intractable if they become conflated with foundational quarrels about sexuality or authority or both.

The come-let-us-reason-together discourse espoused by John Courtney Murray proved unsteady. This book examines the ideological and organizational aftershocks of the tremors that undid the accord Murray helped put in place at Vatican II.[15]

A compact that hinged on an overarching agreement about the practical virtues of moderation forked in two directions. One road headed toward polarization, swept up in feuding about abortion and the culture wars over family values and the role of government. On the intramural front, clashes surrounding the celibate male priesthood and the role of women, which many expected were up for revision with Vatican II, smoldered on, as did demands for gay rights.

A second route has followed a generally more circuitous and organizationally cluttered path. It has accompanied the exponential growth and professionalization of church-sponsored ministries in education, health care, and other social services, where the main issues have been financing and transparency. These developments have been driven not only by government regulations but also by the rise of a nonprofit sector—grant makers and advocacy groups—that strive to raise the bar of performance that church operations are expected to live up to. They want to be listened to and to hold the church accountable for how it spends money.

The underbrush of interest and advocacy groups is not free of ideological conflict. Back-room disputes can find their way into the courts, and even the threat of litigation may magnify otherwise pedestrian dust-ups into battles over principle. The judicial venue is public but remains outside an electoral framework, a process that favors unpopular causes. (The flap that arose in 2012 over the obligation to provide contraceptives in church-affiliated health and educational facilities is a case in point.) Still, though it may be a close thing, friction in this area has as often as not less to do with the dogma than the operational craft, the case law, of Catholicism. A lot depends on how specific issues are framed.[16]

Both narratives—loosely, the passing game and the ground game—have conditioned the strategies of groups vying for influence in the church. The politics of cultural assimilation and consensus associated with Murray shattered when the Supreme Court reshaped the political landscape by legalizing abortion in 1973.[17] The decision, coming on top of the ecumenism licensed by Vatican II, created huge incentives for conservative Catholics to align themselves with like-minded peers across denominational lines.[18] Besides strengthening their hand in cross-denominational coalition building and electoral politics, the mobilization of pro-life forces gave conservatives an edge inside the church. The revival of family values that attracted a broader public became virtually synonymous with the revanchism sponsored by John Paul II to combat excesses, as he saw them, committed in the name of Vatican II. The ordination of women and similar causes dear to Catholic progressives were stymied.[19]

The upwelling of conservative Catholicism went beyond sexual and right-to-life issues. It resonated with a concern about welfare measures and expansive state policies that, conservatives feared, would undermine family integrity. Seemingly technical issues of public policy underwent a kind of political moralization.[20] Anxieties about cultural decay, the usurpation of religious values by a secular government, and the threat to the American ethos of self-reliance entered into a fusion of conservative Catholic and evangelical interests with the passage, under Republican pressure, of the Welfare Reform Act of 1996.

Much of this controversy was fueled by concern about what post-conciliar Catholicism stands for, about what it is. "Moral clarity" became a mantra among critics of runaway *aggiornamento*. The backlash and counterbacklash over Roe v. Wade became staples of conservative and liberal identity politics.[21]

The second path is more obviously taken up with what the church does, working through parishes and outreach ministries. Here, too, the tectonic shift began in the late 1960s, when Catholic colleges and universities set up lay-dominated boards of trustees, legally dissociating themselves from ownership by the religious orders that had founded them. By doing so, they made themselves eligible for student aid, research support, and institutional grants from federal and state agencies. They were able to recruit more lay people to make up for the dwindling cadres of priests and nuns. They became more professional. Catholic hospitals quickly followed suit.[22] "Separate incorporation" was as momentous for institutional Catholicism in the United States as Vatican II was for it theoretically. It represented a "second disestablishment" within a church that once had all-encompassing aspirations.[23]

Few of these changes filtered down to the parishes and dioceses and their network of elementary and secondary schools, which the courts defined as "pervasively religious" and hence practically without access to public support (with the exception of bussing). By the end of the twentieth century, many of the schools were in terrible financial shape and, while still predominantly Catholic, several that remained took on more non-Catholic pupils. The schools, parishes, and dioceses were protected from direct government intrusion into how they ran their affairs by constitutional provisions safeguarding the separation of church and state, but it soon became clear that these provisions also deprived them of almost all public funding.[24]

This is the setting, inflamed by the sexual abuse scandals, that reform groups like Voice of the Faithful and the Leadership Roundtable encountered in the early decades of the twenty-first century. The advent of the Roundtable is predicated on the coming of age of philanthropists, many of whom made their fortunes in the 1980s and 1990s, bringing with them business-like ideas about crisis management and professional expertise for social improvement.[25] Similarly, both VOTF and SNAP, as well as the Roundtable, make up less than a handful among thousands of tax-exempt organizations that have mushroomed in the postwar years, especially since the 1970s. Barely noticeable at the time Murray was writing, many of the 501(c)s now form a complex world of advocacy groups, watchdogs, fund-raising professionals, and charitable foundations in pursuit of mushrooming causes. Staggering sums of money are in play. Estimates place the transfer of wealth across the Greatest Generation to the Baby Boomer generation at just over $40 trillion and change.[26]

So, the political culture in which Catholic conservative and reform networks operate is ideologically hard-edged, and the institutional environment of these groups is more organizationally complicated, rule-bound, and studded with litigation. The ambience is riven by left-right conflicts of a ferocity that Murray yearned to mitigate, and his cordial pluralism looks a little ingenuous in the midst of the nearly trackless welter of interests and power brokers that has taken hold in and around American Catholicism since Vatican II. The problem-solving path has split into multiple specialized branches. Majorities are elusive.[27]

The next section of this book considers the blossoming of conservative Catholicism during the eighties and nineties in the United States. While this part of the story is framed around the late Richard John Neuhaus, founding editor of *First Things*, in fact it ranges across more than half a dozen conservative and neoconservative Catholic thinkers and a few of their non-Catholic allies. Rather than being the center of the narrative, *First Things* is treated as a hitching post for the analysis of Catholic conservatives and their associates. Their story is told in Chapters Three, Four, and Five.

After looking at the preoccupation with relativism and the cultural sabotage associated with modernity, concerns that have animated the topical coverage in *First Things*, Chapter Three turns to the work of James Q. Wilson and John DiIulio. As public intellectuals and government advisers, both were instrumental in calling attention to the role of family structure in shaping the chances for social improvement. Their writings not only found favor among Catholics aghast at the sixties; Wilson and DiIulio also influenced wider debates over the culture of poverty, as compared to its economic determinants, that have been crucial to the formulation of welfare policy.[28]

Chapter Four reiterates a theme that runs through the conservative revival in American Catholicism: its alliance with conservative Protestantism. The evangelical scholar James Kurth matters not only because of the forcefulness with which he has argued against feminism and what he judges to be its destructive impact on the family and, indeed, on the fiber of Western civilization. Kurth has also been central to the intellectual development of Robert George, now, since the death of Richard John Neuhaus in 2009, at the forefront of Catholic conservatism in the United States.

The chapter also considers the contribution of the considerably more moderate Daniel Patrick Moynihan in the struggle over family life as the fulcrum of social outcomes. An examination of the role of Mary Ann Glendon, ambassador to the Vatican under George W. Bush, rounds out the chapter. A hard-line conservative regarding clerical authority within the church, Glendon is best known for her demolition of the premium Americans place on individual rights and the consequences this has for women and children cast aside in divorce. She blames the divorce courts as much as the welfare system for the feminization of poverty and the destitution of children.

Chapter Five highlights the welfare reform bill that President Clinton signed off on in 1996—the cumbrously titled Personal Responsibility and Work Opportunity Reconciliation Act. The analysis comes full circle with a look at the triumphs and limitations of Catholic conservatism, for politics in as well as outside the church, as seen in over-the-shoulder perspective by Richard John Neuhaus.

Chapters Six and Seven form a bridge between the treatment of Catholic conservatism and later chapters dedicated to groups involved, to one degree or another, in pushing the church in a progressive direction. The objective is to lay out the variably legitimate, frequently shadowy, and sometimes forgotten forms of participation and resistance that Catholics have been able to draw on and occasionally reinvent.

Chapter Six provides an overview of a collegial tradition that challenged, though it never prevailed against, the monarchical hierarchy now identified with Roman Catholicism. The conciliar legacy still echoes among liberal Catholics. The chapter also treats a less familiar variant of Catholicism that is actually more prevalent in the organizational culture of the church. Unlike conciliarism, which aimed at replacing a regal papacy, this management style concentrates not on the overall structure of governance in Catholicism but on the administration of its parts. In times gone by, "trusteeism" and "corporatism" were names for low-key, usually consultative arrangements between clergy and devout, mostly well-to-do laymen. "Dialogue" was about practical affairs—the granular "temporalities of the church"—like revenues, expenditures, and personnel. Though they had a whiff of Protestant congregationalism about them, these arrangements were generally temperate, problem-solving associations. The Leadership Roundtable is a modern-day case in point.

Chapter Six also looks at a common though (at least in English) nameless element of Catholic culture. This is the demimonde of off-the-record understandings, unwritten rules, double-dealing, and ambitions craving to be assuaged that suffuses the unspoken mores of Catholicism. A word combining "display" and "subterfuge"—*Romanitá* say, or what Stendhal called *espagnolisme*—would come close. To some, it is the cynical, film noir side of the church. To others it is just a realistic expression of how bureaucracies actually work. In a slightly different view, it reflects the deep Mediterranean, clientelistic strain in the Catholic ethos. From yet another perspective, the manner hints at a more benevolent, pastoral style of conflict resolution than by-the-book regulation. The subculture captures an enduring penchant for backstage maneuvering in the still heavily Baroque theatrics of the church. Transparency is the enemy. Straight talk is reckless. The grown-up action goes on offstage.[29]

The ethos reflects the paramount significance of appearances, of stage management and showmanship, in Catholicism. The calculus of interests may play out behind the scenes, but images and perceptions are crucial for sustaining the appeal of the system. If the fourth wall vanishes, actors and audience are no longer distinct, and demystification sets in. Among other things, Catholicism is staged to be a grand *Gesamtkunstwerk*, a show of shows.[30]

The subculture's persistence offers an explanation—a partial though still important one—for the puzzle of the Catholic deficit and the generally feeble protests of ordinary Catholics against the failings of clericalism. The mentality is pessimistic about institutional reform and grassroots effort, in balance with evasive action, off-the-record deals, cronyism, and simply lying low. It searches out the paths of least resistance. It embodies a near-fatalistic shrewdness that has more to do with self-help and therapeutic uplift than collective and comparatively costly challenges to the status quo.

After taking a look at the antecedents of ministerial managerialism in the reforms of higher education and health care that were launched in the sixties, Chapter Seven follows up on the riddle of the participatory deficit among Catholics. The deficit is at the center of the debate about the apathy with which many Catholics have met attempts to generate support for reform. Two claims are in play. First, Catholics do indeed tend to be less active than most of their Protestant counterparts as far as involvement in church affairs is concerned. Organized dissent is unlikely to be effective when decision-making authority is confined to the top of the clerical establishment. The experience of futility does not encourage organized defiance, and habits of deference die hard.

The second claim, that the participatory deficit has grown worse, is more doubtful. The image of a golden age of parish involvement during the years of immigrant Catholicism is not utterly fanciful; a fall-off in volunteerism by way of the bureaucratization of services cannot be dismissed out of hand. But the trend does not appear to be confined to Catholics. Besides, such a diagnosis overlooks changes in the types of engagement—toward support groups, in particular—that probably outpace change in the sheer extent of participation. Little of this is political in the ordinary sense, but neither were parish activities in pre–Vatican II days.[31]

Part Four initiates analysis of the reform groups themselves. Chapter Eight looks at the Survivors Network of those Abused by Priests. Chapter Nine examines Voice of the Faithful and Chapter Ten the Leadership Roundtable.

The manifest difference between all these organizations and Catholic conservatives is that the liberals usually skirt doctrinal sensitivities as best they can. (An important exception is Call to Action, a progressive group that traces its lineage to the decade following Vatican II; CTA makes no bones about its dissent from the magisterium.) Catholic conservatives can be expected to speak in unison with official teaching, certainly on core matters like sexuality.[32] Many reformers, by contrast, occasionally trim their demands for the sake of inching forward.

The reform groups have somewhat different reasons for downplaying their misgivings about matters of belief. The attitude of the Roundtable is that discussion in this area is simply unhelpful. It detracts from their primary mission, which is to improve the administrative capacity of the church. Most members of SNAP, on the other hand, literally don't give a damn about the teachings of the church. Their self-proclaimed métier is speaking truth to power, and theological debate is irrelevant to curbing sexual abuse. What matters is the imposition of legally binding restraints on miscreant behavior. Adherents of Voice of the Faithful lean closer to the motivational middle, more doctrinally conflicted than members of SNAP and, arguably, the Roundtable.

How reform groups approach the normative parameters of Catholicism, then, affects how they draw up their roadmaps for change. But two other factors also influence approaches to reform. One consists of the resources, usually economic, that actors like the Leadership Roundtable bring to the arena. The financial clout of the Roundtable guarantees it a hearing.[33]

Another asset is the array of professional standards and legal procedures within which the church in the United States finds itself embedded. The civil and criminal liabilities to which child sex abuse has exposed the church provide one example. So too does the ease with which organizational entrepreneurs and reform-minded professionals can assemble nonprofit advocacy groups that target areas of the church for change (or single them out for preservation, as conservative action groups do). Interest associations and watchdog groups can form rather quickly out of a legally sanctioned opportunity structure favoring nonprofit innovation.[34] The agenda of organizational best practices and organizational protocols espoused by the Leadership Roundtable and some of the ideas for "structural change" advanced by Voice of the Faithful typify this chipping away at the possible.

The openness of the organizational environment does not ensure a proliferation of advocacy associations or growth in their membership. Nor does it guarantee results, since adherence to constitutional principles shields the church from most outside demands for internal reform. But the existence of even letterhead pressure groups means that the church is no longer able to keep as many secrets as it once did. Like Gulliver tied down among the Lilliputians, the hierarchy has reason to feel alarmed and sorry for itself.

Viewing social movements and reform groups in Catholicism as putting theological issues on hold and seeking their main chance through economic power and legal pressure is a reasonable approach. The perspective is crude in a few respects, however.

Chapters Eight, Nine, and Ten suggest that reform runs along a continuum. To begin with, strategies can fix on changing behavior. For the most part SNAP focuses its energies on altering the actions of bishops and priests; it all but ignores the organizational innards of the church. The Leadership Roundtable takes strategy toward a second level. It targets selected organizational as well as behavioral features of the church—for example, the setup of diocesan budgetary deliberations, committees to determine merit-based performance incentives, and the like. None of the Roundtable's moves amount to a frontal attack on clerical privilege, yet cumulatively such measures may be transformative. They have the potential to alter the balance of power between clergy and laity. This is what happened over a few decades with the reforms introduced in Catholic higher education and health care in the United States soon after Vatican II, when a de facto passing of the baton occurred.[35]

A third zone along the reform spectrum touches on doctrine or on something that, while not technically doctrinal, remains a ceremonial sore point. The questions of the celibacy requirement for the priesthood and of the female diaconate fall in this third-rail zone. (The diaconate—or "deaconate," as it would be called if Latin weighed less heavily on the argot of the church—is a step above the "lay state," to which expriests are "reduced," but below the priesthood and the episcopacy, that is, bishops.) The persistence of these iconic carryovers is more than a theoretical curiosity. The conventions are impediments to solving the shortfall of priests in a demographically expansive Catholicism.[36]

Whatever prohibitions hang over the female diaconate have more to do with the cake of custom than theological principle. The convention is analogous, in the shakiness of its conceptual underpinnings and its practical dysfunction, to preconciliar Catholicism's preference for a union of church and state.[37] It was this pipe dream that John Courtney Murray helped explode. Vatican officialdom today is in the same state of denial about the drawbacks of its internal regulations, such as the celibacy requirement, as it was about its fustian ideals regarding external relations with American democracy before Murray came along.

The continuum of reform from behavioral to institutional to doctrinal strategies can be expressed in simpler terms, as a rough division between variable and zero-sum understandings of change. Doctrinal transformation has a menacing edge inasmuch as it entails a clear-cut redistribution of power, for example, between clerical and lay interests. This is less likely to be the case for changes in behavioral and institutional rearrangements. The distinction will become central to understanding the priority placed by the Roundtable on growing the size of the pie—on improving church finances and facilitating lateral communication within tiers of the hierarchy—over pressing for relatively incendiary causes like gender equity.

Chapter Eleven examines one small organization, FutureChurch, that devotes considerable attention to incendiary causes. Objections to reforms like the female diaconate are less a matter of absolute prohibition than of reservations about any change that threatens to accelerate decline in numbers. This is the lesson in timidity taken from the shrinkage of liberal Protestant denominations, and it is one that seems to be confirmed by the hydra-headed nature of unintended consequences following on Vatican II.

The church's willingness to stick with beliefs that are past their expiration date in popular culture is hard to separate from the impression that it is dedicated mainly to its own preservation. The intellectual defense for an all-male celibate priesthood is weak, and its practice is no longer workable. Many priests and prelates say as much off the record. The fear is that the proposed solution might make things worse for the institution, on top of trepidation about incurring the wrath of their superiors personally. The result is organizational petrification.[38] "Low-level equilibrium" is a term that will recur through the analysis to describe a predicament that is difficult to distinguish from an absurdist dilemma. "Don't make waves," as the prisoner about to be executed by firing squad whispered to a condemned comrade who had asked the officer in charge for a last cigarette.

There is a hopeful, unapologetic realism to FutureChurch. The organization combines two virtues not always joined in reforms groups: attention to changes that have concrete implications for the running of the church and dedication to doing the right thing. The combination has the makings of an ideal with mobilizational leverage. The program of FutureChurch offers institutional remedies that carry intellectual weight, a potentially legitimate vision, within a conservative tradition. Its case against convention, like the one Murray raised against confessional monarchy, is discussable—well, thinkable—on practical and doctrinal grounds.

We may never know if women actually served as priests in the ancient church. But there is enough doubt to justify a judgment call and sufficient urgency in the reduced numbers of male candidates for questioning how literally precedent, if one can be discerned, should be taken. The church has changed its mind before without publicizing the fact that it is doing so, and operatives are used to asking forgiveness rather than requesting permission beforehand in order to work around the forbidden. That naughty ritual is still observable, even if the time is probably past when it is possible to avoid an uproar about the case at hand. The decision is political. The status quo, meanwhile, has become increasingly dysfunctional.[39]

The aim of Part Five—Chapters Twelve and Thirteen—is to round out the coverage of the interests and advocacy groups as they follow the paths that split off from the spirit of consensus propounded by John Courtney Murray.

Some of these branches are ideological, some are circumstantial and expedient, some crisscross one another.

For the sake of simplicity, the division between the conservatives examined in the early chapters (Three through Five) and the interests treated in Chapters Eight through Thirteen can be depicted as ideological. The tension within the later chapters, from the coverage of SNAP forward, is of another kind. It is one between a theoretical master frame of any stripe, left or right, and pragmatism.

These different ways of looking at things—one worldview versus another, as compared to a tendency to frame conflicts ideologically versus an inclination to handle them empirically—have not converged. In the first, one camp squares off against another; in the second, conflict tends to be oblique. Even then, the world of American Catholicism is more complex than a showdown between true believers and opportunists. Perhaps the most striking indication of this pas de deux between dogmatism and pragmatism is how tortured or simply at a loss Catholics in positions of influence can be as they try to come to grips with the tension between religious principle and institutional viability.

"We were not conflicted in our faith," Kathleen Kennedy Townsend wrote of the irretrievable innocence of simpler times.[40] The newer doubts do not constitute a consensus. They form an irreducible heterodoxy with many adherents and few forthright proponents.

Under analogous circumstances, when faced with the costs of rejecting the mottled benefits of reality in balance with an untenable absolutism, Murray found a way to justify tolerance. Whatever the theory, religious conviction could never afterward be as rock solid as it once was, and religious tolerance as a collective phenomenon could not be understood apart from the individual's freedom of conscience. Dissolution of the ideal of a union between church and state in America was a done deal before Murray came along, even if he did not put to rest doubts about the demarcation between church and state in discrete policy areas. What mattered was his opening toward the primacy of or at least respect for individual choice. I could be wrong, you could be right. Are Catholics better people? Are they on the fast track to heaven? All this made for a paradigm shift in the politics of belief.

Now, as happened with the retrograde ideal of the fusion of church and state, the exclusionary theology of the priesthood has become untenable, but real-world conditions have yet to break the spell of a superannuated vision.

The transition keeps to a holding pattern, running low on fuel, in search of a soft landing.

The following pages unfold in three phases. They start with a focus on ideas—the province par excellence of Catholic conservatives and neoconservatives. The same emphasis holds for most of the transitional Part Three, which treats the conciliarist, corporatist, and, for lack of a nicer word, compliant traditions in Catholicism.

Ideas are the easy part. It is with the case studies of SNAP, VOTF, the Leadership Roundtable, and FutureChurch in Part Four that I shift to a closer look at organizations. These entities spend huge amounts of energy striving to get up and stay running. The effort is indispensable when dealing with a church suspicious of spirited discussion and used to squelching challenges to authority. Even the stabler groups are fairly weak. The situation is reminiscent of the early days of live television, with the recurrent problem of cheap scenery that shook whenever a door was shut.

By the time we get to Part Five, attention shifts from organizations to personalities. Catholicism has refined the art of intimate breakfasts, discreet conversations, and well-placed phone calls. The friends-in-high-places manner is the way things get done in much of the church.

Organizations in Catholicism are not really devoid of ideas. They may be in shambles but they try to be purposeful. Similarly, beneath the organizational patina, despite the lawyered-upness and addiction to propaganda and image-polishing, a few personalities in and around the church happen to be irrepressible in voicing their opinions, whatever the protocols of public life and the imperatives of power enjoin. What we are witnessing is less the irrelevance of organizations in Catholicism as the improvisation, animal spirits, and feel for the fortuitous required to get new ones started in a tradition-bound church. The exercise helps cultivate an appreciation for "slightly mad and dislocated personalities in a time that also was mad and dislocated and filled with unrest."[41]

As the analysis unfolds, I will develop a heuristic device for setting the switchbacks of Catholic reform within a larger trajectory. The conceit involves comparing the institutional church first with authoritarian then with imperial regimes. My thesis is that Catholicism in the United States is straining away from an old-fashioned pyramid in the direction of a better-engineered if not altogether accommodating hierarchy. The transition is toward a kind of neoauthoritarianism.

The evolution is precarious. Large parts of American Catholicism are still run along feudal lines—it is not only much of the architecture that is Gothic—and the consolidation of a refurbished authoritarianism is hardly a sure thing. Nevertheless, the movement gets some lift from a confluence of three economic and cultural trends: a growing sense of urgency about improving the church's service ministries, especially the schools; growing support for these ministries among non-Catholic financial and political interests; and the growing internationalization of Catholicism and the multiethnic, multicultural diversity accompanying it. The circumstances favor a coalitional but less than inclusive Catholicism. The trademark dedication to patriarchal sexism is preserved.

Look on the emerging model as a halfway house, habitable for an indeterminate period. Or look on the hybrid as a streamlined locomotive from the 1930s, an aerodynamic-looking shell retrofitted over an old engine. Except for a suggestion that the mode of transportation itself might survive, this interim solution gave scarcely a hint about where railroad design was headed.

To return to the less fanciful analogy, comparisons between Catholicism and imperial systems or authoritarian regimes are not far-fetched. The church has rightly been called the first multinational corporation and it has maintained a hierarchical culture for centuries. That ethos is unlikely to evaporate soon. The transition underway in Catholicism can be understood as a series of increasingly arduous adjustments in behavior, organization, and beliefs. These fitful processes are not utterly different from those experienced by regimes as they struggle to adapt to political, economic, and cultural pressures.

The fallacy comes in assuming that the transformation of Catholicism has a clear terminus, that continuity is controllable, or that the process is altogether coherent. There is another possibility. The church finds itself enmeshed in a larger institutional and technological setting. Reform tends to unfold more through selective, sometimes adventitious adaptations from the organizational environment—financial innovations, more lateral networks—than by a head-on rearrangement of the power structure.

Under this scenario, growth in the sense of managerial prowess keeps ahead of redistributive fairness. But the side effects and longer-term consequences of even moderate changes are difficult to anticipate. An amplification of resources, were it to take hold, may eventually stimulate profound change, making reforms like the ordination of women and declericalization in general materially affordable, less of a zero-sum operation.

Authoritarian cultures linger in Catholicism, but authoritarian regimes tend to be unstable in the twenty-first century. If they fail to live up to their transformative promise, the practical justification behind top-down control is undermined. If they succeed on their own terms, overcoming the customary dysfunctions, then the social supports of traditional backwardness, including a supine laity, are likely to come undone. The beneficiaries of change sponsored from on high are at least as likely to move on as they are to put their trust in the old ways. Their gratitude might be sincere but confidence in the future of the tried and true is hard to count on.

PART TWO: OVERVIEW

On October 16, 1978, Karol Wotilya became Pope John Paul II. In November 1980, Ronald Reagan won a landslide victory to capture the presidency of the United States. By the end of June 1982, having failed to gain approval in two-thirds of the states, the campaign to ratify the Equal Rights Amendment (ERA) for women went down to defeat. The sixties were on their way out.

Catholic conservatives began to come into their own. They did a couple of things more effectively than their liberal counterparts. They spoke out forcefully about moral issues, with opposition to abortion at the top of the list, and they reached past in-house quarrels to form alliances with non-Catholic groups. In doing so, they caught a wave of popular revulsion against the license of the sixties and rode it to influence within the church and on the American political scene.

Conservatives took advantage of the malleability of Catholic progressivism on economic issues to wed concern about family stability with umbrage at the state of welfare. The conservative platform joined sentiments against abortion, a burning moral issue overlaid in some quarters with resentment against the feminism of the sixties and seventies, with suspicions about the compatibility between public welfare, self-reliance, and economic prosperity. The fusion of economic and moral concerns played well among both Catholics and Protestants. The coalition united around Ronald Reagan, who depicted "liberal activist government as the single devil that is eternally bent on destroying two different sets of sacred values—economic liberty and moral order." The conservative movement went into ideological overdrive.[1]

This program set Catholic conservatives apart from progressives, who worried about ecclesiastical hierarchy, gender bias, and a faith-and-justice agenda that gained little traction in the discourse of American individualism.[2] There was not much contest between the two camps once the papacy of the mediagenic John Paul II got underway. Conservatives could dabble in cafeteria Catholicism just as well as progressives. But their disagreement with church teachings ran toward "prudential"—that is, discretionary—areas like economics. Debate about sex and its sacral twin, authority, stayed off-limits.[3]

Catholic neoconservatism eschews what its adherents term a "paleolithic" reaction tinged with anti-Semitism. The movement is not uniformly in mourning about a lost golden age of premodern values, and it has been reluctant to stay within denominational boundaries.[4] Its core intuition has been that a common threat to the Judeo-Christian tradition overrides tribal-religious divisions. The strident traditionalism of Phyllis Schlafly, a Catholic who spearheaded the defeat of the ERA, played directly to a populist base, with few intellectual frills, but even her appeal crossed denominational lines.[5] Beyond a negative consensus against relativism and the sexual nonchalance associated with the sixties, and beyond abhorrence at what they consider to be the nihilism of the Mapplethorpe–Warhol–Tarantino axis in the arts, Catholic neoconservatives are fairly eclectic, and some who have contributed to the school are not Catholics are all.[6]

James Kurth, the evangelical Protestant academic whose attack on feminism opens Chapter Four, was a teacher of the ardently Catholic Robert George, who went on to become a Princeton law professor and a leading light of Catholic neoconservatism. James Q. Wilson left the church long ago, but his scholarship on the two-parent family as the bedrock of social order has resonated in intellectual circles on the Catholic right. Wilson, in turn, mentored John DiIulio, another Catholic, who was to become the first director of the Office of Faith-Based and Community Initiatives under George W. Bush.

Many of those allied with neoconservatism reject the label as tendentious, and they have a point. Their objection is not with the "neo" prefix, which has chronological significance. William F. Buckley Jr., a Catholic who made his mark in the 1950s, was a conservative. Richard John Neuhaus began to hit his stride in the late seventies, and he was a neoconservative. What holds the movement together, among its Catholic supporters, is rejection of the 1973 Supreme Court decision legalizing abortion and, more broadly, a distaste for the saturnalia of the sixties.[7]

Ampler opportunity for disagreement holds for economics and foreign affairs. Dissent from strict neoconservatism is undeniable in the case of Daniel Patrick Moynihan. He helped found the *Public Interest*, the vanguard journal of the movement, then distanced himself from the coterie in matters of social welfare and aspects of defense policy. Moynihan also came in for condemnation from a few of the bishops because of his stand in support of abortion rights. Buckley, who rolled his thoughts out like a carpet on which words would promenade in solemn procession, made clear his misgivings about papal social teaching early on and demurred from a later pope's ban on artificial contraception.[8] For these luminaries, even the sexual magisterium was open to question.

Further definitional refinements—for example, whether neocons can be distinguished from conservatives for having undergone a conversion from the left—are buried here. It is tempting to characterize neoconservatives as more heterogeneous and less rigid than their predecessors and be done with it. But even that classification is hard to swallow whole, and terminological confusion becomes hopeless once it is realized that "neoconservative" is sometimes used interchangeably with "neoliberal," as in "neoliberal (pro-market) economics."[9]

In the end, neocons are among a generation of postwar, second-wave conservatives, shaped by threats like feminism that emerged some years after the communist menace. They have continued to share several long-standing concerns—the free market and limited government mantras—with their predecessors. New issues have piled on old ones, in good conservative fashion, without replacing them. The movement might be understood as an episode in the ideological radicalization of American politics since the good-tempered conservatism of the Eisenhower era. To the international security concerns they shared with many Cold War Democrats, conservatives have added a series of pivots to the right on domestic issues like gender roles, reproductive rights, and the place of religion in the public sphere—much of this for the sake of damping down "class warfare" over disparities in wealth and income. Social deterioration and moral turpitude on all fronts were cast as the over-arching problem. The result has been cultural polarization.[10]

There is a substantive motif running through my treatment of Catholic conservatism that matters more than the ideological nomenclature. It is a conviction that "culture" surpasses structural, material circumstances in determining behavior.[11] This statement of sociological principle takes concrete form in beliefs, central to debates over welfare policy, about the centrality of the two-parent family for inculcating responsible, productive values. The perspective dominates the thinking of analysts like Moynihan and Wilson, to mention two of the most prominent commentators.

This view of the root causes of social problems is roughly analogous to the way John Courtney Murray privileged the psycho-sexual foundations, as compared to the institutional scaffolding, of social order. It is his under-story, one that has endured beyond his lifetime. In its starkest form, sexual inerrancy is the Catholic fundamentalism that holds a moral society together.

The division of labor between culture and social structure as diagnostic tools parallels the strategic choices facing the reform groups covered later in this book. Reformers recognize the sensitivity of psycho-sexual issues in Catholicism. This is the forbidden zone, as the disaffected would have it, of the theology of the crotch or, as others put it, "pelvic politics."[12] Advocates who seek results aim for changes in clerical behavior and sometimes organizational structures more frequently than transformation in the patriarchal culture of the church.

In practice the domains are not neatly separable. Catholicism *is* a culture. The struggle for change often breaches boundaries. Some doctrines tend to be stickier than others, not just as matters of theory but for political, indeed arbitrary reasons having to do with inherited lines of authority. Just as radicals may defy authority because it is there, for hardliners some cultural relics are worth preserving not because of any beauty they possess, much less for their instrumental value, but for their own sake, as tokens of continuity in the barrens of blighted memory. You can do almost anything with an inheritance except just throw it away.

Power is at stake not far beneath the battle over principle. The rule that celibate males are supposed to retain the final cut is path-dependent, a legacy of turns along the historical road.[13] It is this contested interpenetration of cultural legacy and institutional structure that shapes the limits of reform in the church. Sexism has been baked into the organization for centuries.

CHAPTER THREE

PRISONERS IN THE PROMISED LAND: NEOCONSERVATISM AS CULTURE AND STRATEGY

A striking indicator of the resolutely intellectual strain in neoconservative Catholicism is the quiet that fills the sixth-floor offices of the Institute of Religion and Politics on Fifth Avenue just north of Twentieth Street in Manhattan, where the periodical *First Things* is edited. Except for the walls of an entrance corridor, on which photographs of dignitaries and colleagues at various receptions are hung (including one of the late Cardinal Avery Dulles, wearing a black tee shirt and a Cheshire cat grin), there is no clutter. The setting is more like a library than a city room. It is hard to imagine all-nighters with pizza and canned soda and packs of beer on the premises.

The stringent atmospherics belie the popularity of the neoconservative movement of ideas. The most telling sign of this is the coalition between Catholic conservatives and Protestant evangelicals, particularly in the right-to-life movement. The principles espoused in *First Things* and sister publications like *Crisis* attained crossover appeal beyond a sliver of the intelligentsia.[1]

The alignment of cerebral polemics and mass politics came about in response to the collapse of two pillars that upheld American Catholicism in the decades before the 1960s: the synthesis inscribed in the *Summa Theologica* of Thomas

Aquinas, the church's "perennial philosopher," and the sexual mores—the "little traditions"—built into the ethnic enclaves and kinship ties of the immigrant church.[2] The decay of classicism and tribalism created a vacuum, and the threat seemed all the more frightening because it was coupled with the rise of feminism. The air of social disintegration was hard to distinguish from the troubles of the church itself—the drop in vocations to religious life, the fall-off in religious observance, the loss of credibility following the issuance in 1968 of *Humanae Vitae*. The Roe v. Wade decision taken by the Supreme Court in 1973 catalyzed a counteroffensive against the onslaught of the sixties.

The evaporation of "the world we left behind" was not confined to the church, and the neoconservative project has not envisioned a return to a stand-alone Catholicism.[3] Denominational boundaries matter less than shared beliefs on core issues like abortion and other controversies, such as same-sex marriage, that threaten family values.[4] This is the insight behind the "Catholic and Evangelicals Together" resolutions sponsored by the founding editor of *First Things*, the late Richard John Neuhaus, and his Protestant counterparts. The strategy requires nurturing a "contrast society" of like-minded keepers of the flame. The hope is that the loyal few can lead a tattered Catholic subculture, along with its non-Catholic sympathizers, out of the wilderness of materialism, secular humanism, and disrespect for the Judeo-Christian tradition.[5] Conservatives see themselves as prisoners in a promised land estranged from its moral foundations.

More than trying to fabricate a theme-park Catholicism propped up by retro-ethnic solidarities, a major thrust of conservative strategy is to restore ideas, many of them drawn from the church fathers of late classical times, to a religion torn from its philosophical roots.[6] The dissolution of modernity into decadence and the smithereens of postmodernism has to be averted. The effort to reconstitute a holistic worldview entails both ecumenical outreach and the elaboration of a system of beliefs that cohere across issues. Big Picture Catholicism is a statement of interlocking principles shorn of or at least not reducible to their parochialism and *völkisch* prejudices. To affirm the universality and indeed the superiority of a Judeo-Christian culture and its indispensability to the American way of life—that is the ambition.

On the ground, the program is not all that inclusive. It generates disagreement, not to say indifference, within the fold as well as polarization between those on the inside and outside. Still, philosophically, the assumption of the comprehensiveness of the Catholic *Weltanschauung* stands. John DiIulio, a political scientist with one foot in the neoconservative camp, declares that "Catholicism offers a unifying vision concerning the common good and the good human community." In the next breath, however, DiIulio recognizes that a seamless Catholic bloc is nonexistent:

> church-going Catholics with theologically and politically conservative views are a minority among Catholic voters.... Catholic opinion about politics and political issues tends to be markedly centrist, moderate, or middle-of-the-road.... Politically conservative Catholics tend to favor Church teachings on some issues but not all, and politically liberal Catholics do much the same. Even in cases where politicians may be equally committed to serving the public good as Catholicism requires, and even where they also seek to follow cognate Catholic precepts, prudential considerations and predictions regarding what policies will work best can beget reasonable but irreconcilable policy differences.[7]

Catholicism, in other words, would be a lot more consistent without Catholics or the lax majority of them. The neoconservative position links conservative adepts who appear to be in a minority among Catholics themselves with like-minded individuals from other faiths. Nurturing an ideological affinity across denominational lines turns out to be more feasible, and politically more profitable, than building a consensus within the church.[8]

Plan B to forging a grand coalition around a full-scale philosophy is to rally Catholics against a common enemy. The sixties and their aftermath provide the villain of the piece. "The sixties" represent a portmanteau of pathologies: sexual liberation, in-your-face feminism, elite arrogance, political radicalism, musical and sartorial effrontery, culinary peculiarities, and out-of-control family breakdown.[9]

A complementary device for promoting solidarity is the menace of relativism. Like the Cold War ideology that coincided with the high tide of American Catholicism, the pre–Vatican II church offered an unequivocal catechism of right and wrong, with a clearly delineated set of rewards and punishments. Now the devil lies in a discourse that evades benchmarks for good and evil. A foggy, free-floating empathy that eludes commitment seems to be everywhere. Belligerence and polarization can be identity-defining; they can feel better than anomie, no meaning at all.[10]

Like the sixties, "relativism" is a label for a multitude of bad decisions, almost all of them traceable to a deficit of moral clarity. It is the consummate failure of nerve, the virus that Cardinal Josef Ratzinger singled out in his address at the opening of the conclave that would elect him to the papacy in April, 2005. "How many winds of doctrine have we known in the last decades," the future pope asked, "how many fashions of thought?"

> Every day new sects are born and we see realized what St. Paul says on the deception of men, on the cunning that tends to lead to error.... A dictatorship of relativism is being built that recognizes nothing as definite and which leaves as the ultimate measure only one's ego and desires.[11]

Relativism is the universal nemesis of absolute truth. It is so pervasive that it becomes supremely restrictive, a prison-house of indeterminacy, like the nightmare dinner party in Luis Buñuel's *The Exterminating Angel* that the guests are mysteriously incapable of leaving. In the last moments of that claustrophobic film, the participants stumble outdoors at dawn and find themselves, haggard and bewildered, approaching a church.[12]

Raising the specter of relativism shrinks the middle ground. Ratzinger's view of "the dictatorship of relativism" is itself absolute. What it does effectively is evoke the menace of a loss of control and direction. Routine doubt seems to have disappeared. Relativism sprawls, conjuring up the perils of well-intentioned inadvertence. Tolerance shrivels into a trendy, boundless nonjudgmentalism. If you could be mistaken about the beliefs of others, you might be wrong about your own. Such uncertainty is difficult to sustain.[13]

It is the omen of unintended consequences as much as relativism in the abstract that drives this anxiety. In practice "relativism" is a fancy word for a gnawing sense of a loss of control. If few people exert themselves over the metaphysics, the issue for organized religion becomes not faith as doctrinal sophistication but credulity and the propagation of maxims to live by. These are the guiderails that stand against a corrosive skepticism.

Still another fallback to the restoration of a comprehensive philosophical template is modular Catholicism. It implies a more positive outlook than the condemnation of an omnipresent relativism. Modular Catholicism concentrates on themes—right-to-life and family values are the runaway favorites—that lie somewhere between single issues and overarching ideologies. "Family values" transmits a gestalt about a vital suite of concerns and suggests a characteristic stance toward the ills of the world. The values are mottoes that smack of home and deep emotions, and they resonate more fully than high-minded abstractions. They provide a moral recipe. They are evocative homespun gods, not lengthy manifestos. Sexual liberation might be all very well, but it doesn't tell you how to raise kids.[14]

This midrange strategy deals less with ideas about beliefs (e.g., the Trinity, the virgin birth, archangels) than with ideas about behavior—or rather with ideas and beliefs that are supposed to have observable consequences. The approach is not just about symbols. It points to tangible harm—personal failure, social breakdown—that follows from erroneous ways of thinking. So defined, modular Catholicism opens up the possibility of cross-denominational alliances without getting into the theological wrangling about final authority and devotional practices—for example, the primacy of the pope—that typically thwarts ecumenical relations.[15]

Alarm at runaway sexuality and the decline of family values bolstered the fortunes of the conservative cause in and outside Catholicism. The unsettling irreverence of the sixties was thought to reflect a larger nihilism and "ontological laissez-faire."[16] But the counteragenda struggles with two difficulties that need to be kept in mind when considering the ideas set forth by conservative thinkers.

First, these commentators are better at identifying problems than solving them. Conservatives themselves are often quick to point out the shortcomings of the remedial equipment at their disposal, and they are keenly attuned to the perils of unintended consequences and earnest, grandiose ambition. These pitfalls are galling to practitioners on the lookout for solutions more than elegant analysis.

Some observers from within conservative ranks suggest that a central postulate of their outlook—caution about state intervention—may prevent their colleagues from giving a hearing to measures that have a government pedigree. This obstacle to applying constructive ideas to social problems may be as much a conceptual blind spot as a reflection of inconclusive or discouraging evidence.

"All conservative critics run up against a fundamental barrier," Elizabeth Arens, the former managing editor of the *Public Interest*, commented. "The principal instrument at our disposal for achieving social change is the state. And the state, for a variously weighted combination of its inefficacy and its coercive tendencies, is more horrible to conservatives than the cultural deficiencies they lament."[17]

A second stumbling block centers on the difficulty of assessing the causes of social failures like family breakdown in the first place. It is one thing to pinpoint a social problem. It is another to discern its causes, and still another to propose remedies that work. All of the neoconservatives covered here share a conviction that a cultural crisis, more than economic disintegration, lurks behind social deviance and the erosion of family structures. The causal path goes from a failure of character, a rip in the moral fiber of the individual, toward an unraveling of the social fabric, more than the other way around. Insofar as neoconservatives can be precise about such things, their claim is that the moral environment matters more than the economic setting.

This raises the bar for problem solving. Cultural pathologies are harder than material deprivation to manage by means of the social science toolkit. A further irony is that, according to one of the foundational works of neoconservatism, many cultural problems verge on the intractable because they are themselves propagated by the dynamics of advanced capitalism as practiced in the United States. American markets are better at producing jaded consumers, credit junkies, self-absorbed fashionistas, and morally clueless children than reliable citizens and solid families. An insatiable capitalism devours its civic overlay.[18]

This despondent assessment, laid out by the eminent neocon Daniel Bell, continues to fester.[19] Second thoughts about the compatibility of free markets, disciplined sexuality, and ethical probity in postindustrial societies surface in reflections, reported later in this chapter, by John DiIulio on over-the-top materialism and cupidity. The corporate greed unleashed in the eighties and nineties sits awkwardly alongside conservative condemnations of the epidemic of sex, drugs, and rock 'n' roll in the sixties and seventies. The economy drives consumption, and consumption drives much of the economy.[20] "There remained a certain dissonance in the religious and social conservatives' advocacy of capitalism," the historian Kim Phillips-Fein noted, "for the communal values of family and tradition they claimed to uphold were inevitably undermined by the logic of laissez-faire and the turbulence of commercial society."[21]

In sum, there are unresolved ambiguities in conservative thinking about the role of family breakdown. To what degree is single parenthood a moral disaster with catastrophic economic and social consequences? To what degree is it a pathology spewed up by destitution in an underclass deprived of options? Many commentators agree that divorce and single parenthood inflict economic hardship and emotional damage on offspring.[22] There is less agreement about the mix of factors—personal weakness, poor decisions, cultural decay, poverty—that foster broken families to begin with. It is easier to assign causal status to a single factor such as family dissolution, and to view it as operating in a single direction, than to work with a feedback loop in which numerous variables reinforce economic failure.

Because ideas about the social repercussions of family structure can be cast not just as eternal verities but as testable hypotheses, the preoccupation with family dissolution and its after-effects has proved to be fertile ground not only for Catholics and evangelicals. It has generated debate in policy circles as well.

George W. Bush awarded James Q. Wilson the Presidential Medal of Freedom in 2003. About a decade earlier, Wilson had served as president of the American Political Science Association. After a distinguished career at Harvard (where one of his buddies was Daniel Patrick Moynihan, like Wilson a regular contributor to the *Public Interest*) and UCLA, he was appointed to the Ronald Reagan chair of public policy at Pepperdine University, overlooking the surf at Malibu.[23]

Wilson, who died in 2012, was best known as the originator of the broken windows theory of social cohesion. If small things (broken windows) are fixed, if trash is collected, lawns mowed, gutters cleaned, if people can lounge on their stoops and porches and if street life can go on in a nonthreatening cityscape, a virtuous cycle sets in. Neatness counts. It shows self-esteem, and it breeds self-esteem. Ticketing misdemeanors prevents bigger crimes. People start to take pride in themselves and feel good about their prospects, and this new-found confidence can help foster economic growth.[24]

The subject that Wilson treated at greater length was family policy.[25] The leap from busted windows to fractured families is thematically coherent. The shared idea is that little fixes can improve social order and the quality of life. Families shape character, and character has a huge effect on life chances, more than government programs or purely economic conditions. "The most important change," Wilson began his landmark essay "The Rediscovery of Character," "in how one defines the public interest that I have witnessed—and experienced—over the last twenty years has been a deepening concern for the development of character in the citizenry."[26]

The argument refurbishes the wisdom that the well-ordered family is the building block of society. Wilson sees family socialization as feeding into another value-transmitting process, the educational system, if it is to be effective. One reinforces the other. "The desirable school ethos... obviously resembles what almost every developmental psychologist describes as the desirable family ethos."

> Parents who are warm and caring but who also use discipline in a fair and consistent manner are those parents who, other things being equal, are least likely to produce delinquent offspring. A decent family is one that instills character in its children; a good school is one that takes up and continues in a constructive manner this development of character.[27]

Since his chief interest was in devising practical policies for real-life problems, Wilson stressed the effects of marital instability and illegitimacy on rates of educational underperformance, unemployment, crime, and social deviance generally. Whether marriage is a romantic ideal or emblematic of religious virtue is neither here nor there. The point is that measurable social consequences follow from the stability of marriage or its failure. Lasting marriages, like repaired windows, are good for society. To the degree that marriages disintegrate or are replaced by alternative unions or none at all, costly society-wide dysfunctions set in. The evidence that Wilson marshaled from a variety of sources indicates that stable marriage more than cohabitation, and certainly more than single parenthood, promotes social betterment.[28]

The trick is to move from diagnosis to remedy. "There is no magic bullet that can revive marriage and enhance its character-forming properties."[29]

Neoconservatives are inclined to be as bleak about the fate of family structures as they are enthusiastic about the blessings of free enterprise and policy solutions inspired by the logic of markets. Whatever Wilson's views about economics, he was gloomy about the prospects of resolving the crisis in family life. Compared to what they can do about unemployment or inflation rates, policy makers have few tools for fixing family structures. "If you believe in the power of culture, you will realize that there is very little one can do."[30]

Wilson recommended piecemeal measures, steadily applied. One solution is to present people with incentives to behave in ways that work to their benefit, without fiddling directly with their mindsets, temperaments, or other intangibles. If character is at the unreachable recesses of the psyche, external cues can still be put in place to encourage actions that, when repeated over and over again, help inculcate sound habits and socially redeeming mores. Skills become virtues. "Changing behavior changes attitudes," the columnist David Brooks argues in the same vein, "not the other way around."[31] "In the short run," Wilson insisted,

> we may do the right thing in order to receive a reward. But if we respond in this way routinely, we internalize a disposition to act in the right way such that the disposition, which is to say our character, comes to control our actions. As Aristotle put it, "We become just by the practice of just actions, self-controlled by exercising self-control."[32]

Again, Wilson recognized that the recommendation has limits. Improvement of "character skills" by way of regimentation and repetitive drill shows greater promise in schools, among captive audiences of youngsters, than among grown-ups, for whom rehabilitation may be too little, too late. Wilson railed against "advocates of a therapeutic state" who "have made the mistake of thinking that a large free society can engage in the kind of character-building that was urged upon small Greek city-states by Aristotle, Plato, and others. A large state can change character, but only to a small degree and by means that are profoundly undemocratic."[33]

The underside of the therapeutic is the punitive state, constructed to protect society rather than improve the lot of deviant individuals. Sanctions replace carrots. Wilson cited one analysis that found "that at least one fourth of America's crime decline can be attributed to prison. We do not know," he concluded with some regret,

> whether the more frequent use of prison has changed people's characters or, instead, merely taken them off the street or deterred them from crime without altering their interest in it. I believe that incapacitation and deterrence have made all the difference, and that only a few timid souls have had their character changed by official penalties. But I may be wrong.[34]

Wilson criticized not only the cultural excesses of the sixties (he had chaired the government department at Harvard at the end of that decade, when radical students went on a rampage) but some of the policy measures promulgated by the Great Society of Lyndon Johnson that he felt did not work or that, like the expansion of welfare, he believed made things worse. When the Welfare Reform Act of 1996 passed into law, he disagreed with Daniel Patrick Moynihan, a kindred spirit on several other causes, in judging the "abolition of welfare as we know it" to be a good and efficacious thing. His great theme, sounded by many reformers of welfare at the time, was personal responsibility.[35]

> The right and best way for a culture to restore itself is for it to be rebuilt, not from the top down by government policies, but from the bottom up by personal decisions. On the side of that effort, we can find churches—or at least many of them—and the common experience of adults that the essence of marriage is not sex, or money, or even children: it is commitment.[36]

From the start of his career Wilson was skeptical about mixing religion and politics. "I happen to think that morality is important," he wrote in 1969, "and that those concerned about it are decent people.... But I fear for the time when politics is seized by the issue," he added, well before the culture wars erupted. "Our system of government cannot handle matters of that sort (can any democratic system?) and it may be torn apart by the effort."[37] The sentiments echo John Courtney Murray's praise of cordiality over zeal. Wilson dreaded cultural polarization. It tended toward political combat without quarter; it could be insanely destructive.

John DiIulio was a graduate student of Wilson at Harvard and became coauthor with him of a best-selling text on American government and politics.

A professor of political science at the University of Pennsylvania, not far from the Philadelphia neighborhood where he grew up, DiIulio is a devout Catholic, and he lets his faith show more than the religiously circumspect Wilson. In 2001, DiIulio became the first head of the Office of Faith-Based and Community Initiatives (OFBCI), only to leave in eight months. The politicization of the agency wore DiIulio down.[38]

An important factor behind DiIulio's decision to sign on to the Bush domestic agenda was a conviction, shared by Wilson, that church-affiliated social services were getting the short end of the stick in the competition for federal funding. "Small, volunteer-staffed faith organizations." he claimed, "supply the lion's share of services but receive no public money."[39] DiIulio draws a line between faith-based organizations, which he sees as an overlooked resource for turning underclass neighborhoods around, and "faith-saturated" operations that bundle social work with evangelization. He ran into trouble not just as a result of spin-meistering by partisan handlers like Karl Rove but also because of the penchant of religious enthusiasts recruited by the Bush administration to infuse programs of social provision with proselytizing features that threatened to violate church-state boundaries.[40]

DiIulio has remained cautious about attributing a socially redeeming advantage to faith-based services. There is no reason to suppose that such programs suffer by comparison with secular service providers, but there is not much evidence that they do any better either. The claim that "other things being equal, faith-based programs that are deeply religious will work better than otherwise comparable programs that are only mildly or nominally religious" remains unsubstantiated. "I would make the same bet," DiIulio concedes in a probabilistic language close to Wilson's, "but at this stage, the relative effectiveness of more strongly faith-based programs remains an informed hypothesis, not a settled fact." Are religious workers more highly motivated than their secular peers? How much does motivation matter compared to knowhow in getting the job done? How does the effectiveness of volunteers stack up with the work of professionals? It's complicated.[41]

The attraction of faith-based organizations is not superefficiency but the fact that so many of them, particularly those linked with African American churches, are already in place providing services. In DiIulio's view it is irresponsible for funding agencies to ignore this resource. Not only can faith-based organizations promote social cohesion. They are out there, in the trenches, available to people in need. As social workers and community organizers can attest, churches are likely to be, along with liquor stores, among the preeminent institutions in inner cities.

With the exception of their stands on the Welfare Reform Act of 1996, which DiIulio initially opposed and eventually came to support, the differences between Wilson and his former student are slight. George W. Bush called both men in to consult on early efforts to flesh out "compassionate conservatism."[42] DiIulio sometimes writes in an evangelical-populist key, quoting scripture, which Wilson never did. For DiIulio, as for Wilson, the heart of the matter in social policy formulation and implementation is moral. In DiIulio's case, however, "moral" has a religious substrate while for Wilson the term was freighted with ethical, more purely secular connotations. "As a public philosophy conservatism is a moral and moralizing social force," DiIulio reasons, "and this morality traces its origins to the divine." Liberals can take it or leave it as far as the existence of a divinity is concerned but "true conservatism flows from a single unifying belief: God."[43]

DiIulio finds support for restraining the scope of centrally administered programs in the Catholic notion of subsidiarity. Local problem-solving should take precedence over referring decision-making and policy implementation to higher authorities. Besides being offensive in principle, centralization is too clumsy to work.

> We [true conservatives] do our utmost to honor our social obligations through families, voluntary associations, churches, and charities. We prefer social cooperation to social engineering; the veneration of subsidiary norms to the proliferation of bureaucratic rules; and the cultivation of civic virtue to the exercise of public authority.[44]

DiIulio spends as much time attacking greedy conservatives as he does lambasting uncritical New Deal liberals. The latter he considers, along with arthritic hippies, close to a dead horse. The vitriol DiIulio reserves for unbridled cupidity derives from his Washington days, when he was able to observe the machinations of lobbyists (and the messianism of born-again zealots) up close from the inside.

> Distance conservatism from its moral roots; strip it of its collective responsibilities—familial, local, and national; reduce it to an intellectual or political hired gun for individualistic, materialistic, utilitarian, and commercial interests; and you are

> left with an irreligious, just leave-me-alone, reflexively antigovernmental libertarianism at home and an unpatriotic, globe-trotting, corporate welfare culture both at home and abroad.[45]

DiIulio's disgust with cutthroat economic interests does not quite jibe with his appreciation of the government-by-proxy style of contracting and outsourcing that has characterized the implementation of public policies and war making in recent years. "This uniquely American hybrid... puzzles our European cousins, but it often works remarkably well, and it is a tribute to the conservative insistence that government power be as decentralized as possible."[46] Expenditures on such arrangements—in health care, in the management of the penal system, in contracts for military provisions—have taken off since the 1960s while the size of government itself, measured in terms of full-time employees, has stayed about the same.[47] But as privatization has accelerated, the cost-effectiveness of the strategy as compared to government-managed programs has come into question. It is not clear that outsourcing works "remarkably well." Health care is the most controversial instance.[48]

DiIulio's preference for private-sector initiatives has stayed intact. But, like many liberals who otherwise irritate him, DiIulio criticizes the bias in funding that favors large, established welfare and service providers over street-level social entrepreneurs. He also explodes a few conservative stereotypes about the negative consequences of well-intentioned public policies. He admits that the evidence behind the myth that rising welfare payments actually drive up out-of-wedlock births is tendentious, ambiguous, or nonexistent.[49]

DiIulio repeatedly emphasizes his passion for action even more than his liking for quantifiable results, and he conveys the impression that he is disinclined to stand on principle if theoretical elegance or ideological consistency gets in the way of helping people. "Liberals still tend to emphasize the structural factors of poverty and joblessness, and conservatives tend to emphasize the problems of single-parent families," he told Jim Wallis, the progressive evangelical, in remarks that capture the difference between structural versus behavioral approaches to social melioration:

> But when you get down to solutions, the liberal-conservative dialogue is being supplanted by a new dialogue between people who are problem-focused and people who are not... On the Right, the people who are the least problem-focused

> are conventional libertarians, who believe that all problems were caused by government intervention and overreach, and all problems can therefore be solved by government withdrawal. They have also argued that the root causes are cultural. You can't have it both ways. You can't say that these are cultural problems and at the same time say it is merely a case of welfare overspending. Criticisms of welfare are justified, but the extent to which it's been implicated in all the various problems and pathologies in the inner city is not supported by the data.

"It's important to be known by your works," DiIulio concludes. "Even college professors are known to have some skills worth something more than hot air!"[50]

Viewed in the round, DiIulio's thinking about social pathology and its remedies can be seen as a response to the twin changes that shook the world in which an older generation of Catholics grew up: the decline of the European immigrant ethnic ghettoes and the loss of the premodern philosophical synthesis. The likes of the Irish-Italian parishes that DiIulio knew as a child have lost most of their clientele to suburban churches now attended by middle- and upper-middle-class Catholics. DiIulio and other scholars have suggested that these escapees from the ward politics of their parents and grandparents are not extravagantly generous in volunteering or lavish in donating to social programs. Inner-city African American congregations, however, show some of the same solidarity with their poor brethren that Catholic parishes did fifty or a hundred years ago for their own. In DiIulio's estimation, these congregations have replaced many parishes as vehicles of social recuperation in the inner cities.[51]

Research and policy recommendations of the sort espoused by Wilson and DiIulio are consistent with and supportive of Catholic teaching on the family. But their work is not identical with that doctrine. It is the disastrous personal and social consequences of marital breakdown and the shortsighted pursuit of hedonism it reflects that make up the modern-day equivalent of punishment for sin. The message comes through as indelibly as it does in Hogarth's engravings of gin-soaked profligates and their bedraggled families in the slums of eighteenth-century London. Reprobates share the same metaphorical hovel with their casual victims. Retribution lies in the tragic collective ramifications of character flaws. Like second-hand smoke, moral failure not only damages individual perpetrators; it endangers those around them as well.

Wilson and DiIulio concentrate on what they judge to be the verifiable consequences of family breakdown for social order and collective progress. By their account, on the average, in the United States, the effects of cohabitation on child protection and the economic sustenance of women are negative, when compared to stable marriage. The consequences of single parenthood are thought to be still more damaging.[52]

Wilson's and DiIulio's investigations embody the refrain that ideas have consequences. They cast into testable form the claim that culture, as transmitted by the family, has repercussions on behavior. The by-their-fruits-you-shall-know-them method makes it possible to break the argument down into parts and see if the pieces can be put back together in such a way that a causal pattern emerges. Wilson and DiIulio are also willing to entertain the reverse proposition, that under certain conditions repeated behavior affects culture. It may succeed in inculcating productive habits.[53]

Several lessons can be drawn from their work. Wilson and DiIulio took elements that go under the rubric of "family values" beyond the level of argument by assertion and anecdote. Scriptural and theological sources may be evoked on the side of virtue but what matters in the formulation of public policy, particularly for Wilson, is secular logic and replicable data.

Both men are aware that this is not how things really work. Both are familiar with "the iron law of evaluation, that the expected value of any net impact assessment on any large scale social program is zero."[54] Technical reports, documentary evidence, and the like are only parts—often minor, purely decorative, and sometimes distorted parts—of the decision-making mix.

But adherence to the facts at hand is not just an academic irrelevance in the face of political manipulation. Some regimes are less cynical about the use of evidence than others. Wilson and DiIulio subscribe to the belief that the professional costs of fudging scientific procedures are even higher than the damage incurred by political spin in the short term or for that matter by follow-up scholarship that challenges their results and inferences. Integrity has its uses, given a long-time horizon. Framing the question clearly moves the enterprise forward even if early results are rejected.[55]

The analysis of family structure and its social ramifications has both symbolic and practical rather than narrowly scientific dimensions. This is what makes the bundle of issues so important to Catholics and the public generally. For Wilson and DiIulio the result of their program of investigation is less a belief system, however, than a set of conditional statements about the links between family structure and social pathologies. They leave us with a handful of tentative, if–then clues about the relation of both these to remedial measures. By treating family breakdown and its consequences as problems to be solved rather than evils to be combated in ideological terms, they added to the sophistication of the neoconservative cause and the credibility of its rhetoric. They demonstrated a flair for actionable takeaways. The result is no more rarefied science than pure belief. Wilson was a public intellectual; so is DiIulio. The kernel of empirical verification becomes a stepping-stone for op-ed conjecture and calls for contingent action. This represents a democratization of moral and policy debate—part sermon, part strategy, part science.[56]

A final lesson: for all the qualifications, the neoconservative diagnosis places the blame for family breakdown and its socially dysfunctional consequences on morally derelict individuals more than on economic circumstances. The latter is no more than one of the hands we're dealt. Belief in the primacy of personal responsibility resonated with the American creed of rugged individualism and helped transform an academic program of research into policy changes with popular support. It is a premise that many on the left have been reluctant to take seriously. "Liberals are uncomfortable," E. J. Dionne, a close friend of DiIulio, argues, "with the idea that a virtuous community depends on virtuous individuals" and Ross Douthat writes dismissively of "the old left-wing suspicion of faith and domesticity."[57] Lisa McGirr, on the other hand, has pointed out that liberal squeamishness on such matters may be more circumstantial than characterological. "In no small part due to the traumatic experience of national prohibition in the 1920s, modern liberals drew a thicker line between private behavior and government regulation than had early twentieth-century reformers. Indeed, liberals' increasing emphasis on personal rights and freedoms opened up a space after World War II for conservative claims to being the champions of 'moral virtue.'"[58]

As DiIulio recognizes, such "debates are, at bottom, more about competing values than they are about competing facts."[59]

CHAPTER FOUR

FEMINISM VERSUS THE FAMILY?

Here falling houses thunder on your head,
And here a female atheist talks you dead.[1]

The modern feminist movement has insisted on women's equality with man in every respect. Women have invaded fields of endeavor once given over entirely to men.... In almost every church, the church work from singing in the choir to financing the church and doing the Bible teaching, is done principally by women. Men sit passively in an occasional service, help pay the bills, and are politely indifferent as to whether the world goes to Hell or not![2]

James Kurth is a transitologist. A graduate of Harvard, where he studied with Samuel Huntington, and a professor of international relations at Swarthmore since 1973, Kurth first caught the attention of the scholarly community by laying out a pivotal transition in world affairs, from economies dedicated to manufacturing and transporting physical products toward economies geared to creating and disseminating intellectual property. Kurth's article about the ascendancy of ideas represents an early statement of his variation on a major theme in conservative thought: that in social and political transformations, culture is the key.[3]

In 1994 the conservative journal *National Interest* published an essay by Kurth, "The Real Clash," that reverberated even more widely. Here the transition is still grander than the one he initially described. An evangelical Protestant and deacon at Proclamation Presbyterian Church in Bryn Mawr, Kurth envisions the United States engulfed in a feminist tidal wave.

> The greatest movement of the second half of the nineteenth century was the movement of men from the farm to the factory.... The greatest movement of the

> second half of the twentieth century has been the movement of women from the home to the office... The movement from farm to factory... brought about the replacement of the extended family with the nuclear family. The movement from home to office... separates the parents from the children, as well as enabling the wife to separate herself from the husband.... It... brings about the replacement of the nuclear family with the non-family ("non-traditional" family, as seen by feminists; no family at all, as seen by conservatives).... [Consider] the behavior of the children of split families or single-parent families, especially where they have reached a critical mass forming more than half the population, as in the large cities of America. In such locales, there is not much evidence of "Western civilization" or even of civility. For thousands of years, the city was the source of civilization. In contemporary America, however, it has become the source of barbarism.[4]

Though he writes in a more vehement register than Wilson and DiIulio, Kurth's dismay resembles theirs. In contrast to the clash of civilizations that Huntington depicted in a *Foreign Affairs* article, later a book, of the same name, the real battle is not between rival cultures (the West versus "the rest") but *within* advanced industrial society, between disaffected intellectuals, epicene multiculturalists, and embittered feminists in one camp and everyone else in the other. Multicultural activists and feminists contemptuous of an intellectual repository handed down from white males reject the construct of Western civilization, and their alienation is seeping through society and infecting ordinary citizens.[5] Kurth's denunciation of the *trahison des clercs* is of a piece with neoconservative criticism generally. The truly poisonous figures are malcontents from within the chattering classes, not the bystanders among regular folks. Morally dilettantish elites, riddled with self-hatred and masochistic impulses, infect their peers with defeatism.[6]

The condemnation is not as grandiose as it sounds. Kurth cares less about Western civilization in the abstract than what he believes is or once was its flagship, the American experiment. "This grand project of Americanization [in the sense of immigrant assimilation] was relentless and even ruthless."

> Many individuals were oppressed and victimized by it, and many rich and meaningful cultural islands were swept away. But the achievements of that project were awesome.... The political elite remained comfortable with the Americanization of the mass population. [But for] the academic elite... in the business of training

> the elite of the future... simple Americanization was too rough and primitive.... [The] new common denominator for both Europeans and Americans... became "Western civilization"... [and] very little in this Western civilization happened to contradict the American creed.[7]

What undid this transatlantic high culture? More than just a history of ideas, Kurth's thesis proposes a sociology of cultural change. The new dispensation is empowered by demographic trends, giving birth to a coalition of the excluded that is on its way to displacing the best and the brightest. The emergence of African Americans, Latinos, and Asian Americans has not been enough to form a dominant bloc by itself. The critical group, "which was not really a group but a majority, was women... who [were] much closer in social and educational background to the existing elite and much more central to the emerging post-industrial economy." The feminist onslaught raced toward a point of no return:

> The multicultural coalition and its feminist core despise the European versions of Western civilization... They also despise the American version of the American creed.... They also in practice reject the separation of church and state, because they want to use the state against the church, especially to attack a male-dominated clergy as a violation of equal opportunity and to attack the refusal of church hospitals to perform abortions as a violation of women's rights. The multicultural project has already succeeded in marginizing [*sic*] Western civilization in its very intellectual core, the universities and the media of America.[8]

The cultural revolution has made a shambles of the American achievement, and the upheaval did not stop with the sixties. Its nihilistic momentum has taken several decades to work its way through the system. Writing before the second Iraq war, Kurth worries that it has gathered strength and has shoved aside the American equivalent of the old regime.[9]

The ship is taking on water at a terrific rate. For Kurth the disaster attains tragic proportions because he cannot make out countervailing forces committed to the defense of the American project. He finds no answer to the question "who will believe in [Western civilization] enough to fight, kill, and die for it in a clash of civilizations?" Prior to the 1990s, whatever their differences, liberals and conservatives stood fast by the Enlightenment ideals of the American creed, and they upheld the version of these principles enshrined in the institutions of the United States. But leaders have suffered a failure of nerve, martial values are in tatters. In Kurth's formulation, liberalism is far-gone in postmodernism, while "conservatism in ceasing to be modern is becoming pre-modern." Kurth rejects religious revivalism as a political way out.

> Neither these liberals nor these conservatives are believers in Western civilization. The liberals identify with multicultural society or a post-Western civilization (such as it is). The conservatives identify with Christianity or a pre-Western civilization.[10]

The postwar amalgam of impartial secularism and foursquare piety, the vigorous union of sturdy creativity and garden-variety conviction in discoverable truths, the patriotism of the greatest generation, all have given way to a crescendo of "deconstruction," "barbarities," ironic sneering, and pop religions of prosperity. The paradigm shift is also a power shift. The enemy is inside the gate. The establishment has turned into an upscale freak show; elites, their epigones and simpering hangers-on, spend too much time camping it up. "This time," as the Catholic philosopher Alasdair MacIntyre put it, "the barbarians are not waiting beyond the frontiers; they have already been governing us for some time."[11]

The comprehensiveness of Kurth's analysis belies its weakness. There are too many pasteboard bad guys—ravenous feminists, sissified intellectuals, shabbily assimilated minorities, all courting the favor of a fickle, postliterate mass public—for the linkages between cultural revolution and a pusillanimous foreign policy to be swallowed whole. The jeremiad warns of collapse from depravity and, as the narrator of *The Great Gatsby* put it, "carelessness." It has the power of a George Grosz cartoon of floozies and fat-cats from the Weimar period, and the argument captures some of the plight of contemporary American culture. ("The fact is," Steve Jobs noted in hyperbolic and possibly gleeful agreement with recent surveys, "people don't read anymore.") There is an ineluctability to Kurth's critique that leaves little room either for impromptu scrambling or concerted planning. There seems nothing to do but throw in Yeats's lament that "things fall apart," from "The Second Coming," take a stiff drink, and duck.[12]

It is just such polemical energy that drives Kurth's message home through the haziness of the causal paths. The tragedy for Kurth is that the very habitat of American political culture is contaminated. While blame can be assigned to one or another set of villains, the degradation of the civil environment is so advanced that, like an ecological implosion, it destroys the options of those trapped in it. The problem is all around us, the cultural equivalent of habitat loss. Unmoored from "Western civilization," the entire culture has undergone a colossal corruption and dumbing-down. The end game is a weird collision of self-destruction and collective despondency.[13]

The air of systemic doom is one we have glimpsed before in the demographic, economic, and cultural vortex—the depletion of clerical numbers, the depreciation of ministerial infrastructures, the drift of opinion, especially among younger cohorts, away from the teachings of the church, the sheer indifference—that threatens to crush American Catholicism. We have seen something like it in the forebodings articulated by John Courtney Murray about an imperiled sexual hierarchy. We will see vestiges of it in the horror expressed by the Leadership Roundtable at the demoralization and spiritual "discombobulation" of the Catholic populace. ("The trouble with the American people," one Roundtable board member opined in reacting to the idea that religious beliefs are extraordinarily widespread in the United States compared to most of Western Europe, "is that they are not religious *enough*.")[14]

Possibly, Kurth has gotten the macrosociology right, even if his condemnation of the transition goes awry in imputing conspiratorial powers and a lethal toxicity to feminists and their fellow travelers. He sounds as distraught as Edmund Burke going on about "the swinish multitude." The power shift he discerns may be correct in broad outline, minus the sinister intentions, debilitating consequences, and overall demonization.[15]

Apocalypse is not a policy, even if its tragic sensibility and visionary fervor can be appreciated. Unless repentance itself is the answer, jeremiads are not motivational speeches. Kurth does not do marching orders, helpful hints, or solace. He sounds overwrought. Pessimistic though some of them are, many conservatives are on the lookout not just for ideas but for usable ideas. This requires experimentation and revision—the methodological credo that runs through the work of Wilson, DiIulio, and their colleagues. But these scholar-practitioners are also committed to the proposition that the problems they deal with are cultural—that is, moral—at the core. Because they are cultural, such problems resist actionable takeaways. Neoconservatives flirt with the same risk as Kurth—insightful despair, trapped in self-awareness without an exit strategy.[16]

One way out of the dilemma is to stress the need for moral clarity. In an interview given toward the end of his life, the social democrat Tony Judt lamented the absence of an equivalent certainty on the left. "Part of the attraction of someone who otherwise didn't appeal to me in the least—like, say, John Paul II—was... his sense of an absolutely, morally uncompromising view about what is right and what is wrong."

> What's missing from public conversation and public policy conversation is precisely a sort of moral underpinning, a sense of the moral purposes that bind people together in functional societies... It seems to me that we need to reintroduce some of that. We need to reintroduce confidently and unashamedly that kind of language into the public realm.[17]

Another option is to punt and muddle through. This involves putting examination of the evidence together with a willingness to spitball about solutions. The latter may be only loosely consistent with the former. Identifying social problems and their causes is difficult enough. Even more serious difficulties—political, budgetary, managerial—accompany the sifting and execution of policy options. Since the link between problem identification and problem solving is so chancy, reliance on deduction pure and simple does not suffice. Brain storming, riffing, and bounded rationality may make up for clinical precision. Eclecticism, imagination, ideological iconoclasm, political chutzpah, and a dose of opportunism are required. The idea is to set solutions in motion and move beyond a paralysis induced as much by a fear of making mistakes as by despair.

None of the Catholic intellectuals and policy makers discussed in the following pages attain the fire-and-brimstone doomsday pitch of James Kurth. In one way or another they are all experimentalists. They were also caught up in the white-hot feuds emanating from the sixties. Though few recognized it at the time, Vatican II (1962–65) was something of a kick-off for that tumultuous decade, and Catholicism was not immune to the turbulence of the Council and its aftermath.[18]

Daniel Patrick Moynihan—scholar, statesman, senator from New York, and ethnic raconteur with a taste for the pleasures of the table and the liquor cabinet—was in on the founding of the sixties. His "Report on the Negro Family" came out in 1965, the same year as the Supreme Court's Griswold v. Connecticut decision that legalized the sale of contraceptives. Moynihan sparked a firestorm by suggesting that rates of illegitimacy in the African American community foreshadowed a crisis in family structure. The report was prescient. By the 1990s the incidence of out-of-wedlock births among whites had skyrocketed to the same level, over 30 percent, that prevailed among African Americans in 1960.[19]

A stunning anomaly almost got lost in the controversy surrounding the report. When Moynihan went over the statistics for black male unemployment and new welfare cases from the late 1940s to the early 1960s, the correlation between the two confirmed that the indicators trended together. The data seemed to prove the obvious: Increases in poverty drove up welfare expenditures. But then, as the unemployment rate among African Americans started to go down in the mid-sixties, the welfare caseload in the same population continued to climb, as did out-of-wedlock births. Something was off-key in the socioeconomic score.

Economic deprivation no longer seemed so evidently to be the cause of family breakdown. This was one of the first empirical inklings that something else—culture?—was amiss. Neoconservatives contemplated a still more drastic possibility. The causal flow might go the other way. At some point, welfare expenditures themselves might encourage family breakdown and out-of-wedlock births, just as the Laffer curve that came a decade later was to predict a net downturn in revenues as a result of over-taxation. Public programs might make poverty worse. Good intentions paved the way to perverse outcomes. That claim would become a truism for critics of bussing and affirmative action. Not culture but government giveaways were the culprit.

Which was not the conclusion that Moynihan drew. But his report did call attention to the ramifications of family breakdown for welfare policy. Moynihan succeeded in transforming change in the family from a predominantly private or therapeutic issue into a public policy matter on a grand scale—what came to be called a "social issue"—with moral overtones.[20] Here the influence of Moynihan on both Wilson and DiIulio is plain to see. The ideas from a memo that Moynihan, himself the child of a broken family, wrote to Lyndon Johnson in the wake of his 1965 report, emphasizing the importance of culture by insisting that "the richest inheritance any child can have is a stable, loving, disciplined family life," can be found rephrased in the work of Wilson and DiIulio.[21]

Moynihan insisted that the looming crisis merited more than transient alarm. It signaled a turning point in the nature of poverty, and it had crucial implications for welfare policy. The United States used to be a welfare laggard compared to the countries of Northern Europe, which had begun to respond to industrialization decades before the Great Depression compelled the Roosevelt administration to adopt social insurance and other public policies for ameliorating economic hardship.[22] By the 1960s, however, the United States had overtaken other Western democracies in one important respect: the American economy had produced the first postindustrial society. The problem was no longer poverty associated with dips in the economic cycle but poverty that persisted amid prosperity. A rising tide did not lift all boats. At the epicenter of this disaster was "the earthquake that shuddered through the American family in the past twenty years... the sudden sustained rise in single parenthood and out-of-wedlock births since the mid-1960s."[23] The aftershocks would soon spread to Europe. But for now the United States had a chance to lead the way in social policy.

Moynihan was at pains to repeat "the great wisdom of American conservatives: Stateways do not change Folkways."[24] Still, he helped design government policies to combat poverty and stem the disintegration of two-parent families anyway. Moynihan held on to more of the New Deal, state-centric progressivism he had grown up with than many of his neoconservative pals. Rather than being an article of faith, his reminder to "expect little of government, especially national government" distilled a skepticism that grew out of first-hand experience with the sausage-making of policy.[25] He had also been beaten up by public opinion. His was a cake-of-custom conservatism that revered the little platoons of local tradition and that dealt with domestic problems by trying to induce incremental reforms rather than a root-and-branch overhaul. Moynihan, an analytical mind with a romantic temperament, was consistent in his eclecticism, favoring abortion rights while upholding Catholic social teaching.[26]

"The central conservative truth," Moynihan wrote sonorously, "is that it is culture, not politics, that determines the success of a society. The central liberal truth," he added, not to be outdone in turning a phrase, "is that politics can change a culture and save it from itself."[27] The two precepts might coexist. Moynihan conceded the validity of the neoconservative claim that culture in some form, rather than only or even mainly economic structures, was at the root of dysfunctional behavior. But he was unwilling to rule out government intervention. "Truths," liberal or conservative, were provisional guidelines for getting things done. There were few hard-and-fast principles, and differences between principles were virtually irresolvable anyway. Visionary inclinations were fine as long as they didn't get in the way of facing the facts, and facts themselves were subject to error and scarcity. What mattered were ingenious speculation and working hypotheses. If one thing didn't work, try something else. It sounded more like seat-of-the-pants pragmatism after the fashion of William James, or frantic inventiveness in the style of FDR, than textbook social doctrine.[28]

Mary Ann Glendon, Learned Hand professor of law at Harvard, first female president of the Pontifical Academy of Social Sciences, and recipient of the National Humanities Medal in 2005, shares a key supposition with neoconservatives. The rupture in traditional values that struck family life has produced several baleful consequences. Glendon's depiction of the change is worth quoting at length for the sharpness of the before-and-after contrast:

> By the turn of the twentieth century, Western family law systems had come to share... a common set of assumptions. Domestic relations law was organized around a unitary conception of the family as marriage-centered and patriarchal... [Marriage] was supposed... to last until the death of a spouse and was made terminable during the lives of the spouses, if at all, only for serious cause.... Within the family, the standard authority structure and pattern of role allocation decreed that the husband-father should predominate in decision-making and should provide for the material needs of the family.... Illegitimate children had hardly any legal existence at all...
>
> Not one of these formerly basic assumptions has survived unchanged. Most have been eliminated, and some have been turned on their heads.... The edifice of traditional family law remained standing until the 1960s, but the cracks in its foundations had appeared much earlier. The past twenty years have witnessed the movement from undercurrent to mainstream in family law of individualistic,

> egalitarian, and secularizing trends that have been gaining power in Western legal systems since the late eighteenth century.[29]

Of special importance here is the genealogy that traces upheavals in family law to changes originating in the Enlightenment and the French Revolution. This vision of a moral *longue durée* is obligatory among conservatives.[30] Yet, somewhat elliptically, Glendon rules out a simple association between the severity or laxity of divorce statutes and marital solidity or instability at any one time. For that matter, she also denies that continental theorists of the French persuasion, who actually made little dent in Anglo-American legal codes, can be blamed for the failures of family policy in the United States. Her interest is in the "long-term, indirect effects of legal norms," on the one hand, and on the other in the unanticipated consequences of "abrupt changes in long-standing legal traditions."[31]

Glendon suggests that it is the rapidity with which legal changes are enacted, not just their content, that makes them harmful, and it is the unforeseen side effects of headlong innovations that lead to disenchantment with emancipatory aims. While her disillusionment with forced-march social engineering is well within the neoconservative mold, Glendon's treatment of the social outcomes of legal systems across countries is uncommonly nuanced. Her appreciation of how governments can mitigate individual misfortune and social catastrophe is closer to the views of Moynihan than to those of most other neoconservatives.[32]

Long remarried after an early divorce, Glendon brings a woman's perspective to the analysis of family breakdown that accentuates the concerns evident in the work of Wilson, DiIulio, and Moynihan. She stresses the fate of children and single mothers under a legal system, that of the United States, that prizes I-gotta-be-me individualism and self-reliance more than is typical in continental, particularly Northern, Europe. Glendon's viewpoint highlights the harsh impact of American judicial wisdom on the unprotected. Her take is a departure from the conservative habit of laying responsibility for social and moral decline on statist reformers, rabidly anticlerical intellectuals, or implacable advocates of women's emancipation.[33] "Anglo-American, and especially American, law has placed greater emphasis on individual rights," Glendon argues, "while the civil law systems [of Europe]... have moderated this emphasis with more attention to social context and individual responsibility."

> The difference in emphasis is subtle, but its spirit penetrates every detail of the respective legal systems.... While Anglo-American common law by the turn of the [nineteenth] century had more readily accepted a mythology of self- reliance, the civil law systems were more influenced by the politics of compassion of Rousseau and his followers.... The individual is envisioned, more than in our legal system, as situated within family and community; rights are viewed as inseparable from corresponding responsibilities; and liberty and equality are seen as coordinate with fraternity.[34]

The cultural revolution of the sixties unfolded at high speed everywhere in the West. What troubles Glendon is that the social reverberations of this revolution played out disastrously in the United States. There, she believes, the consequences for women and children involved in broken marriages have been ruinous. Though "such families (especially if they are headed by women) seem to be in a more or less precarious position everywhere," the blowback from divorce is softened by "long-standing European policies and programs to aid families with children." By comparison, the American social safety net is so miserly that many single mothers and their children, left to fend for themselves, get stuck in poverty. They are abandoned not only by their spouses but by the American ethic of minimalism regarding social protection. (The United States has the highest rate of incarceration and the lowest provision of publicly supported child care in the industrial world.) They are doubly victimized.[35]

The cogency of Glendon's analysis lies in her awareness of the cross-national variations in legal and political cultures. She focuses on the hard-to-undo, historically embedded cast of mind that mistakes American individualism for everyday commonsense, as if that supposition were inscribed in human nature. Her bête noire is the characteristically American device of no-fault divorce and the danger of abandonment to which it exposes women and children.

Again and again Glendon returns to her core theme, that the American case is a not altogether admirable outlier. Vainglorious exceptionalism is not a virtue. It is merely debased chauvinism. "By making a radical version of individual autonomy normative," she insists, in a frontal assault on the mystique of self-reliance,

> we inevitably imply that dependency is something to be avoided in oneself and disdained in others. American distinctiveness in this regard is most evident and problematic with respect to laws in the areas of procreation, family relations and child raising.... [T]he new freedom to terminate marriage is accompanied to a lesser degree in the United States than in most other Western countries by legal protections and social programs that respond to the needs of a spouse who has become dependent for the sake of child raising. Similarly, in the construction and operation of our welfare programs, and with respect to parental leave, child care, and other forms of family assistance, the United States lags behind many other liberal democracies in protecting motherhood and childhood.[36]

At the end of the day, what repels Glendon is the "persistent absoluteness in rights talk that is still more common in the United States than elsewhere." The stubborn legacy of individualism, to the neglect of social costs, reached fearful expression when Roe v. Wade justified abortion on the grounds of privacy, and it crops up in the tunnel-vision libertarianism that mounts attacks against gun control and mandatory seat belts.

> Excessively strong formulations [in claims of absoluteness] express our most infantile instincts rather than our potential to be reasonable men and women. A country where we can do "anything we want" is not a republic of free people attempting to live their lives together.... There is pathos as well as bravado in these attempts to deny the fragility and contingency of human existence, personal freedom, and the possession of worldly goods.... The exaggerated absoluteness of our American rights rhetoric is... bound up with... a near-silence concerning responsibility, and a tendency to envision the rights-bearer as a lone autonomous individual.[37]

"How are self-reliance, individual liberty, and tolerance related to selfish indifference, isolation, and nihilism?" Glendon asks. "At what point does the language of individualism in a society or in a legal system begin crowding out other modes of discourse?"[38] The questions are rhetorical. The tipping point was the 1960s.

The specter of blue-sky rights talk that agitates Glendon is identical in all but name to the dictatorship of relativism condemned by Benedict XVI. Late in 2007, George W. Bush nominated Mary Ann Glendon as ambassador to the Holy See.[39]

Wilson, DiIulio, and Glendon agree that the children of divorce are at risk. Broken families jeopardize their chances of educational attainment and social advancement. But there are two areas of divergence. One concerns the role of character. Like Wilson, DiIulio, and many others who see the sixties as a moral watershed, Glendon stresses personal responsibility and chastises self-indulgence. However, rather than push programs that propose, even indirectly, to rehabilitate character, she singles out the perverse consequences of a legal system that aggravates the social havoc of divorce. The law is rigged; the fault is more structural than personal. The norm of individual choice enshrined in the American judicial code heightens incentives for dissolving unsatisfactory unions; the system is socially reckless and counterproductive. The well-being of children succumbs to the primacy of self-fulfillment and the pursuit of individual happiness. The culprit is a legal code that privileges self-interest and is oblivious to its collective side effects. All this makes marital dissolution too easy. The American ideal is to live the dream at all costs. The pursuit of happiness has become unbridled. The atomizing bias of the divorce courts appears to bear as much of the blame for poverty, at least for female poverty, as the welfare system and the failings of individuals combined.[40]

The differences between Wilson and DiIulio on the one hand and Glendon on the other turn out to be as substantial as their similarities. As far as divorce is concerned, the legal system is for Glendon what the pre-1996 welfare machine was for Wilson and to a lesser extent DiIulio. Both arrangements turn a blind eye toward, and in fact encourage, moral nonchalance and social disorder. Permissiveness is built into them. The systems themselves are socially derelict. The incentives they offer are, in the vocabulary of earlier times, temptations that prove crippling for character development and destructive for the collectivity. But for Glendon the problem comes in the individualizing slant of the justice system and its carelessness about communitarian values. For Wilson and to some extent DiIulio the problem arises from criminally self-destructive communal norms. The remedy for a culture of poverty is a renewal of individual responsibility.

A second area of divergence is that Glendon criticizes the American welfare code not for its profligacy but for its stinginess. She opposes narcissistic rights but not, unlike many neoconservatives, social entitlements. It is the legal rather than the welfare system that makes immorality and poverty worse.

Glendon's argument depends on a cosmopolitan, cross-national perspective that is less prominent in Wilson and DiIulio.[41] In reacting against what they castigated as the self-loathing and America-bashing of radicals and liberals, many conservatives renewed their patriotism by way of a chauvinism that emulates the martial vigor prized by Kurth. Things foreign got discredited, and in the process of shoring up nativist defenses against a hostile world, discriminating judgment about international differences, never very acute, got lost. Like Freedom Fries, American exceptionalism became a reality built partly on a myth concocted by intellectuals wrapped in the flag.

Wilson, DiIulio, and Glendon converge on the indispensability of moral fiber as an ingredient of social order. (Wilson came to focus more on the derelictions of the poor than the misdeeds of the wealthy; "At the root of policy failure," Todd Gitlin, a former student of Wilson wrote in dissent, "was bad character—not the bad character of agents of dispossession but the bad character of the undeserving poor."[42]) They disagree about the responsibility of the public sector for the welfare of citizens. Both themes came into contention during the climactic struggle over the welfare reform of 1996.

CHAPTER FIVE

WELFARE REFORM, AMERICAN VALUES, AND THE TRIUMPH OF CATHOLIC NEOCONSERVATISM

The last two decades of the twentieth century witnessed a ferocious battle over how to rectify the excesses of the sixties and the seventies. In the eyes of conservatives, the cultural revolution that burst forth in the sixties was a one-two punch for a society already burdened by the economic overreaching of government initiated during the thirties. "A smoldering sense of dispossession, cultural as well as economic," the historian Steve Fraser wrote, "fed a conservative populism that committed an act of double counter-revolution: against the New Deal welfare state and against the racial, gender, and cultural upheavals that turned the world upside down in the 60s."[1] Political change would require more than a routine course correction. Permissiveness was rife, government spending was running wild. All hell, it seemed, was breaking loose. Redemption called for a renovation of ideas and values. The success of neoconservatives in casting policy discussion in these terms is a measure of their influence.[2]

Several elements went into the mix. One was abortion. Opposition to Roe v. Wade revitalized religious conservatives. Another pair of controversies also propelled mobilization: the role imputed to family breakdown in the propagation of poverty and the reproduction of social disorder, and the responsibility of government for handling this complex of pathologies. It looked like a short step from combustible issues like these to reevaluating the role of government generally. Moral values, economic choices, and political principles seemed to complement one another. The transformation encompassed a "dramatic erosion of the New Deal liberal-regulatory order and the meteoric rise of a religiously inflected Right."[3]

The centerpiece of this chapter is the debate over social policy that reached its climax in the Personal Responsibility and Work Opportunity Reconciliation Act (PRWORA) of 1996. "A Democratic president presided over the end of the welfare program," the historian Elaine Tyler May concluded, "a rapidly widening gap between rich and poor, and mergers of giant corporations into even more gigantic conglomerates with vast power. Citizens expressed distrust toward their government and each other."[4] Extending over several decades, the saga incorporates almost all the cultural and social issues that burst open in the sixties. Conservatives won the fight over public policy. In the process, their Catholic brethren consolidated their leadership position within the church.

Consequentialist, cause-effect reasoning played a part in the defeat of left-of-center social Catholicism. Within the culture of American pragmatism, this way of thinking had greater intuitive plausibility than talk of "structural sin," which sounded exotically collective and alien. Buttressed by quantitative evidence, the belief that family dynamics conditioned life chances became the new common sense. It sounded like a problem that parents, encouraged by the government's rectification of intrusive policies, could do something about.

Unexceptionable as this accent on the family sounded, and perhaps because it became so taken-for-granted so quickly, the conviction did not stand at the top of the policy agenda espoused by the leadership of the American church. The riveting argument was about abortion, not about a mom-and-apple-pie consensus surrounding the family. The latter was a topic that could appear as flavorless as the statement that the bishops had issued years back in support of traffic safety. At the same time, for many Catholics principles of social justice drawn from papal encyclicals, criticizing market-generated disparities in wealth and income, seemed like side issues, too, non-starters in comparison with abortion. But these priorities had supporters in the upper reaches of the episcopate, especially in the offices of the national bishops' conference.

The back-to-back pastoral letters issued in the mid-eighties on war and peace and the economy laid out the peace-and-justice agenda. Though drawing on Catholic prudential thought concerning "just war," these lofty positions stood apart from the cost-benefit calculus that influenced debate among policy makers. What looked like prophetic radicalism was sidestepped, giving way to probabilistic estimates of cause and effect.[5]

Conservatives could not be described as coolly scientific. A distinctive constellation of values had an even greater impact than empirical reasoning on tilting opinion in favor of their position. It was not just the pro-life commitment of Catholic neoconservatives that matched the position of evangelical Protestants. Their appreciation of personal responsibility suited an American attachment to individualism and self-help, and it reflected a growing skepticism, among a generation of Catholics for whom the New Deal was a distant memory, about government activism.[6] The cultural revolution was a more vivid turning point than the Great Depression. "Hey, hippy! Get a haircut! Get a job!" spoke to cultural and economic demands alike. With moral and value issues in the ascendant after the turmoil of the sixties, progressive Catholics were left with an agenda—clergy-lay consultation, the ordination of women, and other questions of internal reform—that few of the faithful, much less outsiders, cared about.

By joining moral-sexual and economic-social precepts, conservatives managed to outflank the comparatively liberal bishops' conference. Instead of political and economic progressivism, "the adventure of orthodoxy would be stressed."[7] Catholics in the pews seemed to want direction and leadership rather than liberation from the conformity that oppressed the rebels and iconoclasts of the sixties. The historian John McGreevy summarized the ingredients of the moral and empirical cocktail that gained popularity beyond Catholic circles and changed the conversation on welfare:

> John Paul II's conservative views on abortion and sexual ethics generally mirrored a wider withdrawal from 1960s-style liberalism in American intellectual life, certainly in its Catholic variant. At the level of ideas, philosophers such as Alasdair MacIntyre attacked the "Enlightenment project" and a liberalism predicated on a false sense of moral neutrality. At the level of policy, Daniel Patrick Moynihan, Mary Ann Glendon, and James Q. Wilson cast jaundiced eyes on liberal social welfare policies and no-fault divorce. In the narrow world of Catholic polemics,

> neoconservatives such as Michael Novak, Richard John Neuhaus, and George Weigel pushed Catholic liberals to acknowledge the achievements of market capitalism, the importance of the two-parent family, and the unstable foundations of liberal church-state jurisprudence.... The neoconservatives made empirical, not just ideological, arguments and provided an important check to liberal pretensions.[8]

Some policy makers who played lead roles in the showdown over welfare reform believed that the connection between the collapse of the nuclear family and socially damaging behavior made for a selective vision of what had gone wrong with the country. The good family as envisioned by James Q. Wilson, for example, struck some as socially disembodied. One such critic was Mary Jo Bane, professor of public policy and management at Harvard's Kennedy School and former commissioner of the New York Department of Social Services. Just as John DiIulio would later resign from the Republican administration of George W. Busch, Bane, a fellow Catholic, quit the Clinton administration after the Welfare Reform Act of 1996 was signed into law.

In her capacity as Assistant Secretary for Children and Families at the Department of Health and Human Services during the Clinton years, Bane was intimately involved in formulating family policy. She believed that a fixation on family breakdown as a precipitant of poverty got things backwards. Harmful as family dissolution was, the larger problem was worsening income inequality.

When she returned to academia, Bane was quick to point out that the gap between rich and poor, an issue that had been a liberal priority during the sixties and seventies, had dropped out of policy discussion altogether. "The 1980s and 1990s have been... a time of unprecedented economic prosperity," she acknowledged, echoing concerns that Moynihan had expressed in the 1960s and 1970s about poverty amid plenty.

> But the prosperity has not been widely shared. Between 1970 and 1996, the mean income of the top fifth of American families increased from $131,450 to $217,355, while the mean income of the bottom fifth... decreased from $11,640 to $11,388.

> During the same period, the portion of America's children under the age of 6 living in poverty grew from 16.6 to 22.7 percent; and from 1976 to 1996 the portion of Americans without health care coverage grew from 10.9 to 15.6 percent.[9]

The thrust of Bane's argument is not just to restore economic disparities to causal status in the impoverishment of families. She also calls attention to the politically harmful consequences of the widening gap between rich and poor. For conservatives, the dangerous outcome of misguided policy is to make social disintegration worse. Policy gets to be misguided because liberals conflate reducing poverty with narrowing the wealth and income divide when they should focus instead on lifting the absolute level of prosperity. The moral hazard inherent in welfare should be crashingly obvious: It corrupts the poor with expectations of handouts, accustoming them to dependency, laziness, and immorality. By contrast, for progressives like Bane, wrongheaded welfare cutbacks reinforce economic and political oligarchy. The concentration of wealth subverts the republic, distorting the democratic playing field. Politicians deliver the best government that money can buy; democracy morphs into plutocracy.[10] "It is hard to see," she wrote, "how American society, especially our sense of obligation to one another, can thrive in the face of huge and growing inequalities."

> In a "winner take all society"... how will we renew what has been an historically American commitment to building institutions such as public schools and hospitals, offering attainable health coverage and supportive work programs that provide all citizens genuine opportunity and shared prosperity?[11]

In the midst of this condemnation Bane takes note of a puzzle. Disparities in income do not bother Americans very much. "Despite these precipitous trends," she observes, "most Americans do not seem to see economic disparity as a problem. They appear not to begrudge the wealthy their riches, perhaps because popular culture suggests that the rich have earned their rewards, perhaps because aspiring to riches seems such a part of human nature."[12]

Though she does not spell it out, Bane all but admits two cognate facts. By cross-national standards the American public remains extraordinarily tolerant of income differentials. Socialism sounds incurably foreign. And it is conservatives who for a long time have had the backing of what looked like most of the citizenry on the issue. Pundits regularly remind Americans that the United States is a center-right country.[13]

The legacy of individualism is slow to change. Cultural inertia is compounded by the difficulty of grasping remote, relatively impersonal systemic forces. On the other hand, patterns of personal behavior that lend themselves to graphic parables—to exposés of welfare queens, for example—are ready-made illustrations of government gone wrong. In facing the bias in favor of self-reliance and the individualistic creed, Bane ran up against a set of beliefs analogous to the sway of cultural breakdown and personal failings over material circumstance that neoconservatives take as the root of social deviance. Individuals are to be blamed for their economic failures. By the same token, they should not be admonished for personal initiative, even when the rewards for it are astronomic. Pluck and luck rule. Unless traumatized by horrendous shocks such as the financial meltdown that hit toward the end of the first decade of the millennium, citizens have a way of clinging to dream-like convictions over real-world conditions.[14]

Though shaken by cascading bad news toward the end of the first decade of the new century, Americans hold to a kind of economic innocence. Even then, after the Occupy Wall Street demonstrations, William Galston observed that "the vast majority of the public... just don't care that much about income inequality."[15] "In short," Katherine Newman and Elisabeth Jacobs conclude, "compared to other Western nations, Americans are willing to put up with more economic inequality." But if we set aside this persistent cross-national contrast and instead compare citizens over time, drawing on opinions they held several years ago, Americans seem less willing to tolerate a blatant skewing of the income profile: "an overwhelming majority of us believe income differences are too large."[16]

Attitudes like these may seem as flighty as the changes in events they supposedly reflect rather than deep-seated values. They begin to make sense, however, if a threefold distinction is kept in mind. First, in the years since the passage of the Civil Rights Act of 1964, Americans can be credited with near-consensual accord about equality of opportunity. This is the social baseline of democracy, the communal equivalent of political liberty. It is the economic, merit-based side of the American creed. Opportunity corresponds to grace in the American civil religion, and material expansion is its collective consort. The track is supposed to be level. There are to be no discriminatory handicaps at the starting line, even if in practice some classes of competitors—women, for example—are new to the race.[17]

Second, there is substantial though weaker backing for a stronger form of equity: a safety net below which citizens are not supposed to fall. "Americans are historically decided on the importance of protecting individual liberties," Margie DeWeese-Boyd observes, "and less decided on the importance of promoting public goods."[18] Here we are in the realm of social insurance and publicly subsidized health care. These are distributive policies designed to shelter people from the hazards of fortune or, like affirmative action, to provide a hand in evening out points of departure. Though controversial, collective protections like these enjoy a measure of legitimacy and popular support.[19]

Third, imagine amounts of income and wealth above which citizens might not be permitted to rise out of a fear that their distance from the less well-off would endanger the democratic commonweal. A structural distortion that skews economic rewards in one direction and democratic ideals in another is the problem. Concentrated wealth might give the rich too much power. At this point, consensus falls apart. At issue are redistributive policies and the possibility not of squelching mobility from below ("equality of opportunity") but of squashing the top of the pyramid along which upward mobility moves. Capping rewards or the appearance of entertaining such an idea smacks of leveling. "Redistribution" strikes the ear as "revenge" or "class warfare." It blurs into egalitarianism as equality of result, and that is thought to be unproductive, unjust, and un-American. The mythic sky is still the limit. Belief in the contrary is inadmissable.[20]

By the time the consequences of the welfare reform of the mid-nineties were becoming visible, Mary Jo Bane had begun to mellow. The most controversial feature of that reform was the Temporary Assistance for Needy Families (TANF) block grants, imposing work requirements and a five-year limit to cash assistance. TANF replaced the Depression-era program of Aid to Families with Dependent Children (AFDC), which included neither stipulation. The reform was a political success, among other reasons because it saved money by cutting caseloads. As for reducing poverty, the results were uneven. Greater numbers of poor women took jobs but many were unable to retain them, in part because of inadequate child care. And TANF made no dent on reducing income inequality or on driving down nonmarital unions. In fact, income inequality got worse.[21]

Bane conceded the partial efficacy of the work requirement, and she endorsed a modified food stamps program which, though it did not require work, set benefits at a low level. She continued to decry a stinginess that failed to provide "a basic level of food, shelter, and medical care for everyone," even to those "who fail to live up to the expectations of [worthiness] that we rightly build into government programs."[22]

Bane expressed these judgments in a conversation with Lawrence Mead, a political scientist and one of the chief architects of the 1996 reform. An Episcopalian, Mead is curious about the role of religion in public policy. But his skepticism does not sit well with two conservative nostrums. In prizing results over good intentions, Mead relegates faith-based initiatives of the proselytizing variety to the margins of service provision, and he is impatient with philosophical insistence on the small government ideal. The title of *Government Matters*, his study of welfare reform in Wisconsin, headlines the lesson that "solutions to poverty must finally look... to the capacities of government itself.... Social solutions finally depend on statecraft."[23]

The pragmatism that Mead favors regarding poverty reduction puts him closer than many neoconservatives to the Moynihan legacy of thinking about welfare, and his agnosticism about the applicability of religious guidelines to public policy distances him from most evangelicals. Mead's skepticism extends still further. He questions the notion, cherished by conservatives, that single motherhood is a direct cause of poverty. His assessment of the controversy sounds very much like one issued by Bane herself a decade before:[24]

> Long-term poor families tend to become poor because of the behaviors that make poverty controversial: Women have children out of wedlock, and then they or their spouses do not work regularly to support their children. Of the two causes, unwed pregnancy appears to be the less important, contrary to common opinion. Families become poor or go on welfare mainly because they lack earnings, not because they are headed by a woman, and that is especially true for the black poor. Employment problems also help to produce female-headed families, in that failure to provide for their families causes many low-income men to abandon them—or to be driven out by their spouses.[25]

The effect of all this is to make the colloquy between Mead and Bane sound like a cruise toward conciliation. At the technical level, in the details of shaping policies around worthy goals, "[we] differ rather little in our poverty and welfare policy prescriptions." (Bane and Mead call one another "radical incrementalists.") One inference that Bane, a practicing Catholic, draws is that theological differences might not matter very much when it comes to economic and social policy.[26]

Religious traditions can have an impact, Bane argues, in "our tendency to err on different sides in conditions of uncertainty." This is a possibly important effect. It suggests, as DiIulio does, that values become decisive when hard information is ambiguous or unavailable. Falling back on core values can make a difference when priorities have to be rank-ordered on a policy agenda crowded with more or less attractive, or equally unattractive, choices. Both situations are more familiar to politicians than fine-grained data analysis. You go with your gut, or your biases. Moral predispositions come into play.

Bane emphasizes her attachment to a Catholic ethos that recommends "a preferential option for the poor."[27] For his part, while he devotes several pages to an examination of scriptural admonitions about wealth, poverty, and a variety of other issues, Mead states that "the essentials of my viewpoint are, so far as I have read, entirely my own." Then he adds, half in consternation, as if he had expected something less equivocal from his biblical excursion, "I find this quite surprising."[28]

It is possible to make out a softer, tender-hearted tone in Bane and a stricter, tough-minded one in Mead, and the contrast might be attributed to a Catholic-Protestant divide over indulgence versus discipline. But there is at least as much variance within the two perspectives as there is between them, and it is hard to distinguish temperament from tradition.[29] When Rebecca Blank and William McGurn engaged in a similar dialogue, the roles were reversed. Blank, a Protestant, took a liberal line when quoting from scripture, while McGurn, a Catholic, cited papal encyclicals copiously to remind his audience of the dangers of government intrusion in the economy.[30]

Political horse-trading powerfully affected the outcome of welfare reform in 1996. After his party lost the midterm elections of 1994, Bill Clinton chose to sacrifice "welfare as we knew it"—in effect, sustenance without time limits for families with children in poverty—for the sake of preserving Medicaid and Medicare, which Republican budget-cutters also had their eyes on. Entitlements like Medicare affected many more voters than welfare programs. None of these decisions flowed axiomatically from religious beliefs.[31]

For all this, regardless of their religious provenance, the values that policy makers brought to deliberations on welfare were tangled up in the battle over reform during the 1990s. In addition, it is important to consider the restrictions that mass political culture—values and framing assumptions widely held in public opinion over long periods of time—place on advocates and opponents of welfare reform. These views run deeper than fleeting attitudes.[32]

The innovation that Mead and others succeeded in building into PRWORA in 1996 was the imperative of "reciprocity"—the requirement, not just the expectation, that adult recipients work in return for aid. Citizenship entails a social contract, contingent on work, not a guaranteed income.[33] The general public knows next to nothing of the details of the welfare reforms about which Bane and Mead find themselves in rough agreement. But giving priority to the work ethic resonates unassailably, like family values, in the American milieu. Together, they conveyed a powerful political message. This is the sentiment enshrined in the passage of the welfare reform of 1996. PRWORA put traditional standards regarding work obligations, worthiness for public assistance, and family structures back into place.[34]

Voters were predisposed to the packaging of welfare reform as a spur to individual initiative and a reaffirmation of the American way. Catholics were little different from the rest of the electorate in this regard. Alarm about the fate of family values went hand-in-hand with a stern economic sobriety. The broader message of the church about social justice, pressed by the bishops, was taken as optional. It did not make a significant dent on the Catholic electorate.[35]

Finally, philanthropic decision-makers and service providers, including those in charge of managing large operations like Catholic Charities, did not come away empty-handed from the passage of the Personal Responsibility and Work Opportunity Reconciliation Act. While the office of the United States Conference of Catholic Bishops opposed the reform on the grounds that it constituted a flat-out repeal of welfare, the bishops themselves did not uphold this position as forcefully as their opposition to abortion. Section 104 of the welfare act contained a "charitable choice" section that regularized the funding eligibility of faith-based service providers. The trend toward contracting out the provision of welfare that took hold with the War on Poverty in the 1960s now encompassed even more religiously affiliated agencies.[36]

From the outset Catholic conservatives have placed a premium on ideas, at the core of which was loyalty to the wisdom of the church. A rock-like orthodoxy—"fidelity, fidelity, fidelity!" as Richard John Neuhaus insisted—was to be proclaimed with neoscholastic precision. The strategy complemented the restorationist project launched by John Paul II. Family values and right-to-life issues were essential ingredients of the campaign.

Catholic neoconservatives began to hook up with audiences in evangelical and policy-making quarters outside the church.[37] While conservatives continue to feel harassed by what they take to be a secular, progressive animus in academic and media circles, the appeal of the Catholic left to a mass constituency has not been overwhelming. Issues toward the top of the liberal agenda in the church have emphasized in-house power struggles over questions of authority that arouse the curiosity more than the commitment of sympathizers on the outside.[38]

As collaboration with non-Catholics evolved, social scientists and legal scholars extended the conversation about beliefs and culture from presumably intrinsic rights and wrongs toward possibly good and bad effects, that is, toward empirical questions about behavioral pathologies and collective dysfunction. The switch looks like a redirection of moral discourse toward social engineering. In fact, there was a modest change in emphasis that was more applicable to a subset of issues involving family structures—specifically, two-parent families—than to truly divisive controversies like abortion, same-sex marriage, and stem-cell research.[39]

The conceptual shift was vital nonetheless. Scientific language buttressed the traditional wisdom that personal foul-ups were not just individual pathologies but a collective problem that contaminated the body politic. Moral failings produced social fallout. They polluted the cultural environment as surely as industrial waste endangered the water supply. Fixing the negative by-products of undisciplined self-indulgence cost taxpayers money. Even then, expensive remedial programs might not work. The call went out for "a fusion of social and moral well-being," for "a conservatism that recognizes stable families as the foundation of economic growth."[40]

It was not just empirically informed bargaining, then, or rough-and-ready pragmatism that brought Catholic neoconservatives and their sympathizers together in helping pass a welfare reform that undid what they saw as the havoc wrought by the sixties and seventies. The alignment between Catholic veneration of traditional family structures and American reverence for individual responsibility and a small role for government also helped. And, even if they were not widely known, Catholic ideas about the benefits of subsidiarity could furnish a backup for the virtues of small government.[41]

The alliance was disjointed. The work requirement of PRWORA was difficult to square with the primacy given by the Vatican to the domestic role of women. Nor did the stress on individualism sit well with the communitarian leanings of otherwise conservative critics like Mary Ann Glendon. But as a melding of Catholic and American values, especially as these values were understood by the public rather than by the staff of the bishops' conference and those of the faithful who actually read encyclicals, the coalition worked. It played well not only among decision makers but in mass opinion, especially in that part of public opinion prevalent among regular churchgoers. The collective effects of family breakdown, emphasized by conservatives, were easier to understand than the structural causes, like poverty, that liberals argued underlay the problem. The program of welfare reform hit a sweet spot in American culture that joined moral concern and righteous self-interest. In a national discourse dominated by the language of nineteenth-century individualism, it is hard for progressives to weave values, ideas, and policy justifications together with comparable cogency.[42]

Though impressive, neoconservative accomplishments have been circumscribed. The liberalization of sexual behavior and the erosion of family structures that accelerated in the 1960s were followed, starting in the eighties, by economic deregulation. Conservatives have yet to come to terms with the effect of these dynamics on poverty and worsening income inequality. It is conceivable that the sky-high remuneration accorded to corporate executives in the name of return on investment may add as much to disparities in wealth and income as the meager skills that single mothers, their woefully prepared offspring, and assorted entitled spendthrifts and parasites among the 47 percent bring to the job market.[43] All this, together with stubbornly high unemployment and the deflation of credit cushions, eats away at the credibility of advanced capitalism. Even if full-blown progressive solutions to the crisis have not filled the vacuum, programs to raise tax rates on top earners were gaining popularity by the second decade of the twenty-first century.[44]

Enthusiasm for fashioning an across-the-board worldview that could consolidate a grand consensus has dwindled. The triad of social tradition, economic conservatism, and foreign policy realism is unwieldy, and the goal of uniting micro (moral) and macro (geopolitical) conservatisms in the form of a full-service *Weltanschauung* has made little headway.[45] Another blow was the turn of political fortune. The reversals suffered by American policy in the Middle East constituted a reality check for deductive styles of political strategizing; so did Vatican disapproval of the Iraq War. And the financial collapse of 2008 revived concerns about inequalities in wealth and income—even if, again, setting the progressive or conservative direction of the reaction to these developments remains a close thing.[46]

What does remain within the fold of Catholic neoconservatism is a shared commitment to nonnegotiable precepts surrounding pro-life issues. Beyond this, there is more or less cordial disagreement about the specifics of the responsibility of government and the means of implementing social policies and a broad, rather Olympian preference for democratic capitalism. These seem almost tangential compared to the virtual consensus around the core sexual-moral issues, on the norm of the two-parent, male-female family, and on preserving hieratic authority in Catholicism. Once past the essentials, Catholic neoconservative positions are only loosely bound to one another or to a common nucleus.[47] The building blocks of modular Catholicism can fit together in a variety of ways.

Looking back over decades of social activism and political controversy, Richard John Neuhaus conveyed a been-there-done-that bemusement with the ups-and-downs of public life. He expressed "some satisfaction with the way the debate on abortion has been shaped," and he noted that among the rewarding aspects of the quarrels won and lost was "the gathering and support of close friends."

These are no small achievements. Several of the ideas set forth by neoconservatives have been contested and some have been found wanting on evidentiary grounds. But there is no question that neoconservatives reframed the debate over welfare and chipped away at the privacy rationale underlying the legalization of abortion.[48] And they created a formidable network of intellectuals, propagandists, and benefactors to bankroll the spread of their ideas. Yet, a bit disconcertingly for someone who made his name decrying the naked public square, Neuhaus declared that "the church is my country."

> What happens in the church matters most to me, not the peripheral stuff of politics. I am very concerned that a clear distinction be made. The very logic of Catholicism is sharply different from the way a polity works. I'm a minimalist when it comes to pulling out all the stops in politics.[49]

While some of the disavowal of politics can be attributed to discretion, perhaps even to a dash of modesty, the statement also suggests that aspects of Catholic neoconservatism have been more successful among bunkered sectors of the hierarchy and outside the church, among evangelical Protestants, than among Catholics who pay off-again/on-again attention to elements of the magisterium they dislike or to leaders they distrust.[50]

The world according to Christian conservatism continues to be one in which religion, impeded from fully entering the public arena, has felt obliged to challenge the exclusionary rule and move into politics, lowering the wall between church and state.[51] In the face of increasing oversight of church affairs, the conservative priority is to prevent politics from entering the church. Offense has become the best defense. It is hard to shake the impression that there is something self-serving in the effort to keep politics out of religion while putting religion back into politics.

The vigorously intellectual bent among Catholic neoconservative leaders encouraged long-term projects over short-term programs, and this may account both for some of the coyness about the hurly-burly of politics and for the perseverance underlying the neoconservative cause. It also accounts for a certain snootiness regarding the cognitive skills of those who do not share their convictions. "Like shooting fish in a barrel" is how Neuhaus described attacking liberal Catholic intellectuals, who evidently form a perfect trifecta of the loserish, the delusional, and the oxymoronic.[52]

The strategy has meant concentrating conservative firepower on the unswerving truths of sexuality and authority. Such principles are presumed to stand apart from the secular reckoning that has infected segments of the clergy and laity. But the project has proved to be a hard sell among Catholics who acquiesce, on their own terms, for an assortment of reasons, or sit on their hands, or drift away. It has proved easier to find common ground between the ideologically compatible, regardless of denomination, than among Catholics themselves.[53]

One of Neuhaus's heroes was the eighteenth-century man of letters Samuel Johnson, who described himself as an "excessive" character, always "in extremes."[54] Dedicated neoconservatives like Neuhaus give the impression of feeling comfortable dealing with issues they can frame in no-two-ways-about-it categories—in the case of abortion, in terms of life-or-death choices. Tradition and first principles are crucial; so is incisive conceptualization. So is the cutting phrase. They are less at home discussing issues in economics and foreign affairs, where the terms of debate seem more cluttered and empirical. There is a tremulous détente between ideological-philosophical conservatives, almost all of them trained in theology or jurisprudence, and their theoretically less turbocharged colleagues, who are not so squeamish about evidence.[55]

Catholic neoconservatism represents a form of modular Catholicism, concentrating on the basics. It has been most successful when it has stayed on message about the sexual magisterium while managing to hook up with the ascendancy of family values and rugged individualism among Americans generally. The social magisterium is a lesser priority. Even then, within the American church, neoconservatism is a passionate minority among other minority currents. This is tied to the fact that the sexual teaching of the church is difficult to separate from its hierarchical governance. Non-Catholic conservatives are free to accept the former and ignore the latter. They can go their congregational way, admiring the church's moral teachings without having to accept the hierarchical trappings.

Catholics on the other hand are conflicted or inclined to compartmentalize doctrinal issues, good works, and questions of governance. The pro-life stance of neoconservatives attracts Catholics and non-Catholics in a way that school prayer, a predominantly Protestant issue, and access to contraception, mainly a Catholic (and less burning) priority, have never done.[56] Once the range of issues stretches to economic policy and foreign affairs, Catholic neoconservatism becomes diluted, certainly with regard to programmatic specifics if not in polemical virulence.

Plasticity contributes to the durability of the neoconservative cause beyond a Catholic setting. Issues concerning sexuality, the family, and welfare economics developed synergy across denominational boundaries. Even if the logical connections were hard to pin down, conservatives bundled the issues with an aura of moral concern, of doing the right—even countercultural—thing, and that package struck a popular chord.

A case could be made that this climate of opinion culminated in a Supreme Court with a majority of center-right to right-wing Catholics whose actions have helped consolidate economic retrenchment and strengthen the political power of corporations, in addition to whatever comfort they offer to upholders of traditional sexual practice. The outcome might also be understood as an instance of fortuitous timing, reflecting a moment favorable to socially cautious Catholic and evangelical tastes rather than the result of a concerted effort.[57] A world of purposeful behavior where intentions anticipate outcomes need not be the sole standard for a realistic causal chain. The alliance between conservative Catholics, evangelical Protestants, and economic power holders did not just happen, even if its ramifications for public policy were uncertain and hard to envision beforehand. The cultural context for such an eventuality had been building for some time.[58]

The limits of the conservative project are not necessarily good news for Catholic progressives, whose constituency is more latent than active. On matters like contraception and divorce, as well as same-sex marriage and to some extent abortion, Catholics can follow their conscience without having to mount a campaign to change doctrine. Secession is the ultimate "Protestant" strategy along a spectrum that includes quieter forms of accommodation that require less time and effort. Silent resistance mirrors the option that Protestant sympathizers enjoy, supporting facets of Catholic doctrine without paying obeisance to the hierarchy. Socially, culturally, and politically, the sexual ideology of the church is less enforceable than it used to be. The irony is that this leeway lowers the incentives for collective action by Catholics who might otherwise feel put upon by the demands of the magisterium. Many of the church's edicts are simply ignored.

So, while the restorationist agenda sponsored by the Vatican has inflicted damage on theologians and has put a lid on doctrinal discussion generally, the air of repression and potential ostracism that hung over ghetto Catholicism has lifted for most of the laity. The social monitoring of sexual morals has lost its small-town, neighborhood base. The potential for organized dissent and participation has suffered. It is easier to tune out. As the following chapters argue, this calculus contributes to the Catholic deficit in church participation among people in the pews. The deficit appears to be asymmetrical, more prominent among liberal Catholics, who tend to participate less in church affairs than their relatively conservative peers.[59]

Another offshoot of conservative dominance has been to narrow, though not confine, the progressive script to dissent on questions of authority and communal identity: priestly celibacy, women's ordination, and so on. Disputes about symbolic matters upset determined minorities, but their resolution one way or the other appears to have only peripheral effects on the behavior of ordinary Catholics and even less on observers outside the church.

Parish closings bring a priest-poor future closer to home. Many Catholics nonetheless look upon the trend as bad weather that happens somewhere else. In technical terms, the institution of the priesthood is a public good. While opening it to women has the approval of the majority of American Catholics, the incentive to fight for such a change is weak because free-riders would have as much access as activists to an expanded clergy, and few women want to be priests themselves. The result is a low-level equilibrium in which Catholics put up with what feels like a tolerably annoying status quo. Thinking about it would only be more distressing. Restrictive though it is, conservative Catholicism developed a culture and a strategy that resonated beyond an inner circle of adepts. Catholic progressives have yet to reach out so effectively from their cocoon.

The handicap of Catholic progressives can be viewed from a slightly different perspective as well. Neoconservatives tied pro-life thinking to American values about the family and to personal as compared to government responsibility for well-being. The position of Catholic progressives (and of the usually conservative Mary Ann Glendon) is closer than that of neoconservatives to the faith-and-justice rhetoric of the church. The intellectual standing of the progressive agenda inside the church, for social action and the like, looks strong.[60]

But the perception of the communitarian program as an echo of a bygone New Deal era has dampened its appeal to a broad swath of American thinking centered on individualism and self-advancement.[61] Liberal Catholics find themselves in a double bind. Their dissent on matters of authority and sexuality puts them at odds with Rome, and the priority they give to social justice issues sets them at some distance from many of their fellow Americans, at least from many of the more devout among them. If they can nourish hope, it may lie in the fact that actuarial realities do not favor hardcore moral reactionaries. While American Catholic conservatism has not shot its demographic bolt, the movement shows signs of having reached a point of diminishing returns as the twenty-first century unfolds.[62]

PART THREE: OVERVIEW

Catholic conservatives take pride in adhering to what they understand to be a set of interlocking principles about sexuality and authority. Added to this is a loosely coupled array of propositions about economic and political issues. Firmness lends conservatives identity; flexibility helps them reach out to coalition partners. The combination enables many conservatives to pass muster as proponents of universal truths who stick by their guns, without overdoing it.

A related characteristic, touching more on style than substance, is also evident among Catholic conservatives. Some, like Daniel Patrick Moynihan, have been comfortable puttering along with empirical information and partial solutions. Disagreement is not a sign of character flaws or heretical leanings. Others—Richard John Neuhaus came close in his more exalted moments, as does James Kurth among the evangelicals—can sound like terrible simplifiers. Their voices quake with certainty. They thunder. Moral clarity reigns supreme over doubt and equivocation. The coexistence of deductive and empirical-incremental styles probably accounts as much for the protean cast of Catholic neoconservatism as do differences over the substance of policy controversies.

When we turn to Catholics outside the conservative fold, vestiges of even modest commonality are harder to find. There seems to be little connective ideological tissue among reform organizations. The next two chapters explore the nature of this heterogeneity and the reasons for it. The argument is two pronged. One part points to multiple strands in the Catholic tradition itself. The other emphasizes recent developments in how voluntary associations and advocacy groups are organized.

The monarchical hierarchy that has been identified with Roman Catholicism at least since the Counter Reformation can be visualized as the last monument standing in a battle between centralized versus decentralized models of governance. Though undercurrents linger in calls for "dialogue" and the convocation of efforts to find "common ground," the collegial model—"conciliarism"—has shriveled under the colossus of a world-bestriding papacy.[1]

Another tradition has greater significance in the day-to-day running of the church. "Trusteeism" is one description, "corporatism" another. A consultative style of management is prevalent among the ministries—broad tranches of social services, health care, and education—that can no longer be run by clerical personnel. This is the extraparochial world that Catholics and many non-Catholics encounter in the good works of the church.

Catholic managerialism looks ideologically nondescript. The prevalent norms are professionalism and merit. It can be seen as a practical accommodation with and an understated safeguard against the pathologies built into the overweening power that Lord Acton had in mind when he decried papal absolutism. The subordination of outreach activities sponsored by the church to the episcopal hierarchy is often attenuated and sometimes nominal. Universities, to take the obvious case, are harder to control than parishes. Bishops can grouch about the wayward theology of Catholic higher education, but they are apt to think twice about trying to forbid the presence of controversial speakers on campus. Catholic elementary and secondary schools are closer to the parishes in their religious content than many of the colleges and universities, where the secularizing residues of separate incorporation are more than trace elements.

Now supposed to be illegitimate, conciliarism is not completely forgotten as an alternative institutional design for the church. But managerialism is the more widely accepted tradition. While elements of it can be found in medieval guilds, arcane precedents are not the driving force behind the phenomenon.[2] The administrative rationalization of church activities, with its stress on the accountability and transparency of professionalized organizations and its dependence on "outside"—that is, secular or nonsectarian—sources of revenue, is of fairly recent origin and remains a work in progress in the United States.

The political fallout of the managerial entente is ambiguous. Its rationale is economic pragmatism. Reliance on numerous small donations from the faithful close to home (often aging and shrinking in numbers) is obsolescent as a financial model for the delivery of services in a large, underfunded system like the parochial schools. On the other hand, the implications of an arrangement in which benefactors and lay experts have substantial say over how money is spent are uncertain for the structure of ecclesiastical authority. This development has a demystifying and to some prelates threatening edge. With the decline in vocations to religious life, the momentum behind managerialism portends a realignment in the balance of power between clergy and laity. There is a suspicion among some members of the episcopate that they will end up like the British House of Lords, congratulated for doing nothing during World War II, and doing it very well.

Still another tradition can be understood as a reaction against ecclesiastical overreach but, in contrast to a comparatively open managerialism, it is hazy to the point of being nameless. Its reason for being is off the books. It is a form of traditional individualism suited to personal survival under conditions of a hierarchy with all-controlling pretensions and nasty powers of surveillance. The modus operandi is neither confrontation (as sometimes occurs with conciliarism) nor collaboration (the motif of managerialism). The main lesson is the need to cultivate secrecy, indirection, and political savvy. Polite, occasionally unctuous, subterfuge is the motif. Strutting, while permitted now and then, may draw attention in the wrong way. Panache, aplomb, and appearance are the cardinal virtues. Anonymous informants are a serious nuisance. Oleaginous sycophants, too. The best advice in the repertoire of common sense under authoritarianism is to lie low. Don't make sudden moves. Ostensible acquiescence is the rule. Speaking truth to power is extremely dangerous and almost always futile. The default position of the mindset—collective inaction—is conservative. At the same time there is a gristle of resentment to it, inclined to the anti-institutional, with a touch of the anarchic.

These traditions run along a continuum. Conciliarism is supposed to foster a modicum of participation; open assemblies are the ideal. Managerialism favors tidier leadership by elites and specialists. Lastly, except for fleeting eruptions, the culture of individual survival discourages collective action.

The spectrum calls attention to a dynamic that goes at least as deep as divisions between left and right in Catholicism, and that is the gradient running from activity of any sort to passivity. After all, more Catholics are leaving the church than are vying for power or doctrinal vindication within it. The real problem for the majority of civilians, those who are neither clerics nor are in employ of the church, is not fear of retribution but resignation at the uselessness of petitions for reform. Many who remain practice an everyday pluralism with polite dignity and a pleasant face, a tolerance of the I'm-okay-you're okay variety. "Who wants to get in a fight with the bishop?" a guest at a Roundtable meeting once asked with a shrug, of no one in particular. Outside of the conciliarist precedent, little in the Catholic hierarchical tradition spurs involvement in structures of church decision making. Seriously organized activity still requires clerical supervision or a sacerdotal blessing of some sort, titular though it may be.

Layered on to the hierarchical legacy is a more recent, thoroughly secular transformation that has spread to associational life in Catholicism and its legal environment. It is not just the services associated with the church—again, the prime examples come from higher education and health care—that have become increasingly professional and bureaucratic. The mainly lay-led advocacy groups covered in Chapters Eight through Eleven have also been affected by this ethos.

These organizations operate in a rule-laced institutional setting, even if few are bureaucratically elaborate themselves. Groups like the Roundtable and SNAP are at home in this environment because they are products of it. The ambience differs from the image of grass-roots, apparently unsophisticated or self-organizing voluntary associations that observers are apt to bracket with the dense parish life of old-time immigrant Catholicism, and indeed with many intermediate groups, Catholic and non-Catholic, in their heyday prior to the 1960s.[3]

The regulatory changes, changes in liability laws, and reforms in the tax code that propelled this transformation—the shift from "amateur," face-to-face associations to relatively professionalized advocacy groups—are unromantically complex.[4] The task here is to take stock of their effects on popular involvement rather than to provide a full account of their origins. What repercussions have new forms of advocacy and the legal-institutional terrain surrounding them had on the levels and types of participation available to ordinary Catholics, above and beyond the constraints imposed by traditional clerical dominance? What has happened to spontaneous associations and social movements in American Catholicism?

If there is one thing to keep in mind in the following pages, it is the juxtaposition of what social historians call an "agrarian bureaucracy"—in nontechnical language, a feudal hierarchy—and different ways, organizational and personal, of working in and around it. The bishops consider themselves to be divinely ordained. There is not much chance of talking them out of that. But material exigencies have encouraged the professionalization of church-related services (often set in motion by religious orders that are less beholden than parishes to the lines of ecclesiastical authority) without openly challenging the system. The eventual result bears a resemblance to the transition from banana republics to modernizing autocracies of the sort that linger in parts of the developing world.[5]

A closer analogy may be the parallel with efforts to adapt congested medieval towns to modern conveniences and traffic without compromising the antiquarian façade. Sometimes ingenuity works. The graft takes, appearances are preserved. A less benign comparison is between the hierarchy and a brittle exoskeleton that cannot be shed. In this case something has to give.

CHAPTER SIX

CONCILIARISM AND OTHER DORMANT TRADITIONS

On an October afternoon in 2006, in his capacity as prefect of the Congregation for Divine Worship and the Discipline of the Sacraments, Francis Cardinal Arinze addressed a colloquium celebrating the golden jubilee of the Institut Supérieur de Liturgie in Paris. A Nigerian in his seventies with decades of experience in the Vatican, Cardinal Arinze had been a *papabile*, one among the half-dozen or so contenders thought to be in the running for the papal office at the death of John Paul II the year before. Though he rarely gave interviews, and though he was apt to run into headwinds when holding forth on contraception, divorce, abortion, homosexuality, and related topics, the cardinal was in demand as a speaker at assemblies of liturgists around the world. "Darkness is chased away by light," he began winningly, "not by verbal condemnation."

Then suddenly the talk turned into a scolding. The cardinal catalogued the harm that experimentation with ritual had wrought since Vatican II. Arinze had made known the substance of his complaints on several occasions. "Unapproved innovations distract and annoy the people," he had declared two years earlier in his keynote address to the Federation of Diocesan Liturgical Commissions convened in San Antonio.

> [I]n religious matters, people's sensitivity and piety can be hurt by ill-considered and hasty novelties... Spontaneity can manifest itself in many ways.... Distractions and even desacralizations can come through dances that offend against good sense and do not help to raise people's minds to God, loquacious and unnecessary commentaries, over-dosage singing monopolized by the choir which allows no time for personal prayer, and the introduction of bizarre vestments and unacceptable vessels for the Holy Eucharist.[1]

If they thought about it at all, those who demurred from the cardinal's dismay about sexual license may have shared some of his concern about the *ars celebrandi*. "Thirty years after the Council," one historian laments, "many American Catholics have yet to understand what they are doing when they gather for Sunday worship."

> American cultural influences such as individualism, consumerism, and the desire to be entertained cannot be overlooked when considering tensions in American liturgical practice.... We are in the midst of a liturgical malaise... In many parts of the United States, liturgy has become a democratic, middle-class activity.[2]

James Zogby, the pollster and marketing consultant, was even grumpier. "[The sacrament of] confirmation today is like the Walmart-ization of the church."

> It's like everybody goes—whatever! The fear and the mystery that were part of the ritual are gone. One of the problems is that it is done so much by rote and at too early an age: it's become a ritual hollowed out of content... The notion that you got at confirmation that you would be called on to defend the faith, that you would be challenged to do what the martyrs had done, that's not there. It's not understood as a passage into that sacred circle.[3]

In the midst of fulminating at the perils of modern times, Cardinal Arinze coined a neologism. "Some abuses," he fretted during his Paris lecture, "are due to an undue place given to spontaneity, or creativity, or to a wrong idea of freedom, or to the error of *horizontalism* which places man at the center of a liturgical celebration instead of vertically focusing on Christ and his mysteries." Horizontalism takes its place alongside individualism, materialism, atheism, consumerism, hedonism, relativism, indifferentism, nihilism, anarchism, solipsism, feminism, populism, narcissism, presentism, anticlericalism, neopaganism, neoantinomianism, neopelagianism, neoilluminism, New Ageism, trusteeism redivivus, acute humanism, crypto-wannabe-Protestantism, Catholic declinism, unduly moody existentialism, runamuck Americanism, faux historicism, untoward radicalism, and other infectious isms of modernity. They all subvert traditional roles and inherited boundaries. Some insinuate their way into places of worship. The taproot can no longer find the aquifer.

"Non-ordained members of the faithful who are assigned some roles in the absence of a priest," the cardinal went on "... should resist the temptation of trying to get the people accustomed to them as substitutes for priests. There is no place in the Catholic Church for the creation of a sort of parallel lay clergy."[4] The specter of horizontalism is a form of *lèse majesté*. A lack of deference threatens clerical hierarchy, institutional stability, and right order. One is reminded of the cartoon of the British lion, drawn by Ronald Searle during the swinging sixties in London, holding a cocktail in one paw and a cigarette in the other, greeting revelers with "Hi, call me Rex."

At least two undercurrents run counter to the regnant centralism of the church. Conciliarism has roots in the constitutional wrangles of early modern Europe. With the papacy split between two claimants, bishops assembled at the Council of Constance (1414–18), sorted through the rivalries, and chose a pope. If a conciliar body—that is, the bishops acting as a whole—could raise up a pope, the thought was that they could also depose him. Ultimate authority rested with collegial bishops who oversaw the papal office. The documents of the Council resemble a rudimentary bill of rights. Conciliarism meant power sharing and a system of checks and balances. The cardinal electors made up a board of directors that could hire and fire the chief executive officer.[5]

Though it is now more common than memories of conciliarism, another challenge to absolute centralization is less readily labeled. "Creeping congregationalism" (as conservatives call it) is a managerial rather than assertively political process that operates toward the middle rungs of the hierarchy. Its most amply documented episode, "trusteeism," unfolded in American Catholicism during the early decades of the nineteenth century, when lay notables ran several parishes. Rome would have none of it. The arrangement was disbanded as the waves of immigrants began to crest before the Civil War and the supply of priests grew. The venture in home rule came to a halt.[6]

In the later part of the twentieth century, soon after Vatican II, a version of trusteeism was reinvented not by parishes but by Catholic colleges, universities, and hospitals when they severed their legal ties with the religious orders that had founded them. "Separate incorporation" of these institutions, governed by mixed clerical-lay boards of trustees, became standard in Catholic higher education, health care, and parts of secondary education. As the number of priests and nuns has dwindled, comparable pressures for the devolution of authority, the renegotiation of contractual obligations, or some form of power-sharing have mounted in parishes and primary schools.[7] The need to raise large amounts of money has made clerical concessions to lay influence look like a reasonable trade-off.

Conciliar theory was an alternative to the assertion of papal primacy, and the struggle involved confrontation between pope and bishops (and some canon lawyers) more than between clergy and laity.[8] The movement aimed to counterbalance a transcendent monarchy with collegial authority. Administrative devolution is less ambitious. There are no pretenders or usurpers. The device comes down to a division of labor between clergy and laity that reshapes the way ministries and some parishes are managed. Power sharing is more widespread in outreach operations associated with the church (the schools and the hospitals) than in parishes themselves, and the arrangement does not question the concentration of power at the top of the system. Its rationale is instrumental. While the parishes have traditionally been centers of cultic practice and "the care of souls," and while the Vatican and especially the papacy constitute focal points of the sacred, the various ministries provide most of the tangible services of the church and employ most of its professionals. "The pope leaves us alone," Bob Newhart, comedian, graduate of the business school at Loyola University in Chicago, and part-time ecclesiologist, used to say, "we leave the pope alone."

Ostensibly apolitical, silent laicization worries some members of the hierarchy, who fear that sooner or later the trend will redraw the lines of authority and spread to the revision of doctrine. The fear is that beneath all the talk of gradualism, dialogue, and protestations about confining change to "the temporalities," managerial reform menaces institutional Catholicism "as we know it."[9]

In fact, though the term can be misleading to American ears and may be even less well understood than the conciliar tradition itself, managerial Catholicism has a respectable lineage that goes back about as far as conciliarism in the political annals of the church. Unlike democracy or monarchy, collegiality or corporatism is more a style of bargaining than a form of government. It is only tangentially a forum for debate. The accent is on minimizing friction through consultation. Managers chat with supervisors, supervisors with subordinates. They might do lunch. The underlying dynamics of corporate Catholicism are professionalization and "concertation" (working together—in effect, deal making) to come up with a nonpartisan plan. The aim is to fix what's broken and to fine-tune what's not. Managerial Catholicism is one area in a convoluted architecture of governance where form approximates function.[10]

So, while few of its American practitioners would recognize the word in the sense used here, corporatism does capture the muted, usually civil interaction among bishops, benefactors, and ministerial professionals. It involves trade-offs between the powerful and de facto leaders rather than a set-to between incumbents and contenders for power, and it gives greater priority to problem solving, professionalism, and fund raising than participation. Agreement on the problem-solving mission is supposed to finesse sticky questions of power sharing. As much depends on how elites and semielites treat one another as on how they handle their subordinates. The courtesies are observed. Minutes are ordinarily taken, and deliberations are not quite off the record; they are just not widely publicized. Think of a city management mode of getting things gone (when was the last time you watched city council proceedings on local television?), and you have an approximation of corporatism in the American vernacular.[11]

As a process rather than a distinct type of government, corporatism is compatible with less-than-democratic rule, even if its rationalizing tenor cannot handle flat-out cronyism. Due diligence and financial transparency are urged with some seriousness. The Leadership Roundtable is the latest experiment in the corporatist tradition. Meritocracy as a corrective to incompetence, caprice, and wastage is the ideal.

Lying to one side of conciliarism and managerialism are a couple of folkways that leave the organization of the church intact but make it tolerable for those who feel squeezed by rigid hierarchy. The "pastoral approach" seeks to tenderize the application of doctrine. In American Catholicism many of the pastoral methods once monopolized by priests have morphed into services supplied by deacons or support groups run by lay people.[12] However it is handled, a paternalistic bending of the rules gives a human face to a steeply stratified structure of authority. This is the *sfumato* factor, softening an otherwise clinical demarcation between the strong and the supplicant.

Another, almost entirely tacit code represents a more shadowy and possibly sinister side of Catholicism. This is the language of behind-the-scenes maneuvering within the church. There is virtually nothing forthright written about it. The style is the moral equivalent of an underground economy. After taking a closer look at conciliarism, I will examine a classic proponent of "the fine Italian hand." Catholic managerialism will come in for extended consideration in Chapter Ten, which focuses on the Leadership Roundtable.

Because the conciliar tradition is a path not taken in Catholicism, the temptation is to reduce it to a sideshow in the grand march toward papal supremacy. Yet the movement was long lived. By some estimates, it held on longer than the papacy has existed in full imperial regalia. The *coup de grâce* came with the declaration of papal infallibility promulgated at the First Vatican Council in 1871.[13]

Soon after the Great Schism had been put to rest at the Council of Constance early in the fifteenth century, the popes began rebuilding their power over the episcopate. Once the question of rival claimants had been settled, conciliarists lacked a flashpoint around which to mobilize. The constitutional issues that agitated adherents of the movement seemed less urgent, the succession problem had been put to rest, and conciliarism began to look more like a tired insurgency than an inspirational ideal.

An even more powerful suppressant was the impetus to rally round the papal flag during the Reformation.[14] Still another was the qualms that conciliarist ideas aroused among the monarchs of early modern Europe. A theory that could justify taming the papacy could be adapted to press for power sharing between ambitious princes and embryonic legislatures, not to speak of the occasionally more violent usurpation of regal prerogatives.[15] This would not do. Lay and clerical incumbents had a mutual stake in discouraging conciliarist rumblings. Having lost its political cover, conciliarism went into hibernation.

Nevertheless, with the rise of absolutist states, the control exercised by the Vatican over the appointment of bishops waned, and the French Revolution speeded up the attenuation of papal power, not so much within the church as between the church and political authorities. In exchange for underwriting clerical benefices, governments demanded a say over the appointment of bishops.

The decline of papal privilege continued until mounting secularization at last caused governments to lose interest in a weakened church. Around 1870, by the time of the First Vatican Council, power over many appointments to bishoprics had reverted to the Vatican. In some countries—Spain, for example—concordats were worked out so that the state kept a say in nominating bishops. By the time the Vatican promulgated a new, stricter code of canon law in 1917, little more than a decade after its condemnation of the allied heresies of "Modernism" and "Americanism," the monarchical papacy had been restored in full.[16]

All these plot twists reflect a struggle between sacred and secular interests and between factions inside the church. They also suggest the contingency and comparative recency of an outcome that owes "more to the spirit of the Napoleonic Code than to scripture or patristic tradition."[17] The legacy of the drawn-out struggle is gnarled and knotted. Splits between church and state contained the nucleus of an emerging pluralistic order in the West.[18] The church itself settled into an autocratic pattern that was disrupted but not decisively undone by Vatican II. It is as if whatever collegial impulses Catholicism had nurtured migrated out of the church, leaving behind an authoritarian edifice. The struggle deposited a detritus of pluralism in the nascent liberties of a secularizing political system but left only chemical traces within the church itself.[19]

Why the story came out this way is something of a mystery. One factor behind the longevity of the papal monarchy is so prosaic that it is easy to overlook. In contrast to almost all other authoritarian hierarchies, for a long time Catholicism has had a procedure in place—papal election through the college of cardinals—for handling succession at the peak of the system. Transitions are regularized, even if voting is not representative. Catholicism is less prone to succession crises at the top than other nondemocratic systems. For all the shenanigans of the papal court, the ritualized system is simply less subject to coups and countercoups than garden-variety dictatorships.[20]

Further clues can be found in the work of scholars of conciliarism. After spending a career writing about the trials of conciliarism, Francis Oakley turned his attention to imperial monarchy itself. The survival of kingship in Catholicism is exceptional. "[T]he one case," Oakley observes, "where a monarchy can be seen to have gained from the nineteenth century to the present in both power and prestige would appear to be that of the papacy... [T]he papacy... stands out in solitary splendor today as itself the last of the truly great sacral monarchies."[21]

Adroit maneuvering and media-savvy theatrics on the part of the papacy cannot provide a sufficient explanation for the rise and survival of the papacy in the midst of a democratizing environment. Oakley's account suggests that several related factors help sustain the papal office.

First, the papacy functions as a kind of psychological anchor in a tumultuous world. It is emblematic of continuity. Monarchy is "a perspective so deeply encrypted in our histories," Oakley contends, somewhat extravagantly, "as to have become almost subliminal." Modernization that brought "disenchantment" and a world "bereft of numinosity" has called forth yearnings that modernity itself cannot fulfill.[22] A semblance of certainty—rock-solid truth with the inquisitorial apparatus scaled back—has grass-roots appeal. Condemnations of relativism constitute a modern-day version of this strategy.

Second, the papacy gained in authority what it lost in political power and territorial dominion. It enhanced its moral magnetism by getting rid of many of the trappings of coercion associated with traditional church-state alliances. In becoming less absolutist, it became less brittle and vulnerable.[23]

To be sure, the authority of the papacy (and the institutional church) has not come out unscathed. Reliance on moral suasion with scant coercive backup and with diminished reinforcement from once insular ethnic enclaves means that Catholics are freer to make their own choices about how to behave and what to believe. Though not particularly responsive, the church feels less repressive, and this dampens head-on mobilization against clerical dominance. The rights of the laity may be few; by the same token, however, rules promulgated by the clergy often seem like so much huffing and puffing. Among American Catholics disaffection is expressed mainly in individual terms, by degrees, in the dribs and drabs of departures and the dialing down of commitment. The church is no longer close to being the only game in town. Immigration is the great engine of replenishment. The dynamic stops short of collapse.

A third factor, which Oakley's study of kingship does not mention at all, needs to be recognized. The wave of democratization that began to spread in the final quarter of the past century, about a decade after Vatican II, has not made the Anglo-American variant of decentralized government into a political gold standard. Catholicism draws sustenance for top-down control from cultures of deference and populist traditions of strong rule. The moral authority of the church resonates more widely outside Europe and the United States.[24]

Last, the church's autocratic governance might seem anomalous in the United States, "the first democracy," were it not for the hold of constitutional principles regarding the separation of church and state. Supporters of the trustee system appealed to the civil courts to overthrow or relax the traditional Catholic norm of episcopal dominance, to no avail. The bishops successfully argued that "Catholicism was compatible with the American system," the historian Scott Appleby has pointed out,

> not because the church was itself a republican institution, but rather because of the constitutional doctrine of the separation of church and state. Lay trustee control—particularly over the selection of clergy—inhibited the freedom of the priest to carry out his duties. Even worse, the lay involvement of civil authorities, in many bishops' minds, was not only morally wrong, but also went against the separation of church and state.[25]

Instances of self-perpetuating clubbiness, like the exclusion of women from the priesthood, might be contested on human rights grounds. But reform is far from a slam-dunk. Aside from the constitutional protections codified in church-state protocols, many corporate actors outside the church share an interest in keeping government at a distance from their management practices.

Protestants were an enigma to him, all high ideals one minute and ruthless expediency the next. You knew where you were in a Catholic culture: up to your neck in

> *lies, evasions, impenetrable mysteries, double-dealing, back-stabbing and underhand intrigues of every kind.*[26]

Vanquished within Catholicism, conciliarism is nonetheless more than a historical oddity. The conciliarist contribution to constitutional thought remains a vital component of secular democratic polities.[27] And inside the church, the perpetuation of hierarchy generated an antibody that has undermined panoptic control. This is an unspoken code whose purpose is to game the system, not overthrow it.[28] The Spanish saying "*Obedesco pero no cumplo*"—"I obey but I don't comply"—captures the spirit nicely. Because the subculture touches a nerve in church officialdom, it is deemed too unsavory for open discussion, even if chronicles of *Romanitá*—that old-world cocktail of the diplomatic, the devious, and devotion to *la bella figura*—are the stuff of Vaticanology.

The philosophy of dissimulation has had one illustrious expositor. Baltasar Gracián y Morales was a seventeenth-century Spanish Jesuit and professor of theology (1601–1658) who ended up on the outs with his superiors for publishing one too many warts-and-all treatises about mundane topics. His guidebook to the ways of the world became a bestseller during the boom years of the Clinton administration; pocket editions flew off the displays near checkout counters.[29] Well before that time, Gracián had attained classic stature among connoisseurs of the Realpolitik of everyday relationships. He was a student of the game. "What Machiavelli said of the politician," Schopenhauer enthused, "Gracián said of the individual."[30] Almost always, he stands at the nether end of the what-Jesus-would-do scale. Nietzsche was a fan.[31]

It was not Gracián's manner to treat church politics overtly. He lets it be known with a wink and a nod that his best practices are applicable to all hierarchies. Gracián's bullet points about making one's way in a treacherous world aim to be transferable across organizational settings, just as Sun-Tzu's subtle recommendations from the sixth century BC, *The Art of War*, have found an audience among businessmen, military officers, and bureaucrats on the make.

Gracián does not deliver his wisdom serenely. He hops from topic to topic with such abandon that in the words of one critic the "three hundred ill-arranged maxims" of his *Pocket Oracle* are "the most confusing and difficult work in the Spanish language."[32] Yet he could be lucid about the uses of obscurity and inconsistency, and it is with this manipulative awareness that Gracián strikes his master chord. "Don't express yourself too clearly," he warns, hitting a note to warm the academic heart.

> Most people think little of what they understand, and venerate what they do not. To be valued, things must be difficult: if they can't understand you, people will think more highly of you. Intelligent people value brains, but most people demand a certain elevation. Keep them guessing at your meaning. Many praise without being able to say why. They venerate anything hidden or mysterious, and they praise it because they hear it praised.[33]

None of this prevents Gracián from urging elsewhere that you should "express yourself clearly, not only easily but lucidly," only to turn around and qualify the advice with the observation that "sometimes it is good to be obscure, so as not to be vulgar."[34] Along with adherence to principle, sincerity and consistency in human affairs are synonyms for the naïve, the tiresome, and the self-defeating.

Puzzlement at the apparently amoral tenor of Gracián's *mots* vanishes once his books are understood as self-help manuals *avant la lettre,* with the accent on "self." Gracián is more interested in power relationships than formal institutions. Organizations are incurably hierarchical. The conciliarist ideal is a pipe dream. It is the kaleidoscopic cunning of human nature and how to manage it that intrigue Gracián. Slyness is all. The overriding goal is personal survival. Life is a *militia contra malicia,* a war against the scheming and treachery of others. Man is a wolf to man, and the only help for it is prudence, deception, and guile.[35]

Gracián works from two premises. One is the assumption of a zero-sum world; he lived in a rigidly stratified society. Winners gain at the expense of losers. The other is that though hierarchy endures, life is fluid and brutal and full of surprises. The upshot is a disjointed, slack authoritarianism. There is plenty of intrigue. Snares and pitfalls abound. Muddle thickens confusion. Hence the air of half-conspiratorial, half slapdash conservatism. Gracián is a gambler with a system.[36]

The ad hoc, staccato quality of his thought mimics the way Gracián sees things, as if his mind were a strobe light flickering across the dim recesses of the human comedy. Whatever advice he passes on is tactical. "One cannot blindly follow the rules," he says in what amounts to a summary of his philosophy. "A zigzag course is advisable."[37] Opportunism is the only plan. The only rule is the bendability of the rules.

Part of Gracián's fascination stems from a forthrightness that, contrary to his own advice, speaks truth to power, like a mordant court jester. He lauds prudence from the viewpoint of the accident-prone. He worships discretion as he does virtue, from afar. A further irony is that Gracián's frankness stands in the service of deception. Prudence and the polishing of appearances are the keynotes. Sincerity is fine, but a reputation for sincerity is even better. The practice of sincerity as a mask in the sly dance of dissimulation and image promotion is the skill to be admired. One has a persona to market and protect.[38]

Gracián is not a nihilist or wholly unscrupulous, nor is he a sociopath. While he has a connoisseur's eye for artful cut-and-thrust and the well-turned dirty trick, he does not condone black ops—treachery or cruelty—for their own sake. Gracián recommends playing one's cards close to the chest; Bill Clinton, a master practitioner, would understand Gracián perfectly. If you concede that the wiles of a Machiavelli are preferable to the ferocity of an Attila and the zealotry of a religious fanatic, Gracián is your man: he offers a middle way. Careers may be ruined but few people are supposed to get killed. Blood-soaked slaughter is often unneeded. Most sins are venial. Still, at the end of the day, "prudence guides one not to the fixed principles of virtue but rather to the different goals of winning one's way."[39]

How does this differ from the stratagems of a Machiavelli (whom Gracián affected to despise, along with Cervantes)? Most of Gracián's maxims are not about statecraft and only some of them are restricted to the powerful. He offers a good many suggestions to players in competitive settings, whether they are in fear of falling from the top or afraid of being trampled by the high and mighty.[40] Gracián was an equal-opportunity cynic. His sinuous dialectic revolves around bullies and weasels, with gawkers, casualties, simpletons, the meek and the needy, and the rare noncombatant on the side.

The realism that Gracián espouses has a sensible rationale, given the combination of perpetual hierarchy and blind-siding uncertainty he sees as the human condition. He does not so much document or satirize the mores of seventeenth-century Spain as endorse a distillation of them. Like John Courtney Murray, Gracián came to terms with the politics of his day. Murray made his peace with democracy. Gracián understood the absolutism of the Spanish monarchs more as a permanently Hobbesian state of nature than as a man-made design subject to revision. The Spain of the Habsburgs was his microcosm of an unforgiving world, and this perennial reality was no more about to change than the wisdom he culled from his beloved poets and philosophers of antiquity. God was essentially a blind juggler. Intimacy? Gracián's people love display and enjoy the darkness. Only fools fail to understand that.

> *Well, for all that, I think that to try and get into X—, enter his labyrinth and get out again, without a clue derived from some source other than what is known as knowledge of the world—that were hardly possible.... [I]n an average man of the world, his constant rubbing with it blunts that fine spiritual insight indispensable to the essential in certain exceptional characters, whether evil ones or good.. .*
>
> *At the time my inexperience was such that I did not quite see the drift of all this. It may be that I see it now....*
>
> *Civilization, especially if of the austerer sort, is auspicious to it. It folds itself in the mantle of respectability.... Though no flatterer of mankind it never speaks ill of it.... [T]hough the man's even temper and discreet bearing would seem to intimate a mind peculiarly subject to the law of reason, not the less in his heart he would seem to riot in complete exemption from that law, having apparently little to do with reason further than to employ it as an ambidexter implement for effecting the irrational.*
>
> *... [I]t is to the average mind not distinguishable from sanity, and... whatever its aims may be—and the aim is never declared—the method and the outward proceeding are always perfectly rational.*[41]

An agile pessimist regarding human nature, Gracián was a thoroughgoing fatalist about society and collective action generally. If structural reform is unthinkable, then the realistic course is low-profile accommodation, ingratiation, and subterranean resistance.[42] The culture of hierarchy, of "little monarchies," reproduces itself on down the pyramid. "Be part serpent" he declared, "and part dove."[43]

The resemblance between the ethos epitomized by Gracián and aspects of church culture, where room for open conflict is restricted, is close. In a culture of honor, respect is the main prize, and deference and dissembling are the fail-safe social skills. It is essential to avoid giving offense, without seeming to be obsequious. While he touched only glancingly on clerical affairs, the wise-ass, acidic Gracián serves as a corrective to anodyne renditions of religious life and ecclesiastical politics.[44]

The leitmotif of Gracián's thought is its unremitting individualism. He bequeathed a refinement of self-seeking, distrust, and evasiveness to the culture of Catholicism, as disturbing in its way to earnest communitarianism as Darwinism was to Victorian propriety. The ruthlessly egocentric syndrome Gracián registered is a mirror-image of the greater-good ethic espoused by the church.

A corollary of his way of looking at things is skepticism about coordinated involvement in issues having to do with the internal workings of any organization. Gracián is not a team player. Trust is for suckers. A judicious distancing from collective effort, an appreciation of stagecraft, and a cultivation of spectatorship rather than citizenship are consistent with the paltry rates of participation of the laity in the affairs of church governance to this day.

The ironic by-product of inveterate hierarchy is not solidarity among the groundlings but a surreptitious individualism that is at odds with the altruistic sentiments expressed in church documents. In Gracián's jaundiced world, the realistic goal for most people is to try and get away with stuff without being caught rather than to waste energy trying to improve the situation. Duplicity, mendacity, suspicion, and fear complete the palette for the landscape rendered by Gracián. Individual myopia may not be a virtue exactly but it is well to accept it as the way things are and to work with it. Collective irresponsibility, its social counterpart, is endurable for Gracían as a write-off.[45]

This dismal assessment covers a lot of ground. But Gracian's pessimism does not extend to unrelieved melancholy, nor does he quite poison the wells of fellow feeling. His how-to manuals are motivational speeches of a kind—about personal survival and organizational careers, not leadership and organizational growth. Since institutional change is off the table, hope rests in the guile of individuals. Personal success may be insecure—that is the great theme of the *vanitas* of human striving—but it is still within reach.[46] Gracián was not alone, only franker than most, in his cynicism about the pursuit of anything besides personal aggrandizement. It is easy to understand how insidious his way of thinking must have appeared to his religious superiors, for whom not only were rules to be obeyed but the "interior disposition" to obey them was to be sincere. Gracián is willing to recognize hypocrisy for what it is: an instrument of reputational power in the ceaseless masquerade of social competition. It is not as if many of his contemporaries could pass muster as sympathizers of democracy. Gracián is a pre-Enlightenment figure.[47]

And though he is skeptical about cooperation, he is not a devoid of community sentiment. Gracián's was a world of bad faith and pretense. Bullshit was the order of the day. But it was not a gallery of the damned. Nor was it, though only flickers of this appear, without tenderness. The Cloaca Maxima spews, the baths are drained. There is no fixity, only flux. Yet his dalliance with the charms of corruption subverts not compromise but the rigidities of principle. Meddlesome system-builders need not apply. Gracián casts a clinical chill without the sinister leer. He shows none of the rancor of the embittered, broken-hearted idealist. His is a realism with a modicum of honor. Think Henry James with a stronger taste of bile. If reality is a nightmare, it takes skill and a certain courage to avoid going haywire.

It would be even more of a mistake—in Gracián's view, a fatal admission of naïveté—to assume that the culture of misdirection and deceit cannot thrive in systems less flamboyantly hierarchical than the one Gracián lived in. The difference is that the charade may not prevail. The rule of law, checks and balances, the assorted bourgeois decencies provide some protection. The smell-test zones could be marginally larger or smaller, depending on the ruler and the political system. Gracián articulated the unspoken workings of an enduring culture, and one of the forms it takes is a side of Catholicism, its *Schattenseite*, where no one can afford to be innocent and nothing is unspoiled.[48]

If Gracián succeeded in codifying lessons for personal survival in the Catholic church and other hierarchies, few Catholics have heard of the man. His influence, such as it is, must be circuitous. A secretive culture need not derive from conscious awareness. It takes root, unannounced, as individual adaptations in hierarchies that provide almost no hold for autonomous collective leverage. It feeds on complicity. It seems better—that is, less troublesome and dangerous—for everyone, once the rules are intuited, not to shatter the pretense. Truancy from this social compact is forbidden.

Gracián examined the politics of everyday life without religious scruples.[49] In the smarmier regions of religious discourse, praise of self-interest is almost inevitably confused with amoralism, original sin, human-nature-being-what-it-is, and the like. What's more, Gracián appears to consign hope to the wasteland of human folly. This helps explain his status as a nonbeing in Catholic officialdom and the ignorance about him among Catholics generally, but it does not destroy the realism of his analysis.

Before (and well after) Gracián, it has been customary in Catholic circles to talk of "saints" and "sinners" in the church. With the important exception of the pastoral approach, there has been little place in this melodrama for a middle ground inhabited by the routinely self-interested. It is Gracián's obsession with self-interest, and its conflation with cynicism, that makes for scandal not only among the devout but also among those concerned with the rhetoric of commitment to organizations of any kind.[50]

The lesson that can be drawn from Gracián is not that collective action is always futile. That conclusion would violate his disdain for universal laws, his impatience with principle, and his appreciation of contingency. The message is that organizing such efforts requires awareness of the less-than-heroic mix of motives that governs human affairs. The fact that he looked deep into the dark side without formulating an overall strategy that would be recognized as leading toward a happy ending—in other words, an ersatz religion—does not mean that he failed, only that such reassurance cannot come easily, as if it could be picked up in a life-lesson article from an in-flight magazine. Formulaic recourse to the high moral ground is a device not only of hypocritical authority but of groups who, mistaking purity of intent for superior motivation, end up being dismayed by the desertion of their followers.[51]

CHAPTER SEVEN

MANAGERIALISM AND THE CATHOLIC DEFICIT

> *A muffled silence reigned, only broken at times by the shrieks of the storm. Each silent worshipper seemed purposely sitting apart from the other, as if each silent grief were insular and incommunicable. The chaplain had not yet arrived...*[1]

Economic necessity propelled two changes that affected Catholic higher education more than the sit-ins and street protests of the sixties and early seventies. One was the rapid and nearly total switch to coeducation on the part of male-only schools. Part of this was driven by low enrollments during the Vietnam draft. Women's colleges also turned co-ed, more gradually and in smaller proportions.[2] The change was transformative. "For the lifetime of Catholic colleges in the United States," one historian wrote, "coeducation had been a practice forbidden by church authorities..."

> Religious communities, for the most part, taught in schools that were either for men or for women. Yet, almost overnight and without philosophical or theological consideration, their colleges became coeducational. The economic factor seems to have won the day, although ex post facto some fine rationalizations have appeared.[3]

The second big change was separate incorporation: the removal of religious orders and congregations as sole proprietors in Catholic higher education. The colleges and universities took on greater numbers of lay faculty and administrators, and their governing boards were manned largely by trustees from the corporate world. Catholic higher education had become more expensive to run and increasingly subject to government regulation and regional accreditation. The schools needed the counsel of operatives seasoned in the ways of grantsmanship and skilled in eliciting contributions from financial heavyweights.[4]

As with the change to coeducation, the shift toward laicization came about quickly, and it penetrated most of the system. Unlike the high schools, Catholic colleges and universities did not stack up well against their academic peers. Notre Dame was known for its football prowess and maudlin Irishness rather than excellence in research.[5] With the GI Bill and the expansion of the market in higher education, the status of church-sponsored colleges and universities became more than just a matter of bragging rights. Eligibility for public funding depended on getting the schools up to professional snuff, and this meant meeting standards set by secular authorities. The urge to catch up was the impetus behind the Land O' Lakes statement, issued in 1967 by the leaders of American Catholic higher education. The document vowed that "the Catholic university must have true autonomy and academic freedom in the face of authority of whatever kind, lay or clerical, external to the academic community itself."[6]

The push toward laicization gathered steam from economic incentives shaped by court decisions.[7] In the Horace Mann case of 1966 the Maryland Court of Appeals had declared two small Catholic colleges in the state to be ineligible for public construction grants. But, in 1971, in Tilton v. Richardson, the Supreme Court decided that four Catholic colleges in Connecticut were not "pervasively sectarian" and that their students could therefore apply for federal aid. Then, in the 1976 Roemer v. Board of Public Works case, also originating in Maryland, the Supreme Court came down in favor of Catholic higher education. Finally, the colleges and universities could apply for public monies.

The last two were five-to-four decisions. The mandate was narrow, and the financial outlook of many Catholic colleges and universities continued to be touch and go. Almost none of them were viable without access to public funds. The difference between 1966 and 1976, between the Horace Mann and Roemer rulings, hinged on the strategy of dissociating the colleges and universities from religious governance.

The laicization of higher education constituted a second revolution in American Catholicism, comparable in its practical effects to the declaration on religious freedom promulgated at Vatican II that condoned the separation of church and state. Like that declaration, it was formulated and brought to fruition by progressive priests, now operating in a postconciliar environment favorable to change. The climate did not last. Clerical sponsorship of this magnitude would not hold for advocates of reform in subsequent decades.

Similarly rapid and irreversible processes took place in Catholic health care and charitable services at about the same time as the reforms in higher education. These changes grew out of a massive effort by clerical leadership to keep their organizations afloat as their traditionally local, almost completely Catholic-ethnic clientele began to shrink. (The sons and daughters of all those Catholic FBI agents, graduates of Fordham Law, who the renegade priest Dan Berrigan joked were busy chasing him around the underground in the 1960s, would go on to better things, to be replaced—it was rumored—by Mormons.)[8] For their part, postwar governments saw the infrastructure of organizations like Catholic Charities as ready-made conduits for channeling social services to a clientele regardless of creed. The strategy circumvented anxieties about bloated statism. Catholicism could not offhandedly be confused with socialism.

The win-win alliance between church-connected charitable operations and the federal government dates from at least as far back as the Great Depression when, in 1933, "Catholic Charities of Chicago wrested an exemption from the 'public funds to public agencies' rule and was permitted to distribute Federal Emergency Relief Funds." Then, with the Great Society programs of the 1960s, public funding for Catholic Charities and health care took off exponentially, as it did for Catholic higher education.[9]

The move toward professionalization in the ministries of American Catholicism provoked two sorts of negative feedback. The most widely publicized reaction in Catholic circles touched on concerns about the religious identity of the reconfigured institutions. Some were straying far from the mother ship. Critics decried "professionalization" as a euphemism for secularization.[10] A second putative downside of the transition surfaced with the participatory effects of professionalization in charitable work. There seemed to be a connection between the growth of bureaucratic social services and the decline of local volunteerism. Participation in parish activities appeared to suffer.

Though accentuated from the 1960s on, the trend, so it was claimed, went back further. One study of Catholic charitable operations found that "decentralized infrastructures that encourage contributions of direct personal service to those in need have been diminishing since the 1920s." During the long century of European immigrant Catholicism stretching from about the mid-nineteenth to the mid-twentieth centuries, religious sisterhoods kept alive the idea that personal service was at the heart of charitable activity. Thousands of nuns, along with lay benevolent associations like the St. Vincent de Paul Society, were directly involved in running soup kitchens, distributing clothes, and prison visiting. "Because charity work did not require much professional training, lay involvement in the institutions was varied, voluntaristic, and somewhat freewheeling."[11]

These local operations could not keep pace with the burgeoning numbers of urban (and non-Catholic) poor or with the drive toward licensing that was taking hold in social work, nursing, and allied activities. As with academic accreditation, certification required evidence of training and competence. The bishops themselves were among the early advocates for the centralization of charitable activities vis-à-vis the parishes and religious orders, that is, for diocesan control. "Unless bishops were able to monitor and control charitable services and fund-raising within their own dioceses," the economic historian Mary Oates argued, "they could never stand together as the American Catholic hierarchy to present a cohesive 'Catholic position' in public debates about social priorities, welfare policies, and reform legislation."[12] Consolidating a Catholic presence in the formulation of social programs for the poor meant upholding episcopal power.

Centralization for reasons of efficiency and lobbying could come with costs, however. The danger that some critics saw on the horizon differed from the risk of a fading Catholic identity. Skeptics worried that with the professionalization and centralization of services, rank-and-file Catholics would inevitably encounter fewer opportunities for social engagement, and they might contribute less monetarily besides. Professionalism looked to be at odds with parish participation, at least in the guise of charitable associations, and possibly with financial support in the form of mass philanthropy.

> Generous in doing good, they [parishioners] found it hard to explain why they found the new approach so troubling.... Their arguments for the preservation

> of small scale, local control, and community commitment fell before the overriding claims for centralization; its promise of greater efficiency, higher professional standards, and more rapid progress toward collaboration with mainstream and government agencies.... Meaningful service opportunities contracted, and new benevolent projects originated more often in central bureaus than in local initiatives.[13]

This dynamic is not uniquely Catholic. It is part of a transformation "from membership to management" that has come to dominate voluntary organizations from the sixties onward and that is thought to account for a good deal of the drop-off in civic engagement across the United States. Federations established in the nineteenth and early twentieth centuries, with elected representatives at state, regional, and local levels, have seen their membership fall with the profusion of professionally managed advocacy groups and networks. Individuals can write checks or simply contribute online instead of meeting one another face-to-face. Many Lady Bountiful operations and Friday night bingo-for-Jesus get-togethers morphed into or were displaced by professionally run advocacy groups. A touching indicator of this decline was the disappearance, beginning in the sixties, of parish cookbooks: locally printed pamphlets of recipes for food "like grandma used to make." The home-grown, last-good-place aura of much charitable activity was gone. "Because today's advocacy groups are staff-heavy and focused on lobbying, research, and media projects," one sociologist concludes, "they are managed from the top, even when they claim to speak for ordinary people."[14]

It looks like a short step from the bureaucratization of church-sponsored social services to a causal diagnosis of "the Catholic deficit"—a participatory shortfall among parishioners relative to the levels of involvement among members of other denominations. The deficit is in fact perplexing. It has continued after the rhetoric of Vatican II exalted participation on the part of the laity, and even after the sexual abuse scandals sparked movements like Voice of the Faithful (VOTF) that looked a lot like the protests of the 1960s. "The life of Catholic parishes varies considerably," Mary Jo Bane summarizes the situation, "but exhibits levels of organization and activity considerably lower than in other traditions."[15]

Two hypotheses come into play here. One involves the idea that a portion of the participatory shortfall is characteristically Catholic. The hierarchical organization of the church, and the submissive culture that this structure induces, set the faithful apart from generally more activist, congregational Protestants. The blame falls on a system that privileges clerical control over lay participation. "Pray, pay, and obey" is the mantra. Ordinary Catholics are not in the habit of "exercising responsibility," at least within the church itself. The laity is no longer confined, as the diseased were in the ancient days of clerical hegemony, to peeking at church proceedings through a "lepers' window," and American Catholics are less likely to go weak in the knees at the sight of a papal procession. But something of the wallflower etiquette remains, along with memories of correct penmanship, good posture and comportment, chastely buttoned white blouses, sensibly tasteful tailoring, and the Margaret O'Brien demeanor.

The other idea suggests an over-time effect. The professionalization of good works has cut into opportunities for benevolent amateurism everywhere. This second trend need not be peculiar to Catholics. The bureaucratization of services and social advocacy, the story goes, has proceeded across denominational lines. It adds to rather than creates a deficit in participation.[16]

Both ideas home in on the causal side of participatory decline. The other distinction to keep in mind looks at the outcome itself—at what counts as "participation." One gradient runs from consensually charitable activity to political and disputatious mobilization within the church. A less obvious demarcation would be between voluntary involvement, whether charitable or openly political, that is sustained as compared to intermittent.

The conclusion of the following pages is that hierarchical Catholicism, while diminished in practice by the fall-off in the number of priests, retains a significant afterlife. The legacy weighs down lay involvement; the habit of participation is weak. Catholics remain on the average less participant, and contribute less financially, than members of other denominations.[17] In addition, for a time, the professionalization of charitable operations almost certainly contributed to a drop in volunteer participation, though it is unlikely that Catholics have been alone in this regard.

However, some forms of involvement in parish life have probably grown. Once blamed for shunting aside nonprofessional input, Catholic Charities, realizing that contributors can be thought of clients or perhaps stakeholders as much as the needy themselves, has made a point of stimulating parish-level volunteerism. Newer activities like support groups are more personalized. Some of this entails collective commitment, some of it appears to be closer to individual or occasional action.

A final development affects both the cause and the effect sides of the participatory equation. The virtual disappearance of European ethnic immigrant enclaves differs from the professionalization of social services, even though it unfolded over roughly the same period. It has contributed to the thinning of old-style parish community participation. The loss of close-knit in-group surveillance that suburbanization entails has made it easier for Catholics to leave the church altogether or to ignore the exhortations, animadversions, and whims of the clergy—in effect, to scale back commitment and participation. Free-riding is common. The rule of thumb that 20 percent of parishioners contribute 80 percent of the financial support looks unassailable.

These developments probably add to the impression, at least among older Catholics, that parish life is less communal and more segmented than it once was. It is not only the forms of participation that have altered. Younger Catholics feel freer to browse for service opportunities and spiritual nourishment outside the Catholic network. This dynamic, from commitment to a kind of entitlement, reflects a generational shift more than it does the bureaucratization of charitable work. In the process, the ties of newer cohorts of Catholics to the institutional church can be attenuated to the vanishing point. Or younger Catholics can shop around from parish to parish until they find one to their liking.

None of this necessarily means that larger, more variegated parishes are less popular or decisively less participatory than the snug Capra–esque enclaves of nostalgic longing. It suggests that some may simply have learned to be a shade more accommodating to lifestyle and ethnic differences. The texture of sociability has changed. Many of the rosy-cheeked parishioners with salt-and-pepper hair and wind-up watches have gone the way of daily newspapers and war bonds and the smell of roast beef and boiled potatoes.

Most of the conditions identified by Bane to account for subpar participation in Catholic parishes are well known. Clerical hierarchy and its offshoots—"constraints on dialogue," for example—remain intact regardless of the pro forma encouragement of openness and involvement promulgated by Vatican II. It is hard to undo centuries of censorship and surveillance that have depleted the intellectual ozone of popular Catholicism; fumes from the permission-seeking atmosphere of *nihil obstat* linger. Thus, in contrast to most of the colleges and universities affiliated with the church,

> Bishops... own parish churches and schools, control the assignment of clergy, and prescribe many aspects of parish life. Laity and parish-based clergy often defer to higher levels in the church to initiate activities and ministries and are fearful of official sanctions if their initiatives are perceived as inappropriate.... Creating a community of moral deliberation is not something pastors have necessarily viewed as part of their office; the current pope and most bishops do not encourage dissent and debate; nor is moral dialogue something pastors by and large know how to do.[18]

Similarly, the professionalized administration of social services that used to engage ordinary Catholics is supposed to have contributed to sidelining grass-roots engagement. Bane contends that "Catholic Charities, the largest social service network in the country... is professional and centralized and seems to feel little need for participation in its ministries by parishioners."[19] To the extent that bureaucratic restructuring along these lines has taken place, it is not only bishops and parish priests who might feel hemmed in. Evidently some members of the laity also sense that professionalization has shunted them aside. By this account, the managerial revolution that began in Catholic higher education and ministries such as health care has made inroads in diocesan and parish activities through a modernized—that is, more bureaucratic and orderly—delivery of social services. The containerization of American Catholicism is well advanced.[20]

But the argument founded on the depressive effects of professionalization may be more dated than the case against the toxicity of clericalism. Mary Oates and other historians have cautioned against extrapolating from conclusions based on research covering the thirties through the sixties. Unquestionably, the professionalization of social work pushed aside volunteer involvement during this period, but the situation from the final decade of the twentieth century onward is cloudier.[21] Stung by criticisms that its professional approach drove down volunteer activity, Catholic Charities USA launched an aggressive parish outreach program, starting in the mid-1980s. The agency's annual reports regularly estimate volunteers to compose upward of 75 percent of its workforce.[22] The figures are sketchy. The head counts say nothing about time commitments—one hour a week? ten hours a week?—nor are the kinds of activities tallied across volunteers and professionals. If the simple frequency of types of services provided can be taken as a guide, just under half of the work of Catholic Charities is geared to "food distribution services"—food banks, soup kitchens, and the like—topping other programs like clothing assistance, tutoring, and so on. It is a fair surmise that volunteers cluster in the largest, food distribution and similar categories, with professionals concentrated in comparatively specialized but numerically smaller areas like "social support services" and "counseling and mental health."[23]

Even if information about the links between charitable management and variation in parish involvement were abundant, the results would still be open to interpretation. Michael Schudson points up the persistent two-sidedness of the effects of professionalization and bureaucratization on popular engagement, including religiously associated voluntarism. "It is unlikely," Schudson writes,

> that we would... want to criticize the school system for having taken on the professional management of children's education or hospitals for having professionalized home health care or social service agencies for having displaced neighbors, grandmothers, and peer groups in offering counseling, occupational therapy, hot meals for the homeless, and so forth. Is there a social cost to every one of these changes? Yes... But the social gain is substantial, too, and it is difficult to imagine turning back this clock.[24]

Part of low parish activism can be blamed on ecclesiastical caprice rather than the bureaucratic suffocation attributed to a professional style of delivering services. The issue for some parishioners is exasperation with rather than abject fear of the hierarchy. There can be little or no return from quarreling with one or other bishop relative to the expenditure of energy elsewhere. Who needs it? The grief-and-aggravation factor is nontrivial. After a couple of tries, the effort begins to look like a waste of time, and the faithful find better things to do. "There are no turning points," a weary reformer observed, "only sticking points." Writing of advocacy movements in general, one analyst has pointed out that "lack of participation is typically due to... pessimism about the probability of success, skepticism that one's own contribution will make a difference, weak commitments to the collective good itself, and lack of exposure to organizing attempts."[25]

As dissidents and potential troublemakers depart or tune out, parish life becomes weighted toward the conservative and the complacent, together with those who get on with their spiritual lives and works of charity while standing apart from what strikes them as useless bickering. The peace-and-quiet scenario has several advantages, including space for a result-focused dedication to the work at hand. This differs from boosting involvement in matters of internal governance.[26]

Nancy Ammerman, a sociologist whose research is devoted mainly to Protestant congregations, affirms Mary Jo Banes's contention that Catholic parishes serve many ends, short of being the schools of democracy that Protestant congregations are often thought to be. "In spite of Vatican II reforms... many parishes remain cultures of minimal participation." Like Bane, Ammerman points a finger at the lack of "mechanisms of congregational interaction and extensive participation [in Catholicism] that channel larger numbers of Protestants into formal and informal networks of service."[27]

Participation in support groups offers another option, besides simply walking away. Some may be extensions of devotional associations, others may be modeled after Alcoholics Anonymous. These groups concentrate on personal problems that are solvable in the here and now. They can be both expressive and practical. They help people feel good about themselves, and they have tangible payoffs. They build confidence. Everyone's story matters. People make connections. Sharing is important. So is getting better.[28]

Support groups whose objective is personal problem solving rather than politics resemble the evangelical gatherings in Brazil that have provided venues for the down-to-earth concerns of women with troubled children and feckless husbands. Besides being discouraged by the hierarchy, the more politicized *comunidades de base* (grass-roots communities) affiliated with Brazilian Catholicism failed to offer comparable sustenance, and they have gone into decline. The spirit of the support groups also corresponds closely to the varied menu of activities sponsored by full-service Protestant megachurches in the United States.[29]

A few corrections, then, need to be made to the decline-and-fall model of the Catholic deficit. First, these accounts regularly ignore support groups or assume that their therapeutic, Oprah-like agendas constitute a slide from a golden age of engagement on the part of parishioners, the ethnics who built the parish churches, rectories, convents, and grammar schools that are now condemned to a struggle for survival in the inner cities. The newer, often modishly therapeutic groups don't count for much as venues of genuine participation.

There is an elegiac, world-we-have-lost cast to this depiction of a participatory past. The demographics of many Catholic parishes have moved from homogeneous, working-class, and sometimes narrowly tribal enclaves toward a middle-class plus extra-European ethnic mix. Some parishes are suburban oases. Others are more culturally diverse; they vary both along ethnic lines and in their participatory repertoires. As one analyst of the transformation puts it:

> In the nineteenth century, voluntarism meant the construction of Catholic parishes as alternative civic spheres, where immigrants could band together for mutual help and service while affirming their ethnic identity and learning skills needed to survive in their new society. In the post-World War II era, voluntarism has meant that religious institutions have provided resources and a relevant repertoire of beliefs and practices that men and women have used to reconstruct new forms of community that are more appropriate for a more educated, mobile, and modern population.[30]

Mutual help and solidarity are provided but not in the same form as they were during the era of enclave Catholicism, when, moreover, lay influence on church governance could hardly be called decisive. It is not clear how much of the diminution in grassroots parish activities reflects a drop in the supply of self-sacrificing nuns, a decline in Friday-night bingo, or a fall from some more vigorously political baseline. As parishioners have become better off, contributions to charitable and social justice initiatives, especially to those directed outside the fold, may have declined, as DiIulio and others suggest, and the fate of parochial schools, especially those located in inner cities, has become a crisis point in the midst of Catholic migration to the suburbs. Many parishes are ready to help take care of their own and to provide a menu of services for the elderly, alongside support for middle-class faithful going through life crises. None of these activities has much to do with participation in church politics narrowly defined.[31]

Second, church politics may be in the heads and hearts of a few Catholics but it is not in their hands. Explanations of the Catholic deficit correctly emphasize the organizational obstacles to lay participation: the legal hold of bishops on church property, their power over the assignment of priests, the appointive nature and advisory status of parish councils, gag rules regarding doctrinal discussion, and so on. However, they neglect one structural and one cultural factor that also drag down parish involvement: (a) the exit option that has the likely effect of tilting the makeup of parishes in a conservative direction and (b) the depressive legacy of a culture of deference.

These factors come to a head in the feeling that collective action lacking the hierarchy's approval is a waste of time. Mandated by Vatican II, parish councils are in place in many American dioceses. But some have difficulty mustering a quorum; others are dead letters. In the view of some Catholics, believing what Rome says is a sign of credulity, not faith. How much of this is attributable to episcopal neglect or suppression and how much to apathy on the part of frantically busy laypeople is impossible to estimate, given the present state of knowledge.[32]

There is some irony here. Incentives for expressly political organization, of the sort that might call doctrine into question, are low, even for well-educated Catholics. This can be the case not because the repressive capacity of clericalism is exceptionally potent but because it is low. Tradition isn't what it used to be. Complaints on the part of the bishops that they feel powerless cannot be reduced entirely to paranoia and self-pity; that diagnosis is not a mirage of their own making. Indignation is hard to muster on a wide scale when Catholics can do as they please in matters, like family planning and divorce, that touch them where they live. What is the point of getting exercised over a clerical despotism that strikes many as mostly talk, and frequently ridiculous talk at that? And from the perspective of an overworked bishop, it almost certainly seems better to let sleeping dogs lie. The same goes for a shrunken, multitasking priesthood that has no time for doctrinal debate even if the will to indulge it were there.

Why should they? To borrow a phrase from David Denby, we are in the land of the cannily acquiescent.[33]

Third, there is something distinctive in the American context about changes in the time budgets of women that has contributed to the decline of civic associations generally and that can be extrapolated to the Catholic deficit. The participation of women in the labor market has shot up everywhere in industrial societies. But, as Mary Ann Glendon and others have noted, the United States is practically alone in the industrial world in failing to underwrite accessible child care. An enormous squeeze has been put on the time available for sustained engagement in voluntary associations. While it is not confined to Catholics, the pressure adds to the conditions that already impede participation in church affairs among families with children.[34]

Finally, the tendency in discussing the Catholic deficit to suppose that rank-and-file Catholics want to participate in church governance is backed up by evidence from surveys indicating that increasing numbers of parishioners favor consultative styles of clergy-lay relations.[35] But the data include neither opinions about the costs (in time commitments, in grief and aggravation, etc.) nor information about the priority assigned to such participation, especially if it is combative, relative to other activities (support groups, devotional societies, good works, etc.). This is not just a quibble. The responses may reflect wouldn't-it-be-nice ideals unencumbered by real-world constraints.

The deferential mindset is in retreat. But the practice of participation is something else than its approval. When time is scarce, compared to the benefits, low cost, and informal drop-in nature of support groups, volunteering, and other mostly non-political activities, it is uncertain what prospective participants have to gain from taking part in or even paying attention to parish governance—unless they are already dedicated to such chores or in the habit of contemplating church strategy in the long term on such looming crises as the scarcity of priests. The modern expression of the belief that "Father knows best" is a let-them-take-care-of-it mentality. Very few Americans are C-Span junkies; very few Catholics are addicted to following church politics.[36]

Whatever limits the professionalization of church-sponsored social services may exert on volunteer involvement, doing good elicits virtually total enthusiasm among ordinary Catholics (and others) when contrasted with debate over doctrine or griping about the tattered image of the hierarchy. When the reputation of church leadership plummeted as revelations about sexual abuse in Europe appeared early in 2010, coverage of the charitable work sponsored by the church could still be counted on for a favorable reception.[37]

Many of the faithful wouldn't mind having a local church that behaved more democratically. Consultation and dialogue are the mom and apple pie of American Catholicism. But the ideal looks rather casual, not something to stand up and fight for. Most seem content to let parish governance follow an amiable, low-stress, city manager model. The bother of church governance is delegated to clerics, a handful of benefactors, and the usual volunteers. Given the circumstances, the decision looks rational. Inertia probably hinders reform as much as outright repression.[38]

To summarize: any account of a decline in the laity's engagement in parish life has to encompass a number of contributing factors, ranging from the perpetuation of clerical control over appointments to the scarcity of time that married people, especially women, have for participation in church affairs. An essential point is that the nature of participation itself has changed. The changes in kind have been mostly lateral. Opportunities for socializing and camaraderie have opened up through support groups. Vertical mobility—a climb up the ecclesiastical hierarchy on the part of laypeople—is rarer. Women are no longer uncommon as diocesan chancellors. Nevertheless, in dioceses and well as parishes (and in contrast to most Catholic colleges, universities, and hospitals), male clerics still have the final word.

Involvement in parish and finance councils (and some philanthropic ventures) is about as close to participation in church politics as lay people can expect to get. While they remain consultative and prone to bias in the vetting of members by bishops and pastors, the councils can play a serious role in shaping local policies—for example, in determining budgetary priorities for schools and charities. By comparison to volunteer work or managerial involvement, church politics can seem cliquish, and the ratio of factionalism to performance may skyrocket to insupportable proportions. The struggle for power is one among many activities—charitable volunteering, involvement in support groups, ventures in therapeutic self-help, and so on—that compete for the attention of Catholics.[39] It is the expansion in the repertoire of activities with palpable and/or psychic payoffs that makes it possible to speak of "vibrant parishes" in the absence of expressly political participation by the laity. A direct trade-off between organizational efficiency and democratic participation fails to capture the shambolic varieties of mostly nonpolitical participation and personal problem-solving and socializing that animate parish life. They are satisfying in ways that church politics almost never is.[40]

PART FOUR: OVERVIEW

As the millennium dawned, several items high on the agenda of American Catholics, especially conservative Catholics, were in place or seemed well on their way to realization. Passed in 1976 as the first victory of the pro-life movement, the Hyde Amendment, spearheaded by a Catholic Republican from Illinois, cut back on the use of federal funds for abortion. It beat back all challenges, in part because it had the support of Catholics generally.

On the intramural front, the office of the national bishops' conference had been tamed. In comparison to the handful of liberals who lingered from the days of John XXIII (1958–1963) and Paul VI (1963–1978), appointments to the episcopate were unstintingly orthodox. Nearly a decade had passed since the bishops had abandoned their efforts to frame a pastoral letter on the role of women. Progressive groups like Call to Action, founded in the effervescent years that followed Vatican II, were showing their age. Organized dissent was erratic and scarcely visible. What Geoffrey Kabaservice was to say later of the hard right turn of the Republican Party could be applied to the fate of Catholic liberals: "A broad and apparently formidable group suffered progressive decimation until it consisted only of a handful of stunned survivors stumbling into the second decade of the twenty-first century."[1]

One of the few unfinished initiatives favored wholeheartedly by Catholic conservatives was *Ex Corde Ecclesiae* ("From the Heart of the Church"), a document, issued by John Paul II in 1990, aimed at shoring up the religious identity of Catholic higher education. The goal was to refurbish the Catholic brand that the pope and several others felt had been tarnished after the colleges and universities moved toward lay-dominated boards of trustees in the sixties. The American episcopate had gone back and forth with the Vatican about the implementation of *Ex Corde Ecclesiae*. By the end of the nineties Rome had rejected the "dialogic" approach favored by the bishops, who were not anxious to take on the academic establishment. The Vatican called for a *mandatum*, a loyalty oath that theologians would be obliged to sign. The stage was set for confrontation. Then, early in 2002, the sexual abuse scandal broke open, and *Ex Corde Ecclesiae* was put on the back burner.[2]

The scandals created opportunities for disaffected Catholics. The revelations revived the fortunes of the Survivors Networks of those Abused by Priests. Founded in the late 1980s, SNAP had barely hung on until media coverage of the church's mishandling of sexual abuse brought the organization back to life. Voice of the Faithful (VOTF) sprung into being directly as a result of investigative reporting published in the *Boston Globe*. The Leadership Roundtable was up and running by 2005.

A striking feature of the groups that emerged in response to the scandals—and of some, like SNAP and FutureChurch, that antedate the catalytic event—is how ideologically heterogeneous they are. (Over a decade before the *Boston Globe* exposed such abuse and its cover-up, SNAP was established by victims of sexual molestation at the hands of priests with the aim of bringing this behavior to public attention; FutureChurch came into being with a separate mission, to challenge rules against the ordination of women and married men.) Whatever disaffection members of the Leadership Roundtable feel is infrequently expressed. Circumspection and protestations of love for the church, and organizational discipline, count for a lot. Voice of the Faithful hovers in a left to center-left orbit, where ambivalence about the institutional church runs deep. SNAP espouses no doctrinal program at all.

Doctrinal and ideological differences are unavoidable even among loyalist groups like the Roundtable, where the skew toward strong, unapologetic personalities is manifest. The Roundtable tries to keep quiet about such matters not only to avoid upsetting a nervous episcopate but to prevent its own members from quarreling among themselves. The bishops need to know where a group with the heft of the Roundtable, regardless of the individual opinions of its associates, comes down organizationally. If the crucial signal to be sent is a willingness to collaborate with the hierarchy, SNAP remains on the outs. VOTF is hard to pin down. Its fondness for nuance can look like elusiveness. The bishops have no time for an organization whose loyalty is in question and whose resources are nebulous.

Perhaps more important than the handling of ideological diversity is the variation in personal histories and resources that the groups bring to reform. (Both SNAP and the Roundtable eschew the word "reform" altogether—SNAP because the leadership believes that institutional Catholicism is essentially unreformable and the Roundtable because some bishops are inclined to load the word with schismatic, reformation-like connotations.) SNAP has few connections to the church except for the victimhood of most of its members.

By contrast, a significant fraction of VOTF members have ongoing relations or extensive histories with the church, as former priests or nuns or well-educated laypeople engaged in parish activities. Some have scores to settle. The long-standing, impassioned, and sometimes checkered ties of many adherents of VOTF to the institutional church contribute to their difficulty in sticking with a disciplined agenda. VOTF's slogan—"Change the Church, Keep the Faith"—reflects these divided loyalties.

The Leadership Roundtable is a case apart. The wealth and organizational expertise of its members, their stock of contacts and knowhow, put it in a more exclusive league than SNAP or VOTF. The leadership of the Roundtable has an extensive record in Catholic philanthropy, and the higher echelons are well connected in church circles. They are also closely linked to one another by reputation and sometimes by cross-generational ties. Kerry Robinson, the executive director of the Roundtable, is the daughter of Peter Robinson, one of the creators of Foundations and Donors Interested in Catholic Activities (FADICA), a consortium of Catholic benefactors. Robinson's great-grandfather, John K. Raskob, pushed through the construction of the Empire State Building during the Great Depression.[3] Frank Butler, a former seminarian and Peter Robinson's successor as president at FADICA and afterwards secretary of the Roundtable, began his career at the bishops' conference during the 1970s after a stint as a congressional aide. FADICA and the Roundtable have offices across from one another in the same building in Washington. Tom Healey, like Geoff Boisi, retired as a partner from Goldman Sachs; he has served as treasurer for the Roundtable and has been a driving force behind initiatives for training young priests in financial management.

And so it goes. Numerous Roundtable associates hold seats on the boards of Catholic institutions. Several belong to the exclusive Knights of Malta, a few to Opus Dei. It is hard to dismiss the membership roster of the Roundtable as interlopers from the business world without a clue about the arcana of church culture.[4]

In the end, the impact of variations in ideology (another word that, like "reform," many activists dislike), in personal histories, and in financial resources depends on the uses to which they are put. All organizations with a pretense to fostering change in Catholicism have to choose among three broad strategies. While they overlap a bit, the strategies are fundamentally different.

The most clearly focused approach targets change in the behavior of church officials. This is the hallmark of SNAP. The strategy leaves the institutional edifice of Catholicism virtually untouched. (The safe-touch programs and review boards that the bishops have put in place can be understood in part as a response to SNAP, but they do not tip the balance of power in the hierarchy.) The clerical system is believed to be set in its ways, and the law generally shields the internal structure of religious groups from external challenges. SNAP is not out for an institutional fix envisioned as a root-and-branch organizational realignment. It is the possibility of going after bad behavior by way of legally imposed penalties and mobilizing public opinion that is the fuse. If the institutional peculiarities of the church cannot be corrected, malfeasance can be punished and possibly, over time, prevented. The incentive structure can be changed.

A second, potentially broader option is to take on institutional transformation. The strategy is more like a spectrum than a category, so broad that it is easier to define in terms of what it is not: it rules out doctrine. The Leadership Roundtable concentrates on administrative best practices, financial accountability, human resource training, and wealth management. The zone runs from the doctrinally innocuous to the potentially contentious.

Aside from business models themselves, the clearest precedent for the Roundtable is the modernization of Catholic higher education and health services that began in the late sixties, when the institutions were reformed in such a way that their management practices came to satisfy professional standards without, it is presumed, violating their religious identity.[5] The primary schools and especially the parishes are a different story. But even there, with economic collapse in the wings, objections to overhauling the parochial schools and to a lesser extent the parishes tend to be as much about technical feasibility, fund raising, and willpower as principle pure and simple.

If doctrine is off limits, however, involvement in policy making is not, and sometimes the boundaries become hard to make out, as happened in 2010, when Sister Carol Keehan, CEO of the Catholic Health Association and a Roundtable board member, endorsed the Obama-sponsored health-care reform in defiance of the opposition of the American bishops.[6] Such deviance is still less ominous-sounding to the episcopal ear, however, than the "structural change" that Voice of the Faithful adopted as one of its core priorities. The expansive strategy has led Voice of the Faithful to reconnoiter areas like the election of bishops and the celibacy requirement for priests, both of which enter ideologically touchier grounds.

Strictly speaking, neither episcopal appointments nor sacerdotal celibacy are doctrinal issues. They are "questions of discipline"—inherited conventions that come with the weight of tradition rather than revelation. In principle, they are subject to revision. Politically, however, such distinctions get lost. Controversies like these fall within a third, contested zone of institutional symbolism that brushes up against doctrinal integrity. They hint not just of change in behavior or of upgrading organizational practices but of regime transformation or at least of a serious realignment of power. The lines of conflict are not merely about this or that policy. They correspond to positions for or against upending the lines of authority. Requirements for the priesthood cannot be modified without altering the chain of command. The celibate priesthood and the appointment of bishops are emblematic markers of governance. They are sensitive in a way that managerial reforms may approach—for example, when the collegiality built into the lay-dominated boards of Catholic universities impinges on clerical privilege—but stop short of trespassing.

CHAPTER EIGHT

SNAP AND THE STRATEGY OF CONFRONTATION

Catholic conservatives are apt to spend as much energy attacking the evils ascribed to society at large—abortion, misguided welfare programs, headlong secularization, metastasizing neopaganism—as they are defending their religion from dissidents within. The Survivors Network of those Abused by Priests (SNAP) pursues a reverse strategy, working from outside to press its demands on the church.

SNAP does not claim to be a Catholic group. It is an association of mostly alienated or ex-Catholics, with a mission "to meet the needs of membership through moral support, information, and advocacy." (Barbara Blaine, a former Catholic Worker who founded SNAP in 1988, remains a Catholic.) Though it has Baptist and Presbyterian offshoots, SNAP more often than not targets the Catholic church.

SNAP's stance is adversarial. The assumption is that the institutional church is beyond fixing if left to its own devices or to the blandishments of its friends. The organization may be of divine origin but human decency can rarely be expected of it. "The bottom line is this," according to David Clohessy, a community organizer by training and the group's national director since 1991.[1] "Those in decision-making capacities in the church hierarchy have no incentive to reform... [and] they will probably never reform."

Why is this? Careers are made from within, accountability flows upward, responsiveness to popular pressure for realigning the structure of power is nonexistent. The church is what it is, an impenetrable monument to inertia and ensconced privilege. Expecting it to do the right thing for reasons of conscience flies in the face of the experience of the survivors that SNAP claims to represent.[2] "Monarchs change," Clohessy reasons, "but monarchies do not."[3]

The reaction of SNAP to the impasse has been litigation, in combination with the pursuit of media coverage. The idea is to alter the structure of incentives, of penalties and rewards, that surround the church. The point is to change the *behavior* of priests and church authorities, regardless of their creedal tics and organizational mores. The sexual abuse of minors is an indictable outrage. The only attitude adjustment required on the part of church leaders is a recognition that, besides the loss of esteem involved, the hierarchy is in fact vulnerable to civil and criminal justice. A pugnacious SNAP constitutes a reality check against clerical insularity. Absolute immunity is delusional even under the generous protection of the First Amendment.[4]

So, stonewalling, negligence, and malfeasance have tangible costs. Pain can be inflicted. It is primarily lawsuits, the threat of lawsuits, costly settlements, and the shaming effects of bad publicity that SNAP counts on for the creation of reliable procedures to protect children and punish wrong-doers. "The bottom line," as Frank Douglas, a former Voice of the Faithful (VOTF) member and victim of abuse who migrated to SNAP, put it, "is the bottom line." Fraternal correction, a meeting of the minds between advocates and bishops, and simple good will are pleasantries that obscure the need for hardball tactics. Like pedophiles themselves, the church as seen by SNAP may be treatable, but it is not curable. Mendacity, as Jason Berry characterizes it, is systemic. Evasiveness, the flip side of absolutism, is ingrained, and recidivism is both an institutional and a personal reversion to type.[5]

SNAP was not an overnight success.[6] It is a product neither of the earlier, emancipatory wave of Catholic reform, represented by Call to Action, that followed on Vatican II, nor of the mobilization ignited later by the *Boston Globe*'s revelations of sexual abuse. SNAP dates from the 1980s. It was during this decade, one that coincided with the first years of the papacy of John Paul II, that some of the American bishops began to realize that the sexual abuse of minors by priests might not be a one-in-a-million aberration. By 1981 the St. Luke Institute, funded by the bishops, went into operation outside Washington as a treatment center for pedophile clergy. The thinking at the time was that therapy could straighten out sexual predators, that they might be recycled back into ministry, and that lawsuits could be avoided or settled quietly and even amicably. At around the same time, Jeff Anderson, a trial lawyer, began to take on clients as plaintiffs against the diocese of Minneapolis in cases of sexual abuse. In 1985 Thomas Doyle, a Dominican priest, coauthored a report warning the bishops that the church in the United States would face billions of dollars in damages if clerical molestation of minors was not stopped.[7]

By the mid-1980s, after the first widely publicized child molestation scandal struck, in Louisiana, it was no longer possible for the church to purchase affordable insurance for covering claims of sexual abuse, and in 1987 over sixty dioceses and archdioceses became shareholders in the National Catholic Risk Retention Group, to protect themselves against catastrophic losses. In 1989 Anderson won the first punitive damage award against the church for clergy sexual abuse. In the same year SNAP was incorporated as a nonprofit organization.

Progress was slow. During its first decade SNAP operated mostly as a support network, putting survivors in touch with one another. Barbara Blaine took success stories about women setting up their own businesses, mutual aid and self-help societies as morale-boosting models for the movement that she and David Clohessy were trying to build. As far as getting the church to mend its ways, "We were very naive," Clohessy remembers. "We thought that the bishops would empathize with their pain once they listened to the stories of the survivors. That didn't happen. They circled the wagons around the institution."[8] When an accusation of sexual abuse leveled against Cardinal Bernardin of Chicago fell apart in 1993, after the plaintiff admitted that his recollections were baseless, the survivors' movement almost folded.

Then in 2001 attention turned to California.[9] After five years of litigation, Ryan DiMaria, a product of the Southern California's parochial school system, won an unprecedented $5.2 million judgment against the diocese of Orange County. The settlement became a template for subsequent legal actions. It required not only Orange but the Los Angeles archdiocese to establish a zero-tolerance policy and a toll-free number for reporting sexual assaults.[10] The judgment also stipulated that the church had to release records of transactions between predator priests and their superiors. The days of appealing to the higher motives of bishops and relying on their sympathy were over.[11]

After this, events came in a rush. Whatever the nature of sexual abuse as a pathology of individuals, attempts to conceal and deny the behavior were beginning to look like an organization-wide pattern. The *Globe* released its exposé of the cover-up engineered by the Boston archdiocese in January 2002. In the uproar over the DiMaria and Boston cases, the California legislature lifted the statue of limitations on civil suits for the year 2003. In 2005, the diocese of Orange agreed to a $100 million settlement with dozens of plaintiffs.[12] In the summer of 2007 came the largest but not the last of the settlements. The Los Angeles archdiocese settled its multiple suits for a total of $660 million.

Patrick Wall is senior consultant at the law firm of Manly & Stewart of Newport Beach, south of Los Angeles. The city, laced with sky-blue marinas and glossy malls, ranks as the richest in the United States. Besides his practice in commercial real estate and business law, John Manly was also a lead litigant in the DiMaria suit, and he was acclaimed "most buzz-worthy attorney" by an Orange County magazine. A former Benedictine priest, now married, Wall looks to be in his late forties. His office furniture is plain and sturdy. The office itself overflows with books, yellow legal pads, bound volumes of canon law journals, and photocopies and other papers stacked in bookcases, on the floor and across a desk. Wall has the build of a linebacker and the intensity of a man on a mission. His job is to dig up information about the cover-up of clerical sexual abuse.

The firm has worked on three bankruptcy cases that span, Wall explains, a full spectrum of sexual abuse scenarios. Fairbanks, in northern Alaska ("25,000 miles from Rome"), is a missionary diocese. Then there was the bankruptcy declared by the Oregon province of the Society of Jesus, the preeminent men's religious order. And finally, the bankruptcy of a conventional diocese, that of Wilmington in Delaware.

What matters across these cases, Wall insists, is the information from discovery procedures that might provide documentation about further instances of cover-up and that in turn might make possible a jump from civil to criminal charges involving conspiracy.[13] That is the prize. The church, however, has allies that make such digging difficult. "The church is large," Wall says, "embedded in state and local government through Catholic Charities. And a provincial or a bishop who cooperates with secular authorities is not promoted. Bishops and provincials will never do the right thing. They wear you down, they rope-a-dope you."

The church's modus operandi, as Wall sees it, is delay ("You rarely differ, you mildly deny, most of the time you maintain silence") and evasion: "On the whole West coast, if they have a Spanish-speaking priest suspected of abuse, they get him to Tijuana, into parish work there, with a PO box across the border in Texas, where he receives payment."

On his blog, Wall denounces something he calls "the numerator/denominator shuffle" in reports that claim to document a decline in cases of sexual abuse. He sees the drop as a deliberate mystification. The ideal solution would be for government to "Get out of the business of supporting the Roman Catholic church through grants to Catholic Charities and related services. There are other groups who can perform the same task with equal professionalism. No quantity or quality of good done by Catholic Charities personnel can cancel or forgive the criminal conduct condoned by the U.S. bishops."[14]

On the walls of the reception hall are six large watercolors of heroically angular battleships and aircraft carriers forging their way through white-capped seas. (John Manly, the senior partner, was an officer in the naval reserve.) One picture portrays a fantasy scene with a centuries-old galleon and a modern destroyer tossing through seething waves; a helicopter tilts overhead, below bombastic clouds, amid sea birds the size of condors. The furniture in the waiting area is pale and plush. Mounted on the receptionist's beige desk is a brass plaque, dating from 1920, of Teddy Roosevelt in profile, with the inscription "Aggressive fighting for the right is the noblest sport the world provides."

The confrontational strategy adopted by SNAP proved to be a game changer. Even a few of SNAP's targets, like the diocese of Little Rock, acknowledge the group's contribution:

> SNAP and the diocese basically want the same thing: We want children protected, and we do not want pedophiles or ephebophiles in a position to prey upon innocent youth. We disagree on the method to obtain this end. The disagreement

> may stem from a distrust of the Church on SNAP's part based upon its past history in the handling of sexual misconduct cases. In some instances, SNAP's suspicions were well founded. Times have changed. And, frankly, vigilant watchdogs like SNAP helped to provoke those changes.[15]

SNAP's strategy grew out of a learning experience. The lesson was that victims of clerical sexual abuse could not get justice simply by petitioning for redress within the church, no matter how much they pleaded. The church would never change on its own. SNAP came to realize that while the hierarchy was as slippery about the complaints of victims as it was unshakeable in matters of doctrine, tort law could provide leverage for bringing the ecclesiastical establishment to terms. If Catholicism would not change, its managers could be held to account. Victims were no longer to be supplicants.

These victories came at a cost. SNAP did not endear itself to many Catholics. The organization aimed its attacks at religious orders and, even more, at dioceses. It was in the dioceses, run directly by bishops, where wealth in property and power over financial allocations lay, that decisions were made. Diocesan chanceries oversaw clerical appointments in the parishes and usually held ownership of parish buildings and belongings under "corporation sole" arrangements.[16] Yet, while the far more numerous parishes were smaller fry, they had to bear some of the damage from litigation aimed at the dioceses. Even with compensation from insurance companies factored in, settlements reached by dioceses spilled over as expenses for parishes. School programs were cut back, obligatory contributions to the diocesan fund were hiked. Some dioceses, like Tucson and Wilmington, Delaware, chose bankruptcy in order to avoid having to pay out punitive damages.[17]

In the eyes of otherwise sympathetic Catholics, like members of VOTF, the fixation of SNAP on the dioceses risked being too blunt a weapon. Parishes in jeopardy tended to see themselves as collateral damage in a far-off war between the courts and the bishops. They had problems of their own. School enrollments were falling, only the number of funerals seemed to be going up. The perception was that SNAP's belligerence threatened to bring down already struggling churches and schools, along with chancery operations that were removed from everyday contact with the faithful and that few Catholics cared much about. (Catholics identify themselves as "parishioners"; there is no comparable noun for members of dioceses.)

One result was to set rank-and-file Catholics who wanted desperately to preserve their parishes at odds with SNAP and to align them by default with bishops who had their own reasons to separate diocesan from parish property.[18] Parishes that had to fend for themselves were not liable for judgments against dioceses; if the parishes were on their own financially, they could not be caught up in suits against the bishops. Parishes were rarely worth suing separately.[19] For their part, dioceses could declare bankruptcy more readily, avoiding the heaviest penalties, if their holdings did not include the assets associated with parish property.

Scenarios like these cast SNAP as an interloper in the intensely local politics of the church. The reaction of Catholics in the pews might appear myopic in light of parish and school closings mandated under diocesan auspices. But resentment against SNAP as an outside agitator lingered. The fear was that SNAP's aggressiveness made a precarious situation worse, and it was not unusual for the organization to be met with what it considered a kill-the-messenger reaction. When SNAP supporters showed up to pass out leaflets at a parochial school on the outskirts of Los Angeles where a perpetrator was alleged to be working, angry mothers shouted that they were frightening the children. An associate pastor offered the handful of protesters soft drinks and coffee as long as they kept to their place filing back and forth on the sidewalk.

Weak support among Catholics attached to their parishes narrowed the options of SNAP to media coverage and the courts. Outside of California, Delaware, and Hawaii, where the push to extend statutes of limitation succeeded, the leadership of SNAP and litigators allied with the organization came to the judgment that petitioning state legislators and rallying their constituents was better than doing nothing but, at the end of the day, only marginally efficient. The church was usually able to deploy considerable resources in that arena, and victories that overturned statute of limitations deadlines remained very rare.[20]

Zero-tolerance for priests credibly accused of child sexual abuse turned out to be another blunt instrument. Adopted by the bishops as part of their Dallas Charter for the Protection of Children and Young People in mid-2002, when pressure for remedial action was at its peak, the measure requires suspending suspected priests from active ministry, as would happen if a police officer were charged with brutality on the job. The policy came in for criticism by the Vatican and others on the grounds of circumventing due process.[21]

SNAP argues that zero-tolerance does not go far enough. Though it may help keep suspected perpetrators away from children, no such norm extends to bishops who may have been involved in the higher-order offense of covering up misconduct. In Dallas, the bishops signed off on a policy that cost them little personally except a sense of betrayal among the men in the trenches. They let it be known that among themselves "fraternal correction" would suffice. SNAP stipulates that in any case, even after the Dallas meeting, "a quiet regression has been going on" because of loopholes in the accord.

As cases of actionable abuse faded into the past, while documentation of behind-the-scenes efforts by higher-ups to conceal them continued to surface, the policy of zero-tolerance began to look lopsided. Prelates suspected of hushing things up were buffered from the fate of ordinary clergy, some of whom felt they had been hung out to dry.[22] It was not until the spring of 2011 that the first "enabler," a monsignor from the Philadelphia archdiocese, was indicted on charges of hiding cases of sexual abuse and helping shuttle suspected perpetrators from one parish to another. A few months later, in October, the bishop of Kansas City–St. Joseph in Missouri was hit with a misdemeanor charge of failing to report child abuse.[23]

Fissures between the bishops and middle management may be a precondition for opening up Catholicism, as the defection of priests who signed a public statement of nonsupport during the run-up to the ouster of Cardinal Law from the Boston archdiocese suggests.[24] In the end, however, SNAP's methods have not won many allies among the clergy, and SNAP probably never contemplated such an alliance to begin with. Distrust is nearly total on both sides. Exacting justice is one thing; enacting reform is another. SNAP's triumph has been to raise the costs of negligence and criminal behavior on the part of the church, not to remake the organization.

A Republican stronghold for years, Orange County, south of Los Angeles, retains much of its conservative ambience. At noon, on Sunday, January 7, 2007, down the road from the Naval Munitions Depot and a Boeing Defense Industries plant, about eighty people showed up for a surprise lunch in honor of Mary Grant, then southwest regional coordinator for SNAP. It was a balmy

Southern California afternoon. The grounds of the Old Ranch Country Club in Seal Beach, surrounded by golf links, were bedecked with fountains and date palms. A soft scent of morning humidity lingered, wafting up from the ocean.[25]

Six large framed quilts hung on the walls of the banquet room. Each quilt had thirty-two childhood photographs of men and women who had been violated by priests, and in the middle of the quilts were caption-titles: "Broken Hearts," "Betrayed Trust," "Stolen Souls," "Lost Innocence," "Shattered Lives."

The first speaker was Erin Brady, who had arranged the quilts. She had been a postulant, a "nun in the making," in a novitiate when she had met Grant fourteen years before. "She didn't judge me for being in the church. She told me 'You're not alone.' Those words changed my life. Survivors are my true community."

Brady described her flashbacks and panic attacks. "Mary, you talked me out of blowing up the chancery... only kidding!"

"You talked me out of *suicide*," she added. "You picked me up after that betrayal. You were always on call, 24/7."

"In 1994, at the Religious Education Conference, we did our first leafleting. 'Oh Mary,' one of the bishops told you, 'you were a provocative 13-year-old.' Not the right thing to say to Mary Grant!"[26]

Barbara Blaine, the founder of SNAP, came to the podium. "I first met Mary Grant in 1991. She showed up in Saint Louis, with three kids. Mary looked frightened, a mouse that plopped down in a room full of cats. Look at her today, a model of strength and courage. Back in the early nineties, it was not the same. There wasn't any Internet. Then we found a way to build a movement. California had the best laws to help victims of abuse, and Mahony could be exposed for complicity and cover-up."

Something reminds Blaine of being drowned out while leafleting on the sidewalk outside Our Lady of the Angels Cathedral in downtown Los Angeles, where she had been leading a small demonstration that morning. The noise sounded like insane calliope music. "The sound of the bells, the bells ringing in the cathedral. At the moment you're making a point, what happens? These bells start ringing! Could they be any louder? Those bells. There's sometimes we want to be left alone."

At the end of the speeches Grant is given a present, an elaborately packaged alarm clock. After unwrapping it, she smiles and holds up the clock like an

Oscar. The laughter quiets down, and she talks about "trying to rebuild trust, without having to explain." She pauses and concludes, "How hard it is to get survivors in a room together. Without this group I would be so alone today."

A few months later, exhausted, Grant began an extended leave of absence.

Scrappiness is not the only tactic separating SNAP from other Catholic advocacy groups. Call to Action can be cantankerous too. SNAP is a gadfly with some clout. The organization's effectiveness must draw on something more than being abrasive.

First, SNAP has concentrated on an understandable goal: vindication and compensation for survivors. Court cases and legal wrangling, like police procedurals, provide riveting narratives with visible outcomes. Second, that goal is tangible—not just material (although survivors sometimes admit that the money is part of it) but set within a finite time horizon. While far from guaranteed, results are foreseeable and there is a plausible perception of a cause-effect link between effort and outcome. There is a chance that culpable priests will be ousted and that compensation for damages will be paid. There is also a chance that such outcomes will discourage child abuse in the future.

Third, many of the protagonists have multiple motives. The leadership of SNAP does not have to rely solely on the promise of righting wrongs; it can also hold out the promise of delivering palpable benefits. Recourse to the tort system has made this strategy feasible.

Fourth, SNAP operates as a support group. It provides venues for venting and bonding among people many of whom have histories of relationships stunted or crippled as a result of their abuse. Listening sessions offer a release, intimacy, and a sense that one is not freakishly alone. A few survivors will drive to meetings only to stay in their cars, unable to enter, paralyzed with shame. Others cannot make it to the door, because they have lost their drivers' licenses for DUI convictions. For some survivors, legal depositions and financial settlements, however empowering, cannot provide relief. Both Clohessy and Blaine insist that the hours spent consoling survivors of abuse by phone or in person far exceed the time taken up in litigation and legislative advocacy.[27]

It is the combination of organizational clarity, objective benefits, and personal recognition, rather than any one of these elements, that has helped SNAP sustain its operations as long as it has. Other advocacy groups also provide affective sustenance. Even if such backup is rarely a stated objective, chatting with the like-minded reinforces fellowship especially, perhaps, in the absence of realizable goals. Groups like VOTF tend to rely almost exclusively on whatever fulfillment comes from straining to do what they feel has to be done. Unadulterated idealism, prophetic heroism, and A-for-effort dedication are too demanding for sustained commitment. Or they may be too difficult to live with organizationally, as the history of faction-prone reform movements indicates. Spontaneous democracy begins to burn people out.

SNAP's strength, then, comes from a mixture of disciplined vision, specificity of aims, and emotional sustenance. A certain psychic autonomy helps too. The organization is nondenominational, though not determinedly secular. Other reform groups—again, VOTF comes to mind—have at least a foot in the doctrinal pew, and they worry about keeping up orthodoxy of a kind.[28] An organization like the Leadership Roundtable has enough material resources to flex some muscle on its own but it has chosen, as part of a strategy of long-term influence, not to mess with the magisterium. Only SNAP is indifferent to, indeed dismissive of, doctrine. It is the actions of the church, not its organizational peculiarities or its beliefs, that matter.

To the public, and certainly in the eyes of the bishops, SNAP stands out among Catholic advocacy groups for the relentlessness of its tactics and its aggressive appeal to legal sanctions. But the power of SNAP needs to be put in perspective. Its resources, like those of most other such groups, pale when compared to the money behind conservative interests.

Consider a sample of Catholic associations, ranging from the long-established Knights of Columbus across right-wing stalwarts like the Catholic League and Legatus, this last a group of entrepreneurs and managers set up by Domino's Pizza founder Tom Monaghan "to promote business ethics and support for an intimate union between faith and life." We can then add the organizations highlighted in this and accompanying chapters—SNAP, VOTF, the Leadership Roundtable, and FutureChurch—and top them off with Call to Action (CTA) and Foundations and Donors Interested in Catholic Activities (FADICA), the consortium of benefactors that works closely with the Roundtable. Table 8.1 ranks the nine groups in terms of their net assets.

TABLE 8.1.
Net Assets (in $000s) of Catholic Interest and Advocacy Groups

	2005	2006	2007	2008	2009	2010
K of C	38,209	41,503	42,020	37,636	45,860	51,582
Catholic League	7,951	22,055	26,098	22,714	26,202	28,689
FADICA	1,854	2,994	5,756	4,754	5,173	5,842
Legatus	1,673	1,739	1,410	654	1,116	1,412
Roundtable	401	−210	385	1,101	675	698
CTA	750	217	−131	77	604	611
VOTF	191	84	76	24	209	156
SNAP	—	430	210	281	203	35
Future Church	115	110	97	102	107	102

Source: National Center for Charitable Statistics at the Urban Institute, IRS Form 990 statements, http://nccsdataweb.urban.org/PubApps/.

The Knights of Columbus are far and away the dominant organization. The assets of the K of C total more than those of all the other groups combined. The Knights are the most formidable lay presence in American Catholicism.[29] Of the remaining organizations, the Leadership Roundtable comes out significantly ahead, especially if we join it to FADICA. Were we to employ a metric indexing the scope of the expertise on tap in the Roundtable's network, the group would approach the standing of the Catholic League and Legatus, whose goals look narrower.[30]

SNAP comes in toward the bottom, a step above FutureChurch, at least until 2010, when its fortunes really plummeted. Like the other groups, SNAP experienced some slippage with the financial meltdown of 2008. It also hit a pothole in 2007—evidently once the contributions of trial lawyers went down after the multimillion dollar settlement in the Los Angeles archdiocese—and another in 2009. By 2011 and 2012, SNAP's financial trouble worsened in the face of diocesan litigation requiring it, at great expense, to hand over years of documentation.

But the striking revelation remains the overall distance between the two leading organizations, the Knights of Columbus and the Catholic League, and the rest of the pack. Together with Legatus, they pull the economic center of

American Catholicism in a conservative direction. While the Catholic League is vociferous in condemning enemies of the church, real and imagined, the profile of organizations such as the Knights of Columbus or Opus Dei is generally quieter.[31] The concentration of resources in a group like the Knights of Columbus appears to be much more at the disposal of the Vatican than it is available to the American episcopate as a whole; financially, each diocese remains pretty much on its own. Another way of putting this is to underline the fact that the operations of the K of C are truly international, with dispersals to Catholic and church-related activities in numerous countries. (One of the Knights' benefactions has been to pay for refurbishing Bernini's colonnades in Saint Peter's Square.) The Knights and Opus Dei can underwrite relatively modernized operations of the church that controvert the identification of the Vatican with *opera buffa* inefficiency. The leaders of Catholic colleges and universities, for example, are aware that even with *Ex Corde Ecclesiae* on hold Rome monitors them carefully. The Knights of Columbus are also reported to have underwritten the investigation of American nuns (the "apostolic visitation of religious communities") in 2009 to the tune of one million dollars.[32]

The capacity of a group like the Knights of Columbus to throw its weight around must itself be set in context. Information of the sort arrayed in Table 8.1 refers to Catholic associations defined as interest groups. The data do not encompass charitable organizations—even though, as in the case of the K of C, there can be significant overlap between the categories. Were advocacy groups and foundations to be lumped together, the Knights would be a jumbo frog in a mostly uncharted pond. In recent years the Knights have amped up their support for conservative causes. From 2005 through 2012, the organization channeled over six million dollars into campaigns against same-sex marriage, stressing that during the same period they donated more than one billion dollars to charities.[33]

Not much is known about Catholic foundations in the United States, except that they are numerous, mostly family run, and typically localized. Their cultural and political impact in the aggregate appears to be less than their financial influence on specific parishes, dioceses, and ministerial operations of the church. At least, it is not systematic.[34]

Yet this dispersed collection of local notables adds to the conservative texture of intramural Catholic politics, somewhat as the "stealth" campaigns of conservative groups whatever their religious affiliation have borne fruit at the state level. There is no doubt that even small Catholic foundations carry more weight than activist groups on the left and that the Knights of Columbus make up a right-wing colossus. In addition to the ready access which the organization enjoys at the Vatican, K of C clubs are spread throughout American dioceses and parishes.[35] The overall effect is to reinforce the conservative aura of American Catholicism. That effect would be magnified still further were we to take into account the influence of strong-willed Catholics—the careers of William Baroody *père* and *fils*, Paul Weyrich, and Ed Feulner come to mind—in building institutions like the American Enterprise Institute and the Heritage Foundation.[36]

The reach of such operations remains elusive even to some insiders. Their influence is not limited to the in-house politics of the church. There are lunches with the papal nuncio and the bonhomie of the annual Alfred E. Smith Memorial Foundation dinner at the Waldorf Astoria, and there are well-placed phone calls.[37] There are also the comparatively above-board activities of the bishops' conferences positioned as lobbies in several state capitals. The operative words are "texture" and "aura," not blatant power, even if over-reach has become more frequent.

The bog is mapless and fogged in. The details vary but the ambience differs little from the world and netherworld portrayed by John Gregory Dunne in *True Confessions*. Transparency has yet to become a prominent feature of Catholic philanthropies in the aggregate. The line between "charity" and "advocacy" is fuzzy.[38]

To a degree, SNAP has become a victim of its own success. The programs of enhanced vigilance that the church has come to adopt have almost certainly speeded the drop-off recorded in the sexual abuse of children. The impact of these efforts is hard to pin down, relative to the role of other forces such as a culture-wide sea change in sensitivity to crimes against children, and in some dioceses procedures have been shown to be out of compliance with the monitoring of safe environment—that is, child protection—programs.[39] Furthermore, the oversight process relies on self-reports. With self-reports, the absolute level of abuse is apt to underestimate the real level, though the downward trend, a relative pattern comparing estimates over time, is less prone to bias. On balance, progress has been made. Self-reports are now more dangerous to fake.[40]

Most revelations of instances of sexual abuse originate in cases that are decades old. This is typical as well of the crimes behind the scandals in Ireland

and elsewhere in Europe that came to light late in 2009 and on into 2010. The tendency for victims, frozen in trauma and abasement, to wait years to report their abuse is generally recognized, but it cannot account fully for the decline in the number of cases reported during a period when there are fewer inhibitions against stepping forward. The incidence of sexual abuse shows signs of bottoming out. The infestation has subsided.[41]

Two things continue to fuel the dogged skepticism of SNAP. Leadership at the highest levels of the church has a habit of lapsing into denial, characterizing accusations of abuse as "the petty gossip of idle opinion."[42] The Vatican's statement in 2010 that the ordination of women is as grave a sin as the sexual abuse of children attained self-parody, winning the insensitivity sweepstakes going away. A command structure of such ineptness does not inspire confidence in the apparatus it has put in place for preventing abuse down through the tiers of the organization.[43]

Even with gradual enlightenment or an eventual changing of the guard in Rome, however, SNAP faces hurdles besides the downward trend in sexual abuse in tandem with fatigue from hearing about it. SNAP's breakthrough, engineered jointly with trial lawyers, was to show that the church was not above the law. Covering up sexual abuse is now more penalty-ridden, and hence less feasible, as an option for church managers. But the execution of sanctions continues to be problematic. It is doubtful whether letting up will promote implementation any more than deference, dulcet dialogue, and the rest of Catholic etiquette succeeded in bringing the church to judgment in the first place. The obligation to report instances of sexual abuse to civil authorities had to be imposed on the church in the teeth of a culture that punishes whistle-blowing, and that disincentive to transparency remains.[44]

So, SNAP keeps up the pressure. Even if the sexual abuse of children is in decline, the anachronistic machinery of much of the church hierarchy and a deep, seemingly ineradicable culture of institutional protectiveness do not inspire confidence in self-vigilance. Pique at what the hierarchy regards as insolence from demagogues, adventurers, and gold diggers, the likelihood that many of those implicated in the cover-up remain in positions of authority, the spotty human resources available for implementing safeguards at various levels of the church bureaucracy, and the whiff of bad faith clinging to an old boy's club, all make a case for sustained surveillance. The judgment is shared beyond the confines of SNAP. "The more relaxed the institution," Peggy Noonan, a

Reagan Catholic and hagiographer of John Paul II, wrote of the church, "the less likely it will reform."[45] SNAP's critical audacity has become common sense in unexpected quarters. The center of gravity of respectable opinion has shifted away from awe-struck loyalty toward vigilance and prudential evaluation.

Confrontation is the trademark of a generation of leaders who have been in charge since the founding of SNAP. Almost all of their experience has taught them to stay with what they know best, and there is enough evidence to indicate that they are doing something right. "Don't assume that things will get better," Clohessy urges, "Time is neutral."[46] "Like Ahab, after years of therapy," a reluctant admirer cracked about him.

Even the cost associated with a take-no-prisoners mode of advocacy—the loss of potential allies among elements of the clergy and churchgoers from threatened parishes—may be acceptable if bargaining with sympathetic groups means diverting energy from child protection and the pursuit of financial settlements. Growing coalitions takes time, and size is not necessarily a productive asset for getting the results SNAP aims for.

The penchant for going it alone is not simply a function of recrimination between SNAP and church authorities or of the reluctance of groups like VOTF to go after the clerical edifice as if loaded for bear. The suspicion that a gay subculture may have contributed to sexual abuse in the church persists as a scab that irritates some otherwise sympathetic partners, like the advocates of LGBT rights in Call to Action, as well as many within the hierarchy itself. Let-the-chips-fall-where-they-may research on the nexus, if any, between mandatory celibacy, homosexuality, and the sexual abuse of minors has yet to overcome an atmosphere of character assassination, unfounded assertion, and pop science, compounded by innumeracy.[47]

In any event, courage and tenacity in the face of numerous setbacks can pay off for SNAP and its supporters in the media. After years of litigation (the decisive complaint was brought by the Associated Press and the LA Times), a superior court judge finally ruled that the Los Angeles archdiocese had to release the names of high-ranking church officials mentioned in confidential records about priests accused of abusing children. The files confirmed what had long been suspected, that Cardinal Mahony, who retired in 2011, had shielded sexually predatory priests from law enforcement.[48]

On the other hand, the tactics favored by SNAP start to look monotonous as sexual abuse within the church has fallen off and SNAP's apparently heavy reliance on trial lawyers for funding restricts its resource base.[49] It is still common to dismiss SNAP's strategy as gotcha politics. There seems to be little political will for extending statute of limitation regulations beyond the few states where that change was enacted. As fewer victims of sexual abuse step forward, the number of court cases diminishes, and media exposure becomes an increasingly important strategy. Philadelphia and Kansas City replaced Boston and Los Angeles as cases of spectacular wrongdoing and neglect on the part of the church. But such cases show few signs of spreading.[50]

A division of labor has evolved among reform groups in and around Catholicism. SNAP, beyond the Catholic pale, has little to gain from softening its tactics if other groups are already filling that niche and if the effectiveness of these groups in curbing the wrongdoing of the church has not proved superior. SNAP's record shows some success attacking from the outside, on its own terms. A loyal organized opposition has yet to be granted safe passage in the church. There are no fully autonomous in-between mechanisms that might discourage anything-goes tactics on either side. There are hotspots but no venues for contestation.

The agents of reform at the edges and under the skin of the church form a loose ecology of pressure groups offering partial alternatives and small-group solidarity. More often than not they function as support groups rather than as advocates with significant leverage. They lack the attributes of a coalition with a plausible alternative vision to the status quo.

The chief lesson emerging from SNAP's crusade is that facts never speak for themselves. The even greater lesson is that, before this, the facts have to be extracted—"disemboweled" would not be too picturesque a word—from an adversary schooled in centuries of secrecy and misdirection.[51] "Propaganda" is after all a term made famous by Rome. Then, once exposed, the data have to be adjudicated in courts of law. The evidence cannot simply lie there in steaming heaps, as if the stench would compel people toward the truth, to take resolute action. On the contrary, quiescence has been a bigger part of popular reaction than active indignation. Catholic politics begins to look bipolar, swinging between vituperation and apathy.

Aside from stick-to-itiveness (one of Clohessy's slightly ironic heroes is Calvin Coolidge, who praised the virtue tersely but repeatedly), the hallmark of SNAP is skepticism and suspicion. Neither Clohessy nor Blaine is a fan of rapport, if "rapport" means caving in, in order to be liked. The influence of Saul Alinsky's organizing style is clear. The method takes a toll. The stance does not encourage coalition building. In one way or another almost all reform groups that call themselves Catholic *want* to trust the church, or at least to conceive of and help build a church that they are able to trust.

To cynics and some partisans of SNAP, this looks like gullibility—selective gullibility perhaps, but gullibility all the same—and demeaning to boot. The dream of reconciliation seems like an inconclusive nightmare or sad mirage shared by the vile and the pathetic. The apologies and admissions of wrongdoing by the church are perceived as mostly inoculations to immunize the faithful against the disease of growing up. Charlie Brown, who should know better, keeps trying to kick the football held by the reliably manipulative Lucy Van Pelt. A hapless Wile E. Coyote keeps pursuing—out of love? out of hunger?—a grinning Roadrunner.

But even when they have reason to distrust the hierarchy, many dissidents and moderate reformers can envision a church that is worthy of trust, after a fashion. Polarization helps get out the troops, but it is also fatiguing. With a substantial emotional and at times practical investment in institutional Catholicism (many are church employees), they feel half trapped and half in love with an organization they cannot quite abandon. Bereavement subsists with outrage. It is this longing for a beloved, somehow Catholic community that separates Voice of the Faithful and the Leadership Roundtable, discussed in the following chapters, from SNAP.

"There's all this confusion," the man says. "Like putting your head in a dryer that's going around at top speed. Round and round. It never ends."

Another man reminisces about the reaction he got when he first reported his abuse as a teenager. "'I understand certain things happened,' the priest's superior tells me. 'You'd better think very carefully about what you say, young man. You're a very smart lad. I don't want to get into specifics. I hope you understand me.'"

An older woman rocks in her chair. "I don't know who I could have been," she says.

"I scream at my husband one morning," another says, "and by the time I get home from work I'm fine. Or vice versa."

The man who's been talking about his high school abuse leans forward. "Even when I won, I wasn't happy. I was waiting for the harpies to descend from heaven, or ascend from hell, whatever, and tear the defendants limb from limb, their arms and legs dangling from the telephone wires. That didn't happen." He sits back. "You find that some people have been emotionally damaged, and that sometimes the same people get it wrong."

"Fucking pope," someone says.

There is a long silence. "If only they lived up to the things they taught us," another says. "I have come to the very sad conclusion that we are not going to make a dent."[52]

CHAPTER NINE

VOICE OF THE FAITHFUL AND THE STRUGGLE FOR CATHOLIC PLURALISM

As a matter of fact, the Phrygian Montanists, the infamous Adamites, the Ophiolaters, the two-faced Manicheans, standing all of them in the middle ground between an emergent Christianity and ancient Buddhism, the disciples of Marcus, the abstinent Encratites, the Flagellants, and all the numerous sects into which the nascent religion was split up, with their hysterical doctors and hyperbolic exegeses—all these would be looked upon today as repugnant cases of insanity. Yet they were normal.[1]

Voice of the Faithful was born in the equivalent of American Catholicism's log cabin, the basement of a parish church. The *Boston Globe* broke the story of sexual abuse by priests and its cover-up by the archdiocese on Sunday morning, January 6, 2002. The same day, after the 11 o'clock mass at St. John the Evangelist church in suburban Wellesley, James Post, a professor of management at Boston University who was to become president of VOTF, spotted Msgr. John Philbin muttering to himself on the sidewalk. "We'll find a way to get through this," Post said. "We always do."

"I hope so," Philbin said, "I hope so," then walked away.

The next evening, parishioners began to swarm into the basement hall at St. John the Evangelist. VOTF quickly found itself in the thick of what was to become a drive to oust Cardinal Bernard Law from the leadership of the Boston archdiocese. The sessions in the basement went to standing room only, and the group ran out of space.

"That great meeting at Boston Garden," the historian David O'Brien recalled, referring to the rally called by VOTF in late July, "we thought a huge social movement was being born."[2] Paul Baier, a dot-com entrepreneur who had set up VOTF's website, put $10,000 on his credit card and reserved the Hynes Convention Center.[3] Over 4,000 people took part in the event. "The current crisis marks the beginning death throes of the medieval monarchical model," Fr. Tom Doyle thundered from the podium. "VOTF was on a growth juggernaut," Jim Post recalled. "We raised lots of money."[4]

Two days after the Hynes Center assembly, Cardinal Law released a statement to the press. VOTF was banned in Boston. The organization was forbidden to meet on church property. Several dioceses along the East Coast—Bridgeport, Newark, Camden, and Rockville Center in Long Island—announced similar prohibitions.

After that, donations to the Cardinal's Appeal plummeted. Over the following months, the Catholic Charities office in Boston declared de facto independence and began to accept donations earmarked directly for its activities, without having them filtered through the chancery. VOTF set up a "Voice of Compassion" fund to accept donations that would otherwise be distributed by Cardinal Law's office. Law's finance committee, stacked with executive heavyweights, refused to accept his budget proposal, and dozens of priests submitted a public letter calling for his resignation. The cardinal took the celebrity exit, landing in exile in Rome, just before the end of the year. The winds had shifted against clerical hauteur.[5]

Less than a decade later, Voice of the Faithful was all but burned out. National membership had dwindled to a fraction of a nominal 30,000 plus. Bill Donohue, the Yosemite Sam of the Catholic right, proclaimed that "VOTF is toast."[6] Voice of the Faithful looked like a social movement in the sense that Pluto was thought to be a planet. Its adherents were aging and its coffers nearly empty. Claims of moral victory, of having changed the conversation, rang hollow. The mobilizational juggernaut could not gain traction. In the words of one member, "the line between hanging in there and being ignored to death was fine."[7]

Early in 2010, revelations of sexual abuse and its cover-up in Europe and elsewhere promised to reenergize a dispirited VOTF. Bursts of horrific publicity about the church lit up the trench warfare like night flares. Just as reports of sexual misdeeds in Ireland and Germany were reaching a climax in March and April, the Baltimore archdiocese announced a series of school closings, parish consolidations, and lay-offs. The spectacle of the "Premier See" of the

American church, the historic cradle of Catholicism in the United States, being brought to its knees made the devastation of the physical plant all the more painful.[8] As the pope boarded a plane on his way back from a tour of Fatima, Homeboy Industries, the organization founded in East Los Angeles over twenty years before by the social-justice Jesuit Greg Boyle, was forced to lay off three-quarters of its staff. "Our shop is still open," Boyle remarked, "we do a decent business. Maybe the Vatican can sell some of its art treasures."[9]

Similarly dismal stories about parish consolidation and school closings rolled in from Cleveland, Paterson, Wilmington, and other corners of the rust belt and beyond. Even after the thinning ethnic demographics and the statistics of an aging priesthood and disappearing nuns were taken into account, some of the wreckage could be seen as comeuppance for poor management and self-destructive obstinacy when it came to ceding authority to competent lay people. Financially, vocationally, and morally, the church was teetering on a sink hole.[10]

Yet the rejuvenation of Voice of the Faithful did not take place. It was as if the accumulation of disasters had crushed realistic expectations that ordinary parishioners might work together and set things right. Hopes for lay-clerical collaboration seemed like relics of a vanished innocence; members tired of straddling rage and resignation. The humiliations kept coming. Just after New Year's Day, 2011, the archdiocese of Milwaukee filed for bankruptcy protection. "Priest-perpetrators sexually abused minors," Archbishop Listecki wrote to his parishioners. "As a result, there are financial claims pending against the archdiocese that exceed our means."[11]

Of all the reform groups that came to prominence around the time of the sexual abuse crisis, Voice of the Faithful bears the closest resemblance to a spontaneous grass-roots uprising. The roots were suburban and the shoots well educated, from middle- and upper-middle-class settings. Many members had grown up in neighborhoods where the faithful walked to Mass. Older residents knew one another and their family histories. VOTF members liked to identify themselves by the names of the parishes where they went to church, even if now they did most of their shopping not in neighborhood stores and delicatessens but in outlying big-box malls with acres of parking.[12] Many of the faces were familiar as parishioners streamed into the basement of St. John the Evangelist. The discussion groups and rallies organized by Voice of the Faithful in the Boston area were not assemblies of total strangers.

So the diversity in attitudes about where the movement should be headed came as a surprise. Shared outrage at Cardinal Law did not translate into cohesiveness of purpose once he was gone. The clamor of opinion seemed novel in comparison to the days when Catholics refrained from discussing church policy at all. Fewer soul mates were in the crowds than expected. Parish life was no longer the urban simulacrum of a homogenous village. Potential leaders were not used to leading, at least not in the church, and not all parishioners took well to spirited argumentation. Strangers seemed to come out of hiding.

Beneath the vow to "Keep the Faith, Change the Church," VOTF was pulled in multiple directions. The emerging agenda covered three goals: to defend victims of sexual abuse, promote structural change in the church, and support "priests of integrity." The last objective was plainly intended to demonstrate cooperation with the clergy; the first two were potentially conflictive. "Supporting victims" usually meant siding with survivors in their claims against the church, and several bishops were quick to construe "structural change" as open-ended sedition. The tensions involved in coordinating these priorities wore away at VOTF as the organization tried to expand beyond its New England base.

Less literally, Voice of the Faithful encountered ongoing battles over three classes of issues. One was internal governance. Some members were former priests, and a few of them felt strongly about building on the organization's spontaneous beginnings to forge a full-blown participatory democracy, in defiance of a steeply stratified church. There was the clerical hierarchy, invariably labeled as "feudal," on one side and an amorphous "people of God" or "the grass roots" on the other, with nothing in between. The binary split within VOTF between mere progressives and full-blown zealots mirrored a division, imputed to many lay groups by the bishops, between lukewarm respect and rabid skepticism.[13]

Adherents of VOTF were fond of comparing their insurgency to the civil rights movement of the sixties. If that sounded unconvincing, hope shifted to the Internet as a weapon of mass mobilization. Antibureaucratic sentiment ran up against the sometimes venomous politics and burdensome mechanics of orchestrating a national organization. The struggle between the populist impulse and a more directive style of governance, together with a degree of magical thinking about new technologies of participation, kept VOTF tangled up in procedural questions for years. When Paul Baier claimed that "what our Web site is doing is connecting the two percent of outraged Catholics in every parish who simply will not tolerate the lack of moral character among our U.S. bishops," he acknowledged the unevenness of support for the movement and a certain vaporware quality to its organization.[14] Though many VOTF adherents were professionals in their working lives, as institution builders they behaved like amateurs.[15]

A second, related difficulty arose from the geographical spread of parishes across the United States and their tenacious parochialism. Almost none of the leaders of VOTF had visibility or connections outside a few parishes in the Northeast. The lack of name recognition among potential leaders in VOTF stands in contrast to the thickly woven ties among the financiers, industrialists, and others of like prominence who have shaped the Leadership Roundtable. Almost all of the latter have national and international stature. They are visible by reputation among their peers even if they are not well known outside elite circles, and most of them employ a common idiom drawn from business and management. They have managed complex organizations. This sets up a certain self-leveraging clubbability—these are the right people, with the right stuff—that helps bypass the awkwardness of having to deal with unknown figures on vital issues.

The organizational paradox of Catholicism is that parishes share many similar yet stubbornly hived-off problems. The imposition of a new pastor without consultation from around the diocese is a frequent complaint. This became a particularly sensitive irritant once it was discovered that Cardinal Law and other prelates had moved predator priests from parish to parish without informing the faithful. But the stories of each parish were sensed as incomparably its own. The anecdotes had common patterns, the most ironic of which was that each parish felt itself to be unique.

The paradox was not purely imaginary. No matter what the regularities across parishes, the organizational means for resolving problems lay ultimately in the hands of individual bishops, some of whom were idiosyncratic autocrats. Leverage across dioceses was very rare, the diffusion of protest erratic. Parishioners from across the country might strike up how-about-them-Cubbies-style conversations but all the while their loyalties and psychic energies were with the home team. Scaling up and coordinating reform proved exceptionally difficult.[16]

A contrast is worth noting here. SNAP has maintained a tight focus on a clutch of objectives, giving perfunctory attention to the niceties of popular attachments to the parishes. The style of VOTF approaches the opposite. It has struggled with diffuse, hard-to-operationalize goals, over a base that strains without much success to see beyond the singular delicacies of individual parishes and their impassioned attachments to them. There is a structural reason for this, besides whatever flukes of personality might be at work. SNAP is managed, like most advocacy groups, without elected directors, while for a long time VOTF hewed to an elected delegate format (detailed in the following section). The whole point, it seemed at the outset, was to give *voice* to the faithful. People wanted to express themselves, but that turned out to be different from being heard. The clamor was deafening.

The third set of controversies revolved around the multiple missions of VOTF. There was a tendency among those who favored supporting the victims of sexual abuse as their top priority—"the original, primary inspiration of VOTF," as they called it—not only to align themselves with SNAP but also to dismiss other goals as vague, superfluous, distracting, insufficiently surgical. They were not interested in supporting priests or in striving for structural reform, whatever that was. Siding with SNAP channeled grievances toward tangible outcomes, toward a vision of organizational action that promised results which were, moreover, motivationally pristine, and that the moderate wing of VOTF seemed unable to supply.

Veterans of the sixties can recall similarly competitive, more-radical-than-thou infighting on the left. The virtues and modishness of the civil rights struggle in balance with protests against the war in Vietnam were once hotly contested. Cutting-edginess was a political fashion statement. Factionalism in Voice of the Faithful grew to cats-in-a-sack proportions with the influx of older cohorts of veteran reformers, who were about the same age, fifty and over, as many political newbies who flocked to VOTF. Radicals bloodied in earlier church reform efforts found it difficult to abide those with fewer recriminatory feelings, and vice versa. Scabs from old wounds had never quite healed, old battles were refought. The ordination of women, optional celibacy, and "the abolition of the clerical caste" were not dead memories of impenitent firebrands or impassioned adherents of organizations like Call to Action. They were live demands, carried over from the Vatican II generation.[17]

VOTF strained to keep a lid on feuds over doctrinal disagreements. The hope was that a consensual gag rule—"making nice" as critics called it—would keep attention on concrete actions and allay the misgivings of the bishops. But aside from the option, which better-off chapters could afford, of inviting guest speakers in to rally the troops, coming up with such "actions"—the word was often used to mean "events" or "programs"—turned out to be difficult. "What is this?" an infuriated member complained about the good manners, "a revolution of church mice?" The effect was to add another level of discord about what the organization should or should not be doing, and none of the wrangling assuaged episcopal suspicions anyway.[18]

For much of its first decade Voice of the Faithful lacked a business model. It was not until 2008 that something like a mandatory system for collecting dues was put in place. A movement-like aura and virtually unadulterated voluntarism at all levels did not pay the bills. Inadvertently comical elements sometimes came into play. Early in the process, John Ryan, a former priest and retired businessman from the Midwest, sat down for breakfast with Jim Post in Newton, a suburb adjacent to Boston. Post wanted to know whether Ryan would like to get involved in the internal governance of VOTF. Ryan, who is somewhat hard of hearing, heard "organizational governance of the church." "That's how I became chair of VOTF's governance committee," Ryan recalled.[19]

Voice of the Faithful experimented with a two-track model of governance. A board of trustees, appointed by an elected president, was to set priorities and oversee implementation. This was in line with the nonprofit status of the organization. But VOTF also established a National Representative Council. In deference to the populist ideal, the NRC was to be an elected body made up of delegates chosen from geographical units aligned with the regional division of dioceses created by the American bishops. The number of delegates totaled eighteen.

Besides being difficult to mesh with the board of trustees, elections and electoral campaigns proved to be clumsy mechanisms in themselves. Since almost none of the Catholic laity were visible outside their parishes as church leaders or aspirants to leadership positions, slates of serious candidates were interlarded with cranks, true believers, and a few provocateurs. Of the 30,000–35,000 members on the books of Voice of the Faithful, slightly more than 2,000—about 5 percent—voted to elect delegates to the National Representative Council. Keeping the attention of constituents was a problem.

The difficulty of bringing coherence to the mission of VOTF did not reflect ideological differences alone. Lawyers advised VOTF headquarters that if the affiliates (in effect, chapters, once numbering about 200) were associated closely with the national office, the entire organization could be held liable if a bishop decided to bring suit against one of them. So the network remained "a loose federation of stand-alone entities," as one former trustee put it, entitled to use the name of VOTF and its logo as long as they subscribed to the three overarching goals. No further obligations were implied. This averted litigation but undercut the coordination of mission. National decisions lacked teeth.

Of the eighteen-member council about half were "from SNAP or SNAP sympathizers." The ethos of conciliation that many adherents of VOTF inherited from the pastoral and healing ministries they were often involved in ran up against the confrontational style of SNAP. At one point, Bill Casey, a board member and professional mediator, tried to bring the sides together. Casey acknowledged SNAP's breakthrough contribution. While working to alter statute of limitations legislation in Delaware, he came to recognize that "the real thrust came from the survivor community. SNAP had developed relationships with people in the press and people in the legal arena, whatever their motives. The only way there was going to be real change was by holding the feet of church leaders to the fire." Casey then formulated the quandary that several of his colleagues in VOTF sensed:

> How do we support the survivors' issues in a way that is faithful to our own mission? What happens if we bankrupt the church? We file lawsuit after lawsuit. If we bankrupt the church, how is this a strategy? We could win the battles and lose the war.[20]

In 2007 Delaware created a one-year window for reporting claims of sexual abuse. (California had passed its own window earlier in the decade.) Casey explained that "We framed it not just as a Catholic but as a human rights issue." That political maneuver, combined with personal contacts among a few legislators who had first-hand knowledge of clergy abuse from relatives or friends, worked. But similar lobbying efforts in more than half a dozen other states failed, and Casey was unable to persuade his peers in VOTF that aggressive legal tactics would not endanger the solvency of the church.

Eventually, by 2008, the National Representative Council collapsed of its own unwieldiness and acrimony. David O'Brien, a board member for several years, remembered "the tremendous internal divisions" within and between the council and the trustees. "You had the most vocal, the noisiest people getting elected. Are we here to advocate on behalf of victims, or to reform the church? Some of them were very angry. They'd yell and keep on yelling. 'You keep on yelling,' I told them, 'fewer people come to the next meeting.' We couldn't agree." Controlling the behavior of priests and bishops, as SNAP tried to do, was a daring yet definable objective, for a group without religious ties to Catholicism. Reforming the institutional structure of the church, even when it did not involve legal pressure, was a task of a different stripe for an organization bent on remaining within the Catholic fold.

Though the two groups did not sever relations, SNAP kept to its own path. Relations between the organizations continued to blow hot and cold. When VOTF held a national convention on Long Island at the end of October 2009, the National Representative Council no longer existed, and the board of trustees laid out a five-part strategic plan entitled "Voices in Action," one of which included "child protection and survivor support."

> *He had "moral taste"—a particular aesthetic sensibility to innocence—which is in keeping with his character. ("Moral taste" is interesting: only highly civilized and really rather morally neutral people have it: it is the stuff of James and Turgenev novels.)*[21]

Almost willy-nilly, Voice of the Faithful became an omnibus movement, as much a Petri dish of ideas and aspirations as an organization. Its equivocal variety sets VOTF apart from other, more sharply delineated reform groups like SNAP and the Roundtable by a series of institutional criteria.

The contrast is clearest with regard to strategy. SNAP's position is plainly adversarial, that of the Roundtable assiduously collaborative. VOTF falls somewhere in between. The variation cannot be attributed solely to the way third-rail controversies are handled. The Roundtable avoids such questions, VOTF has managed to do much the same, while SNAP cares next to nothing about what the magisterium says. The distinctiveness of VOTF is that from time to time the organization allows itself to be publicly critical of how the church operates, without openly questioning its teachings or trying to drag it into court. The target that VOTF tries to hit is not the ideals of Catholicism but the failure of the church to live up to them. It is the honorable thing to do.

The operative model of Voice of the Faithful is that of a loyal opposition in all but name. In the conscience of individual members this amounts to a psychological compartmentalization redolent of the distinction between "religion" (organized) and "spirituality" (personalized). VOTF members are "people of conscience." Personal authenticity trumps organizational loyalty. But segmentation that suits individuals is hard to ramp up and sustain collectively. The existential cure is not a management solution. "Split identification" can wreak havoc on a movement trying to build organizational wallop.[22]

Sometime in mid-2004, when he was well into putting together the Leadership Roundtable, Geoffrey Boisi (*bwah-zee*) met with Jim Post, by then the president of VOTF. Boisi, a trustee of Boston College and benefactor of the campus Center for Religion and American Public Life that bears his name, talked with Post in the office of Fr. Donald Monan, the chancellor of Boston College and a close advisor. Boisi and Post discussed the complementarity of their respective organizations. Boisi noted that Voice of the Faithful's initiative in standing up as lay Catholics had helped pave the way for the Roundtable. "VOTF was to be a voice of criticism," Post recalls the conversation, "very public." The Roundtable, for its part, "was in a cooperative game with the bishops. Think of an inside game, as compared to an outside game. The church really needs both its 'loyal critics' and the professional talent of the laity to improve the system, to clean up the messes."[23]

In academia such a distinction is routine. In the world of Catholic politics, tolerance for nuance of this sort is less elastically construed. The difficulty Jews experience in criticizing Israeli policies toward the Palestinians is comparably severe. Negative interpretations about motives, not subtleties about intentions, take hold when the church is challenged. Disagreement about a particular policy or specific doctrine can rarely be just that. There can be no opposition that is not sabotage. Quarreling is potentially lethal, simply too divisive. Dissent escalates into a rebuke of authority in general. Like relativism, signs of disrespect lurk everywhere.[24]

It was not enough for VOTF to refrain from overtly doctrinal disagreements—"to stay clear of the orthodoxy trap," as activists phrased their silence.

Accusations of harboring an agenda, together with a taint of ambiguity in goals like "structural reform," helped make the dissident label stick. Proof of sinister intent was unnecessary. When the goals—notoriously, structural reform—were unfamiliar to most Catholics, and as long as public disagreement was thought to be in bad form, peremptory defamation did the trick.

More than this, VOTF had almost nothing in the way of material resources to offer. Few of the bishops felt any need to listen to talk of reform and degrees of assent coming from a dubious assortment of lay people with an uncertain following and without lavish lines of credit. Less than a year after it had come into existence, toward the end of VOTF's campaign against Cardinal Law, the archbishop of Newark attacked the organization for using "the current crisis in the Church as a springboard for presenting an agenda that is anti-Church and, ultimately, anti-Catholic." John Myers wrote in his archdiocesan newspaper that VOTF "has as its purposes to act as a cover for dissent and to openly attack the Church hierarchy." It mattered little that the charge was overblown; it was enough to unsettle Catholics in the pews. VOTF was cast as a fifth column.[25]

The effort to keep one's counsel on doctrinal controversies while chiding the church in public on mundane matters ran aground once the strategy became entangled with the sensitivities aroused by two of VOTF's three grand objectives. "Supporting victims of abuse" linked middle-grounders with SNAP's legal assault, and the open-ended advocacy of structural change swiped at clerical dominance. Not only did Voice of the Faithful seem to have an agenda in the sense of concealing its ultimate goals; some proponents of that agenda sounded unappeasably angry at the church. The objections of conservatives like Myers had less to do with the doctrinal refinements than with organizational loyalty and deference to authority or, more simply, with the braiding of doctrine and deference. Respect for authority and adherence to the magisterium were one and the same thing. Neither was negotiable.

Indignation at reports of sexual abuse and its cover-up was not unique to VOTF. Similar sentiments also stirred members of the Roundtable. But the perception that justifiable outrage had mutated into inconsolable fury with the ways of the hierarchy and a deeper disenchantment with the institutional church among members of VOTF was hard to shake.

The political optics were confusing. "There are two kinds of people in Catholicism," one Roundtable leader declared crisply. "There are those of us who love the church, and there are those who feel betrayed by it." The only good Catholic was the consummate stand-by-your-man Catholic. From this love-it-or-leave-it standpoint the bobbing and weaving of VOTF made no sense. The posture sent unbusinesslike signals. There could be pragmatists in the church, and there were always a few purists. But pluralists bred uncertainty and indecision. They sounded like mealy-mouthed mollifiers.

Plus, the costs of taking potshots at "the VOTF crowd" were minimal. It was easy to cast them as spiritual elitists, so many connoisseurs of recreational sailing, yachting for the few in the age of mass steam and diesel.

In 2004 VOTF commissioned a survey of its membership, partly to dispel the imputation of disloyalty. A team of social scientists from Catholic University demonstrated that VOTF members were overwhelmingly white, up in years, and concentrated in the Northeast. What comforted the study's sponsors was the less obvious finding that the followers of Voice of the Faithful did not cede place to other Catholics in piety, devotion, and involvement in the church. The widely touted inference was that rumors of rampant heterodoxy in VOTF were exaggerated.[26]

The inferential fallacy was twofold. For whatever reason, while they devised adequate measures of church attendance and other indicators of engagement, the investigators declined to ask respondents directly for their opinions on doctrinal questions, including the usual suspects like contraception and divorce, so there was no way of telling from the evidence what the VOTF membership thought on such matters or, as critics put it, "what they *really* stood for." A realistic surmise was that members leaned toward the moderate left but were not prepared to press their views for prudential reasons.

A related problem is statistically trickier. There need be no contradiction between devotional observance and less-than-strict-adherence to doctrine; in this sense the inference that VOTF members are faithful Catholics fits the facts. Observant Catholics may disagree with this or that teaching of the church as long as they are not outspoken about it. They go to Mass and say their prayers without advertising their qualms.

Yet the mixture of piety and progressivism doesn't warrant the conclusion that its members can pass as typical Catholics. While a representative member of VOTF probably does tend to be both devout and on the borderline of dissent, such a profile seems relatively latent among Catholics, especially the ardent ones. The numerically more typical combination is cool-to-lukewarm devotion and doctrinal skepticism. The mix represented by VOTF, though not off-the-charts rare, seems to be less common than the incidence of those who are both devout and orthodox, on the one hand, or doctrinally slack and virtually nonpracticing on the other. The dominant pattern is that the more practicing Catholics are, the more religiously conservative they tend to be—that is, the likelier they are to buy into the core teachings of the church on sexuality and authority. By the same token, on the average, progressive Catholics attend Mass less regularly than their conservative counterparts. This said, only about one-quarter of all American Catholics are estimated to attend weekly Mass, so conservatives themselves fall short of being a strong majority.[27]

VOTF members are not garden variety Catholics. The amalgam of vocal disagreement alongside steady observance and genuine spirituality can be understood as a logically possible but modestly populated cell in a cross-classification of agreement/disagreement and devotion/nondevotion. The profile of love for the church *and* a sense of betrayal is psychologically intriguing—consider Erasmus, for one, or Kierkegaard perhaps—but politically disturbing.[28] Sustained attention to the mechanics of church reform strikes a few strongly committed but deeply conflicted Catholics like writing poetry in PowerPoint. It seems an affront to the soul. Something's missing; gravitas perhaps, gravitas with Gregorian chant, *basso profundo* power. A periodic romance with pragmatism is not enough.

The big difference between members of VOTF and ordinary Catholics is not so much that they disagree—after all, Catholics in general approve of relaxing the rules for ordination—but that feelings about such hot-button issues run stronger among the former than the latter, many of whom are nominal practitioners. The sensibilities differ. "The sheeple" give off a waxwork spirituality. This helps explain why VOTF loyalists feel estranged not only from the hierarchy but also from "Catholics in the pews."[29]

VOTF is one among several segmented interests, not a completely isolated band of malcontents. Catholic conservatives form another, equally intense and (to the bishops) more visible minority. At least notionally, most American Catholics have no objection to getting rid of the celibacy requirement for the priesthood and similar restrictions.[30] The agenda promoted by VOTF has some popularity. But public opinion is not a social movement. The stumbling block facing VOTF, somewhat like the pitfalls facing the Occupy Wall Street movement, concerns Realpolitik. The organization does not make for an attractive coalitional partner. A big reason for this comes as much from its weak command of resources as its equivocal image. Sometimes, as Gracián taught, flip-flopping can work for you. Ambiguity regarding intentions can signify political sagacity if one is holding a strong hand.[31]

Some bishops have been more patient than others with the importunings of VOTF. In one instance representatives of a major diocesan office and VOTF stopped meeting out of mutual accord, recognizing that they didn't disagree on much. Both parties felt that the bishop and his staff had almost no power to make meaningful changes anyway. There was little to be gained from having the bishop hold their hand.

The reaction of another bishop—"You don't get anything done whining on the church steps"—is probably more typical. The hierarchy tends to look on VOTF as they would the feral cats that prowl the ruins of Rome—a little creepy perhaps, surly and impossible to befriend, and often vicious among themselves, but barely worth the effort of shooing away. "We could stand a little incense around here," one prelate said half seriously, "and some corporal punishment to boot." Even if many of them haven't taken its reputation for theological well-poisoning to heart, the bishops as a whole have calculated that they have more to lose than gain by dealing with VOTF as a worthy interlocutor.

The distancing of the bishops from VOTF underscores a central drawback of the organization besides its thread-the-needle strategy regarding doctrinal correctness. It lacks hard resources. "VOTF," one cardinal airily concluded, "is simply irrelevant." SNAP can draw on its legal arsenal. The Leadership Roundtable can offer managerial expertise and access to financial support. Voice of the Faithful occupies neither of these niches. VOTF has nothing that the institutional church fears or feels its needs. The bishops and VOTF have nothing to do business about.

Voice of the Faithful has tried to overcome its resource deficit by exploiting the mobilizational promise of the Internet, but the MoveOn.org model has proved inadequate. Virtual politics seems to have been more effective for the organization as a venting mechanism than as a device for fostering leadership.[32]

VOTF's goals are more sprawling than the objectives that keep SNAP or the Roundtable on track, and its message is correspondingly less actionable. Malaise is hard to market. Fund-raising and pumping up opinion can pay off when tangible objectives—supporting or defeating individual candidates, for example—are clear and not overwhelmingly out of reach. Even fairly task-bound tactics like these become less effective when they turn away from win-lose campaigns (such as electoral contests) toward shaping policy and institutional reform, where the path to results is roundabout.[33] The connection between risking investment in resources for reform and the prospect of feasible outcomes in policy change is indirect and frequently hard to make out. It is difficult to keep score when the end game is unclear.

The fact that the arena is shaped by the institutional church, which no longer has much capacity for mass coercion but retains (thanks in part to First Amendment protections) an ability to ignore or put off demands, compounds the difficulty of building usable assets and closing the desirability/feasibility gap. Constitutional law is not on VOTF's side. There is also the fact of apathy among Catholics who wear their faith lightly. This is an audience for which SNAP and the Roundtable have learned to have less hope than VOTF. Indifference is as lethal coming from the public as it is from the bishops. Nonresponse—"being ignored to death"—is deadlier than repression.

No groups working to reform the church ignore the Internet. But the technology serves better as a public-relations and educational tool than as a fund-raising device or a political catalyst in the absence of other advantages. It may be a necessary but it is hardly a sufficient factor in successful insurrection. Taken alone, the Internet is the political weapon of outsiders. SNAP, a quintessential outsider group, can deploy at least one other weapon—legal action—from its arsenal. The Leadership Roundtable, whose most sedulously nurtured asset may be its insider status, gets face time with episcopal powerhouses. It employs the Internet mainly to disseminate information about managerial best practices—"Webinars" that use the WWW as forums for updating professional skills, are a recent venture—and secondarily as a fund-raising tool.

Though not contradictory to the reasons just mentioned, there is another set of explanations for the failure of the Internet to live up to the mobilizing expectations that VOTF placed on it. VOTF is contact-poor in areas where contacts matter. The biggest block in the way of expanding VOTF beyond its East Coast base is the intensely local nature of parish life itself. When the goal is sustaining political opposition, the weak ties that the social media are so efficient at forging are no match for the strong ties built into parishes that are, like those in New England, located fairly close to one another. But satisfying as they are as small groups, and as much as they resemble one another in the abstract, parish associations themselves tend to be politically myopic. They resist strategic scaling-up. They look alike but, as Marx noted grandly of French peasants, they have no more unity than potatoes in a sack.

"No one believes that the articulation of a coherent social philosophy is best handled by a sprawling, leaderless organizational system," Malcolm Gladwell has contended, in words that might be directed at the experimentalism of VOTF. "They [social networks] can't think strategically; they are chronically prone to error and conflict. How do you make difficult choices about tactics or strategy or philosophical direction when everyone has an equal say?"[34] The temptation that the Internet provides for instantaneous popping-off seems as strong as its capacity to generate collective direction is weak.

But why exactly did initial promise fall short so markedly in the case of VOTF? After all, the Internet furnishes connections. It puts more people in touch with one another than would otherwise be possible, and it facilitates the exchange of information. It reduces pluralistic ignorance. Yet its performance is so-so as a device for improving coordination. That requires a point of view. The Internet does indeed facilitate connections with people but it is less skillful at connecting conceptual dots on its own. The problem is not exactly a lack of focus. On the contrary, the danger stems from flooding the receptive field with innumerable points that are all competing for attention. Foci are everywhere. Everything is foregrounded, as if seen through an extreme wide angle lens. Information splatters and congeals into spam.

The solidarity that grows out of parish ties tends to be mostly affective, and that doesn't go far when other organizational ingredients are absent. Members of SNAP and the Roundtable have emotional links, too, but layered over them are shared functional objectives. They prize a common ideology that itself downplays ideology and "emoting" of the nonstructured variety, and they confine themselves to sectioned-off chunks of the problem spectrum. Mass support doesn't hurt but it is not crucial to their operations.

Voice of the Faithful also tries to avoid zealotry. Its problems began with a virtue. VOTF is tolerant of a diversity of beliefs, and in this respect the group is not unrepresentative of a significant slice of the American Catholic public. But sincerity is not the same as moral consensus or staying on message. Even if that hurdle could be overcome, morale is difficult to sustain once past the populist paroxysm stage. The problem seems to be less a lack of unanimity about the need for reform than skepticism about the possibility of advancing reform under the auspices of a mass movement. There is an awareness among sympathizers of VOTF that such movements have a high mortality rate. The organization was never far from becoming an *omnium gatherum* of miscellaneous grievances and the soreness of age. VOTF struck observers like a faintly risible West Coast city—Los Angeles, perhaps, or San Francisco—full of people with random obscure diets.

This pessimism, induced by severe barriers to entry, joined to unfamiliarity with and suspicion of dissent in a culture of acquiescence, has probably impeded organizational takeoff as much as any diversity of opinion. In some cases, diagnosis of what ailed the church seemed clear enough. Ironically, however, it was not evident how concrete tales of local woe, almost monotonous in their similarity, that proliferated alongside programmatic agendas ("structural change") were to add up. Solutions were not obvious, conflict over priorities seemed unending. The Internet can help overcome pluralistic ignorance—the sense of being alone in one's opinions—but not necessarily demoralization. VOTF bloggers were best at singing the blues. The prospects of success for large-scale collective action seemed remote when, in addition to the opposition of the incumbents, the logistics of organizing that action democratically were themselves daunting.[35]

SNAP, by contrast, has a cast of villains against which its members can rally and an institutional mechanism—the tort system—through which it can press its demands. The members of the Roundtable have mostly stayed in formation, too, in part because of the organization's restricted mission, but also because they have remarkably similar skill-sets and preexisting leadership networks. They share a culture not just of professionalism but of managerial discipline. They are at ease with power and its uses. For the Roundtable, the Internet has been an adjunct to the deployment of comparatively conventional resources and the execution of fairly clear operational goals.

Appreciable, if rather disconnected, numbers of American Catholics sympathize with progressive reforms of the kind advocated or hinted at it by Voice of the Faithful. But subjunctive support differs from a conviction that VOTF offers a viable institutional alternative or that it can convince political influentials in Catholicism to join in and tip the balance. In her prelude to *Middlemarch*, George Eliot might have been writing of VOTF members when she described the heroines of Victorian fiction who harbored "a certain spiritual grandeur ill-matched to meanness of opportunity." "You cannot build a church," a woman from the ranks of VOTF repeated "out of bullying and broken hearts."

Without a broad, un-atomized popular base, with very limited economic backup, with no stomach for pursuing the church in the courts, and with a radioactive image among insiders, Voice of the Faithful remains at the margin of the game, raising questions, a dissonant Greek chorus trailing off in doubt. "Is celibacy the issue or part of a larger issue?" Bill Casey, a board member, asked, groping to pin down the panoramic notion of structural change and bracket clerical sore points at the same time.

> Are we a group of dissenters? We're interested in the governance system that allowed this [the abuse scandals] to happen. We've tried to straddle extra-church issues like the death penalty, immigration. But what happens when you get into married priests, women priests? Wasn't celibacy itself a potential contributor to the scandal of sexual abuse? How can you have a reform organization and call yourself legitimate and ignore such issues in the church?[36]

"The experience," Casey added, "has tested everyone."

On the hopeful side, he stressed that "we are a voice in the public square. The bishops haven't been able to shape this thing." He paused, dissatisfied with the moral victory argument. "But are we a significant presence?" He reminisced about the early days of the organization.

> The rank and file were just stunned, just felt we needed to do something about this. We were people in the thick of things, estranged. It became an enormous

burden to accommodate people in the pews, and also across the spectrum. It became very difficult to define VOTF's identity—to collaborate with the bishops *and* to hold the bishops accountable. Some moved to [being] a challenge group. When you form your identity around something different from the church, you have to grow from the bottom up. I've never seen it work. The idealism is fine, but the reality is extraordinarily difficult.

CHAPTER TEN

THE LEADERSHIP ROUNDTABLE AND THE LONG MARCH THROUGH THE INSTITUTIONS

Inside baseball plays just as important a part in America's National Game as Outside or ordinary baseball if I may so term it. No baseball club whether it be the average sandlot club or the Big Major League World's Champion team can hope to be successful if members of the team do not thoroughly understand the inside workings of the game as well as the actual playing of the game on the field itself.[1]

For the United States Conference of Catholic Bishops (USCCB), the early eighties of the last century were a brief golden age. In 1984, a year after they issued their pastoral letter on war and peace, the USCCB began working on a follow-up document entitled "Economic Justice for All." J. Bryan Hehir, a Harvard-trained diocesan priest, would win a MacArthur Foundation genius award for his role in orchestrating the pastorals.

The drafts of the bishops' letter on the economy struck prominent conservatives as little more than a wish list patched together by the left wing of the Democratic Party. William Simon, bond trader, pioneer of the leveraged buyout, and Secretary of the Treasury under Presidents Nixon and Ford, put together a "lay commission on Catholic social teaching and the U.S. economy." Before the final version of the pastoral on the economy was released in 1986, the lay theologian Michael Novak testified before the bishops' panel on behalf of the group and managed to get a few modifications incorporated in the text. Novak would go on to win the Templeton Prize, worth one million pounds sterling, awarded in 1994 for his "exceptional contribution to affirming life's spiritual dimension."[2]

In 1990 Simon and his colleagues came out with a volume of essays that catalogued their differences with the bishops, laying out a tutorial on the workings of the free market. By that time the popularity of the Reagan revolution in economic policy had taken the wind out of the bishops' initiative and Simon's lay committee, its mission no longer so pressing, had all but folded.[3] Then, in 1992, the bishops shelved a projected letter on the status of women in the church. They had been able to come to a working agreement in matters of economics and international politics but their deliberations stalled on the question of gender roles.

By the end of the decade episcopal conferences around the world were in decline. The final blow came in the form of an apostolic letter shaped by Josef Cardinal Ratzinger and issued over the signature of John Paul II, in 1998. *Apostolos Suos*, "On the Theological and Juridical Nature of Episcopal Conferences," put an end to pronouncements by the bishops' conferences on doctrinal matters unless they could reach unanimity.[4] Immaculate consensus was unattainable. As a collective entity, the USCCB had become—in the words of Robert Bennett, the Washington trial lawyer who was to direct the report on sexual abuse that the conference commissioned in 2002—"a loose trade association with virtually no influence."[5] The American bishops went back to being what they were most of the time, a collection of individuals acting on their own, each one answerable separately to Rome.[6]

While the critique of episcopal thinking propagated by Simon, Novak, and their fellow conservatives aimed to score points against doctrinal tendentiousness, economic justice was not usually considered to be at the core of Catholic teaching. It does not "implicate revelation," as theologians say. The dispute touched mainly on public policy—on issues *ad extra*, outside the church. The bishops were chastised for offering recommendations beyond their sphere of competence. Simon's group was pointedly a lay commission. The bishops' venture in economic thinking, so the message went, was impractical and theoretically amateurish. As an aside, the commission could not resist tweaking the bishops about one spectacular in-house improvidence: their failure to see that funds were set aside for the retirement and health care of aging nuns.[7]

When they launched the National Leadership Roundtable on Church Management two decades later, comparably wealthy and influential Catholics defined their task differently. Many of the Wall Street executives behind the Roundtable seemed just as displeased as Simon and Novak had been with the bishops; now, however, the quarrel was internal and related to economic philosophy only indirectly. The source of their irritation was the managerial bungling of the hierarchy, on display in the exposés of attempts to cover up sexual abuse and transfer perpetrators from parish to parish.

In some instances, moreover, the troubles had nothing to do with the abuse of children. Greed, not sex, was the culprit. On other occasions, both were involved. One pastor in Connecticut was convicted of embezzling over a million dollars to support his vacation lifestyle in Florida, and cases of skimming off the collection plate by laypeople as well as clerics turned out to be fairly common. The Connecticut episode caught the attention of the Roundtable in part because it occurred in a wealthy parish where several of its members lived.[8]

It soon became clear that the tribulations of the church went deeper than incidental thievery, sexual perversion, and the administrative ineptitude of one or another prelate, priest, or lay employee. Well before reports of clergy sexual abuse and other failings made the headlines, signs of systemic deficiencies—the dwindling of religious vocations, the difficulty of recruiting and retaining lay personnel, the economic prostration of many parish elementary schools—had been mounting. Added to this was an indifference toward the institutional church that was increasingly evident among younger Catholics. The real problem was not so much the sexual and financial scandals, bad as they were, but serious doubts about whether the church had the organizational capacity to overcome them. Defeatism itself was an issue.

The demographics were appalling (see Figure 10.1). Catholic elementary and high school enrollment had dropped from 5.2 million in the 1960s to 2.3 million by 2010. After the peak of the 1960s, the share of Catholic children attending church schools dropped from one-half to one-sixth.[9] According to some reports the priest shortage was becoming so severe that close to half of the parishes in the United States shared a pastor with at least one other parish.[10]

Even with priests drawn from Africa, India, and other regions, there were not enough celibate males to go around. Some of the slack was taken up by

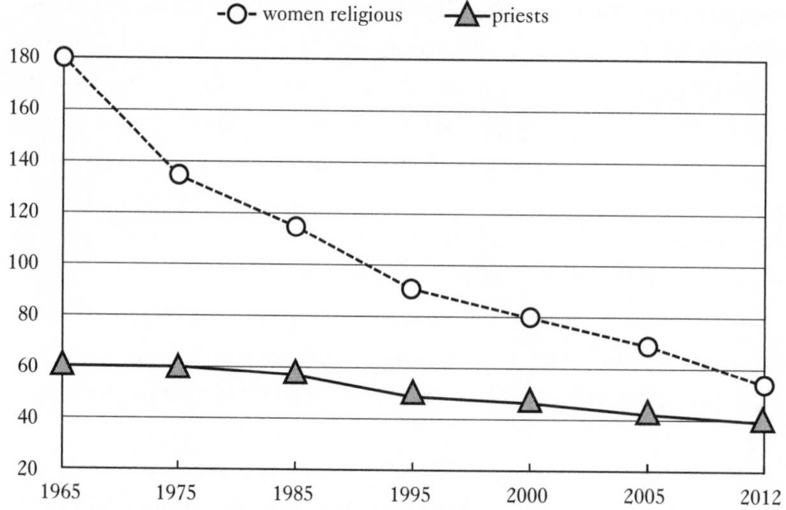

Figure 10.1. Nuns and priests in the United States (in thousands) since Vatican II
Source: Center for Applied Research on the Apostolate,
http://cara.georgetown.edu/CARAservices/requestedchurchstats.html

lay pastoral ministers—religious education teachers, music directors, and so on—estimated to have surpassed, at 30,000 plus, the number of active priests in the United States. Of these ministers, over 80 percent were women. More people were working for the church than ever before and, mostly because of immigration, there were greater numbers of Catholics.[11] The bad news was that compensation packages, including retirement and health care benefits, did not stack up with comparable plans for professionals elsewhere. The scarcity of applicants at the leadership level made recruitment feel more like scraping the bottom of a barrel than turning on a spigot.[12]

Finally, since so many Catholics had moved to the suburbs, supporting the parochial schools established during the high tide of Irish, German, Italian, and Eastern European immigration had become the equivalent of bearing the legacy costs—the medical benefits and pensions negotiated for retirees during the years of postwar prosperity—that weighed on the manufacturing industries of the rust belt.[13] With the wilting of the old-time ethnic neighborhoods, and without the nuns who had served as the cheap oil of Catholic social mobility, fewer and fewer of these schools were sustainable. (As late as the 1960s, nuns made up over 90 percent of Catholic grade school staff; by 2005, 90 percent of the staff were lay people.) Hispanic immigrants gave an impetus to numbers but expenses rose even faster. "The income to parishes goes up 1–2 percent a year," a director of diocesan planning in the Midwest observed. "The costs of the schools go up 6–8 percent a year. Do the math."[14]

Once the magnitude of what Geoffrey Boisi gently termed "the unfortunate demographics" of American Catholicism dawned on them, the indignation that initially flared up among some members of the Roundtable gave way to a realization that lay benefactors and episcopal authorities might be in the same boat. The future of the institutional church, Boisi and his colleagues worried, was at risk. "I will say as a parent of four, and as a grandparent," Boisi announced to the 2010 meeting of the Roundtable,

> part of the reason why we do this is not only our responsibility and obligation to the faith but also for our kids and grandkids... I don't know about you, but the notion of responsibility that we have to pass on this faith to those kids in the future to me is a very important thing. I think it's the reason why a lot of folks are involved with us, because we are nervous, if not scared, about our ability to do this in an effective way.[15]

Impending calamity posed a classic challenge in crisis management. Too many of the socially beneficial ministries attached to the parishes—the schools, in particular—were going under. Institutional Catholicism as an intergenerational transmission belt for a moral inheritance was at risk. There was real distress, a historical catastrophe potentially as traumatic as the sexual abuse cover-up, to be overcome. It was this sense of urgency that got the blood running among organizers of the Roundtable, and it was this that imparted a sense of moral grandeur to the enterprise. How their generation of philanthropists responded to an organizational catastrophe in the making would determine their legacy. The preservation of the values to be passed on to their children and grandchildren was at stake.[16]

The central premise of the consortium of benefactors, bishops, heads of ministerial groups, and other professionals that came to be known as the National Leadership Roundtable on Church Management was a call for participants "to be agents of change with and within the church, to work towards transforming the church that we love."[17] They saw themselves as cooperative insiders, bent on helping an institution in extremis. Besides this overall commitment, interests converged on a couple of concrete strategic areas.

Many lay participants in the Roundtable were products of Catholic primary and secondary education. Their allegiance to "the good nuns" who staffed the parochial schools and to "the Jebbies" who typically taught them in high school was heartfelt. The church had shown a dedication to fostering talents that helped students make their way in the world. Now it was time, when schools were being shuttered, to find ways to spread these skills to sectors, many of them non-Catholic, on their way up and to nurture the character formation associated with this experience. The leaders of the Roundtable and the bishops shared an understanding about the primacy of human capital.

The Roundtable entrepreneurs and many of the bishops also sensed that if the church didn't get its house in order, the government would step in and force it to do so. Many had been repelled by the excesses of the sixties, and almost all of the business leaders adhered to orthodox principles regarding free markets. Some were innovators of genius. But they were no more about to rethink the fundamentals of capitalism than they were to question the core precepts of Catholicism. Keeping the government from intruding into the business of the church was a cause that members of the Roundtable had no trouble identifying with.

When he spoke at the 2007 meeting of the Roundtable, Fay Vincent, the former commissioner of baseball, opened with an assortment of haiku-like tales ("Ralph Branca says to Yogi, 'I'll come to your funeral, so you'll come to mine'") capped with mini-parables of dos and don'ts for business ("Never confuse brilliance with a bull market. Billy Martin told me 'I played for Casey Stengel before and after he was a genius.'")[18] Vincent grew serious as he went along, building up to the plight of the church. "In my parish in Connecticut," he said, referring to the wayward pastor with condos in Florida, "our position was compromised to the tune of a million and a half dollars. The fact is, there's a very bad problem. We are getting no information."

Vincent's remedy was proactive house cleaning. "When I was young, I knew who the bad guys were, those renegade CEOs. Keep it up and the government will step in. Guys who are smart, tough, and aggressive will step in. Almost everything becomes over-legalized." The allusion to Enron and the ensuing regulatory backlash, to Eliot Spitzer and other zealous prosecutors, was unmistakable. "There will come a day when stupidity and negligence become crimes. We all have our fiduciary responsibilities. The corporate world is showing you what's going to happen in the nonprofit world." Anticipatory change could be a prophylactic against worse alternatives, which included the regressive consequences of no change at all or reform imposed from the outside.

Vincent paused, resting on the cane he had used since a childhood accident; he had undergone surgery recently. "The church is about getting home. Baseball is about getting home. "You can push it too far," he added. "Baseball is a game." Kerry Robinson knew Vincent as a benefactor at Yale. "As always," she said, "Fay has hit a home run."

> *The whole club must work as a unit. Every man should know what is expected of him and he must follow instructions or coaching to perfection. Any other big league manager will reiterate what I have said. Every club in both the big leagues will tell you that they play the game from the inside as well as from the outside.*[19]

Almost from the beginning, then, the diagnosis of what afflicted the church that prevailed among leaders of the Roundtable stressed incompetence and denial more than criminality and sexual pathology. But this was a point of departure, not a blueprint for action, and the whiff of chastisement began to recede as the organization turned up success stories, isolated though they were, in the church. There were islands of excellence in primary and secondary education, and some dioceses had experts in human resources and sound accounting methods in place. Though the phrasing is a bit too abrasive for the Roundtable palate, the pattern corresponds to the phenomenon of "reform mongers" scattered in the far stretches of otherwise backward countries.[20] Part of the problem was that the diehard habits of diocesan autonomy worked against the exchange of information. The American church was as much a scattered archipelago as a hierarchy.

Members of the Roundtable could not alter doctrine, they could not fire anybody in the church, and the latest management theory told them that they would get nowhere hectoring people about what a bad job they were doing. They had to keep up a balancing act along several cultural and organizational coordinates. The Roundtable has followed an experimental path that reflects an effort to meld multiple strategies.

First, there is the cost-saving norm. The Roundtable lays out a grand spread for its June meetings, and individual members are generous patrons of Catholic philanthropies; a few have been awarded papal honors and belong to invitation-only associations like the Knights of Malta. Yet many also emerged as members of a generation of donors bent on monitoring the performance of their beneficiaries. They want to keep their money away from "another prince of the church out to buy a $100,000 chandelier."[21]

More than a giveaway, philanthropic giving should be an investment. The Raskob Foundation for Catholic Activities, something of a precursor to the Roundtable, once convened a small gathering of consultants to figure out why it wasn't getting credible applications for funding instead of just pleas for money. The Roundtable started out with a barebones staff of three in its Washington headquarters and a just okay annual operating budget of a little over a million dollars: seed money. Potential backers needed to gauge how many actionable ideas came over the transom and how the Roundtable might shape them before deciding to join forces. If the bishops needed reassurance that the Roundtable was on board doctrinally, supporters of the Roundtable needed to know how their money and expertise would be used.[22]

Second, there is the low- to no-controversy rule. Organizational problem-solving is difficult enough without theological bickering. The bishops are worried clients who need to be spared further reason for alarm. The word "reform" is nowhere to be found on the Roundtable's website. "We made up our minds to stay positive," Boisi reminds his audience. "We're solutions-oriented."

The imperative of discretion reflects more than delicacy about the perils of venting on third-rail issues. Roundtable members have been unanimous about the dangers of demoralization. A close corollary of the no-controversy rule is that it is important to impel the good news/bad news ratio upward. Low morale—institutional acedia—ranks next to lack of trust as an obstacle to getting things done. Catholics need to start feeling good about themselves again. The climate of disappointment, of what the Irish used to call "miserabilism," has to change. Crepe hangers are not welcome.

The third norm involves demonstrable results. The first two rules have to do with minimizing potential losses, with avoiding wasted effort and dead ends. Now the emphasis turns to maximizing the impact of prospective change.

Here the Roundtable finds itself in a tight spot. The more it focuses on the needs of diocesan and parish life as compared to the relatively professionalized outer boroughs of higher education and health care, the closer it moves toward the sacramental core of Catholicism. This is the province of priests, and it touches on the perquisites of bishops.

Even when they might appear threatening, however, changes in this zone are attractive. They promise decisive solutions for practical issues, like the shortage of priests, where the demographics are crushing. The introduction of a female diaconate, a reform that would enable women to take on many of the chores reserved to priests, is a good example of one such proposal. The Roundtable has refrained from endorsing such recommendations.

All changes in this domain are sensitive, but some are less symbolically charged than others. Foundations and endowments with predominantly lay boards of trustees, put in place to guide the disbursement of funds to parishes and programs in need, have caught on in many dioceses. Like their counterparts in Catholic colleges and universities, these hybrid arrangements have the capacity to counterbalance clerical prerogatives. They have the same logic as vested pensions for priests, another financial mechanism that is still uncommon in Catholicism. But they don't broach areas that touch on the ordination of women, and they work well in conjunction with bishops strapped for money. The Roundtable has smiled on these ventures.[23]

Such innovations gather momentum for two reasons: the Catholic public is untroubled by them and they take on the appeal of win-win solutions as the demographic and financial straits of the church become desperate. With the institutional church in a downward spiral, conventional rules begin to look inadequate. Besides accountability, transparency, and the other mantras of the new philanthropy, the bold stroke matters. Benefactors wary of reckless ventures in reform and disdainful of radicals who they feel propose them can also lose interest in stitching and mending around the edges. They want to find meaning in their contributions and they do not want to waste time doing so. Cost consciousness, doctrinal chasteness, and making a difference are the occasionally competing grand priorities of the Roundtable.

The main course is crab cakes at a table in Dalesio's, in the Little Italy section of Baltimore, with a friend from high school, now a priest in the area, and his pastoral associate and business manager, a former nun. Up the road in Catonsville, in 1968, Philip Berrigan, a Josephite priest, had shoved aside Mrs. Mary Murphy, chief clerk at the draft board, knocking her down, before he and eight companions, including his brother Dan, a Jesuit, poured homemade napalm on the files and set them afire.[24] Close by, also in Catonsville, the Dominican Sisters of St. Cecilia, in full traditional habit, teach at Mount de Sales Academy where they "form young women in the spirit of Saint Francis de Sales and in fidelity to the Sacred Scripture and the Sacred Tradition of the Roman Catholic Church though a college preparatory education that nurtures the whole person."[25] The pastoral associate at dinner with us sits on the board of the school.

My friend is wearing a Roman collar, and two heavy-set men at the onset of middle age are buying us drinks from the bar. They run a furniture business downtown. "Your money's no good here, Father." They are sipping Crown Royal and soda. One of them goes into an exceptionally convoluted version of the shaggy dog story about a character who assures a pal that he knows everybody that matters, including the pope. The story winds up with the pope and the main character waving to the befuddled friend in the crowd beneath the balcony in St. Peter's.

That morning, a domestic situation had come up. The priest and his pastoral associate rushed to a dilapidated frame row house, called by the mother of a teenage boy threatening suicide. The older brother has been beating up on him again. The father is a drunk, a junkie, and jobless, and can't be found. The mother is yelling at the despondent son. "Do you know what happens if you kill yourself? You go straight to hell, that's what!"

The son eventually calms down. The windows rattle. The house is drafty and poorly heated, it's early November, and concern is expressed about the cold that's coming. The priest drives back to the rectory and opens a safe the size of a vault in the wall of the basement. The safe contains gold chalices, elaborately embroidered vestments, and silver ornaments bedizened with jewels and filigree from decades past. He unrolls several hundred dollars from a wad of twenties and fifties. He hands the bills to the pastoral associate, who goes off to buy winter clothes for the family at "Burlington Coat Factory or someplace."

"They see the Lord in you," the priest observes, "not in the church."

The cash is donated by parishioners with a handshake and an envelope. "They pick up a little on the ponies, they tell me." The contributors make up an informal group whom the priest calls "The Elves." One of them proclaimed, the priest recalls, that "I'm going to daily Mass until my granddaughter has triplets," after she had lost a son in childbirth. At the 7:45 Mass that morning, the day after New York had defeated Philadelphia for the World Series title, the priest dropped a noncommittal word in his homily about the Yankee victory. "The hell with the Yankees!" the same gent objected softly several times before the closing prayers.

Larry Bossidy is an elder statesmen of American industry. A one-time professional baseball prospect, a devout Catholic, with six daughters, three sons, and thirty grandchildren, he worked for decades with another business legend, Jack Welch, before retiring as chair and CEO at Honeywell. When Geoff Boisi invited him to address the annual meeting of the Roundtable, Bossidy's first reaction was astonishment. Getting the church to change its ways, he responded, was "like trying to haul water uphill."

American dioceses constitute dozens of local markets, with little interaction between them. At its peak, in Rome, the church has virtually no checks and balances. But the tiers below, the dioceses and most of the parishes, might as well be separate worlds.[26] Just as there are few channels for processing conflict, there are few mechanisms and politically fewer incentives for the diffusion of promising innovations. And, as is the case with nonprofits generally, there is as yet no capital market in Catholicism to speak of. Church operations can attract benefactors and volunteers, but terms like "investors" and "stakeholders" don't ring true because profit and risk are not ordinarily in play.[27]

Besides the segmentation of institutional Catholicism, the paucity of funds for upkeep and improvements makes the journey through the institutions a hard slog. Compensation for church employees remains, in Boisi's judgment, "vexing." Even if there were larger than local job markets (as there exist for much of Catholic higher education and for pockets of health care services) and even if guidelines for best practices became normative throughout the church, resources to provide competitive wages and benefits packages for parish and diocesan workers would be difficult to generate.[28]

Sometimes, one pastoral minister observed, "all you can see is a landscape of triage and burnout. The foot soldiers and worker bees are overwhelmed." Problems tend to feed on one another. "When you have multiple parishes and one pastor," she explained, "you have the potential for great upheaval among the staff. Ministry creep, job creep. Say you're the director of religious ed for a small parish. 'I'm taking care of three parishes now,' the pastor says, 'you take care of them too.' There is no change in compensation, no extra remuneration. Mission creep is not part of the job description."

"In the old days," another parish worker said, "a family who provided a priest, they took honor in his sacrifice. It was their sacrifice. It came with a tradition of poverty. Nowadays, though, what does it take to raise a family? We want to be fair, but... The maintenance people [for the rectory and parish school] are the highest paid," she concluded, "because Father feared the boiler would explode."[29]

The parish plant in Baltimore has several nondescript though not unpleasant brick and cement-trimmed structures that look like they date from the Eisenhower era or perhaps from as late as the sixties or early seventies. They include a gym and a two-story parish center with activities rooms and a small library of spiritual readings upstairs. One of the nearby streets follows the route of the antebellum Underground Railway. A few years back, hookers plied their trade behind one of the buildings. "Then we had security put in." The pastor makes sure that Alcoholics Anonymous have room for their meetings. When he was growing up, one of his uncles, a problem drinker, froze to death after his wife threw him out of the house.

The parish school is down to just over 430 students in 2009. "It's the first year below 500," the secretary says. "It's the recession, parents moving for jobs." The boys wear ironed white shirts, solid blue ties, and pressed navy blue pants; the girls are in starched white blouses and green plaid skirts. There is no grime. The children make a little noise during recess. The secretary has a son in the Marines, a first lieutenant in flight school at Camp Pendleton in California. "Pray for him," she asks.

The schools of the Baltimore archdiocese are running through so much money (the deficit was over nine million dollars in 2010) that numerous closings have been in the works. Several of the poorer parishes have quietly suspended sending in monthly payments for health benefits and pensions. "Okay, you're having a rough time," the pastoral associate says. "Our Lady of Perpetual Consternation Parish, it could be, whatever. Everybody understands this. You pay your gas and electric first. But if we get X number of schools not paying in, then what happens?" She complains about the obligatory contribution that the diocese skims from income to the parish, penciling in the figures for me on a scrap of paper. "What don't they understand about taxation without representation?"

"The Roman way," the priest adds, "is not a very ministerial or healthy way."

The next day, he drops me off at the Amtrak station, where a handful of parishioners greet him. They are on their way to Washington to take part in a pro-life rally. They banter a bit, and the priest sends them off with a smile and a reminder that "I don't have enough money on me to bail you out." Just before Wilmington, on the way north, there is a large billboard between the tracks and the wetlands facing east onto the Atlantic. It shows a polychrome St. Michael the Archangel, patron saint of law enforcement, sword poised to skewer Satan, with the prayer "St. Michael Protect Us and Pray for Us" spelled out below.

A trickier roadblock in the way of the reforms advocated by the Roundtable, besides diocesan compartmentalization and threadbare coffers, is the culture of the church. Official tradition aside, the stickiness of church mores derives on the one hand from a penchant for complacency and occasional triumphalism, associated with good times, and on the other a habit of "offering it up" when things go wrong.[30] The effect is to short-circuit a learning process which, according to secular standards, should punish failure in addition to rewarding success. Feedback is weak, denial strong, change is sluggish. Suffering may be providential, a blessing in disguise. The fundamental drive of the church looks not to be efficiency but reproduction and survival. Resurrection follows martyrdom after all. "The possibility of permanent failure," organizational theorists have argued in stronger terms, "high persistence yet low performance, precludes equating performance with survival or, for that matter, reproductive success."[31] To proponents of improvements that smack of High Modernist functionality, the ethos is maddening. For their part, some of the bishops sniffed out what they took to be, in the gospel of the Roundtable, the supple logic of a sales pitch.

When Larry Bossidy delivered his talk at the 2008 meeting of the Roundtable, he urged "a willingness to change even when things are going well" on his audience, and he lauded the courage to face facts as they are. "The sooner you recognize reality, the more options you have. It can be traumatic."

He mentioned the six bankrupt schools in Bridgeport, his home diocese. In 1960, he noted, on the eve of Vatican II, the American church had over five million children in its schools. That total had been cut nearly in half by the present time, with a 14 percent drop since 2000 alone.

Bossidy laid out several suggestions, including one urging every parish to contribute to a nationwide public relations campaign designed to highlight the good things the church is doing. He was "fed up with some of these left-wingers who have to criticize the church." (Bridgeport has an active VOTF affiliate.) Bossidy also recommended holding exit interviews for those who leave the church. His talk created a stir and gave a lift to the room. "The bishops should listen to Larry Bossidy. How can we bottle what this fellow says?"[32]

Bossidy did not dwell on the gloomier passages from his bestseller *Confronting Reality*:

> Many industries today are so crippled by structural change that their problems have no obvious solutions. We call them structurally defective industries. They range from such old economy businesses as autos, commodity chemicals, and electric utilities to airlines, telecommunications, professional baseball and hockey... Companies in these industries are chronically unable to earn enough to be economically successful, no matter how brilliant their strategies may be or how meticulously they execute. Their business models are broken and can't be fixed.
>
> Structurally defective industries limp along waiting for things to get better. Sometimes things do... And yet these industries are purgatories for smart and talented people. Cutting costs and consolidating don't solve their fundamental problems... Each peak is lower, each trough is deeper. Over time they don't earn enough to pay for the cost of their capital, which means they have no financially realistic reason to exist.[33]

> *To begin with, let me caution all would-be players and particularly the captain of whoever runs the team not have too many signals. They are confusing. Have a few ordinary simple ones that can be easily understood by the players, but have them all worked down to perfection.*[34]

The analogy between the structurally defective industries described by Bossidy and a tradition-heavy religion like American Catholicism rings true. A few dioceses are known to have "brilliant, well-executed strategies." The Memphis parochial school system, energized by planning that has attracted big infusions of grant money, provides one instance. Another regularly cited success story is the stewardship-through-tithing program that underwrites the tuition-free schools of the Wichita diocese.[35] But these cases are not "industry-wide." "We still have a lot of wood to chop," Boisi says.

Bossidy's structurally defective industry corresponds to a low-level equilibrium.[36] The situation verges on the catastrophic, but the effort required to overcome the crisis seems so great in comparison to the resources available that interested parties are tempted to put up with the status quo and get on with their lives as best they can, or allocate their energies elsewhere. Incentives to change shrivel in the face of assessments of the risks and costs of actually implementing it. A *sauve qui peut* reaction is liable to take hold; the bishops are more accustomed to going it alone, segmented in their separate dioceses, than working together.

Yet the dire demographics of the priesthood, and the grim statistics of parochial schools, make paralysis itself unstable for American Catholicism. As the last big cohorts of clerics and nuns die off, the bottom is liable to fall out of the services, especially the sacramental rites, that parishes can offer. The actuarial facts push the parochial infrastructure into free fall.

The Roundtable has had success in pressing for the consolidation of procurement practices across neighboring dioceses; multiparish purchasing cooperatives have helped Catholic school systems on the East Coast save money on school supplies. And it has made progress in developing workshops in financial management for newly ordained priests on the track to becoming pastors.[37] In addition, the dearth of pooled information for strategic thinking about American Catholicism prompted the Roundtable to institute ChurchEpedia, a website for sharing best practices at work in parishes, schools, and dioceses.

All of these measures are low-cost (or cost-saving), zero-controversy adaptations that look to long-term results. All of them aim at economic and educational changes that enjoy de facto consensus. Information-sharing procedures like ChurchEpedia.org have made the exchange and diffusion of practical ideas easier. Educational projects designed to upgrade the financial literacy of pastors—crash courses like the "Toolbox for Pastoral Management"—can position the parishes and dioceses that take advantage of them to bear the scrutiny of would-be benefactors as they develop capital campaigns and other funding programs.

Symbolically touchier initiatives have come to fruition on a case-by-case basis. Programs that emulate the diocesan-wide foundation model, with strong lay boards of trustees, may look disruptive, depending on how bishops come to terms with the specifics of power sharing. A lot depends on personal chemistry. On being assured by a Roundtable director that the innovation would free up his time for spiritual and pastoral obligations, one bishop replied that "You've got it wrong. I like to keep my hand in things." Nevertheless, church endowments and foundations have a generally good history. In the increasingly harsh world of church finances, lay-run foundations give bishops fewer administrative nightmares to worry about. Diocesan trusts and endowments rank favorably on the criteria of low cost, manageable controversy, and beneficial outcomes.

Once past initiatives like these, we approach the realm of reforms that cost serious amounts of money or have the potential to spark controversy, or both. (It is significant that not all controversial measures involve doctrine or ideology; turf wars over efforts at coordination across dioceses can be equally bitter.) Inveterate caution and the miasma of fear that surround church employees recommend immobilism.

The wretched demographics of the priesthood, however, make seemingly desperate measures look attractive. The female diaconate comes to mind. Its drawbacks on the cost and controversy dimensions are not absolute. The diaconate is not off limits to women in quite the same way as the priesthood, and its costs do not go beyond part-time salaries.[38] Sympathizers and provisional supporters are apt to hedge their bets until a way out takes shape, one that gains support among key actors and coalitions with resources to put it into practice. This was the case with "pluralism" before John Courtney Murray found reasons for a reluctant church to justify acceptance of what was once a secret that everyone was aware of but reluctant to admit, that the American church had no choice but to live with religious diversity.

Besides being executive director of the Roundtable, Kerry Robinson wears another hat. Along with a few other well-connected women, she periodically visits Rome for off-the-record tête-à-têtes with church officials. But exasperation with the Vatican's hapless reaction to the revelations of sexual abuse that broke across Europe in the early spring of 2010 spilled over into elite Catholic circles, and *Newsweek* devoted a major article to their disaffection, liberally citing associates of the Roundtable network.

Kathleen McChesney, a Roundtable board member, former FBI executive, and first director of the Office for Child and Youth Protection at the USCCB, swiped at the Vatican response as "just men listening to themselves." "It's a pretty good guess," Frank Butler, then secretary of the Roundtable, was quoted as saying, "that we would not be in this same predicament were women involved." Kerry Robinson got in the last words: "It matters how the church is seen. Right now, it's seen as sins and crimes committed by men, covered up by men, and sustained by men. To overcome that, the church has to absolutely include more women."[39]

Robinson was almost certainly urging the promotion of more women to managerial positions, as diocesan chancellors, departmental chairs, and heads of universities, rather than endorsing female deacons, a step that would bring women closer to the altar. But the testiness was there. The message from McChesney and others linked to the Roundtable was critical of discrimination against women in the name of doctrine or in deference to custom. Fred Gluck, former managing director at McKinsey & Company and a longtime member of the Roundtable's board of directors, relinquished circumlocution altogether:

> Many of the clergy (and potential clergy) do not believe that a) celibacy is an essential requirement of the priesthood or b) women should be excluded from the priesthood and other important roles in the church. And they are frustrated and demoralized by the reluctance of the Church to discuss the issues openly.[40]

The women's diaconate is a special, apparently technical case of a class of issues which make the characterization of Catholicism as a structurally defective industry persuasive. The celibate priesthood is another.[41] Reform in these areas has the potential to liberate the human resources of the church in a productive way, putting them to more efficient use. The issues do not pose doctrinal conundrums of the same order as abortion and same-sex marriage.

But they are iconic. They evoke questions of corporate identity that defy mere practicality. Aside from whatever sacredness is attributed to tradition itself, the presumption is that membership based on sexual exclusivity imparts social desirability to the priesthood. So it looks miraculously immune in its indefensibility. The Augusta National Golf Club upheld gender discrimination for analogous reasons. Change came after cultural consensus framed the policy as no longer credible or useful.

Credibility in Catholicism is tied up with reality in a similar though touchier way. Solutions that move from the generically functional idea of "bringing more women into the church" toward the more incendiary, like the female diaconate or the rethinking of the celibacy requirement, are not merely binary contrasts between self-evident problem solving and antediluvian prohibitions. Opposition arises from a fear that altering "decorative" conventions is freighted with negative consequences that might spill over into the practical, organizational realm.

The decline in adherents to liberalized Protestant denominations is the conversation-stopping example of a backfiring nexus between good intentions and damaging outcomes. In matters of faith and tradition, remedial idealism can trigger disaster. Self-intoxication under the guise of blameless enthusiasm is a sure-fire recipe for extinction. The fate of the mainstream Protestant denominations when they started to ordain women is the standard cautionary tale. Reform adds insult to injury; capitulation to wide-eyed liberalism only speeds up the endgame.

Hierarchical Catholicism is in that exclusive league of institutional traditions whose extreme longevity has made it look indestructible, a naturalized part of the environment. It is nice to have an answer to the religious equivalent of Henry Kissinger's question about who you phone when you want to deal with Europe: you try to reach the Vatican, avatar of what Lenny Bruce called the only *the* church, even if the pope is unlikely to return your call.

Except—this is the Catch-22—if tinkering with the arrangement is undertaken, in which case all bets are off. *Ne plus ultra* old age makes the structure of the church a rarity too frail to meddle with. It is not merely exquisite, it is precious beyond price. Like the Parthenon, the church has suffered enough from a toxic environment and man-made destruction without endangering it further by experimenting with "structural improvements." Even efforts to protect it lead to some of the same paradoxical misgivings as wilderness management, though donations are welcome.[42]

So it is politic to change the subject. The fund-raising adage that money follows mission, and that quality attracts customers—that good things go together—is closer to the philosophy of the Roundtable. For many Catholic dioceses and parishes, the connection appears to be reasonable enough, even if much of the evidence remains anecdotal and the causal chain linking mission, money, and a reinvigorated faith is tenuous indeed.[43]

Some traditions have become more equal than others.[44] For Chris Schenk, the leader of FutureChurch whose work will be examined in the next chapter, the church has been captive to a false narrative. (When Schenk heard in mid-2010 that the Vatican had placed advocating women's ordination on a par with pedophilia, her response was pithier than the Roundtable's. "You don't link priest sex abuse with women who want to serve God," she said. "That's like linking manure with fresh fruit and vegetables."[45]) Rich as it is, Catholic tradition is also a graveyard of forsaken alternatives.

Where precedents are remote and marginalized, political will is weak. The problem is not fear of any change whatsoever. It is instead a barely articulated fear of loss of control, of unanticipated byproducts spinning out, that fuels the caution of ecclesiastical decision makers. The problem is not change so much as who controls it and who benefits from it.

CHAPTER ELEVEN

FUTURECHURCH AND THE FOG OF REFORM

When rescuers arrived, he tried to turn them away, even though his men were dying or going mad around him. All he could do was to walk across the last ice that barred the passage. The Northwest Passage was useless to commercial shipping: an unreliable labyrinth through waters which, when not choked by ice, were infested with icebergs.[1]

It's seven o'clock on Friday night, November 6, at the Frontier Airlines Center in downtown Milwaukee. About 2,000 people mill around the assembly hall at the 2009 Call to Action (CTA) conference. There is a Midwestern friendliness to the crowd. A few nuns with walkers and wheelchairs are finding their places in an auditorium as cavernous as an airline hangar. Placards identifying regional groups are held up as they would be at a political convention.

A big banner—"EVERYONE AT THE TABLE!"—hangs above the proscenium. A twelve-person choir, accompanied by piano, guitar, drums, and maracas, is swaying to "Jesus, we are here for you!" Almost all the singers are college-age or thirty-something. Their faces are projected on video screens suspended above either side of the podium.

The lights dim, then come up again. Two CTA officers, portraying "Mr. and Mrs. CTA," relax in leather recliners on the stage. They are Patty Hawkes and Paul Scarborough, members of the board. "Welcome to our home, the Cathedral of the Canonical Rule, Our Lady of Perpetual Authority." Pause for laughter. "Our family is disordered."

A pair of young women who have just returned from performing at a protest vigil at the School of the Americas, a training base for foreign military in Fort Benning, Georgia, replace the choir and the speakers. Pat Humphries and

Sandy O. make up a singing group called Emma's Revolution. Their CDs and peace wear, tank tops and teeshirts, are for sale on the mezzanine. They sing a lyric, "Living Planet," a cappella:

> I don't know where we're going but I know we're going far
> We can change the universe by being who we are.

A watery-eyed Irish priest, who's "been attending ten years now," leans forward in his chair to hear better. A middle-aged woman sitting beside him identifies herself as working in music ministry; she clutches a paperback entitled *Vatican II: Did Anything Happen?*[2]

That afternoon Jim FitzGerald, the newly appointed, fortyish president of CTA, had gone around introducing himself to workshops and small groups of attendees. "In 1997," he remembers, now from the podium, "I drove to my first CTA meeting in Detroit in the middle of a blizzard. 'I'm home!' I said to myself." A CTA member from Chicago introduces himself and whispers, "Tell me Jim FitzGerald doesn't look like Joel Osteen!"

"We can no longer be knocking on the door of the hierarchy," FitzGerald, once a divinity student, continues. "We must be the change we seek to be, we must reach the feminine in all of us."

> This revision of church will happen. The kingdom of God is near. It is to the edge that we are being called to prayer. The poet Guillaume Apollinaire wrote, "Come to the edge." "We can't, we're afraid." They flew, into God's inclusive embrace.

After breakfast on Saturday morning, the participants sort themselves into workshops on the first and second floors of the conference center. Downstairs they file past three cork bulletin boards that make up a Wall of Prayer. The boards are pinned with handwritten index cards and scraps of paper:

> *For my son Johnny, for employment and security for his family*
> *For the safety of my little sister, who is serving in Iraq*
> *That the hearts of the bishop of Arlington, Virginia, and those around him NOT be hardened against welcoming Thomas Gumbleton to celebrate Mass in our community next weekend*[3]

May God send the kidney my sister needs
For Phyllis, who has breast cancer

The best-attended morning event is led by Bob McClory, a retired professor of journalism at Northwestern and a founder of Call to Action. He gives a presentation about the dissident Dominican theologian Edward Schillebeeckx. McClory asked Schillebeeckx, ninety-three at the time they talked in the Netherlands (he died at ninety-five), "Aren't you kind of discouraged?"

> "No, no," Schillebeeckx said. "I believe in God and Jesus Christ."

In the fifties, McClory says, the Kingdom of the Netherlands was the most Catholic country in the world. Schillebeeckx arrived from Belgium in 1958. In 1960 about one-quarter of Catholic marriages were mixed; by 1969 that figure was just shy of 50 percent. By the mid-seventies church attendance had just about collapsed.[4] In the 1960s the Dutch episcopate had issued a new catechism stressing, McClory notes, "the potential goodness of human nature, the experiences of live people, not abstract principles. It was pastoral, not absolutist. Out went the traditional idea of the redemption, that God the Father requires a sacrifice. All that sadistic mysticism of suffering... another attractive task for women!

"Smiling as if like a beacon," McClory reports, "a man at peace with himself and with the church," Schillebeeckx proclaimed that "'the old order has to go.' He's so pastoral, so relativistic, that old man.

"Stop bitching about the bishops and the pope," McClory adds.

> It's fairly useless. Stop asking them to live outside the box. Not helpful. US Catholics are mad about something. In Holland they just don't care; about six percent of Catholics there attend Mass. We have a large majority consciousness on the part of people in the US, we have a commitment to the nuns, to intentional Eucharistic communities.

After lunch, more break-out sessions assemble. About twenty-five people gather to hear Ruth Kolpack, a Wisconsin church worker fired from her job as a pastoral associate specializing in religious education. "I support gay marriage and women's ordination in private," Kolpack says. "My thesis was completed in

2003. I was fired on March 3, 2009." Anonymous fliers circulated through St. Thomas the Apostle parish, three reactionary students from Beloit College got involved, and "Bishop Morlino called me in and told me I could not be trusted to teach authentic Catholic teaching."

> Our diocese is very dysfunctional. They fired one-third of the pastoral staff. They had a fund-raising campaign for over $3 million, they got $1 million. New pastors routinely fire people. You're supposed to have administrative recourse. The canon law tribunal is a kangaroo court. Does the pastor have the right to do anything he damn well pleases? If the bishop says it's a horse, it's a horse.

Nicole Sotelo, a CTA staffer, helped organized the session "Injustices in the Catholic Work Place." "Unless we get enough princes and peasants to rise up," she says, "the king will do as he pleases. Ruth is our Rosa Parks."

"We have a saying in North Carolina," a man in the audience interjects. "Don't teach a pig to sing. Because it irritates you and annoys the pig. Is reform possible?"

This kicks off a discussion of strategy. The legal system is ruled out, Sotelo reminds the group, because employees like Ruth Kolpack fall under "the ministerial exemption." In addition to being able to fire at will, like other supervisors who manage nonunionized workers, a bishop can dismiss pastoral employees without having to demonstrate cause. To challenge this convention would require getting entangled in constitutional issues about the boundaries between church and state. "So that leaves financial pressure," Sotelo argues. "Dioceses have multiple financial concerns. And there's pressure from the media, a people-power strategy. So we have two courses of action: people-power boycotts, and we can provide a context of support. They can have a confidential room, like this one, the victims of wrongful dismissal."

At the end of the session, as the room empties, Kolpack lingers toward the front, and a few people come up to her with words of encouragement.[5]

A week before the CTA meeting in Milwaukee, the Long Island chapter of Voice of the Faithful hosted a conference at the Huntington Hilton in Suffolk County, about a forty-five-minute ride from Queens on the LIRR. It is a few miles down the road from Levittown, over in Nassau County. Along with the subdivisions that sprouted in Orange County, California, "the Island" encapsulates the classic suburban settlements of the postwar period, outposts now advancing in years, with their own memories and traditions.[6] The conference has been billed as national, but roughly half of those in attendance come from New York, New Jersey, and New England. The big item on the agenda is the kickoff of "Voices in Action," VOTF's new strategic campaign. There are plenty of award recipients, and there are guest speakers, too, among them Joan Chittister, a Benedictine nun with a regular column in the *National Catholic Reporter*.

The officers and core team of VOTF set aside Friday night, Halloween eve, to launch the campaign. After some shuffling with the electronics, the din and the static recede and the meeting gets started with about 300 participants in a first-floor assembly hall. Francis X. Piderit, a graphic designer and public-relations executive in his early fifties who has been with VOTF since the beginning, steps up. He is from St. Ignatius Loyola parish in upper Manhattan, on Park Avenue and 84th Street, where the funeral service for Jacqueline Kennedy Onassis was held. He quotes Oscar Romero, the bishop assassinated in El Salvador: "We plant the seeds, we water, we lay foundations. We cannot do everything." Miniature plastic flower pots with green flags, vaguely evocative of Shirley Temple cocktails, are passed out.

"In the old days," Piderit says

> we had a physical foundation for Catholic life. The task now is to rebuild and transform our parish councils, accept responsibility for the future of the church. Build! Build! Build! Plant! Plant! We're a grassroots movement committed to the seeding of American Catholicism. It's now up to the laity: the management, support and growth of the Catholic community. Too many of the old laity...

"I have a question," a man seated toward the back says. "My question concerns the etymology of the word 'laity'..."

"A useful question," Piderit responds, trying not to miss a beat, "a good to-do. Let's make that a to-be-continued."[7]

Next, Bill Casey talks about the child-protection initiative and the success that VOTF has had with statute of limitations laws in Delaware. "We're trying to keep a schedule here," he insists after a few minutes. "We have so many dynamic programs. We did not start with a prayer. We are a prayerful voice. Amen! Alleluia!"

Then Susan Vogt of the Louisville chapter introduces the networking and partnership initiative set up to build coalitions with other reform groups. She asks for volunteers to come to the stage and play the parts of representatives from various organizations VOTF wants to work with. "Who wants to be an archbishop?" A gray-haired lady steps up to applause. "Now we need a pastor." Another woman, "Pastor Milly," steps up to more cheering. "It's silly," Vogt says,

> rather messy and confusing, and tense. Tell yourself I can do this! There are five organizations we are interested in trying to develop a relationship with. There is a dilemma. Some in VOTF, and outside, some are prophetic. Others are pragmatic. Jesus was *both* prophetic and pragmatic. His was a different way of exercising authority. He decided which battles to fight, which would make the most difference.

The scriptural hermeneutics seem to baffle some in the audience and a few on stage. "Collaboration on one issue," Vogt explains, "does not mean agreement on all issues. What we really need is people who know important people, who can go to them personally."

The presentations go on toward 10 o'clock. There is one called "Staying Attentive to the Spirit" ("Unless we are deeply rooted in the presence of God, we are like a noisy gong, an empty cymbal"), another "Facing Issues that Affect the Universal Church." The selection of bishops tops that agenda. Nick Mazza from the local chapter argues that "Right now the way the system is set up, if the individual is tied to the Vatican, he's in. You have to act a certain way, those individuals are going to act in lockstep. Once you are a bishop, that's it. You're not the guy to change your behavior."

Janet Hauser from Florida outlines plans for the American Catholic Council meeting scheduled for mid-2011 in Detroit. "We're looking forward to maybe 5,000 people."

"A lay synod," Dan Bartley, the VOTF president, chimes in, "it made the hair on the back of our head really stand up, when the idea came forward."

Hauser enumerates some of the particulars. "We've had conference calls. People will say, 'I work for the church; don't use my name.' Trust was a little shaky, a typical Catholic meeting. People expressed dissatisfaction with the governance of the church, that's the root cause. The signs of the times:

parish closings, abuse, financial support, fiscal management, leadership, irresponsibility."

Doctrinal and hot-button issues like celibacy appear to have come up less frequently. Hauser stresses the importance of promoting listening sessions across the country in preparation for the Detroit gathering. "People want to talk about the happy stuff," Hauser says. "Why are you happy about being Catholic? Why are you still Catholic?"

> We're truly positive. Bring ten of your closest friends, living or dead! We want a church that hears us, that walks the justice walk, where the American experience is recognized. It's our time. The US church, American Catholics, we are the biggest contributors to the church. The Detroit meeting is going to cost point-five million, for that one event. We need a shot of insulin. Go to our website.[8]

Leo Cuomo and Noreen Natoli from the local chapter lead the next presentation, about the vigil at the 11 o'clock Mass, celebrated by Bishop William Murphy, on the first Sunday of each month, outside St. Agnes Cathedral in Rockville Center. The action has been coordinated with SNAP. Cuomo, who heads a three-person vigil committee, summarizes the rationale. "Why do we do what we do? 'We're glad you're here,' we say, 'but where are the other Catholics?' We let people know what is wrong and what is going on. The survivors are our priority, the first and primary goal of Voice of the Faithful. Murphy's statements are weapons of mass distraction, he waves us away with a 'God bless you.'" The vigils have not been well received, Natoli reports. "Ridicule, name-calling, outrage. Being eyed up and down. Undercover detectives watching our every move. The devout faithful women not given an ounce of concern from our bishop. We're the vigil Catholics and we dress in all manner of red clothing, a damned soul in such pain."

"Join us outside the cathedral this Sunday morning, All Saint's Day," she concludes.

The evening finishes with a tribute to a VOTF member from the Long Island chapter who died some months earlier. On a screen toward the front of the meeting hall a slide show entitled "A Journey of Revelations, In Loving

Memory of Joseph C. Kern, 1936–2009," produced by Donohue-Cecere funeral directors, begins. "With Joe it was always about other people," the speaker recalls. Clouds appear on the screen, over a becalmed ocean.

> Joe didn't use email, didn't handle a phone too well. He was a child of an alcoholic family. He had electric white hair. He liked this pair of sweat pants, one leg up to his knee. He kept lobbying the New York State legislature, couldn't quit. Soul death in those people.[9]

Joe's widow is given a plaque. "The Lord sent us Joe for a little while," the speaker says. The words *In Memoriam* unfold on the screen, against a background of leafless trees. "A tireless advocate," the speaker says, "a tireless Albany lobbyist for remedial legislation." The trees fade, and now a sailboat can be seen, backlit on the ocean. "I feel tremendous pride in his work," Joe's widow says. "This was in some way his special passion." The sun, deep orange, slips below the water.

Before Saturday's kick-off talk, with about 400 people seated around fifty tables in the main hall at the Huntington, Kevin Connors from the local chapter reminds everyone of "this whole discussion of funds. Please consider signing up for our monthly donation; please consider shopping through our website at Amazon.com." There is a bit of back-and-forth across the room. "I'm sixty-four," one man announces. "Would anybody raise your hand who's younger than me?" Someone from another table brings up the noncooperation problem. "Fear, oh boy, they don't even associate with us. We have moved beyond dependence and expectations with regard to the bishops. We're going to do what we have to do anyway."

"How do you introduce a legend?" Pat Paone, another officer of the local chapter, asks as the room quiets down. With salt-and-pepper hair, wearing a red sweater jacket, Joan Chittister has the presence of a mother superior bent on fulfilling the proclamation in VOTF's brochure that "our conference speakers will talk about how we can initiate positive, meaningful church reform. We expect their words to serve as an inspiration for the foundations we build." Chittister's cadence and logic have an evangelical beat, as if she spoke with an invisible bass player at her side. She bolts rhythmically from anecdote to emotive aperçus to what-to-do exhortations:

> I'm a slightly used history teacher. The Spirit sees the universe, leads us to great things, things just start moving. God is stirring the pot. You can't stop that. We stumble along. We're in a Mixmaster called the twenty-first century.

There is something for everybody. Bureaucrats and office managers, "pretenders," come in for a beating. "White, medieval, male certainties are dead. Maleness is the new golden calf. The male celibate priesthood declines with each passing day," Chittister reminds her audience but—in an allusion to the ongoing Vatican investigation ("Apostolic Visitation") of women religious—"nobody is investigating *that*." A great cheer wells up.

As for the future, "God's gonna get you where God wants you to go." A lot depends on personal awakening. "Even when we lose, we keep the questions alive, the gospel alive. You reform yourself!" This in turn might rekindle popular mobilization, perhaps a charismatic breakthrough after the paradigm shift: "all institutions are in a state of flux, so many absolutes signed with a question mark. The very thought of reform brings people out." But, Chittister warns, "if you are quiet now, it will take another fifty years even to legitimate the questions.

> There is a long, last wail raging for redemption and the type of leadership that matches the coming of God. There is a cry for leadership, the kind of direction that's on the side of the outcasts. Come, o radiant dawn!

Chittister shuttles between poetic exaltation ("scarred by struggle, transformed by hope") and political admonition. Reform is roundabout; it entails compromise, coalition building, and elite concessions, piled on uncertainty. "To reform the clergy, it will take the clergy, whole generations, who are privileged by it. People get the leadership they deserve."

What remain unclear are the specifics of how strategies that require reaching out to disparate interests, or to those who agree on goals but disagree on tactics, are to be marshaled into a unified movement. Adherence to an unsullied consensus doesn't square with an imperfect politics. "The problem for reformers is that reform requires cooperation and the participation of separate sectors. All leaders must lead in the same direction." Metaphor makes better sense than the dull intricacies of power. "We need to step into the future on tiptoe, into minefields on snowshoes." The takeaway is to maneuver adroitly to victory, somehow. The specifics stay mysterious.

The rest of the day is taken up with an award presentation; a talk by a statistician from John Jay College, working on the study of sexual abuse commissioned by the bishops; then more awards, including one to Fr. Donald Cozzens, for his series of books on the pathogens of celibacy, and another to Jason Berry, for his investigative writing on the cover-up of sexual abuse and sordid goings-on by the founder of the Legionaires of Christ. The day is capped with a speech and a final Mass presided over by Tom Reese, the Jesuit fired in 2005 by Cardinal Ratzinger from his editorship of *America* magazine.

After Chittister's oration and the certification of dissenters, Reese's advice to forsake sarcasm for "understanding sympathy" and his insistence on the cyclical nature of church politics—"This is not the first nor the last generation to go through a crisis"—disappoints a few listeners eager for redder meat. The discourse strikes some as so much talk about floods and drought without reference to global warming. "You got to take the good with the bad, right?" someone whispers. "It's a mystery."

Reese's message—stick with the church—is consistent with the counsel delivered earlier by Donald Cozzens. "You have an obligation to speak out in the name of Vatican II," Cozzens says.

> If anyone is listening to your voice, most Catholics in the United States haven't heard of you. They are indifferent or wary of your voice. The bishops see an agenda. As years go by, and your energy ebbs, remember that Jesus of Nazareth asked the same questions. Your voice is of the Spirit. Dear friends, don't give up, though your hearts may be weary. In spite of its deafness, the women of the church need you to stand shoulder to shoulder. The men in Holy Orders are growing old and tired. The lifting of mandatory celibacy is the key to revitalizing the church. You can't give up. Children continue to be abused. You are the voice of hope for countless priests you may never hear of. We are too close to see this transformation, or to hear its muted thunder.

> So carry on. Carry on. Our voice could be strident, whether we mean it or not. We need contemplative leadership, a bedrock of trust, a ring of quiet authenticity. You love the church, and you speak the truth in love. If only we priests were more united...

That afternoon, a few hours earlier, Bill Casey, as chair of VOTF's board of trustees, had presented Jim Post with the 2002 original print of the design for the organization's logo. He praised Post for being "a tremendous strategist, a wise counselor, a great listener."

"I was never trained to do any of this," Post said, waving to the crowd, his wife Jeannette, a physician, at his side. "Yet when awakened I could not go back to sleep. We are a faithful group of Catholics trying to do what is right."

"We are people of conscience," Casey said, picking up the thread, "stirred by a profound injustice." His voice rose:

> We challenged the institutions to change. One of the responsibilities of leadership is to develop the next generation of leadership. The work is not done. We have rolled out the strategic plan.
>
> It's been a huge adrenalin rush for all of us, this huge assembly today.

The Vatican had declared 2009 the Year of the Priest, a venture that some in Voice of the Faithful, Call to Action, and SNAP dismissed as a stunt in bad taste. Why Year of the Priest? Why not Year of the Survivors?

On a Friday afternoon at the Call to Action conference, back in Milwaukee, a week after VOTF held its meeting on Long Island, Sr. Christine Schenk, the director of FutureChurch, was holding forth about the Year of the Priest. She was urging her listeners to sign up and pledge to make a novena in honor of "our priests who need our support. Pray this novena on the first Friday of the month. It's a work of the Spirit. Sign up for an email reminder, you'll get one three days before each Friday."

Schenk traces her roots to the agro-industrial heartland.[10] She is from Lima, once a prosperous grain storage and shipment center in the middle of Ohio. After finishing a bachelor's degree in nursing at Georgetown, taking a master's in nursing education from Boston College, and earning a certificate in midwifery from the Frontier School in Kentucky ("I thought I would be going to India"), Schenk joined the Medical Mission Sisters. In the early seventies she worked for three years as an organizer and interfaith coordinator with the United Farm Workers in Philadelphia. She left the congregation in 1977 and struck out on her own, advocating on behalf of nurse practitioners in Kentucky, pressing for a law that would allow them to prescribe medication.[11]

Schenk returned to the Midwest in 1978. She worked as a nurse-midwife with poor families out of Cleveland MetroHealth, the country hospital, and helped found a masters program in midwifery at Case Western, where she held a clinical appointment at the medical school. "By the 1980s," she says of her years as a laywoman, "Reagonomics was beginning to hit home."

> Babies weren't growing. They were just undernourished. We started a five-city coalition to expand Medicaid for low-income pregnant women. That was a five-year struggle. Simultaneously I worked on a project in the parish to declare a public sanctuary for political refugees from Central America. I did all my community organizing stuff. The Immigration and Naturalization Service let it be known that they weren't coming after us, unless we went driving around in the open with the refugees. We helped over twenty find safe haven in Canada.

By 1988 Schenk was back as a nun, having signed up with the Sisters of Saint Joseph. "Those two efforts, with the midwives and the refugees, gave me the courage to take on the reform of the Catholic church." The experience also helped her hone the techniques of reform, especially "using the mechanisms of the system to change the system. We're ground zero. We're the people they're trying to control. How can we do noncooperation?"

In 1990 FutureChurch was born. The idea was to mobilize parishioners against church closings and along the way to mitigate the priest shortage by petitioning for the ordination of women.[12] As Schenk saw things from Cleveland, the drying up of the supply of priests was the main cause behind the abandonment of local churches. "Two parishes got together. Saint Malachi's and the Church of the Resurrection. Plus twenty-eight other faith communities, mostly parishes, but some women's religious congregations too. The pastor at Resurrection, Fr. Lou Trevison, was a great ally.[13] Fr. Richard McBrien [of Notre Dame] was our first speaker.

"We thought maybe if we had 300 people come to a rubber chicken dinner that would be a great success. Six hundred and eight-nine people showed up for the miracle of the multiplication of the chickens!"

> That's the cardinal rule of community organizing: establish a strong base before you go public. We knew who all the activists were. Vatican II never would have happened here without the Cleveland Council of the Laity. A very empowered lay leadership—the "everything-west-of-Harrisburg" principle, maybe because lay people got out here before the clergy. Bishop Pilla, he wasn't real thrilled. We knew, we let him know that we knew, that "the decision-making authority wasn't up to you." As long as our actions were responsible, as long as we weren't goofy, he let us be. We're close to Voice of the Faithful, pillars-of-the-parish type of people.

Then, in 1994, *Ordinatio Sacerdotalis*—John Paul II's edict "on reserving priestly ordination to men alone"—struck. Talk of women's ordination, not just the act itself, was forbidden. By 2003 ordination to the diaconate joined women's ordination to the priesthood on the agenda of FutureChurch, though Schenk continued to chip away at priestly ordination issues whenever she sniffed a change in the winds. The Cincinnati archdiocese circulated its "Vision 2000," a plan for responding to the deteriorating supply of clerics and the shambles that deferred maintenance was making of parish schools. The chancery turned down FutureChurch's request to consider opening the question of women's ordination in its plan, and the archbishop personally forbade church workers to belong to FutureChurch when he heard that the group was starting a chapter in southwest Ohio.

Schenk saw that the movement had to "connect more broadly; no one was going to listen to a couple of parishes in Ohio. Petitions to Rome with over 2,000 signatures made a U-turn to Bishop Pilla's desk. The Vatican simply sent them back.

> The FutureChurch leadership thought it over, and I went ahead and asked for ministry money from my congregation to underwrite my work in the group, and got a response in five days. They would feed, shelter, and clothe me for three years, to see whether the ministry could stand on its own. Every one of the nuns had worked in parishes or at the diocese. They knew the need, and they knew me.

FutureChurch kept drawing on resources in as well at the margins of the establishment. As a woman religious, Schenk was able to get a ringside seat.

> Fr. Lou taught us a lot about negotiating the diocesan politics, as much as anybody could negotiate them. The priests were so terrific. They knew how to play the politics; they'd been doing it all their lives. It was a clerical club after all. Fr. Lou knew when to push and where to pull back. "That Chris Schenk knows how to make things happen," the word got out. Bishop Pilla didn't stand in the way. He didn't try to get in the face of the activists, he played things straight with us.

Starting in 1995, Schenk spent four years crisscrossing more than sixty dioceses up and down the country until, in 2000, the American bishops made their first public acknowledgment that there was going to be a shortfall of priests. A few years back they had cut off funding for a study of vocations conducted by Richard Schoenherr, a former priest. "A great disservice to the church" was how Cardinal Mahony of Los Angeles characterized the project at the time.

"Bob McClory, who was covering the bishops for the *National Catholic Reporter*, snuck me into the meeting of the bishops conference, where they admitted that their own study confirmed what Schoenherr found." The mandated discipline of celibacy hadn't changed but the pressure of facts had increased. Schenk reflected on the incongruities.

> The bishops are human beings. Some have just got rotten jobs. Clerical culture resists thinking outside the box. There are some really, really good people, you've got to respect that complexity. Many personally have good will. But you need to hold up the mirror to what's not right. You have to respect good data, too, as with clinical trials in midwifery, with the priest shortage. The bishops aren't stupid.

The selling-point of FutureChurch is the causal connection the organization makes between the shortage of priests and parish closings. A standard criticism of protests against parish closings is that, after all, demography is fate. It is not just the number of priests that is falling; the Catholic population of the old parishes themselves is also declining, melting away in suburban migrations. Schenk's response emphasizes the political choices over the structural constraints behind the shutdowns:

> The deal is that parishes are more than Starbucks franchises. Two hundred families is a *huge* Protestant church. Parishes shouldn't be punished because they are small. When you add to the mix that small active urban parishes anchor whole neighborhoods, it becomes apparent that to indiscriminately close them impacts the poorest among us in a very significant way.[14]

The cogency of FutureChurch's case hangs on a commitment to analytical sobriety, a flair for political strategizing, and a sense of violated fairness. Schenk and her colleagues have not been alone in forecasting the arrival of the dual crisis in priests and parishes, but they have been ahead of the curve in challenging the hierarchy to get serious about it. In 2006, Richard Lennon was installed as bishop of Cleveland. "In 2004, after watching the archdiocese of Boston (under Lennon's administration at the time) close perfectly viable parishes to pay bills from clergy sexual abuse," Schenk insists,

> we knew that if he got away with it there, it would be just a matter of time until bishops all over the US followed suit, insofar as so many were reeling from clergy sex-abuse payouts. Our board unanimously voted to build a project providing people with tools to resist the closing of their viable, apostolically solvent parish. Little did we know that we would be using it in Cleveland sooner than we imagined.[15]

The clarity of FutureChurch's program, the organization's feel for political timing, and its mix of ambivalence and determination, are rare qualities. The fact that Schenk is a nun makes the authorities think twice before rolling over her, and it helps that she happens to like priests. "So many priests have been battered so badly by the pedophile thing. We need to support priests. There is a critical mass of priests who believe we should move on optional celibacy."

Almost no one thinks that American Catholicism can be reformed after the fashion of a parlor trick, snapping the tablecloth away without disturbing the place settings.[16] Schenk understands that the effectiveness of FutureChurch is circumscribed. (Before the economy crashed, FutureChurch had four full-time staff and one part-time assistant. By 2010, the group was down to two full-timers, Schenk and an office manager, and three part-timers.) The diligence with which the organization has gone through official channels to get Rome to reconsider the closing of specific parishes, one by one, can be seen as an effort to slow down the inevitable by throwing sand in the gears. Likewise, the postcard campaigns petitioning Rome to put the diaconate for women back on the theological docket might be written off as a ploy to give dissatisfied Catholics a sense that they are doing something, anything, in the hope that in the meantime genuinely promising routes to reform open up.[17]

"We are living now with the failure of leadership," Schenk argues. "This train wreck has been coming for quite some time.

> It's not just the United States. There is a worldwide call for optional celibacy, from Brazil, Austria, Australia... We got on the screen at the bishops' synod.[18] It's an effective strategy, not just going out into the ether. Oh, well, the church is not a democracy. But there is reason to surmise that there are ample numbers who are realistic.

In attacking objections to the female diaconate, Schenk has been scavenging through church history for a doctrinally defensible opening. Her campaign to find historical precedent and theological justification for the move is not unlike the investment John Courtney Murray made in scouring papal writings and theological arcana to legitimize religious tolerance.

Schenk's strategy is to build support in small steps and to link pockets of popular discontent with exhaustion and disenchantment on the inside. "I'm not exactly sure 'how' we do what we do... I track church politics very closely and am always looking for the doable project, something that will empower participants with at least a modicum of success and allow secretly sympathetic folks within the clerical system—there are more than you think—to at least look the other way, at best support it behind the scenes."[19]

Speaking at her workshop at the Call to Action conference, Schenk pointed out that "Pope Benedict is very alarmed at the prospect of married priests. 'Stop the clericalization of the laity,' he said in his visit to Brazil."

Earth to Benedict! Eighty percent of all Sunday celebrations in Brazil are led by lay people! We should encourage the baptized to celebrate the Eucharist, whether ordained by bishops or not. Look, in Rockville Center, Bishop Murphy says there can't be any female communion servers. There are none in Cleveland either. But we have a canonical right to the Eucharist.

What we have is a clerical system. We had Vatican II, and a lot of tension internally. So there is the vision of Vatican II, versus the clerical over-structure. I'm committed to fighting this out. There's a lot of somewhat chaotic stuff going on. I don't know where it's going. I know I'm not going to move. You have to do what you have to do sometimes.

In developing his case for religious tolerance, John Courtney Murray appealed to historical exigency. Insisting on the union of church and state was ludicrous in a democratic republic. Murray uncovered theological justification, buried in papal statements, for the wisdom of strategic noncommitment on the part of the church in matters of government form. These liberalizing glimmers had gone unnoticed or had been selectively forgotten, buried as inconsistent with the Catholicism that stood lugubrious and penitential, mausoleum-like, from the turn to the middle of the twentieth century.[20]

Chris Schenk pursues a similar logic in her call for optional celibacy and women priests, mostly scaled down for the moment to women deacons.[21] The reforms would alleviate the logistical nightmares and perhaps the hemorrhaging disappointment with leadership created by the shortage of priests.

But her argument, unlike Murray's, aims at the internal structure of Catholicism. FutureChurch advocates for fairness—gender equity—as well as practical accommodation. The demand strikes at the marrow of church hierarchy, and the theological cover is thinner. In the eyes of conservatives, reform of this ilk has "concession" written all over it. Instead of the church shaping the social and political environment, as dictated by the fable of universal monarchy, the reverse would happen: democratic habits would contaminate the church. Incumbents could no longer think of themselves, colloquially, as proactive.

Long-term demographics work in favor of FutureChurch. But megatrends don't distinguish the group from other reform organizations, and social scientists are no better at predicting the timing of institutional upheavals than real scientists are at forecasting earthquakes. In the shorter term the impetus for the headier varieties of change in Catholicism comes from damages that the hierarchy has managed to wreak upon itself. The first is the cover-up of the sexual abuse of children. The second emanates from a clericalism so rictus-tight about gender roles and so sycophantic toward higher-ups that it has failed to resolve the problem of human resources, while continuing to pick on women.[22]

Being on the right side of history is not the soundest of arguments for change in Catholicism. Yet it cannot be entirely illegitimate in a tradition that views itself as teleological, guided through history toward a better place. The subject of women deacons, the cardinal of Chicago is reported to have said late in 2011, "is being talked about very slowly." That tidbit (among other now-you-see-it/now-you-don't tidbits, feints, cryptic gestures, whispered hints, and trial balloons) raised eyebrows, fluttered the dovecotes, and led to speculation that "perhaps it won't be very long before the many words spoken about women as deacons will be overtaken by actions."[23]

PART FIVE: OVERVIEW

The stories are about characters orienting themselves to constantly morphing circumstances, and we viewers are deposited into the disorientation with them.[1]

Much of American Catholicism remains in place. If you type "Catholic" in the search box on the web page of most metropolitan newspapers, you will find plenty of items about high school basketball tournaments and football games and lots of obituaries with parish affiliations of the deceased and the times of funeral masses. (Across the sea, Dubliners who might otherwise neglect their Sunday obligations and related devotions say a prayer to St. Anthony, patron of lost things and missing persons, when they can't find their cell phones, and elderly ladies condemn as "un-Christian" the issuance of citations for illegal parking in once cozy, out-of-the-way neighborhoods.) While the number of priests and nuns has dwindled, many of the schools and churches, some in better repair than others, stay open, and they keep up a schedule of work and religious observance. It is not as if momentum has been lost all together, despite the school and parish closings. Especially in the South and Southwest, some dioceses are on a growth tear, and in other areas (like Cleveland and parts of New England) a few churches condemned to shuttering have been reprieved by the Vatican.[2]

The puzzle lies in the direction of change. It is possible to make out the beginnings of concerted efforts to rebuild the infrastructure of the ministries, particularly the distressed parochial schools. The Leadership Roundtable has a stake in this gamble. A second push is aimed at an overhaul of clericalism. The effort centers on the flagging viability of a celibate male priesthood and the downward pull it exerts on the sacramental life of the church and the rational deployment of human resources. VOTF and FutureChurch, along with Call to Action, are the main advocacy groups here.

Attempts to improve the management of the church and movements to undo barriers to the priesthood have one thing in common. The crises do not overlap completely; this is what makes it possible to treat them, in the name of political realism, as if they were distinct. But the challenges are also coming to a head at about the same time. The actuarial tables, the demographics, and the financial accounts indicate that the problems are roughly contemporaneous, partially connected, and about equally disturbing. Sensible as it might be for tactical reasons, the "as if" approach is less than comprehensive.

Even if one or both of the crises can be resolved, no one can be sure whether success will stanch the outflow of Catholics, who leave for a variety of reasons.[3] This doubt is the last refuge of conservatives. There are no guarantees. Institutional, not to say symbolic, reforms may make matters worse, vitiating what's left of the old regime, which clings to its iconicity. The tradition has the feel of a ponderous barge laden with riches, low in the water, in high seas. Rocking the boat doesn't seem wise.

The impasse has produced reactions other than direct conflict. Schism has been mostly latent, limited to the silent departures of separate individuals. Large as the numbers are, the exodus can be read as so much effluvium from a pressure-relief valve, ridding the church of the unreliable and unruly.

Another development falls short of outright departure. Call it "the devout and disgusted" syndrome. The ambivalence is not confined to VOTF. Tenacity alongside dismay occurs among more circumspect Catholics, including members of the Leadership Roundtable.[4] Many Catholics who remain in the church "satisfice." Elements of the hierarchy and their preaching are bothersome, but not insufferably so, and a serious reconnaissance of alternatives does not necessarily lead to an acceptable way out.

The prevalence of mixed motives and misgivings suggests a broader lesson besides the inference that their net contribution is probably to reinforce the resilience of the church, or that such prevarication amounts to little more than miscellaneous velleities. With so much unrest under the surface, outcomes are neither predetermined nor particularly stable. Tunneling from within, almost always uncoordinated, need not weaken the structure decisively, but it does undermine total control. Institutional transformation, if it occurs, may be more the result of political choice and provisional opportunities than of inexorable demographics or the smashing victory of one set of inviolable beliefs over another.

The protagonists examined here differ in resources and skills, and they also vary in their commitment to the institutional church. What they share is the need to act under great uncertainty. The battle rages not only between various contenders and not just within divided souls. Indeterminacy also reflects "a game against nature"; it encompasses efforts to cope with turmoil in the historical environment of the church for which no single villain or tidal trend is to blame. Confusion reflects the magnitude, complexity, novelty, and simultaneity of the demographic and cultural changes sweeping over American Catholicism.

Another thread runs through the following pages. The first part of this book, the chapters devoted to conservative Catholics, emphasized ideas. Neocon intellectuals managed to influence public policy and in the process dominate the plastic culture of the church after Vatican II. Catholic liberals succeeded in doing neither.

The chapters treating reform groups paid less attention to ideas and more to organizational practice. One reason for the altered focus may be so obvious that it seems barely worth mentioning. Conservatives could get away with discussing ideas, including those that touch on the structure of the church, because they were allowed to do so. Their loyalty was never in doubt. Liberals have had no such freedom. The lack of clarity in the ideas expressed by Voice of the Faithful may be less a sign of intellectual incapacity than of a need to maneuver within and around episcopal surveillance. Fear of failing the *nihil obstat* test imposed by one bishop or another made the group seem evasive, even infantile in its hopes for attention and its occasional tantrums, when what it was pleading for was an appreciation of nuance and ideational pluralism.

The argument from repression and censorship comes with a qualification. Ordinary Catholics have not been much taken by the entreaties of the left, however they have been framed. This is not really a reflection of being "fed up with the extremes of both left and right." Rather, disagreement with reformers on substance seems less inhibiting than indifference in the face of the energy required for collective action when individual choice in matters of immediate concern, like contraception, is available. Centuries of deference have had an effect. The resolution of potential discord on a personal, case-by-case basis is comparatively unproblematic, and inertia holds with special force in a culture that has traditionally viewed group initiatives with suspicion. The "why bother?" question is not easy to answer. Why pull together when you can do well enough on your own by ignoring The Problem? Even personal confession, renamed "the rite of reconciliation," has fallen out of fashion. What, exactly, is in it for me?[5]

The focus of the upcoming chapters is more on personalities than ideas and organizations, a shift already evident in the chapter that considered the fortunes of FutureChurch. As the institutional ballast of the church crumbles, as the ideological moorings of Catholicism loosen, and as demographic seismographs pick up cracks and tremors, old guidelines come up for grabs. Strong personalities find themselves with room for maneuver and sense that they have a chance to put their stamp on events.[6]

Reformers face a choice between stark alternatives. Some are convinced that the church has to be liberated from traditional restrictions—chiefly, the male celibate priesthood—that cripple its potential to adapt. Their arch-opponents are persuaded of just the opposite, that meddling of this sort is the proverbial handbasket-to-hell. For others, the task is less one of liberation than of leadership. The goal is to create viable institutions from the leftovers of a perilously obsolescent order. Conventions like sacerdotal celibacy as the lodestar of ecclesial hierarchy are at worst organizational disabilities to be overcome by heroic pragmatism.

Reform movements of whatever stripe confront an organizational vacuum as much as outright opposition from steadfast conservatives. The vacuum takes two forms. One is passivity—not just toward reform but toward collective action of almost any kind—among the Catholic public in matters of church politics. The other is the subsidence of progressive episcopal leadership at the national level. For a variety of reasons—the monitoring of the Vatican, the inertia of uncoordinated fiefdoms, the Grundyism of sleepless conservatives, the fallout from the sexual abuse and financial scandals—the United States Conference of Catholic Bishops has never lived up to the hopes that liberals had for it in the last decades of the twentieth century.

So, while tradition weighs heavily, many reformers find themselves on their own. Some are respectful of but not particularly beholden to religious authorities, as most priests and church employees are, and they also stand at some distance from Catholics in the pews, whose interest in organizational change is intermittent. Most of them do not live in fear of losing their jobs. Their problem is making themselves heard and, in the case of the very well placed, like the philanthropists of the Roundtable, how to exercise a leverage over decision making and events commensurate with their economic stature.

The problem, it should be emphasized, is not simply one of converting hard cash into soft power. In Catholicism the difficulty is often less with the substance of the conversation than with having a conversation in the first place. A papacy used to sucking all the air out of the stadium does not take kindly to lay initiatives as a matter of course and, when it comes to church matters, "externs" (as Jesuits used to call nonclerical—and almost all clerical—outsiders) are not much taken by communication among themselves. In the hierarchal scheme of things, it looks like idle chitchat. Conversations even among concerned civilians tend to fizzle out.

Chapters Twelve and Thirteen depict some of the key actors thinking out loud, scrambling to come to grips with questions for which they have provisional answers or none at all. The occasionally elliptical quality of their discourse reflects a fractured reality. Decision makers have to deal with the underlying problems already mentioned and the emergencies that go with them: the near intractability of doctrinal and paradoctrinal issues involving sex, gender roles, and authority, the inanition of large sectors of the Catholic populace, and the spotty organization of groups that have emerged in response to such issues.

To structure this dynamic requires truncating it in some fashion, and chopping the Catholic transition into manageable chunks entails political choices. If overall consensus is fugitive, loose coordination of a smaller number of priorities looks realizable. Chapters Twelve and Thirteen register the tensions associated with making trade-offs, with assessing the benefits and losses of compartmentalizing institutional Catholicism. The workable strategy would seem to be an allocation of labor that places theological issues in the clergy's court and leaves the laity to deal with the physical plant and the mechanics of organizational maintenance. The simplicity of this division of labor is appealing, and "mere upkeep" isn't as prosaic as it sounds.

It is when "the temporalities" converge with "the intractables," as in the sacralization of celibacy and male identity as preconditions of ordination, that the dilemma becomes acute. The tin-pot Platonism behind a tidy bifurcation of the theological and the tangible has limits. Suppression of constitutive questions like these, the dissociation of apparently unthinkable issues from their practical consequences, resembles the self-intoxication criticized in postmortems of the economic crisis of Western capitalism: "how it is that false illusions of the global financial system's operation and consequences were conferred with sufficient legitimacy to deafen alternative views and stymie real reform?"[7]

The two chapters that follow are devoted mostly to the Leadership Roundtable, for reasons that go beyond the fact that its strategy relies heavily on the institution-building skills of "personalities." The Roundtable has a lot of irons in the fire. Another rationale is to set the premises underpinning the analysis so far in broader perspective.

One of these true-most-of-the-time ideas is that ideological or doctrinal conflicts are more rancorous in Catholicism than issues concerning the temporalities. In fact, however, while turf protection has little to do with ideology, the parallel play across the separate dioceses of American Catholicism seems almost as intractable. The bishops are more accustomed to pronouncing on doctrine, to which fewer of the faithful pay attention, than they are to pursuing national solutions to organizational problems. Yet the material worries of the church—the plight of the schools being the obvious illustration—outrun diocesan and parish-level resources.

The Roundtable's encouragement of nationwide standards and networks, aligned as it is with the usual deference toward hierarchy, is not a paradigm shift. It is not even particularly new. Other organizations, like the National Catholic Education Association, have been there before. Irritation with the Roundtable sometimes sounds like pique at the source of the message—pushy rich guys at it again—rather than disagreement on substance. Nevertheless, the Roundtable continues to prod the default register of the American church beyond what in practice remain dispersed, largely provincial fields of vision.

A second claim is that serious reform in Catholicism requires a redistribution of power. This is true, but the generic idea says nothing very precise about how and when. Few reform agendas go into detail about how transformations like a move away from the celibate priesthood are to be paid for. Once this is acknowledged, growth in material resources becomes as important as the realignment of status hierarchies. The alertness of the Roundtable to the volume of hard resources available to parishes and dioceses outranks the priority it assigns to redistribution, but otherwise it makes an effort to be impartial. The agenda, heavy on resource development and fund-raising, can be turned as much to improving remuneration and benefits for lay employees as to underwriting a married clergy. Without resources, the fairness side of the agenda remains academic.

A third, allied supposition is that (with the partial exception of change in behavior of the sort pressed by SNAP) deliberate reform in Catholicism originates inside the institution, through managerial modernization or less frequently doctrinal revision. It is thought to be endogenous, more or less self-contained. In effect, it is thought to be under control.

This fails to do justice to the growing technological and institutional complexity of the environment surrounding American Catholicism. These developments alter the organizational and financial landscape in which the church is embedded as surely as demographic shifts and cultural upheavals. The institutional terrain and the machinery of money are in motion as much as the ideological climate. Models of wealth management that consolidate previously scattered assets are starting to come on line for dioceses that used to act in stand-alone mode. Similarly, cutbacks in state financing for public education have begun to alter the politics of support for parochial schools, once completely off limits because of constitutional prohibitions against government support for religious entities. Both dynamics require a penchant for dealing with risk that has not been common in the church. The question is not whether such adaptations are in the offing but how they will be organized and managed.[8]

Here the Roundtable has a greater capacity than other reform groups to gamble and explore innovations. Because the institutional setting of American Catholicism is in flux and the noise-to-signal ratio is very high, midcourse corrections—the Roundtable likes to call the process beta-testing—are common. But this eclecticism does not render such improvisations merely incremental. Some of the wheeling and dealing of personalities edges toward transformative institution building. At the same time, their ventures carry significant risk. The sensible-sounding consolidation of investment funds across parishes, dioceses, and ministries must deal with the unimpressive-to-negative returns recorded in recent years by the megafunds that the project is modeled on.[9]

An even harsher trade-off emerges in advocacy and lobbying efforts to modify state-level restrictions against releasing public funds to parochial schools. Catholicism's adherence to the celibacy requirement and male gender for ordination to the priesthood amounts to symbolic dysfunction in the face of practical necessity. The impasse reflects a failure to extricate itself from the condition of a structurally defective industry. Ruling out government support for underprivileged children in religiously sponsored schools comes close to a similarly perverse deadlock in American political culture.

The odds against lifting either restriction are very high. The school stand-off grows out of a protracted conflict between Catholic and American traditions. The sorry tale that has shaped the field of battle goes back to the mid-1860s, when Pius IX issued his "*o tempora o mores*" denunciation of what the world was coming to in the *Syllabus of Errors*. This encyclical of "condemned propositions" gave enthusiastic Protestants ammunition—the Whore of Babylon was at it again—to craft the Blaine Amendments of the mid-1870s, outlawing state aid to Catholic schools on constitutional grounds. The countermoves escalated. By the mid-1880s the Catholic bishops had responded by meeting in Baltimore to institute the parochial school system. From these memories and institutional obligations a tangle of litigation has sprouted that persists through the liberating gestures of Vatican II.[10]

CHAPTER TWELVE

TWO STEPS FORWARD...

The stories that people were to follow like events in the lives of people they knew made no attempt to conceal their conventional and spectacular nature—and, in a word, their purely fictional nature. Letters to Dickens from his readers begging him not to kill off a certain character were not written out of any confusion of fiction and reality, but from enthusiasm for the game, the ancient game between storyteller and listener, demanding the physical presence of a public to act as chorus, as if aroused by the very voice of the narrator.[1]

Francis Piderit, head of the Voice of the Faithful (VOTF) affiliate in New York City, is one of a dozen siblings. An older brother is a Jesuit priest.[2] A sister lives across the Hudson in New Jersey with her husband and six children. Every Thanksgiving Francis's sister takes her youngest offspring to the parish shelter. The destitute love the buckets of ice cream that the children bring, and the children are delighted, though it is a race between the melting provisions and their ability to scoop up the ice cream out and serve it to the clientele.

We are talking over lunch at the Hotel Affinia, a few blocks east of Madison Square Garden. "We Create Change" are the words embossed on the back of Piderit's business card. It is late March, just after St. Patrick's Day. The sleet and slush and piles of taupe snow are not enough to bother the pedestrians dodging one another along the sidewalks.[3]

Piderit's parents "had their own radical Catholic style. They had their way of creating their world. Commitment was there, right in the neighborhood." At first he sounds like any other mourner grieving over a world that no longer exists. Soon, however, it becomes clear that Piderit is a dervish of indignation and generosity, pivoting between tales of ecclesiastical intrigue and a generalized anguish over the plight of Catholicism. He gives the impression of being an impulsive traditionalist.

"How do we know if any of this stuff adds up?" he says, speaking of the state of the church. "We do not. Nobody does. Everything's fractured. And all that gradualism: I've learned that the bishops will not respond. They're distracted, we're distracted. Nobody has the answers."

Piderit has reached the point of exasperation with confrontation and moderation alike. "I used to think that SNAP was wrong," he says. "They were right about keeping up the pressure. Then it turns out, so-and-so told me, I forget his name, they won't be satisfied until the church is finished, destroyed."

He is also fed up with temporizing. "The VOTF affiliate is my real parish."

> A few months ago we wanted to invite Peggy Steinfels to give a talk about women in the church. She demurred. She said, "women in the church is not my area of specialization." Not my area of specialization??? So finally Steinfels agrees to speak, and she spoke for more than half an hour. She said nothing. A friend came up to me and asked, what did she say? She said absolutely nothing.[4]

Attendance fell way below expectations. "About fifty people showed up. We tried hard, we did everything we could to put things together, we beat the drums, we tooted the bugles. Is this all we can muster in the New York area? Fifty people? I was very disappointed."

A while back, the Washington office of the Leadership Roundtable had phoned Piderit at the public-relations firm he runs to set up a meeting with Kerry Robinson during the New York stop of her fund-raising campaign. Piderit replied that he would be happy to talk with Robinson about a donation; he also expressed interest in piggybacking some discussion of collaborative work between VOTF and the Roundtable on to the visit. The Roundtable, alerted to the VOTF connection, did not pursue the matter.

Piderit agrees with the bishops on one thing, that "the church should stick with its celibacy and all the rest, otherwise the church, the hierarchy, will go down hill. It may go down hill anyway, who knows? They're stuck. It's hopeless. As for the institutional church, God will provide. Let it go at that. You might as well... it's all a third rail. The church has so many third rails. So many third, fourth, fifth, six rails." Piderit seems long past hoping for fruitful collaboration even with occasionally accommodating bishops. His attitude toward the hierarchy recalls a remark made by the sportswriter Frank Graham about the taciturn and often grumpy Bob Muesel, a Yankee outfielder, near the end of his career in the late 1920s: "He's learning to say hello when it's time to say good-bye."[5]

When I ask about ways out of the impasse, Piderit waxes enthusiastic. "We're going to start again." Are these intentional communities? "Not exactly. I don't want to live as a neo-catechumen. There's no reviving the prefeudal church. We're starting in the twenty-first century, without first-century values. We need to build self-forming parishes. We're all founders. We need to build a new laity. My heart races."

"Francis," I observe, "you're a freaking anarchist."

The conversation loops back amiably to stories about the local church. Piderit recalls his meeting with Cardinal Egan, enthroned as archbishop of New York in 2000 and reigning until 2009. It is as if he had glimpsed something of the *magnum silencium*, the solitude of a priest's vacant Sunday afternoons. The image, vaguely menacing, is of a patriarch who had outlived his children.

> I had him over for the inauguration of a church center I helped design. "Alpine Eddie" they call him, he's tall and cold. His own priests couldn't stand him. Notorious for stiffing everyone. He sat alone with the monsignor who's assigned to squire him around, not talking to anyone. You wanted to go up and say something to him. He was all alone.[6]

> *... small pictures, either miniatures or larger panel compositions, such as one sees in the tablinum of the Villa of the Mysteries at Pompeii. The third style, as it is called, has all the characteristics which Vitruvius found so distasteful: "paintings of monstrosities rather than truthful representations... yet when people see these frauds they find no fault with them but on the contrary are delighted and do not care whether any of them exist or not."*[7]

The Religious Education Conference, sponsored by the Los Angeles archdiocese and held every March since the 1970s at the Anaheim convention center alongside Disneyland, regularly brings in over 40,000 attendees from across the United States and other parts of the world, mostly the Philippines and Central America. It is the sort of California set piece that stirs French theoreticians to paroxysms of dystopian reflection. The amusements of the Magic Kingdom and the Disney California Adventure nearby are spread across acres of motels and fast-food chain restaurants like cones of polychrome lava. The avenues are jammed with SUVs and family-size wagons, many with catchy bumper stickers ("Freedom Is Not Fear","First My Gun, Then My Dog, Then My Wife"). Everything looks to be hectic profusion amid the aerospace factories and beige rows of tile-roofed housing and dusty palms of Orange County.[8]

The gathering is a two-and-a-half day cornucopia—among other things, an exercise in schlock and awe—of inspirational speeches, liturgical celebration, and workshops in contemplative methods, applied spirituality, and pastoral practice. There are presentations by authors of religious and life-style guides with full schedules of book signings and meet-and-greets. The theme for 2011 is "*Mantente Firme... Confía!*" "Hold Fast... Trust!"

The ground-floor hall is jammed with vendors of religious merchandise and church utensils. One booth displays "Fear and Trust in Jesus" teeshirts and bumper stickers. Young Asian and African nuns in crisp white and powder blue tropical habits bustle from event to event. Friars in flowing brown robes ply the crowds with brochures and DVDs. On Saturday afternoon, in one aisle of the exhibition hall, the retired Cardinal Roger Mahony, who stands about 6′5″, explains the sights to a diminutive, portly archbishop José Gomez, his newly appointed successor. In the corridor just outside the hall, groups of teenagers squat on the carpeted floor, their backpacks scattered at their feet, chattering and texting, and outside the building itself, where spring flowers are in bloom, people relax on benches, drinking soda and snacking away on sandwiches and chips. Cell phones pop open and disappear like disposable organs.

Movement up and down the escalators is nonstop. Conference-goers circulate between the second-floor workshops, the big auditorium for the main speakers downstairs, and the exhibits hall. The to and fro induces something of the intoxication of a pilgrimage site. The ambience is not unlike the venue of the great feast of Francis Xavier in Goa on the southwest coast of India, where throngs of the devout, lounging on humid grass and blankets thick with food stalls and souvenir tents, swarm every December 6. At night the voices of the pilgrims move like fish within the air. When morning comes, the multitude cranes to venerate the missionary saint, whose body is thought to be miraculously preserved. His blackened remains are barely visible. The remnants lie in a coffin-size reliquary raised up on a catafalque with viewing panels of thick glass along the sides.

Several booths at the religious education conference offer "powerful parish management software and web solutions." One promises to "synchronize family contact and upload member details among parishes, schools, and the diocese." The stand for Anaheim Melody features the stylings of Annette Hills, who is available to sing "for weddings, funerals, birthdays, holidays & other events." The booth sponsored by Holy Cross Family Ministries publicizes the outreach founded by Father Patrick Peyton, the rosary priest celebrated for his trademark slogan "the family that prays together stays together." Born in County Mayo, Peyton emigrated to the United States in 1928. In 2001, nine years after his death, the Vatican opened canonization procedures, and Peyton has since been recognized with the official title of Servant of God.

The Verbum Dei display, geared to Hispanic customers, almost all of them women, is very popular. It has brightly decorated statues, some of which differ little stylistically from Hindu gods and goddesses, in lawn-size and smaller models. There are bargain racks of medallions, scapulars, rosaries, miniflasks of holy water, refrigerator magnets, dashboard statuettes, amulets, pocket missals, coasters, and holy cards, including one of San Miguel Arcángel, with a blown-back head of blond hair, sword poised, a foot pressed down on the sweaty balding pate of Satan. Another card commemorates the Precious Blood. The head of Jesus, crowned in thorns and aglow in a cloud, is sweating red drops into a golden chalice, and on the reverse is a prayer in Spanish by Marcial Maciel, Mexican founder of the Legionaires of Christ, beseeching men and women to dedicate themselves *sin reservas*, wholeheartedly, to the work of the church. Mementos of assorted martyrs sell well. (There are no signs, however, of *votos*, the wax models of hands, limbs, ears, noses, and other body parts that can be found at Fatima and Lourdes as offerings for the cure of illnesses and injuries. On the international front, no one has had the heart to remove the monumental statue of Saint Christopher outside Lisbon airport carrying the infant Jesus on his shoulder, even though the Vatican has declared the patron saint of travelers to be a nonauthorized fictional creation, and tinny Saint Christopher medals remain on sale at the bargain table in

Fatima.) Some of the shoppers stack their purchases in carts fashioned out of milk crates joined to sets of wheels.

Bookstands offering material for parishes and parochial schools are plentiful. *Cherub Wings* is a DVD designed for children eight and under. The series "Catholic Heroes of the Faith" includes *The Story of Saint Perpetua* and a follow-up on *The Passion of Perpetua*. There are various deluxe editions of the Bible. There are also specialized readings for grown-ups on theology, scriptural history, and parish ministry, as well as bountiful stocks of self-help videos and confidence-building manuals.[9]

Some booths display equipment for churches and the clergy: embroidered chasubles, for example, draped on headless styrofoam mannequins. There is a panoply, a veritable delirium, of "altar accessories and bishop's appointments" from Gaspard, a company founded in Spain in 1939, now located in Wisconsin. The full-color catalogue advertises a gold- and silver-plated tabernacle at $21,495. A brass gold-plated monstrance for showing the consecrated host, "with red enamel halo around the luna," goes for $3,595.[10]

Along with Noberto Guttierez, Larry Vaughan runs The Wood & Iron Factory based in San Diego. A manufacturer of furniture and sculpture for churches and synagogues, the company has been in business for about twelve years, and Larry has been with it for ten. Standing beside the company's setup of pew-ends and brochures in the convention hall, he explains that he used to run the sales department for a large supplier of store fixtures. "All the counters, all the retail displays for Pier One, Johnson & Murphy Shoes, a lot of stuff for Home Depot," he says. "We had 435 workers making sawdust every day, very hectic, nonstop. Once I got a call from a guy in Baltimore. 'When can you be in my office tomorrow?' he says to me. I thought to myself, 'When? Tomorrow?' I was in his office the next day."

The Wood & Iron Factory's breakthrough came in 2001, when the company was commissioned to make the pews and other furnishings for the new Cathedral of Our Lady of the Angels, the hub of the Los Angeles archdiocese. Larry signed on. "With our company," he says, "I may be working with a customer two years before they place an order. I'm not overreligious, but I like the concept of it."

We work only with solid hardwood. No particleboard, no plywood for us. I'd say we sell Cadillacs. We're not the cheapest. We're on the high end of the market, competitive for our quality. All of our furnishings and all of the finishing are hand-done. With hand-carving we can do what a machine can't do. A machine can only work in one plane. It has to make a short cut, then reset, then go another way. A guy with a chisel is more flexible.

A few weeks after the religious education conference I telephoned Larry; the stories geysered on.

We use lots of ash. That's what baseball bats are made of, a very hard wood. We like it because it's a very white wood that stains well. A padre in Tucson had a parishioner who was a pecan-grower who wanted to have pews of pecan wood. Well, our guys took ash and stained and distressed it, and the padre told us he couldn't tell the difference. The guy felt it was fine, loved it.

After Katrina hit, an Episcopal church in Biloxi calls. "We have Jefferson Davis's family pew," they tell me. Well, one pew-end is intact, the rest is in pieces, a bunch of lumber that looks like driftwood in a box. So we ship it off to our factory. "What is this, wood for a bonfire?" the guys say. It took us eight months to find the right wood. We used cypress. Finally we got it fixed.

The Wood & Iron Factory also helped restore twelve Catholic churches in New Orleans in the wake of Katrina. "'We want to bring it back the way it was,' people would plead with us." The company also worked on St. Louis Cathedral in the middle of the French Quarter, reconstructing the pulpit from photographs taken in the 1920s.

The company's operational base, a union shop with benefits and over forty craftsmen and laborers, is just south of the border. "People stand in line to work for us," Larry says. "It's like it used to be here in the '20s. Sons go to work with their fathers on Saturdays and learn the trade."

We made it through last year in the middle of the recession without a layoff. You can see it in their faces, the work they build. The guy who builds a piece points to it and says to his kids, I worked on that. There are other companies that have C & C machines that will crank out whole pews with carvings. You put a piece of wood in, line it up, and it will do all the grinding and cutting, and out comes a

> pew to be assembled. Our pew-ends are all hand-carved. Exactly alike, of course, but you'll see little differences.

Larry and Noberto are used to dealing with top-of-the-line clients.

> We landed the job for Cardinal Mahony's private chapel in the cathedral [Our Lady of the Angels]. A guy in Laguna calls and says he wants a chapel in his home just like the Cardinal's. "Okay," I tell him, "we can make it like that, but there are other options you might want to look at." The next day I get a call from the cardinal's secretary, asking can you please build a chapel just like the cardinal's for Mr. F. So we do it.

"Every day's a challenge," Larry continues. "I stay in the rectory in New Orleans because the padre's my friend. We develop friendships. We are a small company, not just a business. We have no sales reps, we don't advertise, it's all referrals. We're on our third expansion. You got to look to find us."[11]

Back at the convention center, a few yards in front of the main entrance, about half a dozen people from Call to Action are demonstrating in favor of women's ordination. Like other dissidents, the group is forbidden to present their demands inside the building. The women, holding two long white banners with "Save the Church... Ordain Women" stitched in English on one side and Spanish on the other, get a reasonably friendly reception from passersby. Some, including a couple of security guards, give them a thumbs up. Others read over the CTA pamphlets and ask questions. A few church workers come up to confide that they would stand with the women but "Father might hear about it." A middle-aged Hispanic women rushes by toward the entrance doors, muttering loudly "Leave us alone!" She stops and glares back toward the demonstrators, her face a mask of scorn and fury, then hurries inside.

The Valley Hunt Club, its tennis courts and tended gardens, cover about half a block on the corner of Palmetto Drive and Orange Grove Boulevard, just up from South Pasadena. Next door is the Wrigley Mansion, home of the

Tournament of Roses Association. Gentlemen of the Valley Hunt Club created the Rose Parade in 1890. Their portraits hang on the paneled walls. This is the Pasadena of cool lawns and quiet money.

Early on a February evening in 2008, on the same day that conservative grandee William Buckley Jr. died, Thomas Dillon, then president of Thomas Aquinas College, hosted a reception for several dozen benefactors. After waiters had circulated canapés and glasses of white wine and mineral water, the guests heard a talk from David Appleby, a young professor of history, who reflected on the sorrows of "a lost integralism" and the risks faced by "students trained in skepticism." In 2003, Professor Appleby, a convert, had left an associate professorship at the US Naval Academy to join the faculty as a tutor at Thomas Aquinas. Students at the college, which features a Great Books curriculum, learned "the truth of the matter" and, in a swipe at the waywardness of relativism, not just "what the Incas thought in the eighteenth century."

After Professor Appleby had sat down to applause, President Dillon gave a PowerPoint presentation about work on the construction of Our Lady of the Most Holy Trinity Chapel, nestled in the center of campus in the hills around Santa Paula, about an hour-and-a-half drive north of Los Angeles. Up the road on Highway 150 there is a llama farm, and a few miles in the other direction is the Iglesia del Nazarene Vida Nueva. Sixteen million of the twenty-one million dollars needed to complete the project were in hand. The chapel and other campus buildings, the faculty center, the dorms, are a hybrid of Florentine and neoclassical Spanish motifs. "Do the students know how lucky they are?" one of the donors asked during the Q&A. President Dillon illustrated the special techniques of cutting and drilling the marble for the interior columns of the chapel, and he paused lovingly over the symbolism of the architecture. A series of arches represented the Seven Dolors, the sorrows, of Our Lady.

Msgr. Frank Weber, archivist of the Los Angeles archdiocese, and Fr. Cornelius Buckley ("no relation to Bill, God rest him"), an elderly Jesuit who acted as chaplain and assistant dean for religious studies at the school, were in conversation with Fr. Buckley's brother, a Dominican in charge of a local seminary. "I'm the wise old man who delegates," he smiled, "and gets others to do the work. We have three ordinations this year."

There was some joshing and gossip about figures in the church who were or were not sufficiently orthodox. "Look what's happened to Ireland and Spain," Cornelius Buckley noted sadly. "Franco was a daily communicant. A daily communicant. I would like to think that the Generalissimo wasn't as bad as they say he was."

Fr. Buckley began reminiscing about his time in Ann Arbor working for the devout philanthropist Tom Monaghan, founder of Domino's Pizza. His latest venture was the development of Ave Maria University, now transplanted to Florida. Monaghan proved to be a difficult boss. The local bishop refused to consecrate the chapel of the new university. It was not Monaghan's prerogative, the bishop insisted, to appoint the chaplain without diocesan approval. "A billionaire who believes he has a direct line to the Virgin Mary!" Fr. Buckley observed. "'The Blessed Virgin Mary,' he would say about decision after decision, 'the Blessed Virgin Mary wouldn't like it!'"

Fr. Buckley gave a benediction to end the reception, as he had given a prayer of invocation to start off the evening.

At about six feet tall, Geoffrey T. Boisi looks younger and trimmer than a multi-millionaire investment titan might be expected to look. There is nothing of the air of the portly, watch-and-chain-in-the-vest wise man of marmoreal banking lore about Boisi. Going on sixty-five, he is as lean as his peer and former business partner Robert Rubin. "Intense" is the go-to adjective in journalistic accounts of Boisi; the word was one of his own favorite descriptors during his rise to a partnership at Goldman Sachs at the then unprecedented age of thirty-one. "I'm a naturally aggressive, intense personality," he acknowledged at the time he was becoming known as "the mastermind of the megadeal."[12]

While his pace may have slackened a bit since the days, from the eighties though the early years of the millennium, when he played a starring role in the remaking of Wall Street, multitasking through whirlwinds remains a Boisi touch. His network of high-level contacts flourishes. During the 2008 financial meltdown, then Secretary of the Treasury Hank Paulson recalled an urgent meeting with Richard Syron, the head of mortgage giant Freddie Mac. "Dick Syron had brought his outside counsel, along with a few of his directors, including Geoff Boisi, an old colleague from my Goldman Sachs days."[13]

In 1993, two years after retiring from Goldman at the age of forty-four to pursue his philanthropic interests, Boisi and three partners founded Beacon Group, an investment boutique.[14] Seven years later, Chase Manhattan paid $500 million for the firm, with about half of that going to Boisi, and brought him on as cohead of its investment banking operation.[15] Chase Manhattan then merged to become J. P. Morgan Chase, and Boisi was forced out in two years. Soon after, he founded Roundtable Investment Partners, another private equity company, where he has remained as chairman and senior partner. When the sexual abuse crisis began rattling the windows of the church, Boisi called Cardinal Theodore McCarrick, then archbishop of Washington, scanned through his executive contacts, and began to put together another brainchild—the National Leadership Roundtable in Church Management. The group held its inaugural meeting at the Wharton School, where Boisi is a trustee, in mid-2004.

In the immediate wake of the Boston exposé, the church hierarchy was all but winging it. By the time the Leadership Roundtable began to offer its services in earnest, however, in 2005, the dynamic had shifted toward a steadier crisis management. Diocesan review boards had been put in place, the number of sexual molestations by priests had declined, most of the wreckage seemed to have been swept away.[16]

Boisi and his colleagues pushed toward crisis recuperation. "We're only focused on the temporal issues related to the church," he insists, repeating the credo of the Roundtable. "We try to stick to our knitting because these are things we have some expertise in." The idea was to redeem the cratering credibility of the church by improving and publicizing its good works. The Roundtable went from defense to offense.[17]

Even before retiring as a three-star general, James Dubik had joined the board of the Roundtable and served on several of its subcommittees. A former seminarian with a master's degree in philosophy from Johns Hopkins, his last assignment was the training of Iraqi security forces. On occasion he would telecommunicate with the Roundtable's board directly from the Middle East.

One of Dubik's accomplishments in particular caught the attention of the Roundtable. "After the Vietnam War, when the military went through the nadir of its respect function," Boisi says, "there was a group that was put together to develop a game plan on how to resuscitate the reputation of the military." Dubik's assignment, as Deputy Commanding General for Transformation, US Training and Doctrine Command, was to help the military regain combat prowess and restore its prestige. Reviving morale was as important as rethinking tactics and technique.[18]

> When we first met him, we talked about how the church ought to be thinking about that as well. He's brought a discipline. He's been acting as a quasi chief operating officer for us. At the beginning of each year, when we go through our planning cycle, we have conversations among the board members and the staff and we do listening tours to talk to our council members about what they think is particularly important. What we are trying to do is to identify two to half-a-dozen suggestions and focus on them.

Dubik functions as a gatekeeper as plans and projects vie for recognition. Dubik's substantive recommendations also carry weight. Boisi points to a summer training program, the "Toolbox for Pastoral Management" in parish administration for young priests at Seton Hall University, that has drawn part of its inspiration from the general's military experience.[19] Boisi's account of the mentoring program and the ethos of informal exchange among those with leadership presence captures a lot of the Roundtable's modus operandi.

> They [Dubik and his fellow officers] realized that the platoon leader was the critical on-the-ground leader, and so they developed a technology to enable platoon leaders who were in theater to talk about, to communicate with people who have just come out of theater... and also to identify the successor platoon leaders. So there is a private communication that takes place at a very practical level. We've designed the same thing for pastors. We've identified priest leaders. We did the investment to put it all together, and that's now being disseminated throughout the church.

Some of the Roundtable's initiatives have moved slowly toward implementation. An effort to develop performance reviews for clerics and other pastoral workers in partnership with the National Federation of Priests Councils has struggled with costs and the difficulty of devising workable metrics. The program, adapted from the "360-degree leadership evaluation tool" in use by some corporations, got up and running in the Boston archdiocese after pilot-testing in Pennsylvania and New Jersey.[20] Aside from the expense, which can reach $1,000 per head, Dubik acknowledges that "Leadership 360" is the kind of assessment that the military itself, as well as many corporations, have resisted. It presents a challenge to hierarchical control. Pastors can draw on the procedure, but no one has asked the bishops to submit to such evaluations.[21]

A push to get the bishops to adopt standards of excellence—in effect, a bill of rights outlining the expectations of benefactors regarding sound management—has advanced more slowly than hoped for. Dioceses, parishes, and nonprofits associated with the church who sign on to the program receive what amounts to a Good Housekeeping Seal of Approval from the philanthropic community. "Checks and balances," however, is not a phrase that sits well with many canon lawyers. Chuck Geschke, who cofounded Adobe Systems and has been a Roundtable board member from the beginning, reminds skeptics that the hit rate for venture capitalists in Silicon Valley is probably no higher than one out of twenty, and it has to be lower in a church not known as a nursery of innovation.[22]

The spread of administrative Standards of Excellence, an objective of the Roundtable from the outset ("our foundational program," in Boisi's words), involves trade-offs between public relations, morale boosting, and figuring out what's actually going on. In 2007 the Roundtable started to explore the possibility of assessing their implementation. The bishop of Gary, Indiana, Dale Melczek, was one of the early adopters of the standards for his seventy-parish diocese. By mid-2010, with the help of a grant from the Carnegie Corporation, researchers from the University of Notre Dame had completed a fifty-three-page report on the Gary experiment.[23] The document concluded that while "there are unquestionably doubters and detractors of this broad effort... there are many more adherents." The report contains frank excerpts from the priests who responded. And it arrives at a causal hypothesis—"episcopal leadership seems to create the overarching tenor for participatory, collegial efforts in the Standards for Excellence initiative"—that rings true anecdotally.

The snag is the response rate. The report notes without comment that only eleven out of sixty-two priests, fewer than one in five, answered the survey. The low response renders determination of the effectiveness or popularity of the standards moot. The fact that overburdened priests, faced with a questionnaire, could not be bothered to handle another sheaf of paperwork suggests (besides concerns about privacy) a lack of enthusiasm and time for, rather than outright opposition to, the standards in the real world of parish chores. "Pastors are stretched too thin," one priest commented. "They want to collaborate. They can't."[24]

Reactions like these adumbrate a complex dilemma. Authority in the church used to depend on disciplinary power and the norm that followers accepted the spiritual rationale behind the sacrifices expected of them. Obedience could be expected not only on an "or else" basis but because the prospect of eternal reward compensated for rough treatment at the hands of superiors.

That incentive structure is now less convincing. Priests, thinner on the ground, are in a better bargaining position. But as believable penalties have declined, so have rewards. From a management standpoint, the new environment resembles a motivational dead zone. Mission creep outpaces compensation. There seems to be too much procedure and filling out of forms, some of them administered by pettifogging borderline incompetents. The rhetoric of the greater good begins to pale before a process of going through the motions and an ethic of self-realization.

The growth path of the Roundtable is shaped in part by the organization's capacity to live out the Ben Franklin-esque slogan that if one thing fails, try something else. The Roundtable is also astute about choosing its battles. The group stresses procedures—best practices that might be transferable from one organization to another—more than substantive demands.

Even this relatively tame approach, however, cannot stay free of controversy when applied to an institution steeped in tradition. In his memoir of his days in high finance and politics, Boisi's former colleague Richard Rubin summarized the dilemma this way: "antagonism and resistance to change [are] inevitable... That's typically the conundrum around significant change in corporate—or any other—setting: it won't happen unless you're willing to break some eggs and incur sharp opposition. But change also won't take hold without broad buy-in. It is usually very difficult—if not impossible—for an outsider to judge whether an effort at change is meeting both these tests or is either too aggressive or not aggressive enough."[25]

On the coffee table in front of a couch in Boisi's twenty-third floor office on Park Avenue,[26] overlooking the Waldorf Astoria, there is commemorative silver tray, a gift from a Wall Street colleague. "The entrepreneur, as a creator of the new and destroyer of the old, is constantly in conflict with convention," the inscription reads.

> He inhabits a world where belief precedes results and where the best possibilities are usually invisible to others. His world is dominated by denial, rejection, difficulty, and doubt. And although as an innovator, he is unceasingly imitated when successful, he always remains an outsider to the "establishment." He is usually found disturbing and irritating, even unemployable.

Boisi, for whom "relentless" is as common a designation as "intense," concedes that some of the criticism leveled against the Roundtable has stung. "We've tried to be a positive force," he says.

> That doesn't mean that we shy away from trying to be factual. Unless you acknowledge the problem, you can't get there. We do acknowledge the problem. But you don't have to personalize it. I would say one thing I find about the Catholic church is that they tend to... it can to get to be very ad hominem very quickly.

Restricted as the focus of the Roundtable might seem, "the temporalities" cover a good deal of ground. Some of this—for example, the notoriously segmented territoriality of diocesan organization that impedes the diffusion of change—constitutes a structural property of the church. Other problems—the demoralization of clergy and lay workers—are hazier.

The response of the Roundtable to both kinds of challenges has been to set actionable initiatives in motion. At one of the earliest Roundtable gatherings in Philadelphia, Boisi could be seen, a set of instructional DVDs on parish management in hand, announcing to anyone who would listen that "We have a product!" The strategy plunged past objections that Roundtable types were foisting inappropriate gimmicks on the church.[27]

Boisi is emphatic about doing what many in the Roundtable's top echelon do best: deal making. The underlying problem is seen as a lack of coordination and feedback between projects that show turnaround potential. Innovators toiling in isolation need to be put in touch with other creative individuals and with leaders who have the wherewithal to green-light imaginative concepts.

"We've made it our business," Boisi says, "to get to know and gain the respect of the executive committee of the United States Conferences of Catholic Bishops." Kerry Robinson has been invited to be an observer at the general assemblies of the USCCB, and the Roundtable keeps in touch with the heads of the umbrella associations for men and women in religious orders—the Jesuits, the Sisters of Charity, and so on.

Deal making—matchmaking would be a less histrionic and in some cases more accurate term—has begun to show promise when brought to bear on the plight of Catholic schools:

> We went around and started asking different people, "What's your biggest problem right now?" We'll have a dozen suggestions but one of them is always related to the education thing. And then they said, "Could you help us?" We said, well, we're not experts in education but what we are pretty good at is bringing leaders together and developing an action plan to deal with it. Some really smart, really high-energy, proactive people had a lot of great ideas, and were doing good things in their area, and making presentations, and so forth. But we found out when we started monkeying around in this whole area that [people in] the church didn't communicate very well with each other. There was no consistent leadership.

Networking gathers momentum from the mingling of dispersed Catholic educators; it also brings in secular philanthropists and members of government eager to find ways to reboot the K–12 system.[28] What was an oncoming train wreck within the church turns out to be a crossover crisis.

> There are some very significant non-Catholic philanthropists who recognize the efficacy and the contribution of the Catholic parochial approach to the schools. On the other hand, people are increasingly recognizing that the financial model of the parochial school system is broken. With the dwindling participation of the laity, the aging of the laity, and the fact that many of the kids who are going to Catholic schools are non-Catholic, there's sort of an existential question going on about what the Catholic community's commitment to the parochial school system should be.

The schools in the inner cities, what's left of them, risk losing the patronage of suburban Catholics while becoming too expensive for non-Catholic minorities who need them most. "I happen to think that we're crazy to abandon something that has been one of the great contributions of the Catholic church to the United States over the last hundred years."

There are the the nuts-and-bolts problems, complex in themselves, of the schools. The schools in turn are the focus for the application of general how-to principles. These are the best practices, analogous to operating procedures from a military manual or engineering text. The two facets, the specific and the formulaic, inch toward solutions by way of feedback between networkers and field experiments, filtered through whatever test results become available. That, in theory, is the drill.

Framed as a set of problems to be solved rather than an insider puzzle to be deciphered, the fate of the schools attracts the interest and the resources of non-Catholics. The ecumenical threshold is comparable to the one reached by Catholic neoconservatives on their way to rallying adherents around a moral crusade, across a field wider than an inner circle of concerned faithful. Yet school reform remains a challenge in marketing and coalition building in and outside the church. "It wasn't part of the Latino culture to go to a private school because they viewed it as elitist. So you have only 3 percent of the Latino kids participating in Catholic school education." These families, Boisi argues, have to feel more like stakeholders.

> There has to be some education there. Because if you can't get the Latino community bought into this, you'll have a really tough time. There have been some breakthroughs in terms of vouchers and tax relief and what not. But there has to be movement on both sides, from the Catholic leadership as well as the government leadership.[29]

Boisi has an inchoate vision that elevates the crisis and the solutions-in-the-making for it into a cause. He ratchets up his perspective from the Catholic scene toward a nationwide predicament compounded by the decline of parochial education.

> It's clear that we [Catholic schools] have been sending more kids to college than anybody else. Now people are really seriously worried about the competitiveness of the United States. You cannot allow the parochial school system

> in the United States to devolve into bankruptcy. This may be a moment in time when we need another Council, like the one held back in the late 1880s in Baltimore, to recommit the Catholic community in the United States to resolve all that.[30]

The challenge is not purely or even mainly technical. The hurdle to overcome is bewilderment in the face of bad news, the discouragement and loss of nerve, that build a crescendo of pessimism. "You're talking about a quarter of the population of the United States, at least nominally," Boisi insists.

> To be honest with you, I feel like my basic supposition is coming true in the sense that it is having an impact. Not just because of what's gone on in the Catholic church. I think risk taking in the United States has been affected by terror, by our financial problems, by the recognition of our structural excesses.

Here Boisi struggles, trying to choose his words carefully.

> But when your spiritual world is discombobulated, that's an underlying term to risk taking. We as a country can't afford to allow that to take place because that's the engine that drives America. And if a quarter of the population is subliminally being negatively impacted, as an American you can't let that happen. And so when I go out talking about that, people get that.

Boisi joins a strategic addendum to his vision of a mutually beneficial interaction between the parochial and public school systems. While most Catholic elementary schools are still attached in one way or another to parishes and dioceses, the parishes also run an assortment of other programs that lie beyond the Roundtable's reach. Religious worship is one. "When you talk about influencing your overall church, the parishes and diocesan levels are the key areas," Boisi says. "But if you can't get at that in an organized way, or if it's slow, there are other ways.

> When you talk about the numbers, and how Catholics interact with what I would call the real church, the Catholic Action–oriented part of the church, it's through religious orders, it's through the education system, the health care system, through welfare. That's where the Good Samaritans operate.[31]

The outreach ministries are more amenable to reform than the cultic features of the church. "How does one apply performance evaluations to Bible study classes?" one diocesan planning director asked. Efforts along these lines might get the Roundtable mixed up in doctrinal or symbolic squabbles. A penchant for tribalism, a conviction that each parish is unique, are also obstacles. But to the extent that the schools, health care operations, and other concrete appendages of the parishes all deliver tangible services comparable to the work of their secular counterparts, they might respond to rational algorithms. This is what Boisi means by the "Catholic Action-oriented part of the church." And because they are tethered less tightly to the local government of the church and not quite so strictly under the thumb of the bishops, the religious orders have shown flexibility and promise of innovation.

A possible downside of the Roundtable's strategy is that it may draw resources away from softer, less quantifiable activities. The fear is that the parishes, while relieved of the legacy cost of the schools, will be bypassed like so many gas stations and grocery stores on back roads near the Interstate. "The emphasis is on marketing and management skills," Mark Mogilka, a Midwestern diocesan official who agrees with much of what the organization does, warns.

> Though the Roundtable didn't quite come out and say it, it was about wrestling the school away from the parish and diocese. You develop a mission statement for the school, recruit the top legal and finance people. Then you go to the big donors and you raise a lot of money. Our parishes are not the best at keeping and nurturing talent anyway. Now explain to me the impact once the schools are taken away from the parishes. You take the talent and the money away from the parishes. God help them.[32]

But the Roundtable has taken up the problems of the parishes, albeit indirectly. The summer training program in management for young priests is an example. Mogilka recognizes the Roundtable's quandary: "For the Roundtable to tackle parish reform probably would take them from their strength, the business side of the church—management, finances, and human resources—and would incur resistance from the bishops. It would almost be like having a carpenter try to tell fishermen how to fish."[33]

One parish problem remains off limits for the Roundtable: the prohibition against ordaining women and married men. This is the structural deficiency that impedes overcoming the shortage of priests. But lifting that restriction would do almost nothing to relieve the problems facing the schools, already lay dominated and expensive to run. Here the Roundtable sees not only a need but an opening, since malaise about education is shared across denominational lines.

The truly formidable obstacle to making serious headway with the schools is political. The economic magnitude of the school crisis surpasses the resources of private philanthropy. Without substantial infusions of public money more closings will have to take place. Whatever their reservations about the Roundtable's pedagogical expertise, groups like the National Catholic Education Association generally stand behind the Roundtable's objectives. Donors, Catholic and non-Catholic, are lined up in support. The Roundtable has the contacts and the financial heft to influence the larger policy debate. It is the constitutional status of government aid to the schools that is problematic. They hover in a no man's land, technically too religious to qualify for public funding, yet with enough utility for the educational system as whole to tempt civil authorities to reconsider the old protocols separating church and state.

"Moving the needle," to use terminology favored by the Roundtable, is a venture in changing public policy in an extremely delicate area. It involves the promotion of tax credits and more controversially the diffusion of voucher systems. Only seven states and the District of Columbia allow voucher programs, and only seven have tax credit policies in place. The strategy may also include devising hybrid models, like the conversion of Catholic to charter schools, which since their introduction in the 1980s have usually been looked upon as rivals to the parochial system. In addition, public school teachers' unions are reluctant to countenance what they see as moves to muscle in on their territory and, more seriously, to violate traditional understandings of the separation of church and state.[34]

Political complexity is compounded by the fact that the number of Catholic schools, once in an overwhelming majority, has shrunk to the point where they represent only one in five non-public schools.[35] The remainder is made up of a menagerie of secular and variously religious (including evangelical) enterprises, some of them with less than sterling credentials.[36] The constituencies with a stake in private-school funding are more heterogeneous than the already diverse coalition between Catholic and non-Catholic benefactors. And it is unclear how uniformly Catholics themselves may back public funding for the system as the number of parishes with direct obligations to parochial schools declines to less than a majority of parishes. School reform as envisaged by the Roundtable has something of a daredevil air.[37]

For eight years, before she became director of the Roche Center for Catholic Education at Boston College in 2010, Patricia Weitzel-O'Neill was superintendent of Catholic schools in Washington, DC. These were difficult times for the archdiocese. About 28,600 students were enrolled in the system when she left, a decline of almost 15 percent from the time she had taken over. She also presided over the creation of a voucher program and the conversion of seven inner-city Catholic schools to charters.[38]

Vouchers were popular with low-income families. Weitzel-O'Neill recalls the testimony of parents at meetings of the city council: "We parents have the opportunity to be with other parents who really care about their children's education and to learn from them and be supported by them, because the environment that we're in, you know, the neighborhood, not everyone is supporting the child succeeding in school." But school choice fostered divisions among card-carrying Catholics that required careful handling.

> We had individuals, when the voucher program began, there were families who did not want poor kids in the schools with their kids. These weren't wealthy families, these were middle-class families who said "I worked really hard to come up with the tuition dollars for my child to go to this school. I don't think it's fair." That's when you have to say, "Let's talk about what it means to be a Catholic school. We're here to serve all of God's children."

Vouchers became a political football at still another level. "What didn't work," Weitzel-O'Neill says, "was the bad behavior of the adults on the Hill."

> The level of political rancor, the lack of understanding of the politicians about the value of giving the family a choice, to choose the school that best fits the needs of

> their son or their daughter, was baffling and continues to baffle me. I know that the politicians are beholden to the unions, but this is not something that is going to take away from public schools. If anything is taking away from [conventional] public schools, it's the charter schools. The traditional public school is being replaced right now by the charter schools. We all know that. There are 5,600 charter schools now in the United States, and they're going to continue to grow.[39]

The Catholic schools that were converted to charters, Weitzel-O'Neill emphasizes, are no longer religious; they are fully public. Even so, "successful charter schools are modeled after Catholic schools, and nobody says that out loud. You walk in and you feel like you're in a Catholic school. What's present is a value-laden culture where respect for one another and discipline and integrity, they're real and they're played out. A real sense of self-discipline and focus. What's missing is the Catholic identity."[40]

Converting more than half a dozen Catholic schools to charters was a Solomonic decision. "If we could only afford four or five schools," Weitzel-O'Neill says,

> which four or five schools should they be and what would happen to the other schools?
>
> The choice we faced was, okay, I'm really sorry, your child is just going to have to go to a failing school. Michelle Rhee [DC school chancellor from 2007 to 2010], when she was testifying before Senator Durban's committee, told him "Do not ask me to stand in front of a parent whose kids are currently enrolled in Catholic schools in the archdiocese, who have vouchers, and tell them I have good seats for them, because I don't. They are located in the neighborhoods where our failing schools are." So it's like Sophie's choice. I'm going to have to cut loose a certain number of schools, for the sake of saving four. At least we can put them in a situation where they know they won't drown.[41]

After a decade in the trenches, Weitzel-O'Neill takes the view that significant taxpayer support for Catholic schools is "very far down the road."

> Individuals will suggest to you that Catholics should just take the money from the public sector and have schools that are value-based, period. People say you could be a charter school and then after school at the end of the day you could teach

> religion and still call yourself a Catholic school. Well, no, you can't. That's not an authentically Catholic school.

Compromise here would exacerbate what Weitzel-O'Neill terms "mission confusion." The phrase caught the attention of her audience when she used it in a keynote address to a conference of Catholic educators in Chicago in 2009, and that led to collaboration with a task force, "National Standards and Benchmarks for Effective Catholic Elementary Schools." The project coordinated its work with the National Catholic Educational Association. After vetting by an assortment of bishops, "domain experts," and "other key stakeholders," the document was released early in 2012.[42]

"There was a lack of understanding," Weitzel-O'Neill insists, "on the part of the general public, people on the Hill that I had been lobbying for the vouchers, donors, people who worked for the charter schools, people in Annapolis where we were working on the tax credit legislation. People don't know what makes a school Catholic. Is it a parish? Is it because there are religious groups sponsoring it?" Catholics are puzzled themselves.

> Why it is so hard to come to an agreement on the mission and stay with it? Why do we get pulled away from it? Well, you got forces... people will say if you take this money and don't adhere to your mission, then I'll give you more money. That's the draw of the charter money.

The standards establish a template. They are a response to the decades-long laicization of Catholic elementary and high schools, experimentation with and proliferation of various types of governance and financing arrangements between parishes, dioceses, and donors, and the political instability and dim prospects of widespread public subsidies. The document profiles an emphatically Catholic school. It is "a school that controls its values."

> Respect for others is based on the gospel, on the way Jesus behaved and what Jesus taught us. Catholic identity is integrated across the curriculum. It's something that you talk about in all subjects. Sacraments are practiced, Mass is attended by all students. In a Catholic school, a teacher can simply turn to a child and say, "Juanita, Sammy, we know you're really angry with each other but what would Jesus do right now?"

Of the nine defining characteristics envisioned for the effective, authentic Catholic school, the first is that it be "centered in the person of Jesus Christ"; the final attribute is that it be "established by the expressed authority of the bishop." On the other hand the declaration does not envision an infusion of nuns and clerics into the staff. The spirituality of the enterprise is supposed to be lay-driven.

In John DiIulio's terms, this is a faith-saturated model, whose primary source of funding has to be private under prevailing readings of the Constitution. The financial implication is a loss of potential revenue that requires explaining among educators at the grass roots, even with the endorsement of the National Catholic Education Association. Where will the money come from? A limited number of quality schools could be sustained; whether they could make a dent on the entrapment of the urban poor on a large scale is another matter. Tax credits for parents and corporations might supplement tuition and direct philanthropic contributions. Advocates can press this strategy on a state-by-state basis.[43] But vouchers run the political risk of having such schools denounced as boutique ventures that drain resources from public education.[44]

CHAPTER THIRTEEN

IN THE LABYRINTH

One day the man emerged from sleep as though from a viscous dream, looked up at the hollow light of the evening (which for a moment he confused with the light of dawn), and realized that he had dreamed... He understood that the task of molding the incoherent and dizzying stuff that dreams are made of is the most difficult work... To be not a man but the projection of another man's dream—what incomparable humiliation, what vertigo![1]

The Roundtable has succeeded in getting some of the bishops to talk with more of the laity, at least with the laity they feel have the appropriate credentials, and it has helped these notables to talk more regularly with one another. Agreement on the overall mission—improving the material performance of the church—acts as an ordering principle, setting a tone rather than establishing a consensus. Compared to the simultaneous atomization and polarization of much of American Catholicism, connectedness of this sort imparts some hope of accomplishment.

The network is as much a culture as an institution. Friendly prelates advised the promoters of the Roundtable at the outset not to seek recognition as an officially Catholic organization. The task was to establish the group's usefulness. The idea was to leverage the resources of the well disposed and the well intentioned to everyone's advantage. Much depended on relationships between personalities whose prime assets were their reputations and connections. "You have certain leaders," Boisi notes, "like Archbishop [now Cardinal] Dolan. A lot of this is personality driven. You have some people who are recognized in the practicalities, in picking up ideas that are necessary. If it's coming from the laity," Boisi adds unabashedly, "people have to start listening—particularly if it's coming from the laity that are providing the support."[2]

Geoffrey Boisi made his name in the seventies and eighties as a master of the "tender defense," business-speak for maneuvers that protect companies from hostile takeovers. Goldman Sachs affirmed its policy against encouraging clients to pursue unsolicited acquisitions, and Boisi was Goldman's point man in finding ways to stick to this commitment while increasing revenues. The policy paid off. As the merger-and-acquisitions movements swept through Wall Street, more and more businesses came under threat and found reasons to retain the services of Boisi and his partners. "With its refusal to take hostile takeover assignments, while its major competitors had all joined in that highly profitable business," Charles Ellis writes, "Goldman Sachs repositioned itself as the trustworthy friend of corporations and management and established investment banking relationships with more and more of America's largest and most prestigious corporations."[3]

In the eyes of church authorities, even those who know little about Boisi's financial exploits, the similarity between hostile takeover attempts and the ambitions of dissident groups seems plain enough. Both place corporations under siege. Three other lessons for his work at the Roundtable can be drawn from Boisi's experience in banking generally and handling takeover ventures in particular.

One is the value of determination, of standing by one's clients even when expediency might counsel otherwise. This is derring-do of a sort appreciated by portfolio managers. On the walls of Boisi's suite of soberly decorated offices on Park Avenue are large framed posters laying out the "five core principles that serve as [the] moral and intellectual guideposts" of Roundtable Investment Partners. "Integrity" comes first, "at the heart of all we do."[4]

Another is an insistence on managing complex ventures as ensemble operations. "This new business, defending companies from unwelcome predators," one analyst commented, "would require all the specialist skills the firm had and a much heightened emphasis on interdepartmental teamwork."[5] The Roundtable's attachment to information exchange and the coordination of notoriously stand-alone dioceses flows from this history. Lateral communication tracks along a different dimension from what institutional Catholicism is used to. The church, like all authoritarian systems, is not fond of transactions that run counter to or aslant top-down control.

A third lesson is counterintuitive. "The message is simple," Boisi and his team would tell prospective clients. "They should figure out what the raider would do and do it themselves."[6] Clients that have become objects of would-be takeovers have probably been targeted for a reason. Rather than remain on the defensive, the organization under siege should beat antagonists to the punch by way of preemptive reform. Staying one step ahead of rivals can be a sign of enlightened leadership—provided that the changes called for would in fact improve market share, offer better products less expensively, and perhaps increase employment.[7] Incumbents maintain control, and keep their jobs, by outflanking challengers and taking charge of selective concessions. "Let us make the revolution," Brazilian elites used to say, "before the people do."

Extending this reasoning to the work of the Roundtable and its relations with the church requires care. To some bishops, words like "appeasement" and "sell-out" come to mind. The closest analogy is with the system of diocesan review boards for monitoring cases of sexual abuse that the church was forced to adopt through legal pressure, a change with which the Roundtable as a body had nothing to do.[8] The Roundtable's advocacy of organizational modernization reflects a climate of opinion favoring proficiency in services as traditional fonts of human and financial resources dry up. Such eat-your-spinach recommendations can scarcely be called adversarial demands. The alternative, possible collapse through obsolescence and penury, seems worse.

The analogy becomes tenuous, however, when the question turns from getting rid of bad bureaucratic habits to issues like lifting the ban on the ordination of married men and women generally. This would eliminate the demographic cul-de-sac of a celibate male priesthood. But convention and adherence to an age-old theology outweigh cost efficiencies. The fear is not only that newcomers would gain power at the expense of an old guard; the suspicion is that the entire edifice would fold were the ornaments of identity abandoned.[9] "The sacramental life of the church in the United States is going to be severely impacted," Boisi admits. The status quo is not sustainable. "If you really want to solve a problem, there are ways to solve the problem. You can solve it pretty quickly. You just have to stand up to it."

Though Boisi would not put it so baldly, the bishops are the Roundtable's chief clients, and the faithful are the customers of the bishops. (Benefactors are stakeholders. There are no citizens in the equation, except in a roundabout way.) The client is still in charge. A certain evasiveness, as well as a culture of confidential deals and side understandings, prevails over collective leadership. "Would I like it," Boisi asks, "if those seventy bishops [the number estimated to have informally backed the Roundtable's program] got together and said, 'Look, these people have proven themselves? Let's do everything we can to support it. And let's go and get this job done.'"

> If all these levels of clerical leadership would actually, instead of being individually supportive, would just be institutionally supportive—they're moving more and more in that direction—we could get a lot more things done.

When Chuck Geschke addressed an audience at Santa Clara University on "my life as an engineer," he gave a presentation about the growth of Adobe Systems, one of the legendary success stories of Silicon Valley. The company that he cofounded in the 1980s earned him, besides a fortune, international acclaim for his role in spearheading a revolution in desktop publishing.[10]

Geschke, whose father and grandfather worked as printers, grew up in Ohio and spent three years as a Jesuit seminarian, then left to finish an undergraduate degree in Latin. Soon he was married, children were on the way, and his other intellectual passions, math and engineering, kicked in. This was during the late sixties and early seventies, and government funds unleashed in response to the launching of Sputnik back in the fifties enabled Geschke to complete his doctorate at Carnegie-Mellon in Pittsburgh. Before long, he and his family had moved to Silicon Valley. He became one of the ARPA brats, bright young scientists and engineers spread across research universities and their start-up satellites under the auspices of the Advanced Research Projects Agency. The venture was designed to cut through bureaucratic torpor and the isolation of lone specialists. One creation it developed would become known as the Internet.

This freewheeling environment steeped Geschke in the virtues of open exchange and recruitment by merit. It also sharpened his confidence in standing up to entrenched interests. When he was still working for Xerox, the company dragged its heels at the printing system that he and his coworker John Warnock had under development.

> We invited all the Xerox executives to come and take a look at what we were doing. Their body language was like this: arms folded. You didn't need a Ph.D. to figure out this is not good. They could not wait to get out of that room. They were afraid of it, they didn't understand it, and all they could figure out is, oh God, I'm going to lose my job![11]

By the summer of 1981 Geschke and his colleagues has put together InterPress, a precursor to PostScript. Their dream was to synchronize everything from design through dissemination; the system would revolutionize the mechanics of printing and publishing. Geschke flew to Xerox headquarters in Stamford, Connecticut. "I said I wanted to talk to people about how we're going to market this."

> They said, "Really? You know, at Xerox, it takes seven years to bring out a product. We start talking about this, all our competitors will beat us to the market place.'
>
> I said, "You're kidding."
>
> They said, "No."
>
> I said, "Well, in our industry, that's two to three to four generations. By the time you bring this stuff out, it'll be so obsolete that it'll be irrelevant."
>
> "No, seven years it takes."[12]

By the end of 1982, Geschke and his partner had left Xerox, and Adobe Systems opened for business.

Geschke is a major benefactor of Catholic institutions, including the Jesuit-sponsored University of San Francisco, where a daughter matriculated, and he takes part in his parish council, besides serving on the board of the Leadership Roundtable, where he is one of the more outspoken advocates of reform. He is the only board member to sport a beard. Typically, he goes without a tie. He is not beset with reticence in the face of existential crises. In 1992 he was kidnapped at gunpoint from the Adobe parking lot and held for ransom. The FBI freed him after four days of captivity, and the kidnappers received life sentences.

When I asked Geschke how the Roundtable was doing, he replied cryptically that "it's a bit hit and miss. The church keeps spending money on things it shouldn't be spending money on." A while later he emailed me a list of specifics "in no particular order" but one that was clearly headed by the Roundtable's preoccupation with poor management:

> The organizational structure—one out-of-touch CEO with 31,178 direct reports each of whom he sees roughly once every five years—makes no sense. Perhaps when the church was constrained to a few countries in what is now Western Europe during the tenth century, this could work. But not now.[13]

The church, Geschke added, has "several [other] major problem areas [and] failure to address them is no longer an option if it wishes to recapture my children and attract my grandchildren." The list tears into the gender stratification and sexual interdictions propagated by the church.[14]

- No women serving as priests is totally unacceptable in the twenty-first century. A woman pope would have nipped the pedophilia in the bud. Raising John Paul II to sainthood when he totally ignored the situation is an embarrassment.
- Our current pastor at St. Nicholas in Los Altos is a grandfather. One of the best priests we have ever had in a parish. Let's pay the priests (male and female) a living wage and let them marry.
- Sex is not the only, and certainly not the most important, sin. Abortion is totally abhorrent, but prohibiting birth control is just plain stupid. Women in the clergy would have figured this out long ago.
- Homosexuality is not a choice. God made (and loves) these people. Embrace them, don't shun them.

Then, for good measure, Geschke takes on the ten commandments. He opts for the Golden Rule:

> My problem with the ten commandments is that they're all negative. They all say, don't do this. Christ came around, he said there's really only two commandments: "Love the Lord your God with all your heart and with all your soul and all your mind, and love your neighbor as yourself." For me, that says it all.

The Roundtable speaks, like the Federal Reserve, with one temperate voice. Its board also encompasses different views about what ails the church. Some members are conflicted, and they do not fit the binary divide between "those who love the church and those who feel betrayed by it" that the Roundtable, in its brusquer moments, holds up as the standard of fidelity.[15]

"The Army is a global deferential hierarchy," James Dubik emphasizes. "So part of what I'm able to contribute is one other global deferential hierarchy's attempts to come to grips with large-scale transformation."[16] When he retired with three stars in 2009, Dubik was in a position to devote more time to the Roundtable. He lives just outside Washington. Besides serving on the board of the Roundtable, he holds the title of Senior Consultant to the organization.[17]

Dubik began methodically considering how to break down the pursuit of a generic "temporal excellence" espoused by the Roundtable into manageable components. To describe the way in which the Roundtable develops projects, he uses a word—"discernment"—inflected with religious associations.[18] The process goes through three stages. "The first stage is, you think about which of these ideas are consistent with our long-term mission of trying to help the church develop excellence in temporal management affairs, writ large."

> If it's a project that will in the near term or long term help the church either realize, understand, or execute temporal management affairs—and this is what you might call in the civilian world basic leadership in management—that's within the mission. Anything else, anything else outside that, that may help the church in one way or another—construction, or real estate, or something like that—might be completely important and legitimate. It's just not something we want to focus our time and effort on.

So, for example, the Roundtable might put a dioceses set on building a new high school in touch with potential donors, but it would not get directly involved in a project of that sort. Much less would it go near programs that bear on theological sore points.

> The second level of discernment is, okay, now we have an idea that we think is consistent, we think it would be good to do: Can we fund it? And we ask ourselves do we have the expertise within the Roundtable—members, board, and staff—to actually do this in a quality way? And if the answers to those questions are yes, then we go to the third level.

The third stage can be brief or protracted, but it typically adheres to a recognizable sequence.

> We put together a proposal for the board that lays out the issue, an overall concept or plan, our estimated cost in terms of dollars and staffing, a rough time line, and a rough kind of description of what we want at the end of the project. The executive board has a discussion. Many times, as a result of the discussion, the project is altered, for the better in my view. And then we go forth and try to find a donor.

Once the first hurdle is past, the second and third stages of discernment become eminently practical. The Roundtable learned not to debate foundational principles of the kind that came close to destroying Voice of the Faithful. This might mean over-thinking the issues.

The organization also seizes opportunities as they arise. Each year it takes on half-a-dozen or so consultancy jobs at the request of dioceses or religious orders. Some may be emergency operations, as in New Orleans or the economically distraught Camden diocese in New Jersey. The Roundtable collects fees for these services, but it typically spends more. Revenues from consulting help underwrite work on programs for dioceses that are eventually funded by donors. This is where the across-the-hall connection between the Roundtable and Foundations and Donors Interested in Catholic Activities (FADICA), the consortium of Catholic benefactors, comes in handy.[19]

During its early years the Roundtable made a point of allaying the fears of bishops that, in Dubik's words, "we were anything else but the laity trying to help our church." One way of doing this was to put out fires, to act as first responders in cases of extreme distress. New Orleans after Katrina was the main instance. The other strategy was to "develop products"—the standards for excellence, performance evaluations, and the like—that parishes and dioceses might or might not adopt but that showed promise. "At least from my standpoint," Dubik says, "I don't see clear patterns."

> We're working with dioceses in California, in the Midwest, from the Southeast, in the Northeast, the Atlantic states, and the only common characteristic that I can see is an openness of the leadership. I don't mean just the bishop. There are the leaders around him, he's got pastors that are not really in senior-subordinate

> relationships the way ecclesiastical rule works [on paper]. It's the set of leaders in a diocese that are more open to innovation.

CatholicPastors.org is a website for priests Dubik modeled after one, "CompanyCommand," that he and his military colleagues developed for junior officers to improve their leadership skills through peer-to-peer feedback.[20] Two years of testing went into CatholicPastors.org.

> We got a bunch of priests together and they designed the prototype website. They identified the principles by which the website would operate. And then in the pilot program, we got some volunteer priests to exchange information to make sure the technology worked, that the format was right, that the space in which the discussion would take place was actually protected. And then once we did all that, we searched for a priest leader. That took longer than we anticipated. But we found a priest who volunteered to do this, and now it's going to be the slow process of expanding the number of members.

CatholicPastors.org, first of all, has the makings of a resolution to the scarcity-of-mentors problem in the priesthood. Rectories that once housed four or five priests now might have only one or possibly two; newly ordained priests are often on their own, and they are likely to become pastors much more quickly than in the old days. Second, the website provides a workaround for some of the pathologies of hierarchy. Peer-to-peer exchange is not supposed to threaten higher-ups. "Our overall MO," Dubik says, "is not to bang against closed doors, but to push against open doors." Third, the instrumentation is inexpensive, relative to the costs and time involved in on-site visitations. Fourth, the technology depends less on breakout moments than cumulative socialization. Twenty or twenty-five years down the road, as Dubik sees it, when clerical leaders-in-the making have moved up the hierarchy, the benefits for church management of communication among peers should become visible.

What changes like this cannot do is increase the number of priests in the pipeline. The recruitment conduit is still confined to celibate males.

> We're very fastidious about that. This is not a group of people who want to change in any way the clerical and lay arranged roles, but to emphasize what the encyclicals

> talk about in terms of lay contribution.... We're laser-focused on our mission.... We're very serious about moving forward in those areas where we and the church leaders think we can move forward. We're not a pie-in-the-sky group. And we're absolutely not some metaphysical organization. This is a business organization.

"We want to be connected to the divine," Dubik concludes, "but we're very, very practical."[21]

Michael Brough, a Scotsman, was recruited early on to the Roundtable from Renew International, a network of parish revitalization programs, where he served as executive director. He became director of planning and member services (retitled "director of strategic engagement") at the Roundtable, commuting to Washington from New Jersey, where he lives with his wife and three daughters. When I sent him a list of questions asking for an update on Roundtable operations, Brough returned a two-page single-spaced summary, then added "on re-reading this, it may appear too generic and boiler-plate, but hopefully it provides the 'big picture' of where we are at."

We went over the details in a phone interview.[22] The parishes, dioceses, and other religious groups who have signed on to the flagship Standards of Excellence program total somewhere north of 500. The number might seem large except for the fact that the denominator comes to about 19,000 such organizations—essentially, the sum of parishes nationwide, with the 195 dioceses that encompass them added in.

Why the slow pace? "What we've got is categories," Brough explains:

> If we go parish by individual parish, it will take us a very long time, and we won't get the majority of parishes. So if the dioceses come on board... you know how it works. The early adopters will say, "I'm for it." Then there are those who are opposed to anything like this. We hope to capture that huge group in the middle, which I'm sure can be, say, 70 or 80 percent, because other people are doing it, and because the diocese is recommending it, and because of access to resources.

Diffusion involves customizing. Parishes and dioceses like to pick and choose among the Roundtable offerings. "Some of them are saying, 'Look, we don't want to rush into this,'" Brough acknowledges. "'We want to take one step at a time.' Fine. Others are saying, 'We want to go with some piece of it.' So I think that's what we'll be able to capture for the next couple of years. I don't think we're there yet."[23]

What strikes Brough is the way dioceses of different sizes respond to the Roundtable. "We have not yet cracked what I would call a major metropolitan archdiocese," he says. "New York, Los Angeles, the Chicagos. These dioceses say, 'We are already doing this stuff, we already have huge departments responsible for this stuff, we don't need this.' We say to them, it's great you have this in place, share that with others, and that will help bring them along. We haven't given up on those large ones." Growth appears to lie among the lesser dioceses. "It's probably accurate to say that so far it's not the larger, it's the medium-size and smaller ones."

> The economic danger of the last couple of years, the hits they've taken: it may be their schools, for some of them it's their Catholic Charities, whatever it happens to have been. Or a growing diocese, some of them are growing like mad. "We are not set up to run this diocese," they'll say. We have an extra hundred thousand or an extra half a million coming in the next ten years—let's say Tennessee or North Carolina, or parts of Florida. Here they are coming to us and saying, "We recognize that we need to build capacity."

The largest dioceses, on the other hand, might be better able to afford a few of the more expensive Roundtable products like Catholic Leadership 360, a personnel evaluation package. "The chancellor, or vicar general, they'll come to us and they want to do leadership development. 'We don't want it across the board,' they'll say. But one of the particular programs or services that we have fills a gap that we sorely need taken care of. We've got some of the larger dioceses that pick up on things."

This takes the conversation to costs and funding. FADICA, next door to the Roundtable, has been "hugely supportive. We report to their board every time they meet. Many of the players, they're involved in both organizations. So that has been just tremendous."

But there are at least two limits to the interlocking directorates model. One reflects the fact that venture capitalists with a taste for high risk undertakings are rare in Catholic philanthropic circles.[24]

> It would be lovely to think that donors would bring the development phase along, and it would catch fire and run. In reality it's taken Catholic Leaders 360 and

> CatholicPastors.org a couple of years to get a level of awareness out there, a level of use and participation, a level of funding. They're not funding the development, they're funding the implementation of something, because they see it's got a track record that's fairly good.

As a result, the Roundtable relies "on a relatively small number of major donors, both individuals and Catholic foundations, and I would the add the Lilly Endowment to that."

The other departure from going back to the same well-stocked larder entails the pursuit of "sellanthropic dollars." Like many other such enterprises, the Roundtable finances part of its operations by charging fees. The strategy is motivated by organizational sustainability. "When it comes to being a non-profit, we're probably beyond the start-up stage now," Brough says. "But we're definitely still at the point where we have to go out and seek funding and donations.

The complementary rationale for sellanthropy is the rule that giveaways don't work.[25] "We do not want costs to be an obstacle to people participating. So anything that we can promote for free, on our website, we will do. The costs of something like Standards of Excellence, or CatholicPastors.org, are very, very minimal. The costs of the booklets, whatever."

> The flip side, though, is that we want dioceses to commit resources in church management and leadership development and best practices. Because, you know the church, there's been an expectation that we'll get it for free. And sometimes you get what you pay for, right? Sometimes it's a total waste. It's not a surprise you don't get returns.

Brough rises to his theme:

> If a parish or parishes put into practice our best practices, our Standards for Excellence, they will see larger donations. Over the years, if you're transparent in your fundraising, if you tell people what you're spending money for, what you're spending their last dollar on, then you will get larger donations. If you invest in your leaders, in your pastors, if you make sure that you've got this type of procedures in place, your human resources looked after, you won't find yourself being sued for firing somebody, or being embezzled, losing dollars that way.

Brough's comments about hiring and keeping qualified staff came about a month before serious cases of embezzlement hit the New York and Philadelphia archdioceses.[26]

What else besides structural differences across dioceses and parishes, the diverse makeup of their leadership, and the caution of benefactors themselves might affect adhesion to the Roundtable way? The developmental arc of CatholicPastors.org is particularly intriguing. Though the project looks inexpensive and nonthreatening, the road to adoption has been slow. "Funding is not the issue," Brough says. "We got funding from an individual donor, we got a small grant from the Catholic Extension Society, that enabled us to develop the concept. We've secured three years' funding from the Lilly Endowment for a project coordinator and paying for the online platform and so on."

> What is taking time is finding the right priest-leaders for the overall project and then forum leaders for different subjects. Once you've got those in place, and that's happening now, with that in place, I think we'll move forward from the kind of numbers we have fairly quickly.

After a pause, Brough picks up the thread. He is careful to avoid words like "empowerment."

> One thing in my conversations with priests is that there's a generic caution that these forums be secure and safe and protected. And by that we mean that they're not going to be slammed for expressing opinions. This is not in any way a dissent thing, there is not in any way a betrayal. But there does seem to be a concern. And so I think until we have the conversations flourishing, and people can come on and see how the conversations are going, believe that they can make a contribution to it, we've not yet seen that, we've not got to that tipping point.[27]

Anything else? "What if Michael Brough had to summarize the toughest challenges facing the Roundtable, what would you say?"

"We are bringing about cultural change," Brough responds. "I think that's our biggest challenge right now."

> It's a generational thing, and it goes on at multiple levels. I think we can point to people talking about best practices, bringing some of those resources in, doing some good stuff. But I think what we'll ultimately be measured on is changing the culture. And that takes time, and that takes patience, and it takes guts, and it takes sustainable models for ourselves.

When Robert Bennett gave a talk to one of the first meetings of the Roundtable at the Wharton School, he had just come off his assignment as head of the National Review Board's task force looking into the sexual abuse of children. At the time the Review Board was composed entirely of lay people, and it had a free hand. In the Q & A after Bennett's presentation, one of the bishops in attendance remarked that the episcopate as a whole was being blamed for a scandal that was largely confined to one area. The entire church was being "Bostonized." Cardinal Law, the chief culprit, had settled in Rome, where he was put in charge of a basilica. The implication was that if the Cardinal hadn't been punished, he was at least neutralized.

"Well," Bennett responded, "he's not just going around lighting candles."

Bennett's reputation for pugnacity goes back a long way. After studying at Georgetown and Harvard and serving as a federal prosecutor in the District of Columbia, Bennett gained national prominence as a trial lawyer specializing in white-collar criminal cases. By the mid-1980s his clients included Clark Clifford, Washington wise man and counselor to presidents, and Defense Secretary Caspar Weinberger. In the 1990s he became Bill Clinton's personal attorney in the Paula Jones case. Bennett is the lawyer people want to have by their side at the Last Judgment.[28]

When we got together in his Washington office, close by the Reagan Building off Columbia Square, Bob wanted to reminiscence about old times. We had been classmates at Brooklyn Prep, a Jesuit school in Crown Heights, now (since the early seventies) Medgar Evers Community College.[29] The 1957 yearbook dubbed him "The Demosthenes of Brooklyn" for his accomplishments on the debate team. "It was the time of my life when I could have gone this way or that way. I learned more in those four years at Brooklyn Prep, it had more impact on my life than anything. It was a golden age."[30]

Times have changed:

> The pedophile crisis hit so close to the bone, it was just so outrageous that people were willing to take it on. Prosecutors are willing to go after the church. Before, they heard there was a fraud case, some Irish cop would go and talk to the bishop or the pastor and straighten it out. It was an extension of the priest who gets drunk and the cops drive him home and don't charge him with driving while intoxicated. That happened in Brooklyn all the Goddamned time. But when you start messing around with kids, it crosses the line.

Part of the reason, in addition to lawyerly discretion, for his hesitation about holding forth on Catholicism is that Bennett has distanced himself from church affairs. (When the bishops conference invited him to head the sexual abuse task force, he replied, "Don't you want my brother Bill, the moral one?")[31] "I'm sure kids are much safer today in the church than they ever were," Bennett emphasizes. "They were sort of forced into it, the bishops. Things were so bad they had to do something, so they called in this lay review board, and I don't know that they expected us to be as honest as we were. We certainly gave them a playbook. But in fairness to them, I have not gone back to see how well they've carried it out."

The magnitude of wrongdoing astonished the lay board. "To a person we were shocked at what we found. Everybody was hoping, including myself, that we would have found that this was exaggerated by the press. But all of us were sick about it, I mean really sick about it." In the course of preparing the report, Bennett got to know David Clohessy, SNAP's national director. "The positive thing is that SNAP has kept it up. They're always available to talk to the press, they've kept things on the front burner, and I think that that was to the good.

"But my experience with them, as happens probably with a lot of organizations, they become institutionalized and they go too far. I said, 'David, you know just once maybe, you should say the church did something right. Just once you should say that was a really good report.' I'm not saying it should be enough, like there's no more problem. But it was never enough. It would always be, you know, almost justifying their existence. And I think they lost a lot of effectiveness. They certainly lost effectiveness with me."

Bennett's service on the review board left him skeptical about elements in the hierarchy as well. "They're both closed clubs," Bob says, referring to the US Senate, whose Ethics Committee he helped put in place, as well as the church.[32] "They [the bishops] get a lot of credit for having the review board and this investigation. But they were both, Senate and church, forced into it, and the bishops didn't do that much with the results of our report. That's my sense of it. I don't think it's in their *gut* to do it."

At the end of the day, Bennett reasons, "we didn't have the authority to fix anything. The church has been around for a couple of thousand years and they figure, this'll pass too. It's that attitude."

> It's such a secret society, the church. It's so closed. I think the great tragedy, the great tragedy of the church, I really think, is that there are so many lay people who would love to really get in there and help. I still contribute to Catholic causes, and that's how my wife and I have sort of reached an accommodation with our past. But God gave me a brain and reason, and I just can't... There's always a piece of you, no matter how angry you are, you see a collar, you know, there's an automatic...

Bennett rubs something invisible on the table, then flicks it away. The conversation switches back to old times. He is so notorious for interjecting lavish praise of his three daughters into trial proceedings that judges regularly indulge his arch non sequiturs. "We used to live in Arlington when they were little, and we had an incredibly conservative bishop who said girls couldn't be altar girls. My Peggy, I remember, now a lawyer, said 'Daddy, why can't I be an altar girl?' What do you say? 'Well, the bible says something...' So we don't."

If the launching of the Leadership Roundtable required doctrinal uniformity, the organization would never have gotten off the ground. The diplomatic solution has been to avoid theological discussion; here, aside from the occasional *sotto voce* remark, the Roundtable keeps mum. Since the lid cannot be kept on all the time, certain procedures come into play to contain recurrent tension. Most simply, energies are directed elsewhere. The clearest priority is "a laser focus" on projects with potentially measurable payoffs on which managerial expertise, regardless of ideology, can be brought to bear. Metrics can be applied. CatholicPastors.org and the Toolbox for Pastoral Management typify such undertakings.

A related approach searches out projects that aim to expand the institutional pie rather than redistribute power within the organization directly. The earliest Roundtable program of this sort, ChurchEpedia.org, promoted a fairly unstructured exchange of information about managerial innovation; the format has since morphed into about half a dozen task-specific online discussion groups, each assigned a monitor to help keep debate on topic. All along, the objective has been to oxygenate a system whose components had grown stale for lack of a circulation of ideas.

A more recent pair of ventures—the Catholic Philanthropic Leadership Consortium and the Catholic Investment Partnership—are designed to pool economic resources—financial capital—rather than information alone. The scope is projected to be nationwide. "Catholic institutions are badly underfinanced," Boisi points out. Except for one or two of the very largest dioceses, almost no Catholic organizations come close to an economic threshold capable of attracting world-class wealth managers, as Yale, Harvard, the Carnegie Corporation, and some branches of Judaism and major Protestant denominations have done. The task is to coordinate the growth of assets for dioceses, parishes, and charitable works with wildly divergent resources and needs. The goal, according to Boisi, is to make the Partnership "the investment option of choice for the Catholic market."[33]

A third major route involves the parochial schools. Advocates remind policy makers that the system contributes billions of dollars to the nation as a whole by educating children who would otherwise have to be handled by an overburdened public school system.[34] Many Catholic primary schools perform well when compared to their publicly funded counterparts in poor neighborhoods.[35]

But the economics of primary school education are daunting even for the grandest philanthropic investments, and constitutional principles make it difficult to direct state funds toward schools defined as "pervasively religious." Forging alliances with legislators is a grueling undertaking. Nevertheless, the priority given by the Roundtable to gathering non-Catholic and public support for the hard-pressed parochial school system signals a certain coming-of-age. The organization has enough initiatives in place or on their way to consolidation to launch a genuinely tall-order project that reaches beyond the church itself. The problem is not one of avoiding this or that sensitive spot in the doctrinal canon but of redefining traditional relations between church and state.

The campaign is as much ideological as technical. The Wall Street adage that "who has the gold rules" becomes a necessary but not a sufficient condition for success. The need is for money (and expertise), but the quandary becomes genuinely complicated for reasons deep in American political culture. The problem is traceable to strict wall-of-separation readings of a constitutional theory that sets the United States apart from other democracies in which governments are freer to underwrite denominationally affiliated schools.

Much of the problem, but not all. As with the church's reluctance to yield on the question of clerical celibacy despite evidence that relinquishing the tradition could alleviate the shortage of priests, concrete interests and ingrained customs also enter into the task of turning the Catholic schools around. Unions, "Blaine amendment laws" written long ago into more than thirty state constitutions that inhibit the use of public monies for "sectarian education," off-and-on concern among Catholics themselves, as well as the odd imperious declaration by one or another bishop all condition the course of reform. So does skepticism about the motives of wealthy backers behind the push toward privatization in school policy. The politics are inextricable from the principle of the thing.[36] The stalemate is not simply between rational problem solving and irrational tradition, whether religious or secular.[37] Politics, too, has its logic. "Sometimes," Bob Bennett is fond of saying, "you have to rise above principle."

PART SIX

CONCLUSION

Complete tone-deafness is probably as rare as the possession of absolute pitch. The problem was... that... he proved to be morbidly insensitive to any auditory proportions and perhaps because of that was incapable of listening to others or hearing himself properly.[1]

What has endured in American Catholicism since the 1960s? What has changed?

The identity of the institutional church, defined in terms of its sexual culture and its views on male authority and the role of women, has remained intact since Vatican II. Catholicism has drawn a red line round traditional family structures and the celibate male priesthood. Regardless of actual practice among Catholics and others, the sexual canon has barely yielded ground. Upholding the value of the male-female nucleus of domesticity and parenthood represents a triumph of preservation. Traditional family values persist as a warning beacon among rival practices.

On the other hand, a visitor from the 1950s would be hard-pressed to recognize many of the ministries associated with the church as Catholic. Some of the changes—the separation of the colleges, universities, and hospitals from their founding religious orders—have been deliberate. The attenuation of Catholic-with-a-capital-C identity came about as an unanticipated by-product of this initiative and of other causes such as population shifts. Clericalism has subsided in the church's satellite operations. Few priests are active in secondary and higher education, few nuns serve in the parochial schools and hospitals, and the clientele of both is increasingly non-Catholic. Tribalism has been diluted through exogamy, education, and economic necessity. Catholicism has become demographically more catholic with a small c. At the same time, because their lay employees are predominantly stalwart practitioners, the climate of some services (elementary school education, for example) remains palpably Catholic, despite the decline in nuns and clerical personnel. On the whole, whatever the strength or infirmity of their religious character, the performance of church-related organizations is more professional.[2]

The internal politics of the church ranges between battles over corporate identity, centered on clerical dominance and sexual stasis, and the chores of fund-raising and problem solving in the ministries, where the hold of the bishops is generally weaker. Priests, their numbers greatly reduced, still get the last word in parish governance. The ministries are a gray area. They get more input—more advice and de facto consent—from the laity.

Deference lingers along with dissent, modulated by cynicism and apathy. Many progressives, their ranks aging, their expectations dashed at the retrenchment following Vatican II, feel defeated. Alienation is mostly quiet and apolitical. Catholics understand that they have options. Doctrine is not worth arguing about if personal choice is available at close to zero cost. A good deal of what was deviant has entered the mainstream. Now that the traditional mores built into pre-sixties neighborhoods have eroded, an unspoken entente regarding the no-nos of the magisterium is the norm. The episcopal stonewalling that greets organized dissent is reciprocated by a perception, pronounced among younger cohorts, of the irrelevance of institutional Catholicism. Acquiescence is remotely though tellingly analogous to the old crack about the Soviet system, whose citizens pretended to work for supervisors who pretended to pay them. Attendance at weekly Mass is down to around 20–25 percent of American Catholics.

By 2012, the approval ratings of the bishops were back up to prescandal levels. Most of the faithful seemed to be satisfied with the preventive measures that had been put in place. But there was still no evidence that, except for frequent church-goers, Catholics paid attention to the magisterium. Like an off-stage character in *Death of a Salesman*, the hierarchy is liked, but not well liked. Or they are like the Irish who, as the Irish themselves suspect, everyone likes and no one takes seriously.[3]

There is an irony here. Widespread distaste for sexual prohibitions that can be skirted on individual terms does not translate into an advantage for liberals in the church. Following the path of least resistance undercuts the capacity of the laity to act jointly on problems, like the refusal to open up the priesthood, that have collective ramifications and that require a strategic sense and organizing effort. Partly this is because there is real doubt whether organized action on the part of the laity challenging the customs that govern priestly ordination can change them under any circumstances. Low participation favors the status quo. Most Catholics find that they have other things to worry about. There is no politics in the ordinary sense. For many adherents, Catholicism remains a spectator rather than a participant religion.

So, while collective assaults on the sexual values of Catholicism almost always fail, their failure is supremely ambiguous. Orchestrated confrontation has been largely unnecessary to begin with. Catholic conservatives triumphed not only because they took the side of religious orthodoxy (and of popular revulsion against the sexual license of the sixties) but also because dissidents and their sympathizers had little incentive to argue a case that in practice, in the realm of everyday behavior impacting their lives, had already been won. Bystanders had it as good as activists, among whom empathy and a certain amount of mutual support, but not political efficacy, flowed. Abortion stayed on as a hot-button issue but not, or much less so, birth control and divorce. If concerted reform of the church's line on psychosexual matters did not happen, liberalization of sexual norms succeeded anyway—not as a result of deliberate strategy but as the outcome of "a million little schisms," a multiplicity of individual decisions swept up in a cultural tidal wave. The church stuck to its guns, but the bullets were mostly blanks. For their part, ordinary Catholics felt liberated rather than empowered.[4]

Apart from nuns-on-the-bus–style episodes, the remnants of organized liberalism in the church have concentrated mostly on matters of intramural gender roles—rules regulating priestly celibacy, the ordination of women, and so forth—that generate passion among a handful of activists.[5] Broader mobilization on these issues requires a popular connection with collective interests, an appreciation of institutional consequences and a sense of personal responsibility for them. The business-as-usual mode is an ergonomic, individually customized religious consumerism.[6]

Spontaneous rejection and self-interest do not suffice, as they have when ignoring the official condemnation of birth control, for organizational reform in the church. Support for the ordination of women is shallow; public "demand" is broad but not pressing; very few women themselves desire ordination. But in fact only a few thousand ordained women are needed to mitigate the priest shortage, and keeping a gag rule on the issue cannot improve the access of Catholics to religious observance.

What strategies of reform work?

Adversarial tactics have produced some results in cases of clergy sexual abuse. First Amendment rights still protect the church against reforms aimed at its internal organization, and in most states statute of limitation laws and lobbying for keeping them in place by church officials impede the prosecution of decades-old instances of sexual abuse. After some experimentation, the Survivors Network for those Abused by Priests concluded that it could not change the institutional church, certainly not without allies on the inside. SNAP turned its weakness into a strength. It became the quintessential outsider group.

SNAP seeks to force change in behavior, through the courts and media exposure rather than through transformation in the hierarchical structure of the church or its beliefs and culture. Popular mobilization, though desirable, is less important than establishing a judicial beachhead. "How do you build a critical mass? You don't need a critical mass," Barbara Blaine contends, "you need a case that gains publicity."[7] A few dioceses have had to pay out punishing settlements. Some predator priests have gone to jail. Such penalties have alerted the bishops to the costs of bureaucratic carelessness, and they have probably discouraged clerical child abusers from violating minors.

The effectiveness of the national and diocesan review boards set up by the bishops in response to the revelations of sexual abuse depends on the threat of legal sanctions by civilian authorities. The prosecution of predatory priests and their enabling supervisors in Philadelphia came about not through the diocesan review board, which was kept mostly in the dark, but by the actions of a grand jury.

Clerical behavior, not the organizational reconfiguration of the church, continues to be the target of SNAP's advocacy; its policy is one of containment rather than direct, in-house reform.[8] Since the First Amendment shields the church against having institutional change foisted upon it, the limits of SNAP's policy are not wholly a matter of choice. Whatever the reasons, the limits entail costs. Convinced by experience that it would lose whatever leverage it has by working on the inside to improve the performance of a habitually unforthcoming bureaucracy, SNAP burned that bridge long ago. Accusations that the church cannot act in good faith reinforce clerical hostility to any institutional overhaul it feels unable to influence or shape. The result is a downward spiral of mutual recrimination and contempt. The scenario begins to feel like a slide from lace-curtain Catholicism to Jacobean revenge tragedy. In more contemporary terms, the bishops seem about as trustworthy to many SNAP associates as the character played by the porcine Sidney Greenstreet in criminal melodramas from the '40s and '50s, patting the sweat from his neck, under a slowly turning fan, talking about "import–export" in sinister periodic sentences.

The bishops, feeling cornered, close ranks.[9] The hierarchy clings to the right to control the careers of priests, to reassign them more or less at will, and to hire and fire church employees in general. This is the same discretionary power that lay behind the cover-up of sexual abuse.

Nevertheless, the change initiated by SNAP represents a breakthrough. A turning point came in the summer of 2012. More than a reform of the church itself, the Philadelphia verdict against Msgr. William Lynn constituted a realignment in the balance of power between church and state. The conviction and sentencing of a senior church official for negligence in cases of child abuse concluded a battle not over sexuality but sovereignty. The church lost, as it did a few months later with the conviction of Bishop Robert Finn of Kansas City for essentially the same offense.[10]

SNAP wields a stick; the Leadership Roundtable offers a carrot. Selective institutional improvements have topped the agenda of the Roundtable. The signature Roundtable product is an organizational implant that works around rather than displaces existing arrangements. CatholicPastors.org, the peer-to-peer network set up to facilitate communication and information exchange among junior pastors, is among the most ingenious of these devices. Designed to bypass hierarchical monitoring altogether, CatholicPastors.org doesn't overtly threaten traditional authority, and it doesn't involve filling out forms. Yet it still has to overcome a culture of fear instilled by centuries of surveillance from higher-ups and their "sources." The innovation exemplifies the lateral communication among underlings and middle managers that hierarchical systems have always distrusted.[11]

Like SNAP, from which it otherwise differs, and unlike reform movements such as Voice of the Faithful, FutureChurch, or Call to Action, the Roundtable is not burdened with the task of forging an alternative Catholicism. It does not insist on doctrinal or politically sensitive options that would require a realignment of the permissible. For SNAP, the restriction boils down to treating Catholicism not as the object of an organizational makeover but as a chronic condition whose toxic effects are to be isolated and minimized. The illness is managed, not cured. The Roundtable's diagnosis is organizational backwardness rather than malignancy. A managerial turnaround is the order of the day. The anatomy of Catholicism can be reengineered.

It is indicative of the constraints surrounding the Roundtable's efforts that its leadership hesitates to use the words "institutional" and "reform." Its caution reflects an assessment of political reality, traceable to a managerial ethos, that sets "excellence"—efficiency and organizational trim—ahead of fairness. Consolidating parishes, for example, is justifiable to the degree that it is dictated by demographic flight more than by the unavailability of priests caused by Rome's refusal to ordain women and married men. Introducing gender equity into the recruitment channels of the church would be the practical thing to do under either diagnosis. But politically, the trade-off is obvious. Pressing a solution of this sort might jinx whatever progress is being made in other areas. Roundtable decision makers are finely tuned to the dilemma. "This is the right thing to do" is a refrain that comes up in reflective moments, "now pass the hemlock." In reality, the hemlock moment is put off.

Some element of justice is sacrificed in balance with prospective gains in efficiency. The calculus is not meticulously dispassionate; it comes trailing predispositions from business practice and a culture of success.[12] As much as actually setting things right, decisions need to exude sound judgment, to radiate an awareness of reasons of state, of how the world works. The posture is not unpopular. Catholics disposed to reform are weary of authoritarianism; they are also tired of losing. Under conditions of autocratic hierarchy, political wisdom regarding the chances of reform is thought to require a certain *froideur*. The Roundtable addresses what it gauges is within its reach to influence.

Spirituality melds with an analytical temper. "God," the neorealist theologian Reinhold Niebuhr prayed, "grant me the serenity to accept the things that cannot be changed, the courage to change the things I can, and the wisdom to know the difference."[13]

If there is a cultural transition in Catholicism, it is one that has stalled. The impasse is over sexual ethics, the rights of women, and the entanglement of both these questions with the permanence of male hierarchy as a constitutive element of church organization. These are the fundamentals. Stagnation on issues like women's ordination and the role of women in general has started to spill over from the symbolically dubious to the severely dysfunctional. The shortage of priests is acute.[14]

From a liberal perspective the transition has not only stalled, it has deteriorated. A policy of studied neglect regarding the delivery of contraceptive services by church-affiliated ministries has escalated into a controversy framed as a threat to religious autonomy, the Constitution, and the sovereignty of natural law.[15]

Among many Catholics reaction to the stand-off has been less like a tinderbox than a festering torpor. At the opposite end, there is the exile politics, intense but to all appearances ineffectual, of groups like Call to Action, Voice of the Faithful, and FutureChurch. At still another level, among the occasionally disgruntled associates of the Roundtable, the strategy is to nudge the church toward a meritocratic, relatively rational hierarchy.

Gradualism has its critics. Intransigence confined to sexual norms, the role of women, and male authority could be what makes efficiencies in the ministries possible while preventing the church from flying apart. It may keep Christianity's message of resurrection, redemption, and brotherly love from careening out of control. Without careful steering the church would be on a blind curve to eternity.

This is the ultra-conservative case, starkly put. The emblematic product of Catholicism is not really good works, however beneficial. Nor is it reasoned accommodation. It is the church's patrimony, and what makes the patrimony distinctive is sexual hierarchy and clerical authority. One is inextricable from the other. Cleaving to a sacred trust in the face of common sense, enlightened opinion, and similarly functional reasoning demonstrates that the church's primary realm is not of this world. The institutional church is a numinous avatar of eternal truths. It is a different category of reality, a Platonic empyrean. Bishops are curators of a priceless treasure. Gender hierarchy is a supreme cultural marker, the last inviolable tradition, the final taboo. This is what is unique about Roman Catholicism among the great religions of the West. The Gestalt evokes the specter of the Grand Inquisitor.[16]

An equally blunt version of the liberal position is that immobilism on this scale is not just wrong; it has become mean-spirited and self-destructive in the face of irreversible social change. When conservatives signal a willingness to follow their convictions or their interests off a cliff, they set up an ultimately suicidal bargaining position. A vindictive fixation on sex, gender, and patriarchal legitimacy shrinks the patrimony of the church to memories of a primordial fable.

The caveat to the liberal position is not that the argument against sticking with archaisms is untrue but that the future is unclear. The argument is actually twofold. First, liberalizing change of the sort undertaken by other denominations might send Catholicism's loss of membership down an even steeper slope.[17] Though reform might be justified out of adherence to the principle of fairness, the implication is that the move would be foolhardy, risking institutional martyrdom. It teeters on a real world tipping point.[18]

Second, even if such change were to be undertaken, what would fill the void? It is hard to replace the sexual mythos of Catholicism with a drama of comparable atavistic power. The *Commedia* needs its *Inferno* as much as its *Paradiso*. Symbolic capital with tentacles deep in the psychic magma is not fabricated overnight. At this level, reform is like trying to reshape an archetype. The traditional vision has all the exquisite simplicity of a medieval *mappa mundi*, a chart of the premodern world with Rome at the center. It is no longer a credible navigational guide. Still, it is recognizably a map.[19]

Arguably it is the stability of the sexual magisterium, and its precognitive undertow, more than its literal content, that lends it appeal beyond a circle of scrupulous traditionalists. Somewhere between transcendence and therapy, the inheritance serves as an emotional place holder in a world of primordial insecurities.[20] Those wraiths and gargoyles, the chthonic formalism and sexual savagery out of Hieronymus Bosch, mate with sainthood, charity, puerility, complacency, kindness, and cries for social justice. "Is it really the closest model we have to our condition?" the novelist Zadie Smith asks of a kind of fiction. "Or simply the bedtime story that comforts us most?"[21]

The last question can be cast another way, putting the emphasis on dread and trembling instead of consolation and serenity. The inference would be that, to endure, no religion can neglect the cruelest and basest instincts of humanity, or more precisely what Graham Greene called "a sense of evil religious in its intensity." This view could appear over-ripe in what pass for normal times, among adjusted temperaments, a miniflirtation with the wild side. It could reflect a panic attack, to be suppressed on the grounds of turning experience into bathos or fever-pitch sublimity. Either way, a nonstop Great Awakening would be insupportable.

Or we could be dealing, as with artistic masterpieces, with the cathartic expression of visceral anxieties, not their resolution. Or the lesson might be the paradoxical one that strict religions do better than the warm fuzzies because they steel people against adversity. Or that the religious enterprise really does have to give an account of the extremes of human experience and to supply moral guidelines for some in-between dilemmas as well.[22]

Concerns like these give both progressives and traditionalists pause. There are very few plug-and-play fixes in Catholicism. There are many adherents who can detail how one innovation or another violates tradition or offends those who simply want things to stay the same, without fuss. Apprehension can stifle thinking about the unthinkable. The status quo has been in place for a very long time. It has provided succor against tremendous stress. The obliteration of tradition is felt to be a genuine threat. Catholicism liberalized looks to many like Catholicism unhinged. The link between religious reform and institutional decline, understood as a drop in membership, has empirical backing, even if the causal mechanism at work could be clearer.[23]

But the equation between organizational collapse—specifically, the evaporation of clerical hierarchy—and the moral disintegration of a world turned upside-down is doubtful. Nondisaster prevails in the ministries, which get along well on their own. They are overwhelmingly the province of the laity. As for "handing on the faith," it is hard to distinguish between lapses from orthodoxy and growing up, as sociologists, to the consternation of church authorities, have indicated for some time.[24]

On the one hand, the cause–effect path from improving the "temporal" operations of the church toward a restoration of trust and religious belief (curiously reminiscent of the old dispute between "faith and works") is questionable, for all its commonsensical ring. On the other hand, the connection ascribed to the erosion of clerical order and the loss of moral compass is also suspect; one need not follow the other, even if rough anomic weather can be expected. The spell cast by the conviction that both ideas are self-evidently true is part of the problem. Other possibilities are worth contemplating.[25]

There is no easy answer. The creative appropriation of the genius of tradition is usually left to virtuosi. Organizationally, delving into the human songbook with an eye to making it new brings unpredictable, spasmodic transformation. Primeval Cycladic gods reappear. In the least, it can be disruptive. The viability of institutional vehicles for cultural transmission remains to be sorted out. The fear is that the rails along which they travel have themselves been wrecked and scrapped.

American Catholicism has been moving from a regime in which beliefs were relatively uniform and administration fairly decentralized toward something like the opposite. The faithful pick and choose among beliefs—the sexual magisterium after all has several components—while management of the church's far-flung operations is starting to become more standardized under the impress of legal liabilities and professional norms. As the slippage between practice and dogma attests, the operation has lots of moving parts.

There is an instructive resemblance between the status quo ante and the way the Roman Empire was run. Not exactly beliefs but culture and language were common, and governors, like bishops, had a free hand in ruling the provinces.[26] Now there are signs that the equivalent of that equilibrium has started to come undone in the church. The reversal also suggests similarities with the decay of authoritarian governments, so long as democracy is not taken to be the inevitable terminus of the disintegration of the old regime. An imperial system in the throes of losing its encompassing powers offers a parallel with fewer suppositions regarding the destination of change. For some conservatives, that prospect looks like the onset of the Dark Ages. For progressives the forecast is ambiguous at best.

The dynamic in which American Catholicism is caught up is closer to institutional differentiation than formal democratization.[27] Not many of the ministries affiliated with the American church remain under the unequivocal control of the bishops. Higher education and health care tend to follow norms of their own, set by their peers. Similarly, with fewer priests, the capacity of the church to run parishes and schools in the absence of significant leadership from the laity has diminished. The everyday politics of the church at the parish level is less reliably clerical. Parishes are no longer the cultural equivalents of company towns, and Catholics don't pay a lot of attention to what the bishops endorse or forbid. Outside of the rules governing self-selection into its own fraternity, the clerical elite is on the verge of losing control.

The reassertion of episcopal autonomy is one of the reasons why the bishops take a hard line on issues like the ban on providing contraceptives for which there is scant enthusiasm among the faithful. Neither the content nor even the stability of the sexual magisterium seems to matter as much politically as the subtext of "the new evangelization," namely, that the institutional church remains a demographic powerhouse to be reckoned with. The 2012 elections revealed holes in that supposition.[28] Much of the evangelization campaign is sophistry. It hangs on a strategy of product placement, with puff pieces planted in receptive organs of the Catholic press, with critical views suppressed.

The reason why prediction is so problematic—why "drift" sounds more reasonable than "direction"—is not only that agreement about sex and gender roles has been shattered and the persuasiveness of the church been damaged. The managerial standardization implied in the remedies set forth to modernize institutional Catholicism has yet to take hold in a big way. Some bishops continue to resist these measures as a threat to their prerogatives or ignore them as useless or supererogatory. Some priests and parishioners are simply not interested in or haven't got the time for experiments that break routine. To others, the whole enterprise has a brave-new-world flavor; the vision is of parishes as variations on supermarkets and big-box stores.[29] Whatever its eventual efficiencies, the consolidation of organizational pragmatism in many of the parishes and dioceses is a way off.

Even were such criteria to win out, it is doubtful whether administrative rationalization will restore the credibility of the bishops or enhance commitment to the magisterium.[30] The idea that efficiency generates legitimacy betrays some wishful thinking. The restored-attachment-to-the-faith part of the equation does not appear to hold up. In contrast to the practice in the United States, Catholic primary and secondary schools operating under church auspices in several European countries receive state support and they perform pretty well, yet this has done nothing to improve church attendance.

The comparison is inexact. Church schools in Europe channel resources supplied by the state, and they pay a price for these funds in the form of greater public control over curriculum and personnel. It is not clear that the church is in charge. Nevertheless, the experience with an alternative model of church–state relations for the delivery of services is telling enough. Beneficence may lead to gratitude or reciprocity so diffuse that the wished-for payoff in trust and solidarity is undetectable.

A new normative and functional arrangement—a paradigm shift with teeth—has yet to emerge from the decomposition of the old regime. At the same time, the analogy of institutional Catholicism with a structurally defective industry is just that, an analogy. The implication is that the church, incapable of fundamental change, will devour its reformers. The jury is out.

Faced with a de facto pluralism that could not be squeezed into the Procrustean bed of Catholic ideas about the desirable polity, John Courtney Murray played two gambits. He argued with some justification and considerable ingenuity that the political tradition of the church could not be identified with a single type of regime. However anomalous it might be in continental Europe, a republic respectful of religion was the American norm.[31]

Murray's second move was to assume an underlying consensus that prized moderation if not as a *summum bonum* then as a lesser evil for getting things done. The relevant players were supposed to share a capacious, self-assured tolerance. Their common understanding rendered commitment to reasoned discussion and good manners feasible. The theory, though circular, had a practical, let's-get-on-with-business flavor. There was an American optimism to it. Bargaining might be theoretically second-best but it was better than the real-life alternatives.[32]

The church has difficulty accommodating this line of reasoning when it is applied to its own turf. Especially since the Counter-Reformation, Catholicism has evolved into a towering patriarchy that its leaders and many adherents feel has served it well. It matters little that some monarchies—England or Spain, for example—are less than absolutist yet work well enough. A turn to the merely ornamental is unacceptable to a church that takes ceremony very seriously. Make-believe is a big part of reality.

Models of the relationship between church and state might vary, but the form of Catholicism itself is not compatible with alternative designs. The papacy is a charismatic institution. The system is not constructed to be efficient, and it is not fair. But it lends a sense of order and destination to a streaming diversity. An indulgent absolutism, fertile with deep-seated hopes, sunk commitments, and hard-earned intoxications, attains the wisdom of an indispensable fiction. Some of the disenchanted feel a rueful attachment to it.

The opening that groups like the Roundtable pursue is not touted as a halfway house to democracy. In fact, however, the strategy does imply some redistribution of power. It is a way of coping with—"managing" conveys too strong a sense of control—a transition toward lay empowerment that leaves the clergy with a limited yet somehow significant role. At a minimum, it is a bow to a dual, deeply ambiguous demographic reality: a drop in the absolute number of priests and growth in the net number of relatively conservative Catholics. In its expansive guise, the strategy also acknowledges the draining away of disaffected Catholics.

The fact that there is no grand bargain among the protagonists testifies to the uncertainty of the transition. But the process goes on anyway and the courtesies are kept up. The hope is that the details can be worked out while the fundamentals stay lock-boxed. *Faute de mieux*, a combination of managerial strategizing and muddling through buys time, tugging the church to a place where lay leadership may attain fuller acceptance.

The authority behind such an arrangement is problematic, more like a truce than a settlement. The legitimacy of revised gender roles remains an issue for another day. Discretion is as much a part of the strategy as action. The intellectual wattage goes down a bit. Focusing on "the temporalities" means, somewhat paradoxically and unpredictably, staking out the long-term. The understanding is not completely at odds with Murray's faith in elites and his simultaneous willingness to cut deals with pluralism. Like all "temporalities," the settlement is provisional.

The rightward shift documented in the early chapters was more than a matter of propping up tradition. The activation of ideas and opinion in the name of family values during the seventies, eighties, and nineties entailed a vigorous campaign to recover from a free fall in moral conventions during the 1960s. The old rules seemed shredded and scattered like so much confetti the morning after a wild all-nighter. The movement succeeded in joining cultural and material conservatism in the public consciousness. It felt as much like a moral as an economic crusade, and it gained popular traction.[33]

By contrast, movements at the center and the left of Catholicism have followed comparatively segmented strategies or they have lurched along, like VOTF, in pursuit of a broader emancipatory agenda. The relatively integrated approach adopted by neoconservative Catholics grew out of a premonition of chaos emanating not just from mephitic hippies and their dissipations. Alarm also arose from apprehension at the unforeseen consequences cascading out of Vatican II itself, on top of economic disorder and sexual pandemonium. The Roe v. Wade decision dates from the same year, 1973, as the oil crisis. In hindsight both seem like death knells for the binging sixties.[34]

Within the church the restorationist program benefited from traditional passivity in matters that require collective action. A bloc of progressive Catholics was difficult to conjure up out of individuals who were in effect reasonably contented scofflaws without much experience or credibility in projecting a coherent voice. "If the public interest is nothing more than the unintended outcome of millions of individuals pursuing their private interests," an observer of neoauthoritarian Russia has commented, "then any sacrifice in the name of the public interest is a waste."[35]

A closely related lesson touches on how the various groups have mobilized supporters. Neoconservatives spelled out a cause and targeted a clear-cut set of enemies. So did SNAP. The difference is that the neocons tapped into deep-seated, widely shared beliefs about family life and economic worthiness. The appeal of SNAP has been narrower, and the implications of its message for preserving traditional arrangements—Catholicism itself—have raised warning flags. The mobilizational success of Catholic neoconservatism qualifies it as a social movement, a status that none of the other groups quite attains. They are all advocacy and to some extent support groups, and secondarily membership organizations. SNAP counts on media opinion and the judicial process more than on the development of a mass of determined citizens to press its demands.

The Roundtable is *sui generis*. It marshals resources—funding, expertise, its network of elite contacts. Associates of the Roundtable are organizations and representatives of organizations as often as they are individuals, a property that confounds measures of influence like head-counts of members. "They have staked out a position," a director of development for a religious order remarked, "they stay away from the theological quagmire. They're able to bring the heavy hitters into the same room." The Roundtable, a network of networks, has significant convening power.[36]

It would be a mistake to underestimate the moral resonance behind the problem-solving thrust of the Roundtable in the American setting. Its compartmentalization of "the temporalities" and the eternal verities may lack existential pizzazz. Its accentuation of the positive can make its version of spirituality sound as military music does to music. But confidence building has organizational utility, and the Roundtable gains stature in comparison to the floundering and fragility of resource-poor reform groups.[37] The most powerful feature of such emotional appeal as the Roundtable has, however, lies in its union of respect for the past and responsibility for posterity, demonstrated in the group's concern for the cross-generational transmission of values. It is Roman *pietas* cast in modern guise, an agile managerial hybrid dominated by an ethos of private-sector problem solving.

Voice of the Faithful and FutureChurch originated as grass-roots movements with a spark of spontaneous anger directed at child abuse and a caste-like priesthood. They have struggled to overcome their local provenance and above all the low involvement of Catholics generally in church affairs. The net effect of departures from the church appears to have tilted membership slightly more to the right than would otherwise be the case.

Passivity is as much a brooding presence as repression in church politics. Apathy is a two-edged sword, giving leaders room for maneuver but raising questions about the popular buy-in regarding decisions—progressive, conservative, or merely managerial—taken from on high. (Some of the appeal of the Roundtable, for example, comes not from its pragmatism, the actual workings of which can be difficult to pin down, but from the idea of pragmatism, which enjoys a certain inarguability in decision-making circles.) Given the ease of the exit option, leakage in membership has to be a major source of both inertia and unintended change in Catholicism.[38]

If individualism and low participation are important features of the environment inhabited by advocacy groups in Catholicism, a pair of other contextual characteristics also needs to be recognized. One, highlighted in Chapter Eight, is the modest size of the organizations examined here, compared to the dimensions of strong and customarily silent groups like Opus Dei and the Knights of Columbus. The organizational arena of church politics does not encircle a level playing field. The tilt is toward the right. The thematic emphasis on moral clarity and economic sobriety has gained Catholic conservatives a popular base, and the movement has deep pockets. Yet, if we focus on the inevitable replacement of older cohorts in the church, the clock is ticking against a decisive conservative victory in the culture wars.

A concurrent element, apart from a demographic dynamic framed purely around generations, that conditions the impact of advocacy groups is the changing ethnic composition of American Catholicism. Parsing the crisis of the American church without at least a nod toward immigration is like analyzing the financial meltdown in the United States without considering globalization. The decline in the number of priests and the simultaneous growth in the number of Catholics, attributable mostly to immigration, have been amply documented. So has the falling off in attachment to the institutional church among the young. Secularism, measured by the number of persons without religious affiliation, is also on the rise.[39] Immigration, of course, is not new to the American church. But newcomers bring fewer priests with them than did their nineteenth-century predecessors.[40]

Immigration, together with differential fertility between immigrants and nonimmigrants, will curb secularizing tendencies among the population at large. Traditional values regarding church and family, including gender inequality, are on the average more prominent among immigrant sectors, like Latino Catholics, with high fertility. The majority of American Catholics under nineteen are Hispanic.[41]

This said, such developments set up broad parameters that condition the viability of reform scenarios in roundabout fashion. Whatever the population estimates, cultural predispositions are wobbly guides to value profiles ascribed to demographic sectors, and ethnic stereotypes regarding family ideals become even more attenuated when actual behavior that relates to specific public policies is involved. The "Hispanic church," so far, has been a relatively inert presence in the intramural politics of American Catholicism.[42] It is unlikely to remain so.

CONJECTURE

This was a tainted, mainly obsequious age. The greatest figures had to protect their positions by subserviency; and, in addition to them, all ex-consuls, most ex-praetors, even many junior senators competed with each other's offensively sycophantic proposals. There is a tradition that whenever Tiberius left the senate-house he exclaimed in Greek, 'Men fit to be slaves!' Even he, freedom's enemy, became impatient of such abject servility.
Then, gradually, self-abasement turned into persecution.[1]

How much of a difference have the advocacy groups made in driving change in the church, relative to a roster of other causal agents? If the idea is to extrapolate from a series of organizational cases to the transformation of American Catholicism writ large, the impact of these groups needs to be set weighed. Do the pressure groups matter?

A mental experiment helps sort out the puzzle. Array potential sources of change in provisional order of importance. The five listed here are ranked according to the magnitude of the effects, from large to small, that we might assign to them intuitively.

At the top is Vatican II. The transformation was proclaimed from the peak of the hierarchy, and it reshaped the external relations of the church and redrew parts of its intellectual map. Vatican II was change on a grand scale that affected the rhetoric and the self-understanding of the church more than the design of the institution. Many effects of the Council were unintended. It generated a massive drop in recruits to "the consecrated life," a radicalization of some dedicated Catholics, and a conservative backlash.

Close behind comes a raft of forces that have precipitated change from the outside: demographic and cultural shifts like the Hispanicization of the American church, the break-up of sexual guidelines, and the feminization of the work force. The ambience of everyday life in and around parishes has been transformed.[2]

The sway of a few very large benefactor groups can be ranked close to the same level of importance. Insider organizations like Opus Dei, the Knights of Malta, and the Knights of Columbus are gray eminences. Their reputation for being so is as much a part of their power as their exercise of it. They set a tone. It is not their way to be strident. They provide financial ballast, and some direction, to Peter's barque.

Attributions of leadership to such megagroups must be accompanied with a caveat: there is not much systematic evidence about their activities. The aura of power associated with them reflects the economic support they give to the Vatican, and by extension to the centralizing ambitions of Rome, and only indirectly their influence within American Catholicism and on the operations of specific dioceses. Recently, though, groups like the Knights of Columbus have adopted a more aggressive stance in the domestic politics of the American church—on issues like same-sex marriage and on the neutralization of left-leaning nuns, for example. Coordinated or not, conservative interests large and small keep alive a vision of American Catholicism that conjures up a Norman Rockwell–Frederic Remington picture of domesticity and powerhouse patriotism.[3]

Next, a large but fragmented series of changes has transpired on the inside of the church, in the hearts and minds of parishioners. Many Catholics pick and choose what to accept and reject in the church, when they do not simply opt out and quit. The dynamic operates case by case, from individual to individual. We are in the realm of a nearly deinstitutionalized spirituality. The aggregate result is substantial but uncoordinated. Apathy cannot help donations. But indifference does not constitute a formula for challenging authority through concerted action. It is has no anthem. There are no lawn signs proclaiming "UNDECIDED." The process of departure and decommitment feels like a safety valve as much as resistance. The net outcome of the drain in membership appears to be a slightly greater residue of conservatism among those who stay on.[4]

Finally, we come to the advocacy and interest groups. Their impact has been uneven and modest. Various cliques and associations on the right have done well. They have secured favor with the leadership of the church, they have left their imprint on its internal politics, reinforcing hierarchical values, and they have redirected public policy on moral and some economic issues.

The record among groups outside the conservative sphere is less impressive. The impact of Survivors Network of those Abused by Priests (SNAP) has been significant and irreversible but the organization carries on a step ahead of extinction. Voice of the Faithful practically disintegrated after its initial success. FutureChurch continues to cry in the wilderness, as does Call to Action. There is a certain echo-chamber quality to these movements. Catholicism may no longer be a religion of polite spectators but it is not one of effective participants either.[5]

The results of the Roundtable's efforts are difficult to evaluate in the organization's own return-on-investment language. Value added in church administration is often elusive not only because it takes time to show up but also because indicators of achievement can be ambiguous. It is hard to isolate some of the contributions of Roundtable programs from managerial changes that would be going on anyway, if a bit more slowly, and the scoreboard is sometimes obscured by public-relations hype.

A realistic appraisal would begin by recognizing the Roundtable's proficiency in building networks across the operations of the church. Lines of communication that speak to real needs have been opened. The expansion of the organization and its capacity to innovate can be counted as significant achievements. In a field where threadbare persistence and mortality are high, growth itself is a sign of accomplishment. But it is not alchemy.

What is wrong with this picture? The list is a mechanical concatenation, a string of beads. We need something that takes into account the interaction across macro-trends, meso- and micro-actors. In English: we need to get a fuller sense of how the advocacy groups deal with specific opportunities and constraints. How do the groups react to one another and their cultural and political environment? Where does indifference fit in the cause-effect chain? And what can the experience of other embattled hierarchies tell us about the Catholic predicament?

In searching for practical guides to institutional change in Catholicism, examples drawn from Judaism and Protestant churches might seem promising. They might work, if not exactly as precedents, then as latent models to be tinkered with and adapted. Variants within these traditions provide blueprints for organizational formats that encourage lay participation, access for women, and similar issues that have bothered liberal adherents of Catholicism for decades.

But the obstacles against drawing on such solutions are formidable. Aside from the fear that well-intentioned changes will cause membership to tank, as is thought to have happened with mainstream Protestants, or exacerbate tendencies toward schism, much of the unity that holds across fundamentalist, conservative, orthodox, and reform currents in Judaism relies on ethnic solidarity.[6] This is a foundation that a big-tent, proselytizing Catholicism could not abide.

More generally: improvements that appear to threaten identity are rarely meliorist transactions open to quiet bargaining. Emulation on the ministerial periphery is acceptable. This is what legitimizes efforts to pool financial assets, as a few Protestant denominations and branches of Judaism have done for some time. But comparing denominations in order to search out ways of transferring good-sense practices into the clerical core of authority in Catholicism raises too-close-for-comfort qualms. Hierarchy, deference, and the rest of the panoply of time-immemorial fealty and obeisance are placed at risk. The semiotics seems un-Catholic. The church has difficulty enough with the idea of being reduced to the rank of a mere denomination; in the eyes of some adherents that condition is already too close to the religious equivalent of professional wrestling.

Setting the Catholic condition alongside authoritarian regimes and empires reaches farther from home. These institutions are not religions, or not primarily so, and Catholicism is not often thought of as a political system, or not only as one. Nevertheless, the analogy—in particular, the resemblance to long-lived empires—is worth pursuing.

The Ottoman Empire provides an intriguing if unfamiliar example; the comparison is exotic but so too is Catholicism. The sultanate lasted a very long time, from the end of the thirteenth century to the third decade of the twentieth.[7] The fact that it eventually perished points to roads taken and mistakes made that Catholicism might wish to avoid. In particular, global Catholicism has no reason to repeat the efforts at ethnic homogenization that overtook the Ottomans in their last days and that persisted in aggravated form through the republic implanted by the Young Turks. On the contrary. Motives for the Vatican operate, often enough, on an international scale. The overriding incentive is to welcome candidates for leadership from Latin America, Africa, and Asia. Up-and-coming leaders from these areas are unlikely to bring feminist sympathies with them as they replenish manpower that used to be supplied from the European and North American core.

In short, the cosmopolitan strategy makes up for occasional disruptions that can be expected from newcomers outside the Roman orbit. Representativeness on one dimension—racial and ethic heterogeneity—trumps fairness as gender parity. This geopolitical calculus brings good news for power holders in the church. Subordination of women and gays may operate as the sheet anchor for what is otherwise an inclusive Catholicism.

But this is to put the moral ahead of the story. For now let's focus on similarities in imperial longevity and the reasons for eventual decline. The resilience of Catholicism, its American branch included, has to be at least as impressive as its weaknesses. The lessons turn out to be sobering.

Several factors contributed to the long arc of the sultanate. Culturally, the Ottomans forged an identity founded on a hybrid, partly religious, partly negotiated tradition. They cultivated sensitivity to local variations bordering on syncretism. In their prime the authorities seated in Istanbul were more ecumenical toward nonbelievers than they were clement to dissenters within their own fold. Organizationally, they followed a divide-and-rule policy. The empire was designed like the spokes of a rimless wheel, centralized around the hub and integrating regional elites who had spotty lateral communication across their ranks. Rulers cultivated tolerance of religious and ethnic minorities, absorbing capable managers from a range of backgrounds.[8] The result was a shrewd, nervous resilience. As with the long history of Catholicism, endurance should not be confused with stability or tranquility. The empire was not optimal as a corporate enterprise, but it hung on for centuries.[9]

There are instructive parallels between what scholars of the Ottoman empire have termed (1) "productive control and integration of elites," (2) a decent respect for "diversity," and (3) "legitimacy," and what I have called the imperatives of American Catholicism, respectively: (1) performance, (2) fairness, and (3) identity. In its heyday the sultanate worked as a brokered authoritarianism.

The hybrid started to come apart when it tried to impose stricter religious coherence as a surrogate for a slipping cultural consensus—this in the midst of runaway revenue shortfalls, unmanageably large inflows of migrants, and growing lateral interaction among local notables who were once hived off from one another.[10]

In American Catholicism administrative operations that were decentralized, under the discretion of bishops, each more accustomed to reporting directly to Rome than consulting and forming alliances with one another, are slowly becoming standardized under the influence of lay cadres, funding pressures, and demands for civil accountability. Consensus about the cultural core of Catholicism—mostly, its sexual teachings and cognate ideas about reverence for authority—has given way to individual choice. A common language—not just Latin but an understanding across generations—has grown thin. Complaints about inequity regarding gender roles have become insistent. The imperial template is not yet breaking up, but the squeeze is on.[11]

The Ottomans were enmeshed in problems on multiple fronts so entangled with one another that extraction was difficult. Decline eventuated not merely in collapse, however. The regime underwent a metamorphosis. Though subsequent republican reforms were far from simply different renditions of the imperial past, a new type of authoritarian system arose out of the detritus of the old.[12] The transformation was strung out over decades.

True, the trauma of rupture and revolution was severe, and this is where the Ottoman-Catholicism analogy breaks down. The empire did not last. Yet the collapse of the sultanate was one denouement among a whirl of precursors and anticlimaxes. Continuities in institutional style and political culture were significant. Authoritarian habits formed over centuries exerted significant clawback on the Young Turks and their followers.[13]

The analogy with a transit from one variant of authoritarianism to a comparatively up-to-date adaptation of "revolution from above" has a real bearing on Catholicism. The moral of the story is consistent with strategies in reach of conservatives. The Vatican can respond with open arms to the globalization of Catholicism, speeding the assimilation of cadres from outside Europe and the United States, without lifting its strictures on gender parity. Strong traces of authoritarian culture persist, minus racial bias. This is the least disruptive and most benign accommodation with modernity that a cosmopolitan tradition saturated in a culture of deference and sexual hierarchy may be able to handle. The enforcement of a doctrinal orthodoxy fixated on sexual tradition is not universally seen as a spiteful move. The traditional spirit and hierarchical accoutrements of institutional Catholicism retain a certain mystique.[14]

What alternatives are there for liberals in the American church? Looking at the situation in terms of a gap between seemingly reasonable preferences and historical constraints—above all, the institutional and cultural inertia of tradition—doesn't tell us much except the obvious, that some people are dissatisfied, or get us beyond time-will-tell, expected-the-unexpected forecasts. But if we imagine a cultural realignment of the permissible, we catch glimpses of a new territory.

Not wholly new, however. Such awakenings have occurred before. One emerged from the cultural wetlands that John Courtney Murray plied. The predicament he faced was similar to the unstable zone that the abolitionist movement trod in the eighteenth and nineteenth centuries.[15] Murray saw that a theology espousing the union of religion and politics under one true monarchy was a dumb idea for church and state alike, certainly in the American setting. He could never bring himself to admit that the old intellectual order was defective as a matter of first principles. But the off-chance that it might stay the same had become a dead letter, like the prohibition against usury that the church allowed to lapse in early modern Europe. "The signs of the times" discerned by Vatican II cut deeper than trendiness.

Fashion is knowing the rules; style is knowing when to break them. Similarly, the success of the antislavery movement reflected more than an upswell of popular opinion. Together with the emergence of a new merchant class, it reflected a conceptual reframing of what constituted a just society.[16]

We do what we can, not what we think we should or what we want to do.[17]

Resistance against feminism in the church arises from a mindset that associates adherence to hierarchy with a male-dominated social order; and rather than being simply imposed, the worldview has proved to be fairly popular. It has a global, if recessive, appeal. The prudent strategy for American Catholicism would seem to be a refurbished authoritarianism, given cultural and demographic constraints from in and outside the church, and especially from growth areas outside the United States.[18] From a purely self-protective standpoint, the trade-off probably antagonizes fewer organized interests than other alternatives. In positive terms, the strategy aligns moral caution with charitable interests centered on a character-building transmission of productive values.

Yet the program is only weakly energizing. It is impossible to shake the feeling that something is false. This is what's behind much of the drain in numbers and the chronic sag in participation. Customs like the ban on women's ordination, the reluctance to acknowledge gender parity, and the like that once were relegated to the quaint, the balmy, and the harmlessly arbitrary come to be seen as meanly gratuitous, culturally maladroit, and finally wrong. The tolerably dotty begins to look alarming.

Despite these handicaps, the steady-as-she-goes option has three things going for it. First, the priority given to institutional performance speaks to real needs, like improving primary and secondary education. It is imbued with a let's-pull-together atmosphere that an emphasis on gender parity and fairness seems unable to match within the Catholic tradition. It is teamwork—communitarianism—under an illiberal dispensation. The default condition of American Catholicism may be an indistinct authoritarianism that is not averse to dedicated generosity and good works, even as it gravitates toward becoming an old story for old men, tugging at the heartstrings of a presixties mindset.[19]

Second, the internationalization of Catholicism in as well as outside the United States places the church in an unusually favorable position for numerical expansion. Multicultural growth is a bottom line that Catholic officialdom understands.

Third, the joint emphasis on performance and the welcoming reception of racial and ethnic diversity create opportunities for dominant alliances. The strategy stressing efficiency, "excellence," and other investment goals gives the agenda crossover drawing power. With some tweaking, it could be considered a sophisticated Catholic version of the prosperity gospel.[20] Just as Protestant evangelicals can align with conservative Catholics in defense of family values and economic sobriety, without buying into the church's authority structure, non-Catholic philanthropists (and sometimes state governments) can take part in projects that support the good works of the church without risking theological entanglement. They need not accept papal authority or Catholic doctrine or moral instruction to help promote the church's infrastructure of schools and social services.[21]

Taken together, these three elements—growth in problem-solving efficiencies, growth in numbers, and growth in projects with cross-denominational appeal—provide the undergirding for a dominant coalition. We are no longer comparing the effectiveness of separate pressure groups, relative to one another and to their environment. We have instead a mix of low-conflict ideas, demographic evolution, and strategic partnerships. The correlation of forces favors an emollient authoritarianism.

A dominant coalition is not necessarily a winning coalition. The alliance seems all dressed up but is unsure of its chances and uncertain about where it might go. The arrangement has several moving parts that could become disarticulated. The supposition that Catholics from the southern hemisphere are enduringly antifeminist is tenuous. Besides, the clerical hierarchy could turn indefensibly sour, lashing out as its authority wanes. Some donors who identify with the church's desire to safeguard its institutional integrity are vexed by its attitude toward women; the insistence of the bishops on controlling nuns and access to contraceptives troubles a few benefactors customarily unbothered by doctrinal idiosyncrasies. Also, large sectors of American Catholicism have yet to show much enthusiasm for coordinating the reform of church management and even less for a cramped vision of gender roles and sexual orientation.

Finally, substantial progress toward revitalizing the contribution of Catholic schools to American education depends on the capacity of the alliance of Catholic and non-Catholic benefactors to modify constitutional norms regarding the separation of church and state for "pervasively religious" organizations. This seems to be the highway toward saving the parochial schools and helping them overcome the handicaps of childhood poverty on a big scale.

But just as undoing age-old rules restricting the priesthood to celibate males sounds un-Catholic to purblind conservatives, revisiting constitutional law on the separation of church and state smacks of un-Americanism within the secular heritage of the United States.[22] The obstacle is not just another quirk of democracy American-style, like the pathologies of the electoral college or the plight of third parties, which are hard enough to correct. The separation of church and state is constitutional principle, open to interpretation, but painfully. Scaling that wall is comparable to changing gun-control legislation.[23]

As 2012 drew to a close, the strategy of chipping away at constitutional restrictions on public aid to parochial schools suffered setbacks. The Louisiana courts revoked a program to fund vouchers for parochial schools, a major initiative of a Catholic governor. While the number of government-funded charter schools continued to surge across the United States, this development did not augur well for Catholic elementary and secondary education. Catholic and non-Catholic benefactors had to regroup and rethink a campaign associated with a defeated Republican bid for the presidency.[24]

The liberalism that gives priority to gender parity and sexual tolerance stands at odds with the official wisdom of the church. The vision is one that a growing majority of American Catholics finds more palatable than the status quo. Yet this constituency is dispersed, its disagreement is far from nosediving into thoroughgoing contempt, and prospective reform, in contrast to Murray's breakthrough, menaces the internal structure rather than the external relations of the church. Besides, unlike many of today's lay reformers, Murray was a clerical insider. The notional popularity of reform can be denounced as a typically American (or post-Christian European) fad. And who knows what a more relaxed style of governance would look like for Catholicism on a world scale?[25]

Inaction is reinforced by bemusement in the ranks at rules about sexual behavior that the church has almost no capacity to enforce. Reticence is amplified among lay leaders by a reluctance to challenge authority when agitation might make matters worse, putting noncontroversial upgrades in the ministries, schools, and parishes at risk. There is an eagerness to change the conversation from the suppression of rights for women and gays to the good works of the church, the gregarious charm of a rubicund bishop you wouldn't mind having a beer with, and so on. There is the sumptuous tradition, too.[26]

Among the many propellants that advanced the abolitionist cause was an Enlightenment-inspired appreciation for extending the universe of liberty.[27] A groundswell of this sort is hard to detect in a church where public opinion ignores the hierarchy as much as the hierarchy ignores public opinion. The old culture of obedience and dependency has morphed not into rebellion but into a lame mix of deference and indifference. An attrition of the imaginable occurs. Checks and balances within the church might not be to the Catholic palate after all.

Speculation about a transformation in the church's construal of sexual rectitude and gender roles must acknowledge its improbability. The contours of normative progress regarding religious tolerance were in place for decades in the United States before Murray's case gained cogency, and his position caught an updraft from a historical context shaped by the triumph of the American way in World War II and by revulsion at ethnic and religious persecution. The abolitionist movement also benefited from an antecedent revolution in thinking about human rights. In both instances reformers could contend that it was not only principle but a fresh assessment of practical costs and benefits that vindicated their cause.

The women's movement in Catholicism, not to mention gay liberation, is weaker. Its rudiments in Catholic tradition struggle for legitimacy. The sediment of reaction against the sixties has hardened for many leaders in the church. And because of the interweaving of gender and political status, it is not clear that those in power have more to gain than to lose by relinquishing some of their authority. Transitions can get out of hand. There really is something to be afraid of, and the deposit of faith really is something more serious than the fruitcake that is perpetually regifted but never consumed. Dialogue succumbs before that old standard: *Après moi, le deluge*.

The parallel between Catholicism and a cooptive authoritarian system draws sustenance from these doubts and fears. For the time being, the church is able to celebrate its role as a multinational cultural order without having to bend to demands for the access of women to influence at the top.

"Politics ain't beanbag," Daniel Henninger has noted, "but it also isn't just about politics."[28] Political change in Catholicism is limited, yet viewing the transition through a political lens imposes limits itself.

The metamorphosis of Catholicism, part of it, resembles the shift from sacred to secular art, less a displacement than an alteration in subject matter and sensibility, rather as merit and mobility are supposed to work through rather than utterly replace traditional hierarchy. It resonates outside the usual institutional templates. Outmigrants and half-hearted adherents cannot be written off as self-indulgent seekers with a touch of the vapors. Some could be heralds of spiritualities yet to crystallize, of narratives no longer "representational" after the fashion of Victorian portraiture and landscapes. *Bien pensant* tact is not all there is to cultural transformation. Power does not always smother doubt.

Transitions are rarely smooth or efficient. Change frightens people in Catholicism for two reasons. The first-order fear is of existential consequences more terrible than stagnation. "Poof! It's gone!" is an unbearable kablooey moment for what's counted on to be here. This is the classic "transition cost," of making things worse. The second is a function of distaste and conflict-aversion that runs deeper than a feeling that all the shouting is unproductive. There are multiple, tough-to-negotiate "veto points." The contemplation of change threatens unpleasantness, an arousal of the *non placet* reaction against pushing the limits of received wisdom.

The church could stand a jolt of the underbred brashness and coarse erudition that alarmed Virginia Woolf in the potty-mouth James Joyce. A soupçon of George Carlin would help too. There are conflicts scarier than the one between primness and indecency, there are worse intimidations than charges of carrying out "a great disservice to the church." Muckraking provides some remedy to abject reverence. Exposés fascinate even as they repel, and over time, since the scandals, they have changed the universe of discourse and the terms of what's thinkable about the church. While much of this may discomfort people by failing to lay out turn-key solutions, it is better than no discussion at all.

In a similar vein, the rambling, infinitely digressive *Don Quixote* may be a greater classic of Catholicism than the well-ordered transcendence of the *Divine Comedy*. *Don Quixote* is modern in a way that the *Commedia* is not. Cervantes' tale conveys no surpassing redemptive message. Yet it has a sublime poignancy. It is a story of cruelty, pathos, violence, compassion, incoherence, and off-kilter intelligence. The Don dies disillusioned, probably a virgin, half aware that he is loved. His failure is anticlimactic.[29]

Three concrete ideas emerge from these considerations. The transition from childhood to adulthood is increasingly muddled in Catholicism. The lesson to the story taught to juveniles founders like a paper boat as it approaches moral clarity for grown-ups. The problem is more serious than boredom with and easy rebellion against bossy institutions. The message itself, a good deal of it, lacks credibility. The inscription of sexual dominance in church authority amounts to baby talk. It has the coherence of Lard Lite. Many of the messengers quite reasonably lack conviction.

Second, the facts of sexual fluidity have contributed mightily to discrediting the gospel propagated by the church of virtue as sexual propriety and gender stratification. Elements of the church's positions that are worthy of attention, like some ideas about advanced reproductive technologies, get stuck in a coagulated murk about sexual orientation, contraception, and the like. The high incidence and occluded condition of homosexuals in the ranks of a clergy ultimately charged with upholding absurd doctrines regarding celibacy, who find themselves contorted by an organization known for inflicting emotional immaturity on its cadres, give a fun-house-mirror look to efforts at frank conversation about sexual and gender controversies generally. The politics of it are convoluted in the extreme.

Third, there is a methodological point of substantive consequence here. The division between those who love the church and those who feel betrayed by it, between those who are for it and those who are against it, between the helpful and the hurtful, is so stupefying that it destroys reflection capable of making headway. People want to know whether you're on their side or not. If you're not part of the solution, you're part of the problem.

These are banalities. We wind up with a battle of wits in which—to quote Louis, the grouch played by Danny DeVito in *Taxi*—both sides are disarmed. Scholarship in Catholicism ranges across investigative journalism, social research, meta-analysis, and theological speculation. At almost every point the impulse is to answer the question that science is not supposed to address: to tell people how they should live. Sometimes the implication is that the answer is known beforehand. Research becomes a process of reverse engineering from ideologies set in place. Preconceptions rule.

Many of the questions, it is true, are not merely puzzles to be solved but problems to be fixed. They have a nontrivial urgency to them. It is especially tempting for political scientists, for whom the worst sin is to be deceived, to fall into the trap of a value-free cynicism that mistakes indifference and aloofness from action for wisdom. That demurral is ethically precious.

But the ratio of nostrums to real answers is very high. Things get hortatory and meretricious very quickly. In this milieu, let-'er-rip research is not idle curiosity. It may look obliviously impractical, and possibly unsound. Yet such research has serendipitous potential. It too can raise hackles.

Susan Owaki Berman died at fifty-seven of lupus, a wasting disease, leaving her husband, Jack, and two daughters, Lisa and Clare. The funeral mass was celebrated by Kevin Kester, who was dressed in white vestments, as were two altar girls in surplices, carrying paschal candles, and two altar boys who held books of liturgical readings. About 400 people attended the service at St. Bede the Venerable on a rainy January Saturday morning. St. Bede's is a well-lit, spacious, sixties-ish church in La Cañada, an upscale suburb north of Los Angeles.

Susan had sung alto in the choir and she had worked to rejuvenate the local chapter of Call to Action. (She was one of the women in Chapter Twelve holding up the "ORDAIN WOMEN" banner outside the Religious Education Conference in Los Angeles.) Dr. Bierman read a passage from the mourner's Kaddish, then Fr. Kevin, an associate pastor, spoke. "Take part with us," he said to the mixed congregation, "to the best that your conscience will allow." His voice cracked.

> As a priest my own expression of my faith has been shackled by the hierarchy or by some among the faithful who might take offense at my remarks. I didn't know how sick Susan was. When Susan gave me a petition to sign a few weeks ago, for some priest, I forget just who it was, I just didn't feel like I could get involved.[30]

Fr. Kevin took a moment, then went on.

> She belonged to a group called Call to Action, which some of you might have heard of. She worked for the rights of women, she worked for the rights of gay people. She didn't care what anybody thought or anybody said. When Jack and her daughters asked, I suggested a reading from the Beatitudes. We were blessed by Susan. I knew her as a member of the choir. This is a very sad occasion. Susan was younger than me by five years. I try to be a little upbeat at funerals. Leave with this thought in your mind. Our lives have been blessed because we have known Susan.
>
> Please kneel or if you feel more comfortable be seated.

In addition to the hymnals in the pews, copies of the parish bulletin could be picked up on the way in. A phone number to call for classes in teen spirituality was listed on the first page. So was a roster of Mass times and devotions, including the rosary at 8:30 a.m. on weekdays and prayers to the Mother of Perpetual Help on Tuesday mornings after the 8:10 Mass. A foldout contained invitations to the Bede Fest scheduled for March 10 at the Annandale Golf Club, cocktail attire, black tie optional.

Parishioners are also reminded to save the date for Ken O'Malley and the Twilight Lords Band, set to appear at the St. Paddy's Day traditional dinner with good spirits, and there is an ad to join us for Super Bunco, sponsored by the parish council of women, $20 entry fee, no experience necessary, walk-ins always welcome, though reservations are greatly appreciated. Next week the monthly book club is to discuss *Galileo's Daughter* by Dava Sobel. Next Sunday, Frank Pastore will speak at an open house about his book, the best-selling autobiography *Shattered, Struck Down, But Not Destroyed*, an uplifting story of Frank's life before, during, and after his professional baseball career, and the story of how God can surprise any of us with His goodness and love when we allow Him to make beautiful the shattered fragments of our lives. A box on page eight of the announcements gives a number to reach Sister Marisa to make reservations for a long-held parish tradition, the Annual St. Bede Women's Street Fair, from Friday through Sunday. The facing page lists the fourteen-member parish council with their email addresses, and there is abundant contact information about groups like Bible Study, Justice and Peace, Centering Prayer, Branch 374 of the Italian Catholic Federation (Benvenuti!), Bereavement Ministry, Ushers for Weekend Masses, Moms' Rosary Prayer Group, Respect Life, Spiritual Direction, and the St. Bede's Skidettes who prepare lunches for the people of skid row.

"Well, here we all are, Susan, to celebrate your life." Cindy Yoshitomi, a grandmother, Susan's closest friend, blue-eyed, rosy-cheeked, and married to a Japanese-American, speaks from the lectern. She has been studying for ordination to the priesthood, though outside after Mass she acknowledges that "my real vocation is to be a deacon, I think. So many people to marry and bury in Ventura." Her voice too is shaking.

> I've known Susan since we belonged to a group of radical Catholic women, Bibles and Babies, in Eagle Rock. She went to school at St. Agatha's parish and Notre Dame Academy for Girls. She thrived in school and loved the nuns who taught her. And then she went to Mount Saint Mary's College, where she graduated with

a BS in nursing. She loved being with you, she loved you all, and felt that you loved her in return. St. Bede's was her community of faith. It's where her faith was reestablished, among grown-up loving people. (For a while Susan had attended the liberal All Saints Episcopal Church in Pasadena, which she found to be "very fine, but it just wasn't the same.") Susan was a private person, a gentle person, a gentle voice. She was a faithful friend, and in later years she surprised herself with her own boldness in reorganizing the Los Angeles chapter of Call to Action. Listening to a strong voice is what gave her courage. "This is the way. Take it, Susan." You will remain a mystery to us all, Susan.

Oceanic grief, little hallelujahs. . .
Fr. Kevin closes, calling on "God Who conquers all things, even death itself."

NOTES

PROLOGUE

1. "The Strong Right Arm of the Bishops: The Knights of Columbus and Anti-Marriage Equality Funding," report by Equally Blessed, http://equally-blessed.org/release/knights-columbus-report, October, 2012.

2. See Jennifer Jacobson, "Catholic Group Criticizes Professors," *Chronicle of Higher Education* (September 2, 2005), http://chronicle.com, The Faculty 52 (2), A16.

3. See Ronald Inglehart and Pippa Norris, *Rising Tide: Gender Equality and Cultural Change* (New York: Cambridge University Press, 2003), Susan Thistle, *From Marriage to Market: The Transformation of Women's Lives and Work* (Berkeley: University of California Press, 2006), and Leigh Ann Wheeler, *How Sex Became a Civil Liberty* (New York: Oxford University Press, 2012).

4. See the lament by Cardinal Francis George of Chicago regarding his fears about "how we are losing our freedoms in the name of individual rights," quoted by Sharon Otterman, "In Hero of the Catholic Left, a Conservative Cardinal Sees a Saint," *New York Times* (November 26, 2012).

5. David O'Brien, *U.S. Catholic Historian* 29 (Spring 2011), 5: review of Joseph P. Chinnici, *When Values Collide: The Catholic Church, Sexual Abuse, and the Challenges of Leadership* (Maryknoll, NY: Orbis, 2010). See also Paula Kane, "American Catholic Studies at a Crossroads," *Religion and American Culture* 16 (Summer 2006), especially 264–265.

6. See George Wilson, SJ, "An Examination of Conscience for the Whole People of God," *Human Development* 25 (Summer 2004), 5–8.

INTRODUCTION

1. Tony Pipolo, *Robert Bresson: A Passion for Film* (New York: Oxford University Press, 2010), 10.

2. Garry Wills, *Bare Ruined Choirs: Doubt, Prophecy, and Radical Religion* (Garden City, NY: Doubleday, 1972).

3. "Earthly Concerns: The Catholic Church Is as Big as Any Company in America," *Economist* (August 18, 2012).

4. "Charting a Future for Catholic Education," *City Journal* (October 17, 2012).

5. For an overview of forces sweeping over the American church that respects regional variations and cultural nuance, see Tom Roberts, "Seismic Shifts Reshape US Catholicism," *National Catholic Reporter* (January 17, 2012).

6. M. Kathleen Kaveny, "Retrieving and Reframing Catholic Casuistry," in *The Crisis of Authority in Catholic Modernit* y, ed. Michael J. Lacey and Francis Oakley, 238 (New York: Oxford University Press, 2011). See also Paula M. Kane, *Separation and Subculture: Boston Catholicism, 1900–1920* (Chapel Hill: University of North Carolina Press, 1994) and Jon Gjerde, *Catholicism and the Shaping of Nineteenth-Century America*, ed. S. Debora Kang (New York: Cambridge University Press, 2012).

7. Amitai Etzioni formulated the distinction between coercive, utilitarian, and normative types of power in *A Comparative Analysis of Complex Organizations: On Power, Involvement, and Their Correlates* (Glencoe, IL: Free Press, 1961). In conventional political systems, coercive power is a *sine qua non*, equivalent to Max Weber's view of the state as the institution with a monopoly over the means of violence. Instrumental rewards and sanctions, and legitimacy, follow after. Institutional Catholicism in the United States has the reverse profile at this historical juncture. Its coercive capacity is close to zero, and the hierarchy's control over instrumental goods and services is weak. Leverage resides in its reservoir of moral legitimacy. Hence the church's "they shall not pass!" stance on issues of sexual authority.

8. See Lynne G. Zucker, "The Role of Institutionalization in Cultural Persistence," *American Sociological Review* 42 (October 1977), 726–743.

9. Hugh Heclo has argued that "by the mid-twentieth century the Supreme Court had embarked on the creation of a new and immensely elaborate system of rules, the general thrust of which was to favor a thoroughly secular approach to public life, especially but by no means exclusively in public schools." Heclo's case is sound enough for public schools, but he overlooks the increasingly favorable treatment that religious schools received during the same period. "Christianity and America," in *Christianity in America*, ed. Hugh Heclo et al., 1–144 (Cambridge, MA: Harvard University Press, 2007).

10. See Theo Hobson, "Not Liberal Enough," *Times Literary Supplement* (September 7, 2012) and Goodwin Liu, Pamela S. Karlan, and Christopher H. Schroeder, *Keeping Faith with the Constitution* (New York: Oxford University Press, 2010).

11. Compare David Brooks, "Rules for Craftsmen," *New York Times* (October 15, 2012).

12. Several years later, at a conference in Philadelphia, Hehir pointed out that Vatican II has typically been understood "as a council of renewal and reform." But while renewal was "about ideas, vision... reform is about institutions. Reform takes place not in the library but in the political arena." Compare Charles Simic, "A Master of the In-Between World," *New York Review of Books* (July 12, 2012).

13. The roots of my attention to multiple outcomes lie in social science concerns about "selecting on the dependent variable." The procedure, similar to but not the same as deleting

control groups, truncates the range of what needs to be accounted for and runs the risk of short-circuiting explanation. The compare-and-contrast option assured by multiple outcomes gets lost. Avoiding the fallacy doesn't guarantee an impartial investigation. But if you aren't careful about it, chances are you will be drawn into indicting or defending—engaging in the kind of persuasion that Catholics used to call "apologetics"—rather than explaining.

14. Vivian Gornick, *The Situation and the Story* (New York: Farrar, Straus, and Giroux, 2001), 35.

CHAPTER ONE THE MATRIX OF AMERICAN CATHOLICISM

1. Lawrence Gipson, "A 'Golden' Age for Catholic Center," *Yale Daily News* (February 25, 2009). Golden died in October 2011 at the age of eighty-two.

2. The volume of essays from the 2003 conference appeared as *Governance, Accountability, and the Future of the Catholic Church*, ed. Francis Oakley and Bruce Russett (New York: Continuum, 2004). The quote is from the book jacket.

3. John Courtney Murray, SJ, *The Problem of God, Yesterday and Today* (New Haven: Yale University Press, 1964). The lecture for 2006 was an abbreviated version of M. Cathleen Kaveny, "Prophecy and Casuistry: Abortion, Torture and Moral Discourse," *Villanova Law Review* 51 (2006), 499–579.

4. Peter R. D'Agostino, *Rome in America: Transnational Catholic Ideology from the Risorgimento to Fascism* (Chapel Hill: University of North Carolina Press, 2004).

5. Thomas Banchoff and Robert Wuthnow, eds., *Religion and the Global Politics of Human Rights* (New York: Oxford University Press, 2011).

6. Melissa J. Wilde, *Vatican II: A Sociological Analysis of Religious Change* (Princeton: Princeton University Press, 2007) and Robert Wuthnow, *The Restructuring of American Religion: Society and Faith since World War II* (Princeton: Princeton University Press, 1988).

7. Rochelle Gurstein, *The Repeal of Reticence: A History of America's Cultural and Legal Struggles over Free Speech, Obscenity, Sexual Liberation, and Modern Art* (New York: Hill and Wang, 1997). The landmark decision that made the pill legal for married women, Griswold v. Connecticut, came on June 7, 1965. (The FDA has authorized the pill Enovid for contraceptive use in 1960.) In 1972, Eisenstadt v. Baird made the pill legally, and anticlimactically, accessible to unmarried women in all states. See Elaine Tyler May, "How the Catholic Church Almost Came to Accept Birth Control," *Washington Post* (February 24, 2012).

8. David Courtwright, *No Right Turn: Conservative Politics in a Liberal America* (Cambridge: Harvard University Press, 2010), 40. Another nail in the coffin of a "tuneful, wholesome Catholicism" and the "Victorian Irish Catholic" ethos was the demise, during the 1960s, of the Legion of Decency and the motion picture industry's system of censorship, both run by old-line Catholics. See Thomas Doherty, *Hollywood's Censor: Joseph I. Breen and the Production Code Administration* (New York: Columbia University Press, 2007).

9. Susan F. Martin, *A Nation of Immigrants* (New York: Cambridge University Press, 2011), 183–219.

10. David J. O'Brien, "The Land O'Lakes Statement," *Boston College Magazine* (Winter 1998) and Kevin Sack, "Nuns, a 'Dying Breed,' Fade from Leadership Roles at Catholic Hospitals," *New York Times* (August 20, 2011).

11. See Thomas J. Shelley, "Twentieth-Century American Catholicism and Irish Americans," in *Making the Irish American*, ed. J. J. Lee and Marion R. Casey, 574–608 (New York: New York University Press, 2006) and Michele Dillon, "What Is Core to American Catholics in 2011," *National Catholic Reporter* (special issue on Catholics in America) (October 28–November 10, 2011).

12. See Donna J. Drucker, "An 'Aristocracy of Virtue': Cultural Development of the American Catholic Priesthood, 1884-1920s," *Religion and American Culture* 21 (Summer 2011), 227–258.

13. The seminal account of the "differentiation of the sphere of religious authority" is by Mark Chaves, "Secularization as Declining Religious Authority," *Social Forces* 72 (March 1994), 749–774.

14. John Spano and Jean Guccione, "L.A. Archdioceses Agrees to Pay 60 Million in Abuse Cases," *Los Angeles Times* (December 1, 2006).

15. See David S. Meyer, "Protest and Political Opportunities," *Annual Review of Sociology* 30 (2004), 125–145.

16. See Steven K. Green, *The Bible, the School, and the Constitution: The Clash That Shaped Modern Church-State Doctrine* (New York: Oxford University Press, 2012). Clerical sexual abuse has the potential to raise serious church-state issues insofar as litigation calls into question shields against prosecution provided under freedom-of-religion and statute of limitation norms. The political will to press this course has not been great. See Marci Hamilton, *Fundamentalism, Politics, and the Law* (New York: Palgrave Macmillan, 2011). A related area in which church-state issues continue to fester involves "the ministerial exception," the right of denominations to control the hiring and firing of employees whose duties involve religious activities. See Adam Liptak, "Justices Grant Leeway to Churches in Job Bias Laws," *New York Times* (January 11, 2012). Another area of church-state contention has already been mentioned: the bishops, claiming that religious liberty is under siege, have objected to the provision of family planning services in church-related ministries that receive federal funds. See Michael Kinsley, "Bishops Are Not Exactly Oppressed," *Philadelphia Inquirer* (November 23, 2011), Nicholas P. Cafardi, "Advice for the New Archbishop," *Philadelphia Inquirer* (September 8, 2011), and E. J. Dionne Jr., "Obama's Challenge with Catholics and Health Care," *Washington Post* (November 23, 2011).

17. David Matzo McCarthy, ed., *The Heart of Catholic Social Teaching* (Grand Rapids, MI: Brazos, 2009), and John A. Coleman, SJ, ed., *One Hundred Years of Catholic Social Thought* (Maryknoll, NY: Orbis, 1991). See also David C. Leege et al., *The Politics of Cultural Differences: Social Change and Voter Mobilization Strategies in the Post-New Deal Period* (Princeton: Princeton University Press, 2002) and Corwin W. Smidt et al., eds., *The Disappearing God Gap?* (New York: Oxford University Press, 2010).

18. For a useful if largely unsympathetic account, see Peter Berger, "Is the Vatican About to Occupy Wall Street?" *American Interest* (November 9, 2011), http://blogs.the-american-interest.com/berger/2011/11/09/is-the-vatican-about-to-occupy-wall-street/. Church-sponsored welfare organizations can be traced farther back than the nineteenth century. Networks of *misericórdias*—shelters, food dispensaries, health clinics, and the like—grew up in Mediterranean countries in the sixteenth century, before industrial times. See Maureen Flynn, *Sacred Charity: Confraternities and Social Welfare in Spain, 1400–1700* (Ithaca, NY: Cornell University Press, 1989) and Carlos Dinis da Fonseca, *Historia e Actualidade das Misericórdias* [History and Present Times of the Misericórdias] (Lisbon: Editorial Inquérito, 1996).

19. See, however, Roger Haight, *The Future of Christology* (New York: Continuum, 2005) and Paul Lakeland, "Not So Heterodox," *Commonweal* (January 26, 2007).

20. Richard McBrien, "The Disconnect between Bishops and Other Catholics," *National Catholic Reporter* (January 8, 2012).

21. Compare Michael J. Lacey and Francis Oakley, eds., *The Crisis of Authority in Catholic Modernity* (New York: Oxford University Press, 2011).

22. See D. Paul Sullins, "Gender and Religion: Deconstructing Universality, Constructing Complexity," *American Journal of Sociology* 112 (November 2006), 838–880, and Douglas Farrow, "The Dignifying Family," *First Things* (October 2011). "Imperishable essence" is lifted from an essay on a related topic by Wilfred M. McClay, "Less Boilerplate, More Symmetry," *Journal of American History* 98 (December 2011), 745.

23. Kevin P. Murphy and Jennifer M. Spear, "Historicizing Sexuality and Gender," *Gender & History* 22 (November 2010), 527–537; Jo Renee Formicola, "Globalization: A Twenty-First Century Challenge to Catholicism and its Church," *Journal of Church and State* 54 (Winter 2012), 106–121; and Lisa M. Diamond, *Sexual Fluidity: Understanding Women's Love and Desire* (Cambridge: Harvard University Press, 2008).

24. David M. Buss, *The Evolution of Desire: Strategies of Human Mating* (New York: Basic Books, 2003); Cullen Murphy, *The Word According to Eve: Women in the Bible in Ancient Times and Our Own* (New York: Houghton Mifflin, 1988); Margaret Susan Thompson, "Women, Feminism, and the New Religious History," in *Belief and Behavior: Essays in the New Religious History*, ed. Philip R. Vandermeer and Robert P. Swirenga, 136–163 (New Brunswick, NJ: Rutgers University Press, 1991); and Barbara B. Smuts, "The Evolutionary Origins of Patriarchy," *Human Nature* 6 (March 1995), 1–32.

25. Compare Keith R. Bradley, *Discovering the Roman Family: Studies in Roman Social History* (New York: Oxford University Press, 1991). For discussions of contending theological perspectives on the sexual question, see James F. Kennan, SJ, *A History of Catholic Moral Theology in the Twentieth Century: From Confessing Sins to Liberating Consciences* (New York: Continuum, 2010) and Mark S. Massa, SJ, *The American Catholic Revolution: How the '60s Changed the Church Forever* (New York: Oxford University Press, 2010), 29–74.

26. Quoted by Benjamin J. Friedman, "Chairman Greenspan's Legacy," *New York Review of Books* (March 20, 2008), 25.

27. The shift was not altogether sudden, and the cohesion of pre-sixties days was not total during the search for assimilation; see Mark M. Massa, *Anti-Catholicism in America: The Last Acceptable Prejudice* (New York: Crossroad, 2003).

28. John T. Noonan Jr., *The Church That Can and Cannot Change* (Notre Dame, IN: University of Notre Dame Press, 2005).

29. Paul Vitello, "To Save Them, A Plan to Prune Catholic Schools," *New York Times* (September 21, 2010) and David Gonzalez, "Schools Out, Forever," *New York Times* (June 24, 2011).

30. This is a simplification. The alienation of younger generations from the institutional church is equally serious in the eyes of ecclesiastical authorities. Though related to the two challenges mentioned, it is not reducible to them. See Christian Smith with Patricia Snell, *Soul Searching: The Religious and Spiritual Lives of Emerging Adults* (New York: Oxford University Press, 2009).

31. Damon Linker, *The Theocons: Secular America Under Siege* (New York: Doubleday, 2006).

32. See Mayer N. Zald, "Social Movements and Political Sociology in the Analysis of Organizations and Markets," *Administrative Science Quarterly* 53 (September 2008), 568–574.

33. Eric Hobsbawm, "Diary," *London Review of Books* (January 24, 2008), 35.

34. Richard Schoenherr, *Goodbye Father: The Celibate Male Priesthood and the Future of the Catholic Church* (New York: Oxford University Press, 2002).

35. Russell Shorto, "Keeping the Faith," *New York Times* (April 8, 2007) and Michael A. Hayes, ed., *New Religious Movements in the Catholic Church* (London: Burns & Oates, 2005). An exception is the Sant'Egidio community, founded in Rome in the late sixties, now with about 50,000 members worldwide, and with five branches in the East and Midwest of the United States. See Desmond O'Grady, "Pax Romana: An Interview with Andrea Riccardi," *U.S. Catholic* (July 2010).

36. On the course of Christian Democracy, see Stathis N. Kalyvas and Kees van Kersbergen, "Christian Democracy," *Annual Review of Political Science* 13 (2010), 183–209, Thomas Kselman and Joseph A. Buttigieg, ed., *European Christian Democracy: Historical Legacies and Comparative Perspectives* (Notre Dame, IN: University of Notre Dame Press, 2003) and Wolfram Kaiser, "Christian Democracy in Twentieth Century Europe," *Journal of Contemporary History* 39. (January 2004), 127–135; on Call to Action, Bradford Hinze, *Practices of Dialogue in the Roman Catholic Church* (New York: Continuum, 2006), 64–88; on the Catholic deficit, Mary Jo Bane, "The Catholic Puzzle: Parishes and Civic Life," in *Taking Faith Seriously*, ed. Mary Jo Bane, Brent Coffin, and Richard Higgins, 63–93 (Cambridge, MA: Harvard University Press, 2005); on Vatican II, John W. O'Malley, SJ, "Developments, Reforms, and Two Great Reformations: Towards a Historical Assessment of Vatican II," *Theological Studies* 44 (September 1983), 373–406 and O'Malley, "Opening the Church to the World," *New York Times* (October 10, 2012).

37. Roger Finke and Patricia Wittberg, "Organizational Revival from Within: Explaining Revivalism and Reform in the Roman Catholic Church," *Journal for the Scientific Study of Religion* 39 (June 2000), 154–170. The Society of St. Vincent de Paul, founded by a French layman early in the nineteenth century, is an overwhelmingly lay "confraternity." So are the Knights of Columbus, founded in the United States in the 1880s. The Knights, now at the top of the power ranking of lay groups in the United States, encountered some ecclesiastical opposition in getting started, but they had the advantage of clerical sponsorship. See Douglas Brinkley and Jule M. Fenster, *Parish Priest: Father Michael McGivney and the Knights of Columbus* (New York: William Morrow, 2006).

38. Gerald Berk and Dennis Galvan, "How People Experience and Change Institutions," *Theory and Society* 38 (November 2009), 543–580.

39. For an eloquent demurral, see Eamon Duffy, *Faith of Our Fathers: Reflections on Catholic Tradition* (New York: Continuum, 2004).

40. The archdiocese of Philadelphia is among the most prominent of Catholic franchises to join the ranks of the walking wounded. See David O'Reilly, "School Panel Head: Catholic School Changes Long Overdue," *Philadelphia Inquirer* (January 9, 2012) and Brian Roewe, "Philadelphia Archdiocese Announces Major School Closings," *National Catholic Reporter* (January 6, 2012). In the fall of 2012, the archdiocese announced a major restructuring to energize its school system.

See Jerry Filteau, "Philadelphia Breaks New Ground on Managing Catholic Schools," *National Catholic Reporter* (September 10, 2012).

41. See James Mahoney and Kathleen Thelen, "A Theory of Gradual Institutional Change," in *Explaining Institutional Change: Ambiguity, Agency, and Power*, ed. Mahoney and Thelen, 1–37 (Cambridge: Cambridge University Press, 2010.)

42. "Faith in Flux: Changes in Religious Affiliation in the U.S.," *Pew Forum on Religion and Public Life* (April 27, 2009).

43. Compare Avner Greif and David D. Laitin, "A Theory of Endogenous Institutional Change," *American Political Science Review* 96 (November 2004), 633–652. The cumulative impact of Botts' Dots (invented by Elbert D. Botts in 1953) resembles the butterfly effect made famous by chaos theory: the production of surprisingly large changes traceable to minor initial conditions.

CHAPTER TWO THE DYNAMICS OF TRADITION

1. Quoted in Peter McDonough, *Men Astutely Trained: A History of the Jesuits in the American Century* (New York: Free Press, 1992), 227.

2. Donald E. Pelotte, SSS, *John Courtney Murray: Theologian in Conflict* (New York: Paulist Press, 1976).

3. John T. Noonan Jr., *The Lustre of Our Country: The American Experience of Religious Freedom* (Berkeley: University of California Press, 1998) and Perez Zagorin, *How the Idea of Religious Toleration Came to the West* (Princeton: Princeton University Press, 2003).

4. George Weigel, *Tranquillitas Ordinis: The Present Failure and Future Promise of American Catholic Thought on War and Peace* (New York: Oxford University Press, 1987), 71.

5. Chris Beneke, *Beyond Toleration: The Religious Origins of American Pluralism* (New York: Oxford University Press, 2006), 204–205. For less sunny perspectives, see Susan Jacoby, *Free Thinkers: A History of American Secularism* (New York: Metropolitan, 2004) and J. Judd Owen, "The Struggle between 'Religion and Nonreligion': Jefferson, Backus, and the Dissonance of America's Founding Principles," *American Political Science Review* 101 (August 2007), 493–503.

6. Alfred Stepan, "Religion, Democracy, and the 'Twin Tolerations,'" *Journal of Democracy* 11 (October 2000), 37–57. See also Anthony Gill, *The Political Origins of Religious Liberty* (Cambridge: Cambridge University Press, 2008), Frank Lambert, *The Founding Fathers and the Place of Religion in America* (Princeton: Princeton University Press, 2008), and Gordon W. Wood, "Praying with the Founders," *New York Review of Books* (May 1, 2008).

7. Jack L. Walker, "A Critique of the Elitist Theory of Democracy," *American Political Science Review* 60 (June, 1966), 285–295. Walker's assessment focused on the political thought of Robert Dahl, the leading proponent of "polyarchy." Murray and Dahl got to know each other during Murray's sojourn at Yale in the fifties.

8. Peter McDonough, "On Hierarchies of Conflict and the Possibility of Civil Discourse: Variations on a Theme by John Courtney Murray," *Journal of Church and State* 36 (Winter 1994), 115. A complete catalog of Murray's legacy would have to include other loose ends. He wrote at a time when it seemed reasonable to treat denominations in the United States as plainly demarcated if not small in number. The religious landscape is more varied now, and "religion" is harder to define. As firmly established old-line churches have declined and new ones sprout as

prolifically as banks in strip malls, debate on such issues has begun to include a third, slippery term—vernacular practices, folkways, informal devotions, without clear organizational standing—that elude the polarity between "church" and "state." See Will Herberg, *Protestant Catholic Jew: An Essay in American Religious Sociology* (Garden City, NY: Doubleday,), Winnifred Fallers Sullivan, *The Impossibility of Religious Freedom* (Princeton: Princeton University Press, 2005), and Robert F. Cochran, Jr., ed., *Faith And Law: How Religious Traditions from Calvinism to Islam View American Law* (New York: New York University Press, 2008).

9. See William J. Callahan, *The Catholic Church in Spain, 1875–1998* (Washington, DC: Catholic University of America Press, 2000), 311. At around the same time that Murray was propounding his ideas about historical contingency, his fellow Jesuit, the Canadian Bernard Lonergan, was developing a similar approach; it is hard to tell which way intellectual influence ran.

10. Murray built on an encyclical by Leo XIII, *Graves de Commune*, issued in 1901 but by the mid-twentieth century largely forgotten, that allowed for flexibility regarding monarchical and "republican" forms of government. See the 1953 essay by Murray, "Leo XIII: Separation of Church and State," http://woodstock.georgetown.edu/library/murray/1953c.htm. Leo, writing for a European context, was careful to hedge his opening toward "Christian Democracy" and "Catholic Action" with admonitions about the need for caution, moderation, and deference. He was not a pluralist in the modern sense, as this excerpt from the encyclical makes clear:

> ... it is essential that all refrain from giving any cause of dissension which hurts and divides minds. Hence, in newspapers and in speeches to the people, let them avoid subtle and practically useless questions which are neither easy to solve nor easy to understand except by minds of unusual ability and after the most serious study. Those who sincerely seek after truth will not... let differences of opinion deteriorate into conflicts of wills. Besides, to whatever opinion a man's judgment may incline, if the matter is yet open to discussion, let him keep it, provided he be always disposed to listen with religious obedience to what the Holy See may decide on the question.

11. This is what Walter Ong, Murray's fellow Jesuit, pointed out in statements like "the development of the Roman Catholic ethos... has been [the product of] of a strongly masculinizing era." *Fighting for Life: Context, Sexuality, and Consciousness* (Ithaca, NY: Cornell University Press, 1981), 169.

12. John Courtney Murray, SJ, "The Danger of the Vows: An Encounter with Earth, Woman, and Spirit," *Woodstock Letters* 96 (Fall 1997), 424. The article was pieced together from a talk that Murray gave during a spiritual retreat for seminarians sometime in 1947. Compare Fulton J. Sheen, PhD, DD, *Peace of Soul* (New York: McGraw-Hill, 1949) and Sheen, *Lift Up Your Heart* (New York: McGraw-Hill, 1950).

13. Compare Peter Brown, *Augustine of Hippo: A Biography* (Berkeley: University of California Press, 1969), Ted Hughes, *Shakespeare and the Goddess of Complete Being* (New York: Farrar, Straus, and Giroux, 1992), and Joel-Peter Witkin, *Harms Way: Lust & Madness, Murder & Mayhem* (Santa Fe, NM: Twin Palms, 1994).

14. Cynthia Fuchs Epstein, "Great Divides: The Cultural, Cognitive, and Social Bases of the Global Subordination of Women," *American Sociological Review* 72 (February 2007), 1–22;

Francis Fukuyama, "The Primacy of Culture," *Journal of Democracy* 6 (January 1995), 7–14; James Q. Wilson, "On Gender," *Public Interest* 112 (Summer 1993), 3–26; Don S. Browning et al., eds., *Sex, Marriage, and Family in World Religions* (New York: Columbia University Press, 2006); and "Catholic Perspective on Women in Society and in the Church" (http://www.cco.caltech.edu/~nmcenter/women.html.) The last compilation, put together in 2000 by the Newman Center at Caltech, assembles the views of several Catholic neoconservatives—Mary Ann Glendon, Michael Novak, and others—on the subject.

15. For an unambiguously conservative reading of Murray, see Peter Augustine Lawyer, "John Courtney Murray as Catholic, American Conservative," in *The Dilemmas of American Conservatism*, ed. Kenneth L. Deutsch and Ethan Fishman, 97–124 (Louisville: University Press of Kentucky, 2010).

16. Allen Hertzke, "Religious Interest Groups in American Politics," in *Oxford Handbook of Religion and American Politics*, ed. Corwin E. Smidt, Lyman A. Kellstedt, and James L. Guth, 299–329 (New York: Oxford University Press, 2009) and Allan J. Lichtman, *White Protestant Nation: The Rise of the American Conservative Movement* (New York: Atlantic Monthly Press, 2008).

17. Daniel K. Williams, *God's Own Party: The Making of the Christian Right* (New York: Oxford University Press, 2010).

18. Peter Berger gives a concise history in "Contraception and the Culture War," *American Interest* (February 22, 2012), http://blogs.the-american-interest.com/berger/2012/02/22/contraception-and-the-culture-war/.

19. See John Allen Jr., "Reform Rollback or Emerging Sane Modernity?" *National Catholic Reporter* (August 28, 2007).

20. Laura Kalman, *Right Star Rising: A New Politics, 1974–1980* (New York: W. W. Norton, 2010) and Raymond Tatalovich and Byron W. Daynes, eds., *Moral Controversies in American Politics*, 4th ed. (Armonk, NY: M. E. Sharpe, 2011).

21. Mary Bernstein, "Identity Politics," *Annual Review of Sociology* 31 (2005), 47–74.

22. Charles E. Curran, "The Catholic Identity of Catholic Institutions," *Theological Studies* 58 (March 1997), 90–108. Some Catholic organizations seem to have been more successful than others in safeguarding their religious identity while pursuing professionalization. See Loramy Conradi Gerstbauer, "The Whole Story of NGO Mandate Change: The Peacebuilding Work of World Vision, Catholic Relief Services, and Mennonite Central Committee," *Nonprofit and Voluntary Sector Quarterly* 39 (October 2010), 844–865.

23. Compare Steven K. Green, *The Second Disestablishment: Church and State in Nineteenth-Century America* (New York: Oxford University Press, 2010).

24. See Leonard DeFiore, *Story of the Storm: Catholic Elementary Schools from the 1960s to the Present* (Arlington, VA: National Catholic Education Association, 2011). For a perspective that is critical of the bishops' own failure to address the school crisis with radical measures (including a revision of ordination requirements), see Patrick J. McCloskey and Joseph Claude Harris, "Catholic Education, in Need of Salvation," *New York Times* (January 6, 2013).

25. Hokyu Hwang and Walter W. Powell, "The Rationalization of Charity: The Influences of Professionalism in the Nonprofit Sector," *Administrative Science Quarterly* 54 (June, 2009), 268–298.

26. Andrew S. McFarland, "Neopluralism," *Annual Review of Political Science* 10 (2007), 45–66 and Olivier Zunz, *Philanthropy in America: A History* (Princeton: Princeton University Press, 2012), especially pp. 232–263. The figure is a gross estimate of how much one generation can pass on to the next, not of the net sum available to nonprofits.

27. See "Lobbying for the Faithful: Religious Advocacy Groups in Washington, D.C.," Pew Forum on Religion and Public Life, November 21, 2011, updated May 15, 2012, http://www.pewforum.org/Government/Lobbying-for-the-faithful—exec.aspx; Jeffrey M. Berry, *The New Liberalism: The Rising Power of Citizen Groups* (Washington, DC: Brookings Institution Press, 1999); Ann N. Costain and Andrew S. McFarland, eds., *Social Movements and American Political Institutions* (Lanham, MD: Rowan & Littlefield, 1998); and R. Shep Melnick, "Entrepreneurial Litigation: Advocacy Coalitions and Strategies in the Fragmented American Welfare State," in *Remaking America: Democracy and Public Policy in an Age of Inequality*, ed. Joe Soss, Jacob S. Hacker, and Suzanne Melter, 51–73 (New York: Russell Sage Foundation, 2007).

28. See Rick Santorum, *It Takes a Family: Conservatism and the Common Good* (Wilmington, DE: Intercollegiate Studies Institute, 2006).

29. See Wu Ming, "Berlusconism without Berlusconi," *London Review of Books* (November 18, 2010), blog, http://www.lrb.co.uk/blog/2010/11/18/wu-ming/berlusconism-without-berlusconi/.

30. David E. Apter, "Politics as Theatre," in *Social Performance*, eds. Jeffrey Alexander et al., 218–256 (Cambridge: Cambridge University Press, 2006); David Cannadine, *Ornamentalism* (New York: Oxford University Press, 2001); and Wilfrid Sheed, *The Hack* (New York: Macmillan, 1963).

31. Robert Wuthnow, *Sharing the Journey: Support Groups and America's New Quest for Community* (New York: Free Press, 1994).

32. There are exceptions; see Michael W. Cuneo, *The Smoke of Satan: Conservative and Traditional Dissent* (New York: Oxford University Press, 1997).

33. Compare James Hudnut-Beumler, *In Pursuit of the Almighty's Dollar: A History of Money and American Protestantism* (Chapel Hill: University of North Carolina Press, 2007).

34. See Frank Baumgartner and Beth L. Leech, *Basic Interests* (Princeton: Princeton University Press, 1998).

35. Compare Kathleen Thelen, *How Institutions Evolve: The Political Economy of Skills in Germany, Britain, the United States, and Japan* (Cambridge: Cambridge University Press, 2004).

36. See inter alia John L. Allen, Jr., "Global Priest Shortages, Faith and Reason in the U.K. and a Loss in Ohio," *National Catholic Reporter* (December 9, 2011).

37. Compare Jan Nelis, "The Clerical Response to a Totalitarian Political Religion: *La Civiltá Cattolica* and Italian Fascism," *Journal of Contemporary History* 46 (April 2004), 245–270.

38. Compare Jerry Filteau, "Bishop Urges Change in Teaching Concerning All Sexual Relationships," *National Catholic Reporter* (March 17, 2012).

39. The coverage of FutureChurch is intermingled with a less systematic treatment of the larger Call to Action movement, with which FutureChurch has often been aligned.

40. Kathleen Kennedy Townsend, *Failing America's Faithful: How Today's Churches Are Mixing God with Politics and Losing Their Way* (New York: Warner Books, 2007), 37.

41. The phrase comes from Gregor von Rezzori, *Memoirs of an Anti-Semite* (New York: New York Review of Books, 2008), inside cover, writing about the decades following the collapse of the Austro-Hungarian Empire.

PART TWO

1. Jonathan Haidt, "Forget the Money, Follow the Sacred," *New York Times* (March 17, 2012). See also Anna Marie Smith, *Welfare Reform and Sexual Regulation* (New York: Cambridge University Press, 2010) and Thomas Sugrue, "In Your Guts You Know He's Nuts," *London Review of Books* (January 3, 2008).

2. See David Farber, *The Rise and Fall of American Conservatism* (Princeton: Harvard University Press, 2007) and the essays in Peter Berkowitz, ed., *Varieties of American Conservatism* (Stanford, CA: Hoover Institution Press, 2004). Compare Molly Worthen, "The Power of Political Communion," *New York Times* (September 16, 2012) and the upbeat essays in Michael Kazin, ed., *In Search of Progressive America* (Philadelphia: University of Pennsylvania Press, 2008).

3. For a different ranking of the gravitas of issues, one favored by Catholic progressives, see David Hollenbach, SJ, *The Common Good and Christian Ethics* (New York: Cambridge University Press, 2002).

4. See Patrick Allitt, *Catholic Intellectuals and Conservative Politics in America, 1950–1985* (Ithaca, NY: Cornell University Press, 1993); Paul V. Murphy, *The Rebuke of History: The Southern Agrarians and American Conservative Thought* (Chapel Hill: University of North Carolina Press, 2001); and Joseph Scotchie, ed., *The Paleoconservatives: New Voices of the Old Right* (New Brunswick, NJ: Transaction, 1999).

5. Donald T. Critchlow, *Phyllis Schlafly and Grassroots Conservatism: A Woman's Crusade* (Princeton: Princeton University Press, 2005) and Donald T. Critchlow and Cynthia L. Stachecki, "The Equal Rights Amendment Reconsidered: Politics, Policy, and Social Mobilization in a Democracy," *Journal of Policy History* 20, no. 1 (2008), 157–176. Compare Timothy Stanley, *The Crusader: The Life and Tumultuous Times of Pat Buchanan* (New York: St. Martin's, 2012) and Adam Nagourney, "'Cultural War' of 1992 Moves in from the Fringe," *New York Times* (August 29, 2012).

6. One such figure is the evangelical Michael Gerson, commentator for the Public Broadcasting Service, columnist for the *Washington Post*, and former speechwriter for George W. Bush. In *Age of Fracture* (Cambridge: Belknap/Harvard University Press, 2011), 250ff., Daniel T. Rodgers credits Gerson with having "absorbed a large slice of Catholic social theory." See also Steven Teles, "Compassionate Conservatism, Domestic Policy, and the Politics of Ideational Change," in *Crisis of Conservatism? The Republican Party, the Conservative Movement and American Politics after Bush*, ed. Joel D. Aberbach and Gillian Peele, 178–211 (New York: Oxford University Press, 2011).

7. See Francis Fukuyama, *The Great Disruption: Human Nature and the Reconstitution of Social Order* (New York: Free Press, 1999). Some observers would push the origins of neoconservatism back to the 1930s, when many leftwing intellectuals broke with Stalinism; see Michael Kimmage, *The Conservative Turn: Lionel Trilling, Whittaker Chambers, and the Lessons of Anti-Communism* (Cambridge: Harvard University Press, 2009), 10ff., and Peter Steinfels, who coined the term in his book *The Neoconservatives: The Men Who Are Changing America's Politics* (New York: Simon & Schuster, 1979).

8. Richard Brookhiser, *Right Time, Right Place: Coming of Age with William F. Buckley, Jr. and the Conservative Movement* (New York: Basic Books, 2009). Moynihan's loathing of the

neoconservative label is amply documented by Hendrik Hertzberg, "Politics and Prose: The Letters of Daniel Patrick Moynihan," *New Yorker* (October 25, 2010), 78–82.

9. See Daniel Stedman Jones, *Masters of the Universe: Hayek, Friedman, and the Birth of Neoliberal Politics* (Princeton: Princeton University Press, 2012), Mitch Pearlstein, "Cain's Pain: A Three-Minute History of Neoconservatism," *American Experiment* blog (October 24, 2011), http://www.amexp.org/blog/201110/cains-pain-a-three-minute-history-of-neoconservatism-0, Jason W. Stevens, *God-Fearing and Free: A Spiritual History of America's Cold War* (Cambridge, MA: Harvard University Press, 2010) and Michael Kimmage's critique of Stevens's book in "Guilty of Innocence," *New Republic* (January 6, 2011). Neil Gross, Thomas Medvetz, and Rupert Russell summarize the definitional quarrels in "The Contemporary American Conservative Movement," *Annual Review of Sociology* 37 (2011), 325–354. The situation is still more confused when it comes to defining "the essential idea that holds together all of the various factions [of conservatism]." As Brian J. Glenn and Steven M. Teles write, "even the movement's semi-official historians have recognized that the task is, essentially, hopeless." "Introduction: Studying the Role of Conservatives in American Political Development," in *Conservatism and American Political Development*, ed. Glenn and Teles (New York: Oxford University Press, 2009), 11.

10. For a different yet critical reading of this history, see David Brooks, "The Conservative Mind," *New York Times* (September 24, 2012).

11. See E. L. Jones, "The Revival of Cultural Explanation in Economics," *Economic Affairs* 23 (December 2003), 7–13.

12. Nicholas D. Kristof, "Beyond Pelvic Politics," *New York Times* (February 11, 2012). Compare Geoffrey Kabaservice, "Archie Bunker's America: The GOP Takeover of Family Values," *New Republic* (December 20, 2012), http://www.tnr.com/print/book/review/family-values-robert-self-archie-bunker.

13. Don S. Browning et al., eds., *Sex, Marriage, and Family in World Religions* (New York: Columbia University Press, 2006) and Aline H. Kalbian, *Sexing the Church: Gender, Power, and Ethics in Contemporary Catholicism* (Bloomington: Indiana University Press, 2005),

CHAPTER THREE PRISONERS IN THE PROMISED LAND: NEOCONSERVATISM AS CULTURE AND STRATEGY

1. Donald T. Critchlow, *The Conservative Ascendancy: How the GOP Right Made Political History* (Cambridge: Harvard University Press, 2007) and George Nash, *The Conservative Intellectual Movement in America since 1945*, rev. ed. (Wilmington, DE: Intercollegiate Studies Institute, 1996). The description of the atmospherics dates from late 2006, when I visited the offices.

2. William H. Halsey, *The Survival of American Innocence: Catholicism in an Era of Disillusionment, 1920–1940* (Notre Dame, IN: University of Notre Dame Press, 1980) and Hugh McLeod, *The Religious Crisis of the 1960s* (New York: Oxford University Press, 2007).

3. For accounts that highlight the involvement of American Jews, see Justin Vaïsse, *Neoconservatism: The Biography of a Movement* (Cambridge, MA: Harvard University Press, 2010), especially 271ff., and Samuel C. Heilman, *Sliding to the Right: The Contest for the Future of American Orthodoxy* (Berkeley: University of California Press, 2006).

4. Robert Wuthnow, *The Restructuring of American Religion* (Princeton: Princeton University Press, 1988).

5. Interview with Richard John Neuhaus, New York, December 4, 2006. The title of Neuhaus's final book—*American Babylon: Notes of a Christian Exile* (New York: Basic Books, 2009)—says it all. See also Alasdair MacIntyre, *Against the Self-Image of the Age: Essays on Ideology and Philosophy* (Notre Dame, IN: University of Notre Dame Press, 1978) and any number of statements by Benedict XVI.

6. Robert Louis Wilken, *The Spirit of Early Christian Thought* (New Haven: Yale University Press, 2003). However, at least since the turn of the millennium, the leaders of American Catholicism have dabbled more deeply in obscurantism and outright reaction. See Eugene McCarraher, "Morbid Symptoms: The Catholic Right's False Nostalgia," *Commonweal* (November 5, 2012), http://commonwealmagazine.org/morbid-symptoms.

7. John J. DiIulio Jr., "The American Catholic Voter, Report 06-2," Program for Research on Religion and Urban Civil Society, University of Pennsylvania (April 2006), 3, 5, 9, 12, and DiIulio, "The Catholic Voter," *Commonweal* (April 7, 2006), 10–15.

8. The sociologist Peter Berger, a one-time colleague of Neuhaus, gives a concise account of this outreach in a blog entitled "Contraception and the Culture War," *American Interest* (February 22, 2012), http://blogs.the-american-interest.com/berger/2012/02/22/contraception-and-the-culture-war/.

9. Philip Jenkins, *Decade of Nightmares: The End of the Sixties and the Making of Eighties America* (Oxford: Oxford University Press, 2006) and George Weigel, "The Sixties, Again and Again," *First Things* (April 2008), 32–39.

10. See Christian Smith, *Lost in Transition: The Dark Side of Emerging Adulthood* (New York: Oxford University Press, 2011). Compare the Sisters of St. Joseph of Brentwood, NY, *Brooklyn Catholic Readers: First Book in Reading* (New York: Schwatz, Kirwin, and Fauss, 1933), Rev. Michael A. McGuire, *New Baltimore Catechism and Mass*, no. 2, official revised edition (New York: Benziger, 1953), the slightly updated *Saint Joseph Baltimore Catechism*, official revised edition, no. 2, explained by Rev. Bennet Kelly, CP (New York: Catholic Book Publishing, 1962–9), the Daughters of St. Paul, *Guide to the Revised Baltimore Catechism for Grade One, According to the St. Paul Catechism of Christian Doctrine*, no. 2 (Jamaica Plain, MA: Daughters of St. Paul, 1957), and Gustave Doré, *The Doré Bible Illustrations* (New York: Dover, 1974).

11. Daniel Wakin and Ian Fisher, "Sistine Chapel's Doors Are Closed as Cardinals Begin Conclave," *New York Times* (April 18, 2005).

12. The scene is reminiscent of the conclusion of *La Dolce Vita*, released two years earlier in 1960, also loaded with Catholic symbolism. After a drunken all-night party, Marcello Mastroianni and his companions wind up on a beach, where they inspect a one-eyed blob of a "sea monster" and, off in the distance, an angelic young girl waving to the hero, her voice drowned out by the surf.

13. M. P. Baumgartner, *The Moral Order of a Suburb* (New York: Oxford University Press, 1988) and James Davison Hunter, *The Death of Character: Moral Education in an Age without Good or Evil* (New York: Basic Books, 2000). See also Jennifer Michael Hecht, *Doubt: A History* (New York: HarperCollins, 2003).

14. See Gene Burns, *The Moral Veto: Framing Contraception, Abortion, and Cultural Pluralism in the United States* (New York: Cambridge University Press, 2005) and William J. Bennett, *The Book of Virtues* (New York: Simon and Schuster, 1996).

15. Seth Dowland, "'Family Values' and the Formation of a Christian Right Agenda," *Church History* 78 (August 2009), 606–631, and William M. Shea, *The Lion and the Lamb: Evangelicals and Catholics in America* (New York: Oxford University Press, 2004). The stress on behavior over beliefs corresponds to the philosophical focus on "deontological" as compared to ontological questions. The political scientist Theodore J. Lowi makes a similar distinction between "error" and "sin" in elaborating on his classic typology of public issues: "Foreword: New Dimensions of Policy and Politics," in *Moral Controversies in American Politics*, 4th ed., ed. Raymond Tatalovich and Byron W. Daynes, xvi–xvii (Armonk, NY: M. W. Sharpe, 2011).

16. David Martin, *A General Theory of Secularization* (New York: Harper & Row, 1978).

17. Arens, "The Anxiety of Prosperity," *Policy Review* 104 (December 2000–January 2001), 75–81.

18. Daniel Bell, *The Cultural Contradictions of Capitalism* (New York: Basic Books, 1976). See also John C. Bogle, *The Struggle for the Soul of Capitalism* (New Haven: Yale University Press, 2005) and Lizabeth Cohen, *A Consumers' Republic: The Politics of Mass Consumption in Postwar America* (New York: Alfred A. Knopf, 2003).

19. For rebuttals from the Catholic side, see Michael Novak, *The Spirit of Democratic Capitalism* (New York: Simon & Schuster, 1982), George Weigel and Robert Royal, eds., *Building the Free Society: Democracy, Capitalism, and Catholic Social Teaching* (Grand Rapids, MI: William Eerdmans, 1993), Samuel Gregg, "*Deus Caritas Est*: The Social Message of Pope Benedict XVI," *Economic Affairs* 26 (June 2006), 55–59, and James Q. Wilson, *The Moral Sense* (New York: Free Press, 1993).

20. Jeff Madrick, *Age of Greed: The Triumph of Finance and the Decline of America, 1970 to the Present* (New York: Alfred A. Knopf, 2011).

21. Kim Phillips-Fein, *Invisible Hands: The Making of the Conservative Movement from the New Deal to Reagan* (New York: W. W. Norton, 2009), 235.

22. See Paul Tough, "The Birthplace of Obama the Politician," *New York Times Magazine* (August 19, 2012). For qualifications and dissent, see Scott Forbes, *A Natural History of Families* (Princeton: Princeton University Press, 2005).

23. For a career overview, see Jim Newton, "James Q. Wilson's Moral Sense," *Los Angeles Times* (May 27, 2007). An assessment from a conservative perspective is Matt Delisi, "Conservatism and Common Sense: The Criminological Career of James Q. Wilson," *Justice Quarterly* 20 (September 2003), 661–674. In a personal communication (May 5, 2008), Wilson stated that "I was raised by my parents in the Catholic faith, but as a young man I drifted away from the church. While I admire the church's teachings on many matters, I do not belong to that (or any) faith." Wilson was mistaken for a Catholic several times—by, for example, Murray Friedman, *The Neoconservative Revolution: Jewish Intellectuals and the Shaping of Public Policy* (New York: Cambridge University Press, 2005), 200.

24. James Q. Wilson and George L. Kelling, "Broken Windows: The Police and Neighborhood Safety," *Atlantic Monthly* (March 1982), 29–38. For a positive evaluation of the idea, see Wesley G. Skogan, *Police and Community in Chicago: A Tale of Three Cities* (New York: Oxford University Press, 2006); on the skeptical side, Bernard E. Harcourt and Jens Ludwig, "Broken Windows: New Evidence from New York City and a Five-City Social Experiment," *University of Chicago Law Review* (Winter 2006), 271–320, and D. W. Miller, "Poking Holes in the Theory of 'Broken

Windows,'" *Chronicle of Higher Education* (February 9, 2001). See also Sabrina Tavernise, "For Late 'Mr. Mayor,' A Last Tour of Town," *New York Times* (April 25, 2001). Former Los Angeles police chief William Bratton adapted Wilson's ideas to the community-policing movement, cracking down on minor offenses like turnstile jumping, when he was chief of transit police in New York. See Bratton with Peter Knobler, *The Turnaround: How America's Top Cop Reversed the Crime Epidemic* (New York: Random House, 1998).

25. James Q. Wilson, *The Marriage Problem: How Our Culture Has Weakened Families* (New York: HarperCollins, 2002).

26. Wilson, "The Rediscovery of Character: Private Virtue and Public Policy," *Public Interest* 81 (Fall 1985), 3–17.

27. Ibid., 294.

28. See Barbara Dafoe Whitehead, *The Divorce Culture* (New York: Alfred A. Knopf, 1997). The causal link between single parenthood and children's underperformance has been disputed by Gary Painter and David I. Levine, "Family Structure and Youths' Outcomes: Which Correlations Are Causal?" *Journal of Human Resources* 35 (Summer 2000), 524–549, and Marianne E. Page and Ann Huff Stevens, "The Economic Consequences of Absent Parents, *Journal of Human Resources* 39 (Winter 2004), 80–107. For a study that reinforces the value of both the family and kin for children's social attainment, see Mad Meier Jæger, "The Extended Family and Children's Educational Success," *American Sociological Review* 77 (December 2012), 903–922.

29. James Q. Wilson, "The Ties that Do Not Bind: The Decline of Marriage and Loyalty," *In Character: A Journal of Everyday Virtues* [John Templeton Foundation] (Fall 2005), http://incharacter.org/archives/loyalty/the-ties-that-do-not-bind-the-decline-of-marriage-and-loyalty/.

30. James Q. Wilson, "Why We Don't Marry: The Cultural Trends that Gave Us Enlightenment and Freedom Now Give Us Cohabitation and Divorce," *City Journal* (Winter 2002), http://www.city-journal.org/html/12_1_why_we.html.

31. David Brooks, "When Preaching Flops," *New York Times* (June 22, 2007).

32. James Q. Wilson, "Character and Culture," *Public Interest* 159 (Spring 2005), 45.

33. Ibid., 48.

34. Ibid., 47. Toward the end of his life, Wilson came to suspect that the lock-'em-up policy had overshot its mark and that mass incarceration had become as serious a problem as street crime. See Richard Rosenfield, "The Limits of Crime Control," *Journal of Criminal Law and Criminology* 93 (Fall 2002), 289–298. On the exceptionally high rate of incarceration in the United States, see Adam Liptak, "Inmate Count in U.S. Dwarfs Other Nations," *New York Times* (April 23, 2008). "By the close of the twentieth century," Heather Ann Thompson writes, "almost 5.6 million US adults had served time in a state or federal prison." See "Why Mass Incarceration Matters: Rethinking Crisis, Decline, and Transformation in Postwar American History," *Journal of American History* 97 (December 2010), 734. For studies that highlight the costs of prison time in aggravating racial and class disparities, see Becky Pettit and Bruce Western, "Mass Imprisonment and the Life Course: Race and Class Inequality in Lifetime Risks of Imprisonment," *American Sociological Review* 69 (April 2004), 151–169; John Hagan and Holly Foster, "Intergenerational Educational Effects of Mass Imprisonment in America," *Sociology of Education* 85 (July 2012), 259–286; Jason de Parle, "The American Prison Nightmare," *New York Review of Books* (April

12, 2007). See also Joshua Guetzkow and Bruce Western, "The Political Consequences of Mass Imprisonment," in *Remaking America: Democracy and Public Policy in an Age of Inequality*, eds. Joe Soss et al., 228–242 (New York: Russell Sage Foundation, 2007), and Loïc Acquaint, "Crafting the Neoliberal State: Workfare, Prisonfare, and Social Insecurity," *Sociological Forum* 25 (June 2010), 197–220. One study that dismisses the causal importance of "the imprisonment binge" but attributes positive significance to police tactics inspired by the broken windows thesis is by Franklin E. Zimring, *The Great American Crime Decline* (New York: Oxford University Press, 2007).

35. James Q. Wilson, "Gentlemen, Politician, Scholar," *Public Interest* 152 (Summer 2003).

36. Wilson, "Why We Don't Marry."

37. James Q. Wilson, "A Guide to Reagan Country," *Writers and Issues*, ed. Theodore Solotaroff, 67 (New York: Mentor, 1969).

38. John J. DiIulio Jr., *Godly Republic: A Centrist Blueprint for America's Faith-Based Future* (Berkeley: University of California Press, 2007), 135–136, passim, and conversation, Philadelphia, July 9, 2004.

39. John J. DiIulio Jr., "Getting Faith-Based Programs Right," *Public Interest* 155 (Spring 2004).

40. DiIulio, "Getting Faith-Based Programs Right"; and DiIulio, "The Three Faith Factors," *Public Interest* 149 (Fall 2002). See also Charles Kuo, *Tempting Faith: An Inside Story of Political Seduction* (New York: Free Press, 2006) and Charles Savage, "Bush Aides Say Religious Hiring Doesn't Bar Aid," *New York Times* (October 18, 2008).

41. John J. DiIulio Jr., "Godly People in the Public Square," *Public Interest* 141 (Fall 2000), 114. See also Ram A. Cnaan and Stephanie C. Boddie, "Setting the Context: Assessing the Effectiveness of Faith-Based Social Services," *Journal of Religion and Spirituality in Social Work* 25 (200), 5–18, and Paul Lichterman, "Beyond Dogmas: Religion, Social Service, and Social Life in the United States," *American Journal of Sociology* 113 (July 2007), 243–257.

42. Marvin Olasky, *Compassionate Conservatism: What It Is, What It Does, and How It Can Transform America* (New York: Free Press, 2000), 13–14.

43. John J. DiIulio Jr., "The Moral Compassion of True Conservatism," in *The Fractious Nation? Unity and Division in Contemporary American Life*, ed. Jonathan Rieder, 218 (Berkeley: University of California Press, 2003).

44. Ibid., 220.

45. Ibid., 218.

46. Ibid., 221.

47. DiIulio credits Donald F. Kettl, *Government By Proxy: (Mis?)managing Federal Programs* (Washington, DC: Congressional Quarterly Press, 1988) with pinpointing this phenomenon.

48. See Jacob S. Hacker, *The Divided Welfare State: The Battle over Public and Private Benefits in the United States* (Cambridge: Cambridge University Press, 2002).

49. John DiIulio, "The Prophetic Voice," *Sojourners* (May–June 2001).

50. Ibid. See also E. J. Dionne Jr. and John DiIulio, eds., *What's God Got to do with the American Experiment? Essays on Religion and Politics* (Washington, DC: Brookings Institution, 2000).

51. DiIulio, *Godly Republic*, 165–168. On this point DiIulio seems to ignore the reach of Catholic Charities, whose agencies work independently of parishes.

52. An assessment that tries to retain the link between the "moral" and "scientific" dimensions of social deviance is by William J. Bennett, John J. DiIulio Jr., and John P. Walters, *Body Count: Moral Poverty... And How to Win America's War Against Crime and Drugs* (New York: Simon & Schuster, 1996). The book is full of tables and charts without statistical controls of the kind needed to establish the causal associations on which the authors' argument depends. A more skeptical assessment of the welfare-marital status link is by Francine D. Blau et al., "The Impact of Welfare Benefits on Single Motherhood and Headship of Young Women," *Journal of Human Resources* 39 (Spring 2004), 382–404.

53. In this respect the message of Wilson's work especially seems prescient, anticipating some of the arguments of behavioral economics, with its stress on individual psychology (though less on culture). See Richard H. Thaler and Cass R. Sunstein, *Nudge: Improving Decisions about Health, Wealth, and Happiness* (New Haven: Yale University Press, 2008).

54. Formulated by Peter Rossi, "The Iron Law of Evaluation and Other Metallic Roles," in *Research in Social Problems and Public Policy*, vol. 4, ed. Joann L. Miller and Michael Lewis, 4 (Greenwich, CT: JAI Press, 1987).

55. After falling out of fashion, research of the sort that Wilson pursued on the cultural roots of poverty, as captured in family structures, returned to favor. See Patricia Cohen, "'Culture of Poverty' Makes a Comeback," *New York Times* (October 17, 2010), Sara McLanahan et al., "Fragile Families," *Future of Children* 20 (Fall, 2010), 3–230, and William Julius Wilson, "Why Both Social Structure and Culture Matter in a Holistic Analysis of Inner-City Poverty," *Annals of the American Academy of Political and Social Science* 629 (May 2010), 200–219.

56. The hybrid can go astray. DiIulio gained prominence in conservative circles by forecasting in the mid-1990s, on the basis of demographic projections, that crime rates among African Americans would skyrocket within a decade. He warned of a "ticking time bomb" of "superpredators." The prediction did not pan out. See Elaine Tyler May, "Security against Democracy: The Legacy of the Cold War at Home," *Journal of American History* 97 (March 2011), 952.

57. E. J. Dionne Jr., *Why Americans Hate Politics* (New York: Simon & Schuster/Touchstone, 1992), 14.

58. Lisa McGirr, "Now That Historians Know So Much about the Right, How Should We Best Approach the Study of Conservatism?" *Journal of American History* 98 (December 2011), 770.

59. DiIulio, *Godly Republic*, 190. Compare Bernard Laurent, "*Caritas in Veritate* as a Social Encyclical: A Modest Challenge to Economic, Social, and Political Institutions," *Theological Studies* 71 (September 2010), 515–544.

CHAPTER FOUR FEMINISM VERSUS THE FAMILY?

1. Samuel Johnson, "London: A Poem in Imitation of the Third Satire of Juvenal," lines 17–18, originally published 1738.

2. John E. Rice, DD, *Rebellious Wives and Slacker Husbands: What's Wrong with the Modern Home?* (Wheaton, IL: Sword of the Lord, 1945), 3.

3. James R. Kurth, "The Political Consequences of the Product Cycle: Industrial History and Political Outcomes," *International Organization* 33 (Winter 1979), 1–34; compare Steve Lohr, "Apple and Google as Creative Archetypes," *New York Times* (January 26, 2012).

4. James Kurth, "The Real Clash," *National Interest* 76 (Fall 1994), 3–15.

5. Kurth's mentor went on to write a final book, evidently influenced by his student, about the problems posed by the new ethnic heterogeneity: Samuel P. Huntington, *Who Are We? The Challenges to America's Identity* (New York: Simon & Schuster, 2004). See also Patrick J. Buchanan, *The Death of the West: How Dying Populations and Immigrant Invasions Imperil Our Country and Civilization* (New York: St. Martin's, 2002) and Harvey C. Mansfield, *Manliness* (New Haven: Yale University Press, 2006).

6. See Jim Sleeper, "Gods and Monsters," *Book Forum* (February–March 2012): review of Simon Critchley, *The Faith of the Faithless* (Brooklyn: Verso, 2011); Charles Murray, "The New American Divide," *Wall Street Journal* (January 21, 2012), and Mark Lilla, "The Great Disconnect," *New York Times Book Review* (September 30, 2012).

7. Kurth, "Real Clash."

8. Kurth, "Real Clash." A later version of the piece restates the argument but assigns feminism a less central role in the degradation of the West; see Kurth, "The United States as a Civilizational Leader," in *Civilizations in World Politics*, ed. Peter Katzenstein, 41–66 (London: Routledge, 2010). This toning down may reflect the fact that since 9/11 the prestige of a military ethos has grown. See Karlyn Bowman and Andrew Rugg, "A U.S. Military Worth Saluting: The U.S. Military Is the Most Respected Institution in American Life, According to Several Polls," *Los Angeles Times* (May 30, 2011).

9. See Steve Fraser and Gary Gerstle, eds., *Ruling America: A History of Wealth and Power in a Democracy* (Cambridge, MA: Harvard University Press, 2005).

10. Kurth, "Real Clash." See Joel A. Carpenter, *Revive Us Again: The Reawakening of American Fundamentalism* (New York: Oxford University Press, 1997).

11. Alasdair MacIntyre, *After Virtue* (Notre Dame, IN: University of Notre Dame Press, 1981), 245. Compare Charles Baxter, "A Different Kind of Delirium," *New York Review of Books* (February 9, 2012).

12. John Markoff, "The Passion of Steve Jobs," *New York Times* (January 21, 2008). See also Steven Ozment, "Why We Study Western Civ," *Public Interest* 158 (Winter 2005), 111–124, and John Seabrook, *Nobrow: The Culture of Marketing, the Marketing of Culture* (New York: Random House, 2001).

13. See Chrystia Freeland, *Plutocrats: The Rise of the New Global Super-Rich and the Fall of Everyone Else* (New York: Penguin, 2012).

14. Compare Daniel Patrick Moynihan, "Defining Deviancy Down: How We've Become Accustomed to Alarming Levels of Crime and Destructive Behavior," *American Scholar* 62 (Winter 1993), 17–30, and Andrew Karmen, "'Defining Deviancy Down': How Senator Moynihan's Misleading Phrase About Criminal Justice Is Rapidly Being Incorporated into Popular Culture," *Journal of Criminal Justice and Popular Culture* 2 (1994), 99–112.

15. Christopher Hayes, *Twilight of the Elites* (New York: Crown, 2012) recapitulates much of Kurth's thesis from a liberal perspective, stressing the displacement of the old establishment by an amoral meritocracy.

16. Just as Huntington inspired Kurth, Kurth's article provided the starting point for an attack by Robert George, later expanded into a book, on "lifestyle liberalism" and "secularist orthodoxy" that developed parts of his analysis along the lines of a history of ideas. The article is "A Clash of Orthodoxies," *First Things* (August–September 1999), 33–40.

17. Christine Smallwood, "Talking with Tony Judt," *Nation* (April 29, 2010). See also George Lakoff, *Moral Politics* (Chicago: University of Chicago Press, 2002).

18. Paul Berman, *A Tale of Two Utopias: The Political Journey of the Generation of 1968* (New York: W. W. Norton, 1996).

19. James T. Patterson, *Freedom Is Not Enough: The Moynihan Report and America's Struggle over Black Family Life, from LBJ to Obama* (New York: Basic Books, 2010).

20. Compare Elaine Tyler May, *Homeward Bound: American Families in the Cold War Era*, rev. ed. (New York: Basic Books, 2006).

21. Sam Roberts, "Moynihan in His Own Words," *New York Times* (September 19, 2010).

22. Walter I. Trattner, *From Poor Law to Welfare State: A History of Social Welfare in America*, sixth ed. (New York: Free Press, 1999).

23. Daniel P. Moynihan, "A Dahrendorf Inversion and the Twilight of the Family," in *The Future of the Family*, ed. Daniel P. Moynihan, Timothy M. Smeeding, and Lee Rainwater, xvii (New York: Russell Sage Foundation, 2004).

24. Daniel P. Moynihan, *Miles to Go: A Personal History of Social Policy* (Cambridge, MA: Harvard University Press, 1996), 189. The phrase was coined by William Graham Sumner, one of the founders of American sociology.

25. Ibid., 229.

26. Peter Steinfels, "O'Connor Joins in Protesting a Notre Dame Award for Moynihan," *New York Times* (May 8, 1992).

27. Daniel P. Moynihan, *Family and Nation, Godkin Lectures, Harvard University* (San Diego: Harcourt Brace Jovanovich, 1986).

28. See Louis Menand, *The Metaphysical Club* (New York: Farrar, Straus, and Giroux, 2001).

29. Mary Ann Glendon, *The Transformation of Family Law: State, Law, and Family in the United States and Western Europe* (Chicago: University of Chicago Press, 1989), 291–292.

30. See Darrin M. McMahon, *Enemies of the Enlightenment: The French Counter-Enlightenment and the Making of Modernity* (New York: Oxford University Press, 2001).

31. Glendon, *Transformation of Family Law*, 16. See also Charly Coleman, "Resacralizing the World: The Fate of Secularization in Enlightenment Historiography," *Journal of Modern History* 82 (June 2010), 368–395.

32. See John Summers, "Daniel Bell and The End of Ideology," *Dissent* (Spring 2011).

33. Glendon opposes the ordination of women and similar reforms in Catholicism, but that compartment seems separate from her views on public policy—except that she concurs with the church's deep skepticism regarding divorce. See Garry O'Sullivan and Sarah MacDonald, "McAllen Reveals 'Attack' by Disgraced Cardinal," *Irish Independent* (October 6, 2012).

34. Mary Ann Glendon, *Abortion and Divorce in Western Law* (Cambridge: Harvard University Press, 1987), 132–133. See also Gøsta Esping-Anderson, *The Three Worlds of Welfare Capitalism* (Oxford: Polity, 1990).

35. See Hugh Heclo, "General Welfare and Two American Political Traditions," *Political Science Quarterly* 101 (1986), 179–196.

36. Mary Ann Glendon, *Rights Talk: The Impoverishment of Political Discourse* (New York: Free Press, 1991), 73, and Glendon, "What's Wrong with Welfare Rights," in *Welfare in America:*

Christian Perspectives on a Policy in Crisis, ed. Stanley W. Carlson-Thies and James W. Skillen, 81–94 (Grand Rapids, MI: William Eerdmans, 1996).

37. Glendon, *Rights Talk*, 45. Glendon and James Q. Wilson disagreed on gun control. See Wilson, "In Defense of Guns," *Los Angeles Times* (April 20, 2007).

38. Glendon, *Abortion and Divorce in Western Law*, 114. Compare Steven D. Smith, *The Disenchantment of Secular Discourse* (Cambridge, MA: Harvard University Press, 2010). For a historical treatment of the tensions in legal individualism within American constitutional law, see William J. Novak, *The People's Welfare: Law and Regulation in Nineteenth-Century America* (Chapel Hill: University of North Carolina Press, 1996).

39. The logic of the papal condemnation is strikingly similar to that used by another German scholar, and a radical of the left, the late Herbert Marcuse, to excoriate "repressive tolerance." See the essay entitled "Repressive Tolerance" by Marcuse in Robert Paul Wolff, Barrington Moore Jr., and Herbert Marcuse, *A Critique of Pure Tolerance* (Boston: Beacon Press, 1969), 95–127. George Cardinal Pell of Australia uses the same reasoning in his argument that "modern liberalism has strong totalitarian tendencies," published as "Intolerant Tolerance," *First Things* (August–September 2009).

40. Glendon's critique of narcissism closely resembles the views of the social critic Christopher Lasch; see Eric Miller, *Hope in a Scattering Time: A Life of Christopher Lasch* (Grand Rapids, MI: William Eerdmans, 2010)

41. See however James Q. Wilson and Richard J. Herrnstein, *Crime and Human Nature* (New York: Simon & Schuster, 1985). It would be instructive to see how Glendon's treatment of the condition of women and their children in the United States holds up in light of the growing attention given to human rights more generally. For starters, see Mary Ann Glendon, *A World Made New: Eleanor Roosevelt and the Universal Declaration of Human Rights* (New York: Random House, 2001) and Margaret E. Keck and Kathryn Sikkink, *Activists Beyond Borders: Advocacy Networks in International Politics* (Ithaca, NY: Cornell University Press, 1998).

42. Todd Gitlin, "What My Teacher James Q. Wilson Missed," contribution to the forum "James Q. Wilson, Broken Windows and Los Angeles," Rand Corporation, Santa Monica, CA, June 4, 2012, http://zocalopublicsquare.org/thepublicsquare/2012/06/03/what-my-teacher-james-q-wilson-missed/read/who-we-were/.

CHAPTER FIVE WELFARE REFORM, AMERICAN VALUES, AND THE TRIUMPH OF CATHOLIC NEOCONSERVATISM

1. Steve Fraser, "The Age of Acquiescence," *Salmagundi* 170/171 (Spring 2011), 23.

2. For an overview, see Kim Phillips-Fein, "Conservatism: A State of the Field," *Journal of American History* 98 (December 2011), 723–743. See also Eva Bertram, "Democratic Divisions in the 1960s and the Road to Welfare Reform," *Political Science Quarterly* 126 (Winter 2011–12), 579–610; W. Wesley McDonald, *Russell Kirk and the Age of Ideology* (Columbia: University of Missouri Press, 2004); Mark Blyth, *Great Transformations: Economic Ideas and Institutional Change in the Twentieth Century* (New York: Cambridge University Press, 2002); and Matthew Avery Sutton, "Was FDR the Antichrist? The Birth of Fundamentalist Antiliberalism in a Global Age," *Journal of American History* 98 (March 2012), 1052–1074. For a discussion skeptical of the primacy of ideas in this transition, see Monica Prasad, *The Politics of Free Markets: The*

Rise of Neoliberal Economic Policies in Britain, France, Germany, and the United States (Chicago: University of Chicago Press, 2006).

3. Elizabeth Tandy Shermer, "Origins of the Conservative Ascendancy: Barry Goldwater's Early Senate Career and the De-legitimization of Organized Labor," *Journal of American History* 95 (December 2008), 679. Some analysts have contended that it was a 1978 ruling by the IRS, challenging tax exemptions for Christian schools founded since 1963 (around the time of the Great Society's Civil Rights Act) that drove conservatives to the barricades more than the abortion controversy. See Geoffrey Hodgson, *The World Turned Right Side Up: A History of the Conservative Ascendancy in America* (Boston: Houghton Mifflin, 1996), 177ff. This may have been true for segregationists and some Protestant evangelicals but it was opposition to abortion that helped unite conservative Catholics and evangelicals. See Paul Boyer, "The Evangelical Resurgence in 1970s American Protestantism," in *Rightward Bound: Making America Conservative in the 1970s*, ed. Bruce J. Schulman and Julian E. Zelizer, 29–51 (Cambridge: Harvard University Press, 2008).

4. May, "Security against Democracy," 950.

5. For different takes on Catholic lobbying regarding welfare policy, see John A. Coleman, SJ, "American Catholicism, Catholic Charities U.S.A., and Welfare Reform," *Journal of Policy History* 13 (January 2001), 73–108, and Thomas J. Massaro, SJ, *United States Welfare Policy: A Catholic Response* (Washington, DC: Georgetown University Press, 2007).

6. David M. Kennedy, "What the New Deal Did," *Political Science Quarterly* 124 (Summer 2009), 251–268.

7. George Weigel, "The End of the Bernardin Era: The Rise, Dominance, and Decline of a Culturally Accommodating Catholicism," *First Things* (February 2011).

8. John McGreevy, "Shifting Allegiances: Catholics, Democrats, and the GOP," *Commonweal* (September 22, 2006), 17.

9. Mary Jo Bane and Brent Coffin, Introduction, in *Who Will Provide? The Changing Role of Religion in American Social Welfare*, ed. Mary Jo Bane, Brent Coffin, and Ronald Thiemann (Boulder, CO: Westview, 2000), 8–9.

10. Eduardo Porter, "Inequality Undermines Democracy," *New York Times* (March 20, 2012).

11. Bane and Coffin, *Who Will Provide?*, 9.

12. Ibid.

13. Christopher Howard, "Giving the People What They Want? Age, Class, and Distribution in the United States," in *Divide and Deal: The Politics of Distribution in Democracies*, ed. Ian Shapiro, Peter A. Swenson, and Daniela Donno, 231–235 (New York: New York University Press, 2008); Mary R. Jackman and Robert W. Jackman, *Class Awareness in the United States* (Berkeley: University of California Press, 1983); Herbert McClosky and John Zaller, *The American Ethos: Public Attitudes Toward Capitalism and Democracy* (Cambridge, MA: Harvard University Press, 1984); and Sebastian Mallaby, "Fairer Deal," *New York Times* (September 24, 2010).

14. Larry M. Bartels, *Unequal Democracy: The Political Economy of the New Gilded Age* (New York: Russell Sage Foundation, 2008). Lew Daly makes a case for the persistence of a progressive stream in Catholic variants of the American creed. "In Search of the Common Good: The Catholic Roots of American Liberalism," *Boston Review* 32 (May–June, 2007), 23–27. Daly's

argument would benefit by taking into account the Republicanization of erstwhile Catholic New Deal Democrats.

15. William Galston, "Why the President's Campaign Shouldn't Focus on Inequality," *New Republic* (May 3, 2012).

16. Katherine S. Newman and Elisabeth S. Jacobs, *Who Cares? Public Ambivalence and Government Activism from the New Deal to the Second Gilded Age* (Princeton: Princeton University Press, 2010). See also Greg M. Shaw, "Changes in Public Opinion and the American Welfare State," *Political Science Quarterly* 124 (Winter 2009–10), 627–653, and Daniel J. Hopkins, "Whose Economy? Perceptions of National Economic Performance during Unequal Growth," *Public Opinion Quarterly* 76 (Spring 2012), 50–71.

17. See Michael Jan Rozbicki, *Culture and Liberty in the Age of the American Revolution* (Charlottesville: University of Virginia Press, 2011); Jennifer L. Goloboy, "The Early American Middle Class," *Journal of the Early Republic* 25 (Winter 2005), 537–545; and Andrew Kohut, "Don't Mind the Gap," *New York Times* (January 26, 2012).

18. Margie DeWeese-Boyd, "Re-establishing Poor Law as Public Ethic: Church, Charity, and Poverty Alleviation in the Post-Welfare Era," *Journal of Policy History* 16 (2004), 357.

19. E. J. Dionne Jr., *Our Divided Political Heart: The Battle for the American Idea in an Age of Discontent* (New York: Bloomsbury, 2012).

20. See Stanley Feldman and Marco Steenburgen, "Welfare Attitudes and the Humanitarian Sensibility," in *Citizens and Politics: Perspective from Political Psychology*, ed. James H. Kuklinski, 366–400 (New York: Cambridge University Press, 2001) and in particular the distinction between "abstract conservatism and functional liberalism" in the American public documented by Benjamin I. Page and Lawrence R. Jacobs, *Class War? What Americans Really Think about Economic Inequality* (Chicago: University of Chicago Press, 2009). See also "No Consensus about Whether Nation Is Divided into 'Haves' and 'Have-Nots,'" Pew Research Center for the People & the Press (September 29, 2011) http://people-press.org/2011/09/29. Derek Bok makes a case against "proposals [that] call for massive shifts of income, causing consequences so disruptive and so impossible to anticipate, that they seem both impractical and unwise." At the same time, "unlike redistributing income, both equal opportunity and political equality [by way of campaign finance reform] are goals that Americans support overwhelmingly." See *The Politics of Happiness* (Princeton: Princeton University Press, 2010), 79–98.

21. Rebecca Blank draws attention to the distinction between reducing poverty and reducing the gap between rich and poor in *It Takes a Nation: A New Agenda for Fighting Poverty*, updated (Princeton: Princeton University Press, 1998). See also Blank, "Evaluating Welfare Reform in the United States," National Bureau of Economic Research Working Paper, no. 8983 (Washington, DC: NBER, June 2002), www.nber.org/papers/w8983; David T. Ellwood, "The Impact of Earned Income Tax Credit and Social Policy Reforms on Work, Marriage, and Living Arrangements," Kennedy School, Harvard University (June 2000); Jeffrey Grogger and Lynn A. Karoly, *Welfare Reform: Effects of a Decade of Change* (Cambridge, MA: Harvard University Press, 2005); Jason DeParle, "Welfare Limits Left Poor Adrift as Recession Hit," (April 8, 2012); and Sharon Parrott and Arloc Sherman, "TANF at 10: Program Results Are More Mixed Than Often Understood," Center on Budget and Policy Priorities (August 17, 2006), www.cbpp.org/8-17-06tanf.htm. For an evaluation that includes both political and economic repercussions, see Demetrios J. Caraley,

"Ending Welfare As We Know It: A Reform Still in Progress," *Political Science Quarterly* 116 (Winter 2001–2), 525–559.

22. Mary Jo Bane, "A Reply to Mead," in *Lifting Up the Poor: A Dialogue on Religion, Poverty & Welfare Reform*, ed. Mary Jo Bane and Lawrence M. Mead, 118 (Washington, DC: Brookings Institution Press, 2003).

23. Lawrence M. Mead, *Government Matters: Welfare Reform In Wisconsin* (Princeton: Princeton University Press, 2004), 276. Tommy Thompson, a progressive Republican (and a Catholic), was governor of Wisconsin when Mead conducted his study; the Wisconsin welfare experiments were not representative of measures taken in other states. Thompson later became Secretary of Health and Human Services under George W. Bush.

24. Mary Jo Bane and David T. Ellwood, *Welfare Realities: From Rhetoric to Reform* (Cambridge: Harvard University Press, 1994). See also Kevin Lang and Jay L. Zagorsky, "Does Growing Up with a Parent Absent Really Hurt?" *Journal of Human Resources* 36 (Spring 2001), 253–273. For a review of evidence about the effects of divorce on children, see "The Frayed Knot: Briefing Marriage in America," *Economist* (May 26, 2007), 23–25.

25. Mead, "A Biblical Response to Poverty," in *Lifting Up the Poor*, ed. Bane and Mead, 59–60.

26. Bane, "Personal Responsibility Means Social Responsibility," in *Lifting Up the Poor*, ed. Banes and Mead, 140.

27. See Charles E. Curran, *American Catholic Social Ethics: Twentieth-Century Approaches* (Notre Dame, IN: University of Notre Dame Press, 1982).

28. Mead, "Biblical Response," 98. See also Mead, "The Twilight of Liberal Welfare Reform," *Public Interest* 139 (Spring 2000), 22–34.

29. Philip S. Gorski, *The Disciplinary Revolution: Calvinism and the Rise of the State in Early Modern Europe* (Chicago: University of Chicago Press, 2003). A strong case for the Protestant features behind the 1996 welfare reforms has been made by Kenneth Hudson and Andrea Coukos, "The Dark Side of the Protestant Ethic: A Comparative Analysis of Welfare Reform," *Sociological Theory* 23 (March 2005), 1–24. Sigrun Kahl makes a similar argument from a more broadly cross-national perspective in "The Religious Roots of Modern Poverty Policy: Catholic, Lutheran, and Reformed Protestant Traditions Compared," *European Journal of Sociology* 46 (April 2005), 91–126.

30. Rebecca M. Blank and William McGurn, *Is the Market Moral? A Dialogue on Religion, Economics, and Justice* (Washington, DC: Brookings Institution Press, 2004).

31. Josefina Figueira-McDonough, *The Welfare State and Social Work: Pursuing Social Justice* (Thousand Oaks, CA: Sage, 2007), 184ff.

32. See Monica Prasad et al., "The Undeserving Rich: 'Moral Values' and the White Working Class," *Sociological Forum* 24 (June 2009), 225–253.

33. Lawrence H. Mead, *Beyond Entitlement: The Social Obligations of Citizenship* (New York: Free Press, 1986). For a critique, see Joel F. Handler, *Social Citizenship and Workfare in the United States and Western Europe: The Paradox of Inclusion* (Cambridge: Cambridge University Press, 2004).

34. Joe Soss and Sanford F. Schram, "A Public Transformed? Welfare Reform as Policy Feedback," *American Political Science Review* 101 (February 2007), 111–127.

35. Mary Bendyna et al., "Catholics and the Christian Right," *Journal for Scientific Study of Religion* 39 (September 2000), 321–332.

36. Andrew Morris, "The Voluntary Sector's War on Poverty," *Journal of Policy History* 16 (October 2004), 275–305 and Linda Yankoski, "Common Ground for the Common Good: A Case Study of Church-State Partnership," in *Catholic Charities USA: 100 Years at the Intersection of Charity and Justice*, ed. J. Bryan Hehir, 85–109 (Collegeville, MN: Liturgical Press, 2010).

37. Seth Dowland, "'Family Values' and the Formation of a Christian Right Agenda," *Church History* 78 (August 2009), 606–631.

38. See for example Dominic Sandbrook, *Eugene McCarthy: The Rise and Fall of Postwar American Liberalism* (New York: Alfred A. Knopf, 2004). David A. Hollinger makes a subtler point in his comparison of "ecumenical" and "evangelical" Protestantism, arguing that "ecumenical [liberal] Protestantism actually advanced some of its central goals even while its organizational hegemony disappeared." See Hollinger, "After Cloven Tongues of Fire: Ecumenical Protestantism and the Modern American Encounter with Diversity," *Journal of American History* 98 (June 2011), 21–48.

39. Robert P. George, "Families and First Principles," *National Review* (February 12, 2007), 31–38. George Weigel has extended consequentialist reasoning to argue against "artificial" contraception. The damaging consequence is demographic suicide, evidenced by birth rates in many European countries that have fallen below replacement level. Weigel, *The Cube and the Cathedral: Europe, America, and Politics without God* (New York: Basic Books, 2005). With the exception of William Bennett, no prominent Catholics have mentioned the consequentialist argument that access to abortion as well as the availability of contraceptives have had a significant impact on reducing crime. See Steven D. Levitt, "Understanding Why Crime Fell in the 1990s: Four Factors That Explain the Decline and Six That Do Not," *Journal of Economic Perspectives* 18 (Winter 2004), 163–190, and John J. Donohue III and Steven D. Levitt, "Further Evidence That Legalized Abortion Lowered Crime," *Journal of Human Resources* 34 (2004), 29–49.

40. David Brooks, "The Two Earthquakes," *New York Times* (January 4, 2008).

41. Michael Novak, ed., *Democracy and Mediating Structures: A Theological Inquiry* (Washington, DC: American Enterprise Institute, 1980).

42. Stanley Feldman and John Zaller, "The Political Culture of Ambivalence: Ideological Responses to the Welfare State," *American Journal of Political Science* 36 (February 1992), 268–307.

43. For neoconservative takes on this and related questions, see Michael Novak, "Capitalism and the Human Spirit," *Public Interest* 139 (Spring 2000), 76–83, and James Q. Wilson, "Two Cheers for Capitalism," *Public Interest* 139 (Spring 2000), 72–75. For perspectives from the center-left, see Robert A. Dahl, *On Political Equality* (New Haven: Yale University Press, 2006), Robert H. Frank, *Falling Behind: How Rising Inequality Harms the Middle Class* (Berkeley: University of California Press, 2007); Lawrence R. Jacobs and Theda Skocpol, eds., *Inequality and American Democracy: What We Know and What We Need To Learn* (New York: Russell Sage Foundation, 2005); and Donald Tomaskovic-Dewey and Ken-Hou Lin, "Income Dynamics, Economic Rents, and the Financialization of the U.S. Economy," *American Sociological Review* 76 (August 2011), 538–559.

44. Larry Bartels, "Economic Inequality Is All the Rage," *The Monkey Cage* (January 18, 2012), http://themonkeycage.org/blog/2012/01/18/economic-inequality-is-all-the-rage/ and Bartels, "Occupy's Impact Beyond the Beltway," *World of Ideas* (January 18, 2012), http://billmoyers.com/2012/01/18/has-the-occupy-movement-altered-public-opinion/.

45. Joseph Bottum, "The New Fusionism," *First Things* 154 (June–July 2005), 32–36.

46. Noam Lupu and Jonas Pontusson, "The Structure of Inequality and the Politics of Redistribution," *American Political Science Review* 105 (May 2011), 316–336, Lindsay A. Owens, "Confidence in Banks, Financial Institutions, and Wall Street, 1971–2011," *Public Opinion Quarterly* 76 (Spring 2012), 142–162, and Jacob S. Hacker and Ann O'Leary, eds., *Shared Responsibility, Shared Risk: Government, Markets, and Social Policy in the Twenty-First Century* (New York: Oxford University Press, 2012).

47. This is the gist of the view promoted by Robert George, the McCormick Professor of Jurisprudence at Princeton and Neuhaus's de facto successor. See David R. Kirkpatrick, "The Conservative-Christian Big Thinker," *New York Times Magazine* (December 20, 2009).

48. Joshua Guetzkow, "Beyond Deservingness: Congressional Discourse on Poverty, 1964-1996," *Annals of the American Academy of Political and Social Science* 629 (May 2010), 173–197.

49. Interview, New York, December 4, 2006.

50. Peter Steinfels, *A People Adrift: The Crisis of the Roman Catholic Church* (New York: Simon & Schuster, 2003). An article had appeared about a year prior to the interview identifying "Father John" as a frequent consultant at the Bush White House: Garry Wills, "Fringe Government," *New York Review of Books* (October 6, 2005).

51. The landmark work was Neuhaus's own *The Naked Public Square: Religion and Democracy in America* (Grand Rapids, MI: Eerdmans, 1984).

52. See Francis Cardinal George, "How Liberalism Fails the Church," *Commonweal* (November 19, 1999).

53. See D. Paul Sullins, "Catholic/Protestant Trends on Abortion: Convergence and Polarity," *Journal for the Scientific Study of Religion* 38 (September 1999), 354–369.

54. "He forced these 'excesses,'" one commentator writes about Johnson, "into a sternly classical mode of expression; he tailored the 'extremes,' as best he could, into the semblance of a devout High Churchman and respectable Conservative... Like Swift, Johnson had longed to be more 'respectable,' more unquestionably a member of that fixed hierarchy which he venerated, though the principle of contradiction within him was always impelling him to criticize and satirize in detail what he revered in gross." Patrick Crutwell, Introduction, *Samuel Johnson, Selected Writings* (London: Penguin, 1968), 35–36.

55. James Q. Wilson suggested that "liberals are a bit more likely to let what they want to believe influence what the facts allow them to believe." Foreword, in *The Essential Neoconservative Reader*, ed. Mark Gerson (Reading, MA: Addison-Wesley, 1996). He offered no evidence to back up the claim. Wilson mentioned that "this is, of course, an exaggeration." Wilson weighed in on the debate over inequality encouraged by the Occupy Wall Street movement with an article entitled "Angry About Inequality," *Washington Post* (January 26, 2011), citing the work of Page and Jacobs, *Class War?* Page and Jacobs responded with a letter to the *Post* published on January 31 stating that Wilson had "presented a selective reading of our book... and a mistaken view of

what Americans think about economic inequality." See also James Q. Wilson, "Quit Twisting My Words," *Los Angeles Times* (April 27, 2008).

56. In a predominantly poor, Catholic country like the Philippines, birth control is more of an issue; see Kenneth R. Weiss and Sol Vanzi, "Philippines President Signs Law Easing Access to Contraceptives," *Los Angeles Times* (December 29, 2012).

57. Adam Liptak, "Court under Roberts Is Most Conservative in Decades," *New York Times* (July 24, 2010). For a conspiratorial interpretation, see Betty Clermont, *The Neo-Catholics: Implementing Christian Nationalism in America* (Atlanta: Clarity Press, 2009). See also Chris Suellentrop, "The Rev. John McCloskey: The Catholic Church's K Street Lobbyist," *Slate* (August 9, 2002), http://www.slate.com/articles/news_and_politics/assessment/2002/08/the_rev_john_mccloskey.single.html, and Patricia Zapor, "Catholics Still Largest Congress Denomination; 10 Percent Jesuit Grads," *National Catholic Reporter* (January 8, 2013), http://ncronline.org/print/news/politics/catholics-still-largest-congress-denomination-10-percent-jesuit-grads.

58. Besides Wills, "Fringe Government," see Erwin Chemerinsky, *The Conservative Assault on the Constitution* (New York: Simon & Schuster, 2010); Margaret R. Somers and Fred Block, "From Poverty to Perversity: Ideas, Markets, and Institutions over 200 Years of Welfare Debate," *American Sociological Review* 70 (April 2005), 260–287, and Block, "Understanding the Diverging Trajectories of the United States and Western Europe," *Politics and Society* 35 (March 2007), 3–33.

59. See Mark Regnerus and Christian Smith, "Selective Deprivatization among American Religious Traditions," *Social Forces* 76 (June 1998), 1347–1372.

60. Amy Sullivan, *The Party Faithful: How and Why Democrats Are Closing the God Gap* (New York: Scribner, 2008), E. J. Dionne Jr., *Souled Out: Reclaiming Faith and Politics After the Religious Right* (Princeton: Princeton University Press, 2008), and Michael Sean Winters, *Left at the Altar: How the Democrats Lost the Catholics and How the Catholics Can Save the Democrats* (New York: Basic Books, 2008).

61. Alan Brinkley, *The End of Reform: New Deal Liberalism in Recession and War* (New York: Alfred A. Knopf, 1995), and Steve Fraser and Gary Gerstle, eds., *The Rise and Fall of the New Deal Order, 1930–1980* (Princeton: Princeton University Press, 1989).

62. Robert D. Putnam and David E. Campbell, *American Grace: How Religion Divides and Unites Us* (New York: Simon & Schuster, 2010). See also K. Healan Gaston, "Demarcating Democracy: Liberal Catholics, Protestants, and the Discourse of Secularism," in *American Religious Liberalism*, eds. Leigh E. Schmidt and Sally M. Promey, 337–358 (Bloomington: Indiana University Press, 2012) and John S. Dickerson, "The Decline of Evangelical America," *New York Times* (December 15, 2012).

PART THREE

1. John W. O'Malley, SJ, "The Millennium and the Papalization of Catholicism," *America* (April 8, 2000).

2. S. R. Epstein and Maarten Prak, eds., *Guilds, Innovations, and the European Economy, 1400–1800* (Cambridge: Cambridge University Press, 2008).

3. Michael Young, "Confessional Protest: The Religious Birth of U.S. Social Movements," *American Sociological Review* 67 (October 2002), 660–688.

4. Peter Dobkin Hall has done the groundbreaking research. See Hall, "Blurred Boundaries, Hybrids, and Changelings: The Fortunes of Nonprofit Organizations in the Late Twentieth Century," in *Critical Anthropology Now*, ed. George E. Marcus, 147–202 (Sante Fe, NM: School of American Research Press, 1998); "Philanthropy, the Welfare State, and the Transformation of American Public and Private Institutions, 1945-2000," working paper no. 5, Hauser Center for Nonprofit Organizations, Harvard University (November 2000), and "A Historical Overview of Philanthropy, Voluntary Associations, and Nonprofit Organizations in the United States, 1600-2000," in *The Nonprofit Sector: A Research Handbook*, 2nd ed., ed. Walter W. Powell and Richard Steinberg, 32–65 (New Haven: Yale University Press, 2006).

5. See Barrington Moore Jr., *Social Origins of Dictatorship and Democracy: Lord and Peasant in the Making of the Modern World* (Boston: Beacon, 1966).

CHAPTER SIX CONCILIARISM AND OTHER DORMANT TRADITIONS

1. Keynote address to the convention of the Federation of Diocesan Liturgical Commissions, at the Omni San Antonio Hotel, October 7–11, 2003.

2. Keith F. Pecklers, SJ, *The Unread Vision: The Liturgical Movement in the United States of America: 1926–1955* (Collegeville, MN: Liturgical Press, 1998), 285. See also Dennis Smolarski, SJ, *Eucharist and American Culture: Liturgy, Unity, and Individualism* (Mahwah, NJ: Paulist Press, 2010).

3. Quoted by Arthur J. Magida, *Opening the Doors of Wonder: Reflections on Religious Rites of Passage* (Berkeley: University of California Press, 2006).

4. Address to the Institut Supérieur de Liturgie, October 26, 2006, reported in *ZENIT* online (January 20, 2007), http://www.zenit.org/article-18690?l=english (italics added). The cardinal went on about the same topic on several occasions, all of them documented by the Zenit website under such titles as "Latin Is Concise, Precise, and Poetically Measured" (January 11, 2008), "No Individual Has Authority to Change the Approved Wording" (January 14, 2008), etc.

5. Eugene C. Bianchi and Rosemary Radford Reuther, eds., *A Democratic Catholic Church: The Reconstruction of Roman Catholicism* (New York: Crossroad, 1992); Francis Oakley, *The Conciliarist Tradition: Constitutionalism in the Catholic Church, 1300–1870* (Oxford: Oxford University Press, 2003), iv; and Oakley, "History and the Return of the Repressed in Catholic Modernity," in *The Crisis of Authority in Catholic Modernity*, ed. Michael J. Lacey and Francis Oakley, 29–56 (New York: Oxford University Press, 2011).

6. Patrick W. Carey, *People, Priests, and Prelates: Ecclesiastical Democracy and the Tensions of Trusteeism* (Notre Dame, IN: University of Notre Dame Press, 1987).

7. Patricia Wittberg, *From Piety to Professionalism—And Back? Transformations of Organized Religious Virtuosity* (Lanham, MD: Lexington Books/Rowman & Littlefield, 2006). Seminaries and pontifical universities—the Catholic University of America is one example—are the chief exceptions to separate incorporation in higher education. There are also a few diocesan universities—Seton Hall in New Jersey, for example—that don't fit the norm. These schools are supposed to report directly to local bishops.

8. See John R. Quinn, *The Reform of the Papacy* (New York: Crossroad, 1999).

9. Questions of religious authenticity—that is, of doctrinal fidelity—are at the heart of Vatican attempts to reestablish control over lay-dominated operations like Caritas Internationalis, a

global charitable organization. See John Thavis, "Vatican Presses Caritas on 'Catholic Identity,'" *Catholic News Service* (May 6, 2011), and Lesley-Anne Knight, "The Church We Believe in is Catholic," *Tablet* (March 3, 2011).

10. A classic statement of the general process is by Paul J. DiMaggio and William Powell, "'The Iron Cage Revisited': Institutional Isomorphism and Collective Rationality in Organizational Fields," *American Sociological Review* 48 (April 1983), 147–160. See also Steven Brint, *In an Age of Experts: The Changing Role of Professionals in Politics and Public Life* (Princeton: Princeton University Press, 1994), Magali Sarfatti Larson, *The Rise of Professionalism: A Sociological Analysis* (Berkeley: University of California Press, 1977), and Peter J. Williamson, *Corporatism in Perspective: An Introductory Guide to Corporatist Theory* (Newbury Park, CA: Sage, 1989). Compare Chris Lowney, *Heroic Leadership: Best Practices from a 450-Year-Old Company that Changed the World* (Chicago: Loyola Press, 2003), and Kathleen Thelen, "Varieties of Capitalism and Business History," *Business History Review* 84 (Winter 2010), 646–648.

11. See John Wilson, "Corporatism and the Professionalization of Reform," *Journal of Political and Military Sociology* 11 (Spring 1983), 53–68. Daniel Patrick Moynihan laid out the main lines of corporatist policy making in 1965, in the inaugural issue of *The Public Interest*; he tweaked his ideas in "The Professionalization of Reform II," *Public Interest* 121 (Fall 1995), 23–32.

12. Albert R. Jonsen and Stephen Toulmin, *The Abuse of Casuistry: A History of Moral Reasoning* (Berkeley: University of California Press, 1988); James F. Keenan and Thomas A. Shannons, eds., *The Context of Casuistry* (Washington, DC: Georgetown University Press, 1995); Gianpiero Dalla-Zuanna, "Tacit Consent: Church and Birth Control in Northern Italy," *Population and Development Review* 37 (June 2011), 361–374; and Paul Wilkes, *The Good Enough Catholic: A Guide for the Perplexed* (New York: Ballantine, 1996). Modification of the penalties associated with divorce is an important example of the application of "the pastoral approach" on a large scale. Divorce used to be grounds for excommunication. With the increase in divorce among Catholics, attendance at Sunday Mass, and weekly collections, fell. The bishops found a remedy in the expansion of marriage annulments. See Melissa J. Wilde, "From Excommunication to Nullification: Testing and Extending Supply-Side Theories of Religious Marketing with the Case of Catholic Marital Annulments," *Journal for the Scientific Study of Religion* 40 (June 2001), 235–249, and Paul M. Zulehner, "Remarried Catholics Shouldn't Be Divorced from Communion," *U.S. Catholic Weekly Bulletin* (October 11, 2011).

13. See Brian Tierney, *The Origins of Papal Infallibility, 1150–1350* (Leiden: E. J. Brill, 1988), Hans Küng, *How the Pope Became Infallible: Pius IX and the Politics of Persuasion*, trans. Peter Heinegg (Garden City, NY: Doubleday, 1981), and Garry Wills, "A Democratic Church?" *New York Review of Books* (November 21, 2002).

14. Giuseppe Alberigo, "From the Council of Trent to 'Tridentism,'" in *From Trent to Vatican II: Historical and Theological Investigations*, ed. Raymond F. Bulman and Frederick J. Parrella, 19–37 (Oxford: Oxford University Press, 2006). See also John W. O'Malley, *Trent: What Happened at the Council?* (Cambridge, MA: Harvard University Press, 2013).

15. See Harro Höpfl, *Jesuit Political Thought: The Society of Jesus and the State, c.1540–1630* (Cambridge: Cambridge University Press, 2004).

16. R. Scott Appleby, *"Church and Age Unite!" The Modernist Impulse in American Catholicism* (Notre Dame, IN: University of Notre Dame Press, 1992) and Lester Kurtz, *The Politics of Heresy: The Modernist Crisis in Roman Catholicism* (Berkeley: University of California Press, 1986).

17. Duffy, *Faith of Our Fathers*, 73. That code itself goes back to "the traditions of Roman imperial administration." See Francis Oakley, *Kingship: The Politics of Enchantment* (Oxford: Blackwell, 2006).

18. Brian M. Downy, *The Military Revolution and Political Change: Origins of Democracy and Autocracy in Early Modern Europe* (Princeton: Princeton University Press, 1992), Brian Tierney, *Religion, Law, and the Growth of Constitutional Thought* (Cambridge: Cambridge University Press, 1982), and Francis Fukuyama, *The Origins of Political Order* (New York: Farrar, Straus, and Giroux, 2011).

19. This is a variant of an argument advanced by Charles Taylor, *A Catholic Modernity?* (New York: Oxford University Press, 1999). See also Michael Allen Gillespie, *The Theological Origins of Modernity* (Chicago: University of Chicago Press, 2008) and Eric Nelson, *The Hebrew Republic: Jewish Sources and the Transformation of European Political Thought* (Cambridge, MA: Harvard University Press, 2010).

20. Compare Jennifer Gandhi, *Political Institutions under Dictatorship* (Cambridge: Cambridge University Press, 2008).

21. Oakley, *Kingship*, 160–161. Compare H. A. Drake, "The Church, Society, and Political Power," in *Cambridge History of Christianity*, vol. 2, *Constantine to c. 600*, ed. Augustine Casiday and Frederick W. Norris, 403–428 (Cambridge: Cambridge University Press, 2007).

22. Talal Asad, *Formations of the Secular: Christianity, Islam, Modernity* (Stanford: Stanford University Press, 2003) and Adam B. Seligman, *Modernity's Wager: Authority, the Self, and Transcendence* (Princeton: Princeton University Press, 2000).

23. José Casanova, *Public Religions in the Modern World* (Chicago: University of Chicago Press, 1994).

24. Claudio Veliz, *The Centralist Tradition in Latin America* (Princeton: Princeton University Press, 1980) and Jason Brownlee, *Authoritarianism in an Age of Democratization* (Cambridge: Cambridge University Press, 2007). Compare Walter L. Adamson, *Hegemony and Revolution: A Study of Antonio Gramsci's Political and Cultural Theory* (Berkeley: University of California Press, 1980), Chrystia Freeland, "The New Age of Authoritarianism," *Financial Times* (August 12, 2008), and Kevin Narizny, " Anglo-American Primacy and the Global Spread of Democracy: An International Genealogy," *World Politics* 64 (April 2012), 341–373.

25. R. Scott Appleby, "From Autonomy to Alienation: Lay Involvement in the Governance of the Local Church," in *Common Calling: The Laity and Governance of the Catholic Church*, ed. Stephen L. Pope, 91–92 (Washington, DC: Georgetown University Press, 2004).

26. Michael Dibdin, *And Then You Die* (London: Faber and Faber, 2002), 55.

27. Donald T. Critchlow, "Rethinking American Conservatism: Toward a New Narrative," *Journal of American History* 98 (December 2011), 752–755.

28. See James C. Scott, *Domination and the Arts of Resistance: Hidden Transcripts* (New Haven: Yale University Press, 1990) and Erving Goffman, *Asylums: Essays on the Social Situation of Mental Patients and Other Inmates* (New York: Doubleday, 1961).

29. Baltasar Gracián, *The Art of Worldly Wisdom: A Pocket Oracle*, trans. Christopher Maurer (New York: Doubleday, 1992). The newest translation, entitled *The Pocket Oracle and Art of*

Prudence, is by Jeremy Robbins (London: Penguin, 2011). See also Scott Adams, *Dilbert and the Way of the Weasel* (New York: HarperCollins, 2003).

30. Thomas G. Corvan, ed., *The Best of Gracián* (New York: Philosophical Library, 1964), i.

31. Massimo Ciavolella and Patrick Coleman, eds., *Culture and Authority in the Baroque* (Toronto: University of Toronto Press, 2005).

32. Cited by Aubrey F. G. Bell, *Baltasar Gracián* (Oxford: Oxford University Press, 1921), 28ff.

33. Gracián, *The Art of Worldly Wisdom*, 143.

34. Ibid., 122.

35. For a fuller account, see Peter McDonough, "Clenched Fist or Open Palm? Five Jesuit Perspectives on Pluralism," *Studies in the Spirituality of Jesuits* 37 (Summer 2005).

36. In American fiction, John Kennedy Toole's *Confederacy of Dunces* (Baton Rouge: Louisiana State University Press, 1980), which portrays a line of bumbling Catholic eccentrics centered in New Orleans (one that in reality trails up to St. Louis and further north), catches some of this *mis-en-scène*. John Huston's comic parable *Beat the Devil* from 1954 comes even closer, without dwelling on the tragic murk. A star-studded cast of villains and grifters of various nationalities spin Byzantine schemes to acquire uranium-rich land in British East Africa. In the end, the prize goes to Harry Chelm, the obliviously earnest, stuffed-shirt husband of Gina Lollobrigida. Harry, imbecilic in his purity, telegraphs the faithless Gina, forgiving all and inviting her to share his good fortune. Everyone else goes to jail. See also James Ursini, *The Fabulous Life & Times of Preston Sturges: An American Dreamer* (New York: Curtis, 1973) and Diane Jacobs, *Christmas in July: The Life and Art of Preston Sturges* (Berkeley: University of California Press, 1992).

37. Quoted by Michael Nerlich, "Gracián in the Death Cell," in *Rhetoric and Politics: Baltasar Gracián and the New World Order*, ed. Nicholas Spadaccini and Jenaro Talens, 324 (Minneapolis: University of Minnesota Press, 1997).

38. See Erving Goffman, *The Presentation of Self in Everyday Life* (Garden City, NY: Doubleday Anchor, 1959).

39. Monroe Z. Hafter, *Gracián and Perfection: Spanish Moralists of the Seventeenth Century* (Cambridge, MA: Harvard University Press, 1966), 93.

40. See Umberto Eco, "Les Signes du pouvoir," introduction to *Brévaire des politiciens*, by Cardinal Mazarin, trans. François Rossi (Paris: Arléu, 1997), 7–12, and La Rochefoucauld, *Maxims*, trans L. W. Tancock (Baltimore, MD: Penguin, 1959).

41. Herman Melville on the villain Claggart, *Billy Budd, Sailor*, section 11, ed. Harrison Hayford and Merton M. Sealts Jr. (Chicago: University of Chicago Press, 1962).

42. Albert O. Hirschman, *The Rhetoric of Reaction: Perversity, Futility, Jeopardy* (Cambridge, MA: Harvard University Press, 1991) and James C. Scott, *Weapons of the Weak* (New Haven: Yale University Press, 1985).

43. Gracián, *Art of Worldly Wisdom*, 137.

44. See David G. Schultenover, SJ, *A View from Rome: On the Eve of the Modernist Crisis* (New York: Fordham University Press, 1993) and Wilfrid Sheed, *The Hack* (New York: Macmillan, 1963).

45. For accounts of traditional individualism, see Edward C. Banfield, *The Moral Basis of a Backward Society* (New York: Free Press, 1958, 1967) and Laurence William Wylie, *Village in the Vaucluse*, 3rd ed. (Cambridge: Harvard University Press, 1974).

46. Gracián on a good day might be compared to Don Juan, as depicted by Byron in his poem of the same name. "He [Don Juan] is not a cynic," W. H. Auden argued, "he does not say, for instance, that all love is only lust; all goodness a sham—or all heroism only ambition. What he does attack is what he calls *cant*, the proneness of human beings, in order to think well of themselves, to pretend that their motives and feelings are always of the noblest and purest character, and that lust, greed, social climbing, desire for fame, etc., are vices that beset other people, not themselves." Introduction to George Gordon, Lord Byron, *Selected Poetry and Prose* (New York: Signet Classics, 1966), xxiii.

47. See however the essays by Maurizio Viroli, "Republic and Democracy: On Early Modern Origins of Democratic Theory" and Theodore K. Rabb, "Institutions and Ideas: Planting the Roots of Democracy in Early Modern Europe," in *The Making and Unmaking of Democracy: Lessons from History and World Politics*, ed. Rabb Suleiman and Ezra N. Suleiman (New York: Routledge, 2003).

48. The novels and stories of Gregor von Rezzori (1914–1998), an Eastern European who lived through two wars and a variety of unsavory regimes, convey much the same pessimistic tone as does Gracián about cooperative action, with a bit more humor and considerably greater anti-religious feeling. The following is from an interview he gave to Bruce Wolmerre that appeared in *Boom* 24 (Summer 1988) http://bombsite.com/issues/24/articles/1116:

> Put ten people together and the quota of intelligence is brought down to almost zero. And if you put one hundred thousand together, well, it's all over then. Plant a great idea, a magnificent invention, or a great example in the mass of mankind and it becomes what Jesus Christ became—the Catholic church. Endless chains of misinterpretations and misunderstandings—that's what I call stupidity.... The accumulating and progressive stupidity of mankind is something I fear. And it can't be fought.... The strange thing is that I despise the mass but I love other people.

49. José Antonio Maravall, *Culture of the Baroque: Analysis of a Historical Structure*, trans. Terry Cochran (Minneapolis: University of Minnesota Press, 1986).

50. See Lewis A. Coser, *Greedy Institutions: Patterns of Undivided Commitment* (Glencoe, IL: Free Press, 1974).

51. Jeremy Robbins treats Gracián as more of an ethically scrupulous realist than most interpreters. Robbins's position is that the moral component, largely absent from the writing itself, would be supplied as a matter of course by readers of his time. The argument restores some virtue to political *savoir faire*, ridding it of the unseemliness often attached to it by the devout. See Introduction, in *The Pocket Oracle and Art of Prudence*, trans. Robbins, xxv–xlv. It is instructive to compare Gracián's agnosticism about collective action with Reinhold Niebuhr's classic *Moral Man and Immoral Society* (New York: Charles Scribner's, 1932).

CHAPTER SEVEN MANAGERIALISM AND THE CATHOLIC DEFICIT

1. Herman Melville, from Chapter Seven, "The Chapel," *Moby Dick*.

2. Tracy Schier and Cynthia Russett, eds., *Catholic Women's Colleges in America* (Baltimore: Johns Hopkins University Press, 2002).

3. Alice Gallin, OSU, *Negotiating Identity: Catholic Higher Education since 1960* (Notre Dame, IN: University of Notre Dame Press, 2000), 81. Several private secular colleges and

universities—for example, Yale—went co-ed during the same period. A few Catholic schools, like Saint Louis University, had gone co-ed decades before. The revolution began by way of their professional schools, such as those devoted to training in social work, which attracted large numbers of tuition-paying women.

4. The separate incorporation of Catholic ministries was a belated development relative to trends that had begun decades earlier in the business world. See Mark S. Mizruchi, "Berle and Means Revisited: The Governance and Power of Large U.S. Corporations," *Theory and Society* 33 (October 2004), 579–617.

5. Kathleen A. Mahoney, *Catholic Higher Education in Protestant America* (Baltimore: Johns Hopkins University Press, 2003) and Mark S. Massa, *Catholics and American Culture: Fulton Sheen, Dorothy Day, and the Notre Dame Football Team* (New York: Crossroad, 1999).

6. Quoted by Gallin, *Negotiating Identity*, 56. See also Joseph O'Hare, SJ, "Autonomy and Communion," *America* (May 7, 2007), 10–15.

7. Paul C. Reinert, SJ, and Paul Shore, *Seasons of Change: Reflections on a Half Century at Saint Louis University* (St. Louis, MO: Saint Louis University Press, 1996).

8. See Steve Rosswurm, *The FBI and the Catholic Church, 1935–1962* (Amherst: University of Massachusetts Press, 2009). "There are definitely many Mormons who became FBI agents in the past 30 years or so," according to Kathleen McChesney, former Executive Assistant Director for Law Enforcement at the agency, "but I believe they are still outnumbered by Catholics" (personal communication, January 12, 2013). I am grateful to McChesney for pointing me to Rosswurm's contention that "Mr. Hoover, in the early days of his directorship, preferred to hire white Protestants from small towns.... In 1940, however, he began specifically recruiting in New York City... Jesuit colleges produced a large number of graduates who went on to earn law degrees.... Hoover wanted the men the Jesuits produced because they (and the men who trained them) exhibited the things he 'admired most in men'—'athleticism, toughness, virility, loyalty, and... piety.' Character, a word often used by both Hoover and the Jesuits, was what these grads had: Character, thus initiated and habituated, is not a stucco front but polished granite, unmoved for the most part by the storms of greed, passion or expediency."

9. Andrew J. F. Morris, *The Limits of Volunteerism: Charity and Welfare from the New Deal through the Great Society* (New York: Cambridge University Press, 2009), 219, and Dorothy M. Brown and Elizabeth McKeown, *The Poor Belong to Us: Catholic Charities and American Welfare* (Cambridge: Harvard University Press, 1997). Amendments to the Social Security Act in 1962 and 1967 formalized the ability of the government to purchase services from voluntary agencies, including those with religious affiliations. See Yankoski, "Common Ground for the Common Good," 85–109.

10. Compare James T. Burtchaell, CSC, *The Dying of the Light* (Grand Rapids, MI: Eerdmans, 1998) and David J. O'Brien, *From the Heart of the American Church: Catholic Higher Education and American Culture* (Maryknoll, NY: Orbis Books, 1994). Much of the opposition came from resentment and recrimination over the passing of old-line ethnic Catholicism; see "Rev. William Barnaby Flaherty Dies at 96, Chronicled St. Louis," *St. Louis Post-Dispatch* (August 22, 2011), especially the comment by one reader that "Saint Louis University has become a Jesuit marketing moment... without the Jesuits."

11. Mary J. Oates, *The Catholic Philanthropic Tradition in America* (Bloomington: Indiana University Press, 1995), xiii, 45. See also Carol K. Coburn and Martha Smith, *Spirited Lives: How Nuns Shaped Catholic Culture and American Life, 1836–1920* (Chapel Hill: University of North Carolina Press, 1999).

12. Mary J. Oates, "Faith and Good Works: Catholic Giving and Taking," *in Charity, Philanthropy, and Civility in American History* (New York: Cambridge University Press, 2003), 288.

13. Oates, *Catholic Philanthropic Tradition*, 94.

14. Theda Skocpol, *Diminished Democracy: From Membership to Management* (Norman: University of Oklahoma Press, 2003), 224. The disappearance of parish cooking booklets has parallels not only with the vanishing of Irish and Norwegian bartenders but, more cross-denominationally, with the fall-off in the number of Jewish delicatessens. See Erik Anjou, "Deli Man Trailer," http://vimeo.com/m/53381762 (no date). I am grateful to Jill Wiener and Jack Scott for bringing this video to my attention.

15. Mary Jo Bane, "The Catholic Puzzle: Parishes and Civic Life," in *Taking Faith Seriously*, ed. Mary Jo Bane, Brent Coffin, and Richard Higgins, 86 (Cambridge, MA: Harvard University Press, 2005).

16. A historically low participant culture establishes a baseline. This is the parameter around which recent trends in participation, driven by other forces, operate up or down. See Christian Welzel and Ronald Inglehart, "Mass Beliefs and Democratic Institutions," in *The Oxford Handbook of Comparative Politics*, ed. Carles Boix and Susan C. Stokes, 297–316 (New York: Oxford University Press, 2007).

17. See Sidney Verba, Kay Lehman Schlozman and Henry E. Brady, *Voice and Equality: Civic Voluntarism in American Politics* (Cambridge, MA: Harvard University Press, 1995) and "Candidates Checkbooks... The Nation's Checkbooks... And Those of Worshippers," *New York Times* (January 29, 2012).

18. Bane, "The Catholic Puzzle," 86, 91.

19. Ibid., 88. See also Mary Jo Bane, "Voice and Loyalty in the Church: The People of God, Politics, and Management," in *Common Calling: The Laity and Governance of the Catholic Church*, ed. Stephen J. Pope, 181–193 (Washington, DC: Georgetown University Press, 2004).

20. Compare Eugene McCarraher, "The Saint in the Grey Flannel Suit: The Professional-Managerial Class, 'The Layman,' and American-Catholic-Religious Culture," *U.S. Catholic Historian* 15 (Summer 1997), 99–118.

21. Personal communications from Elizabeth McKeown, December 14, 2010, and from Mary Oates, December 15, 2010.

22. M. Vincentia Joseph and Ann Patrick Conrad, "The Parish Comes Full Circle and Beyond: The Role of Local Parishes in the Work of Catholic Charities," in *Catholic Charities USA:100 Years at the Intersection of Charity and Justice*, ed. J. Bryan Hehir, 64–84 (Collegeville, MN: Liturgical Press, 2010).

23. Mary L. Gautier and Melissa A. Cidade, "Catholic Charities USA, 2009 Annual Survey Final Report," *Center for Applied Research in the Apostolate, Georgetown University* (July 2010), 16.

24. Michael Schudson, "The Varieties of Civic Experience," *Citizenship Studies* 10 (January 2006), 591–606.

25. J. Craig Jenkins, "Nonprofit Organizations and Political Advocacy," in *The Nonprofit Sector*, ed. Walter W. Powell and Richard Steinberg, 2nd edition, 321 (New Haven: Yale University Press, 2006).

26. Katherine E. Stenger, "The Underrepresentation of Liberal Christians: Mobilization Strategies of Religious Interest Groups," *Social Science Journal* 42 (2005), 391–403.

27. Nancy T. Ammerman, "Religious Narratives in the Public Square," in *Taking Faith Seriously*, ed. Mary Jo Bane, Brent Coffin, and Richard Higgins, 166, 169–170 (Cambridge, MA: Harvard University Press, 2005).

28. Robert Wuthnow, *Sharing the Journey: Support Groups and America's New Quest for Community* (New York: Free Press, 1994) and Wuthnow, *Saving America? Faith-Based Services and the Future of Civil Society* (Princeton: Princeton University Press, 2004).

29. John Burdick, *Looking for God in Brazil: The Progressive Catholic Church in Urban Brazil's Religious Arena* (Berkeley: University of California Press, 1993), Manuel Z. Vásquez, *The Brazilian Popular Church and the Crisis of Modernity* (Cambridge: Cambridge University Press, 1998), and Donald E. Miller, *Reinventing American Protestantism: Christianity in the New Millennium* (Berkeley: University of California Press, 1997).

30. Penny Edgell Becker, *Congregations in Conflict: Cultural Models of Religious Life* (Cambridge: Cambridge University Press, 1999), 229. See also Nancy Tatom Ammerman, *Pillars of Faith: American Congregations and Their Partners* (Berkeley: University of California Press, 2005).

31. See Paul Wilkes, *Excellent Catholic Parishes: The Guide to Best Places and Practices* (Rahway, NJ: Paulist Press, 2001).

32. See Corwin E. Smidt et al., *Pews, Prayers, and Participation: Religion and Civic Responsibility in America* (Washington, DC: Georgetown University Press, 2008). Whatever connection the participatory deficit of Catholics in church affairs has with their rates of political participation generally is hard to pin down. While less observant Catholics are less likely to vote than those who attend church regularly, the same correlation holds for members of other denominations as well; note too that "observance" is not equivalent to "involvement in church affairs." I am grateful to Corwin Smidt for providing me with data on this point from the Pew Religious Landscape survey, which polled 35,000 respondents in 2007. See also Peter W. Wielhouwer, "Religion and American Political Participation," in *The Oxford Handbook of Religion and American Politics*, ed. Corwin E. Smidt, Lyman A. Kellstedt, and James L. Guth, 394–426 (New York: Oxford University Press, 2009).

33. David Denby, "Noble Creatures," *New Yorker* (September 5, 2011).

34. Robert Anderson, James Curtis, and Edward Grabb, "Trends in Civic Association Activity in Four Democracies: The Special Case of Women in the United States," *American Sociological Review* 71 (June 2006), 376–401. For an examination of the differences between men and women in modes of congregational involvement, see Penny Edgell, *Religion and Family in a Changing Society* (Princeton: Princeton University Press, 2005).

35. Dean Hoge et al., *Young Adult Catholics: Religion in the Culture of Choice* (Notre Dame, IN: University of Notre Dame Press, 2001) and Nina Eliasoph, *Avoiding Politics: How Americans Produce Apathy in Everyday Life* (Cambridge: Cambridge University Press, 1998).

36. Compare John E. Mueller, *Capitalism, Democracy, and Ralph's Pretty Good Grocery* (Princeton: Princeton University Press, 1999).

37. Nicholas D. Kristof, "Who Can Mock the Church?" *New York Times* (May 2, 2010).

38. The pattern is strikingly similar to the hierarchy of "parochial," "subject," and "participant" citizens identified in studies of political culture. Gabriel A. Almond and Sidney Verba, *The Civic Culture: Political Attitudes and Democracy in Five Nations*, new ed. (Newbury Park, CA: Sage, 1989). See also John R. Hibbing and Elizabeth Theiss-Morse, *Stealth Democracy: Americans' Beliefs about How Government Should Work* (Cambridge: Cambridge University Press, 2002).

39. Paul Burstein et al., "The Success of Political Movements: A Bargaining Perspective," in *The Politics of Social Protest*, ed. J. Craig Jenkins and Bert K. Klandermans, 275–295 (Minneapolis: University of Minnesota Press, 1995) and Frank Dobbin, "The Business of Social Movements," in *Passionate Politics: Emotions and Social Movements*, ed. Jeff Goodwin, James N. Jasper, and Francesca Polletta, 74–80 (Chicago: University of Chicago Press, 2001).

40. Mark Chaves, *Congregations in America* (Cambridge: Harvard University Press, 2004). Becker, *Congregations in Conflict*, 29ff., distinguishes among congregations (and parishes) that struggle to establish their "identity and mission" as primarily "houses of worship," as dedicated to "family devotions and religious education," as "intimate communities of shared values," or as "activist" groups. See also Jerome P. Baggett, *Sense of the Faithful: How American Catholics Live Their Faith* (New York: Oxford University Press, 2009) and Elisabeth S. Clemens, "The Constitution of Citizens: Political Theories of Nonprofit Organizations," in *The Nonprofit Sector*, ed. Walter W. Powell and Richard Steinberg, 2nd ed., 207–220 (New Haven: Yale University Press, 2006).

PART FOUR

1. Geoffrey Kabaservice, *Rule and Ruin: The Downfall of Moderation and the Destruction of the Republican Party* (New York: Oxford University Press, 2012), 363. Compare Jason Berry, "Küng Still Resists the 'Roman Inquisition,'" *National Catholic Reporter* (December 26, 2012), http://ncronline.org/print/news/women-religious/k-ng-still-resists-roman-inquisition.

2. J. Donald Monan and Edward A. Malloy, "'Ex Corde Ecclesiae' Creates an Impasse," *America* (January 30, 1999), 6–12, James L. Heft, "Distinctively Catholic: Keeping the Faith in Higher Education," *Commonweal* (March 26, 2010), 9–13, David B. House, "Catholic Colleges 20 Years After 'Ex Corde,'" *Chronicle of Higher Education* (September 12, 2010), http://chronicle.com.ezproxy1.lib.asu.edu/article/Catholic-Colleges-20-Years/124353/, and—for what reads like a boilerplate summary—Catholic News Service, "Bishops, Colleges Find Good Collaboration in 'Ex Corde' Review," *National Catholic Review* (January 11, 2013), http://ncronline.org/print/news/theology/bishops-colleges-find-good-collaboration-ex-corde-review.

3. See Bob Wells, "I Want to Be Like Them," *Faith & Leadership* (August 17, 2010), http://www.faithandleadership.com/profiles/i-want-be-them.

4. See Bob Wells, "Excellence Is the Standard," *Faith & Leadership* (August 17, 2010), http://www.faithandleadership.com/features/articles/excellence-the-standard?page=0,1.

5. Not all criticisms of these reforms are rearguard actions, however. A handful of back-to-basic Catholic colleges do not accept government money. See Burton Bollag, "Who Is Catholic? New Conservative Colleges Say Existing Institutions Lead Catholics Away from the True Faith," *Chronicle of Higher Education* (April 9, 2004), http://chronicle.com.ezproxy1.lib.asu.edu/article/

Who-Is-Catholic-/31886/. A home-schooling movement has also grown up among parents of primary and high school students.

6. "NCR's Person of the Year for 2010," *National Catholic Reporter* (December 31, 2010), http://ncronline.org/news/people/ncrs-person-year-2010. In 2012 the Catholic Health Association came to side with the bishops in their opposition to "the contraception mandate" set forth by the Obama administration. See David Gibson, "Catholic Hospitals Reject Obama's Birth Control Compromise," *Religious News Service* (June 15, 2012), http://archives.religionnews.com/politics/election/Catholic-hospitals-reject-Obamas-birth-control-compromise.

CHAPTER EIGHT SNAP AND THE STRATEGY OF CONFRONTATION

1. Among the best accounts of Clohessy's life is the report by Bill McClellan, "Unexpected Celebrity Stands Up for Victims," *St. Louis Post-Dispatch* (September 26, 2011).

2. Excerpted from an interview conducted by Jaime Romo, February 11, 2010, http://jjromo.wordpress.com/2010/02/11/an-interview-with-david-clohessy/. See also the interview conducted by Romo with Frank Douglas, a board member of SNAP and organizer of the blog *Voice of the Desert*, September 29, 2010, http://www.jaimeromo.com/blog/archives/291.

3. David Clohessy, "Church Won't Police Itself," *Philadelphia Inquirer* (September 6, 2012).

4. Compare Hindy Lauer Schachter, "Reflections on Political Engagement and Voluntary Association Governance," *Nonprofit and Voluntary Sector Quarterly* 40 (March 2010), 703–719.

5. Interview with Frank Douglas, October 26, 2010. See also the comments of another survivor, "Dan McNevin," in Kerry Kennedy, ed., *Being Catholic Now: Prominent Americans Talk about Change in the Church and the Quest for Meaning* (New York: Crown, 2008), 121–128. Compare Alan Zarembo, "Many Researchers Take a Different View of Pedophila," *Los Angeles Times* (January 14, 2013), latimes.com/news/local/la-me-pedophiles-20130115,0,197689.story.

6. For a good chronology, see Timothy D. Lytton, *Holding Bishops Accountable: How Lawsuits Helped the Catholic Church Confront Clergy Sexual Abuse* (Cambridge: Harvard University Press, 2008), 13–41. The early years of SNAP are also covered by Jason Berry and Gerald Renner, *Vows of Silence: The Abuse of Power in the Papacy of John Paul II* (New York: Free Press, 2004), 78ff. For a contrasting perspective, see Philip Jenkins, *Pedophiles and Priests: Anatomy of a Contemporary Crisis* (New York: Oxford University Press, 1996). Jenkins has served as a paid expert witness for dioceses in abuse cases.

7. Doyle's own account of the period 1984–2010 has been published in eight installments during 2010 and 2011 on the website of Voice of the Faithful, in the *In the Vineyard* monthly newsletter.

8. Interview with David Clohessy, Detroit, June 11, 2011.

9. In 1974, Congress had passed the Child Abuse Prevention and Treatment Act, requiring all states to collect reports of child abuse. Teachers, nurses, police officers, social workers, and others have to report any evidence of abuse of neglect. Most states give those accused of abuse the right to a hearing to contest such reports; California does not. David G. Savage and Carol J. Williams, "Cleared of Child Abuse, But Unable To Clear Name," *Los Angeles Times* (September 30, 2010).

10. Gustavo Arellano, "The Army of God: How a Monk, an Altar Boy, and a Sex-abuse Victim Joined Forces to Battle their Common Enemy, the Catholic Church," *Orange County Weekly* (August 12, 2004).

11. Victoria Kim, Harriet Ryan, and Ashley Powers,"L.A. Archdiocese Personnel Files Could Be Released Next Month," *Los Angeles Times* (December 10, 2012).

12. See Patrice Apodaca, "God's Stand-In," *Orange Coast Magazine* (September 2010). Orange is the fastest-growing diocese in the United States. Its Catholic population doubled in the first decade of the twentieth century, reaching 1.2 million, and in 2012 the diocese purchased the bankrupt Crystal Cathedral in Garden Grove. See Nicole Santa Cruz,"Texas Bishop to Lead O.C. Roman Catholic Diocese," *Los Angeles Times* (September 22, 2012).

13. See for example Gillian Flaccus,"Court Rules on Friars' Records Public in Sex Cases," *Associated Press* (October 1, 2010), Greg Hardesty,"Friars' Files in Sex Cases Going Public," *Orange County Register* (October 1, 2010), and Tony Perry and Paloma Esquivel,"San Diego Diocese Releases Priests' Records in Sex Abuse Cases," *Los Angeles Times* (October 25, 2010).

14. Patrick J. Wall, blog, http://patrickjwall.wordpress.com, January 15, 2008.

15. "Diocese Responds to Arkansas Chapter of SNAP," *Arkansas Catholic* (October 18, 2007).

16. Perry Dane,"The Corporation Sole and the Encounter of Law and Church," in *Sacred Companies: Organizational Aspects of Religion and Religious Aspects of Organizations*, ed. N.J. Demerath III et al., 50–61 (New York: Oxford University Press. 1998).

17. A rounded account of the Wilmington settlement is by Joseph N. DiStefano, "Philly Deals: How Wilmington Diocese Paid for the Abuse Claims," *Philadelphia Inquirer* (September 2, 2012).

18. There is no central listing of dioceses constituted under "corporation sole," essentially mini-monarchies with bishops designated as sole owners of the physical plant, and those in which parishes are separately incorporated. Corporation sole appears to be the modal type in the United States. But many looser arrangements predate the sexual abuse crisis. Baltimore, for example, went to separately incorporated parishes after a disastrous flood in the 1960s put diocesan-wide finances at risk. See Thomas W. Spalding, *The Premier See: A History of the Archdiocese of Baltimore, 1789–1989* (Baltimore, MD: Johns Hopkins University Press, 1989).

19. The big exception is a Delaware parish, St. Elizabeth's, which was found liable for three million dollars in damages (out of a total award ten times that amount) for negligence in the case of former priest Francis DeLuca. Laurie Goodstein "$30 Million Is Awarded Over Abuse by Priest," *New York Times* (December 1, 2010).

20. SNAP has to be wary about legislative lobbying that would transgress the conditions of its nonprofit tax-exempt status. The best study of the tenacity of Catholic parishioners remains Gerald Gamm, *Urban Exodus: Why the Jews Left Boston and the Catholics Stayed* (Cambridge: Harvard University Press, 1999).

21. Avery Dulles, SJ,"Rights of Accused Priests," *America* (June 21, 2004).

22. Compare Susan Pinkus and Peter McDonough,"American Catholics and Their Priests," *Public Perspective* 14 (March–April 2003), 10–12, and Stephen J. Fichter, Mary L. Gautier, and Paul M. Perl, *Same Call, Different Men: The Evolution of the Priesthood since Vatican II* (Collegeville, MN: Liturgical Press, 2012).

23. Mitchell Landsberg, "Charge against Catholic Bishop Unprecedented in Sex Abuse Scandal," *Los Angeles Times* (October 14, 2011)

24. "Letter from Priests to Cardinal Law," *Boston Globe* (December 10, 2002) and Matt Carrol and Michael S. Rosenwald, "Clergy Speaks Out," *Boston Globe* (December 14, 2002).

25. See Lisa McGirr, *Suburban Warriors: The Origins of the New American Right* (Princeton: Princeton University Press, 2001) and Adam Nagourney, "Orange County Is No Longer Nixon Country," *New York Times* (August 29, 2010).

26. The Religious Education Conference, organized by the Los Angeles archdiocese, has been held in Anaheim, next to Disneyland, since the early 1970s. It regularly draws about 40,000 attendees, mostly church workers, from the United States and other countries. The event is described in Chapter Twelve.

27. This argument depends on the fact that, while abuse victims are spread across most of the country, the vulnerability of dioceses to litigation is concentrated in a few states, especially those in which statues of limitations have been lifted or are under severe pressure. Listening sessions and the like are not the sort of news that gets reported in venues like the website of the National Survivor Advocates Coalition.

28. See Paul Wilkes, *The Good Enough Catholic: A Guide for the Perplexed* (New York: Ballantine Books, 1996).

29. The figures reported here underestimate the financial size of the Knights of Columbus. They refer to Knights of Columbus Charities USA only, exclusive of the Supreme Council, which runs its insurance operations, and numerous K of C affiliates. In 2010 the net assets of the Supreme Council stood at over $1,735,435,000—about thirty times the net assets of the Charities USA side of the K of C. See Carl Anderson, *A Civilization of Love: What Every Catholic Can Do to Transform the World* (New York: Harper Collins, 2008). Anderson, supreme knight of the Knights of Columbus, is the CEO and chairman of the board of the organization, "the world's largest Catholic family fraternal service organization." He also serves as a trustee on numerous boards, including the Catholic University of America. See http://www.kofc.org/un/en/executives/sk_bio.html.

30. The rankings shift around slightly depending on which measures—net assets, total revenues, and so on—are used. Data for Opus Dei and the Knights of Malta were not available on public sites like GuideStar and the NCCS. Opus Dei, like the Knights of Malta, qualifies as a religious organization. Legally the IRS treats it as a church, and as such it is not required to file annual returns.

31. Quieter but not silent. The Knights speak out from time to time, in *Reader's Digest* prose, on political issues. See Carl A. Anderson, "What Every Catholic Can Do to Transcend Partisanship," address to the Catholic Press Association, http://www.kofc.org/un/en/news/releases/detail/printer_friendly/cmc-20120623.html, and Dennis Coday, "Knights of Columbus Leader: 'Catholics Can No Longer Accept Politics as Usual,'" *National Catholic Reporter* (June 26, 2012).

32. Comments on Phyllis Zagano, "Following the Money," *National Catholic Reporter*, blog, May 23, 2012, http://ncronline.org/print/blogs/just-catholic/following-money. See also John L. Allen, "Transfers Fuels Doubts about Vatican's Line on Sex Abuse, US Nuns," *National Catholic Reporter* (October 18, 2012), http://ncronline.org/print/news/vatican/transfers-fuel-doubts-about-vaticans-line-sex-abuse-us-nuns, Phyllis Zagano, "Ministry by Women Religious and the U.S. Apostolic Visitation," *New Blackfriars* 92 (September 2011), 591–606, and Zagano, "Fighting

Talk," *The Tablet* (August 18, 2012). The K of C informed Zagano that the organization supplied "PR assistance, stationery, and web design, initially worth about $25K." Her understanding is that the Knights "gave $1 million after Mother [Mary] Clare [Millea, superior general of the Apostles of the Sacred Heart of Jesus] went begging to the bishops; the money would have gone either to her order or to CICLASL [the Congregation for Institutes of Consecrated Life and Societies of Apostolic Life at the Vatican, popularly known as the Congregation for Religious] or to some US entity to wash it" (personal communications from Zagano to McDonough, January 10, 2013). A report by Jason Berry on the troubles of the nuns does not mention the Knights; see "The New Inquisition: The Vatican Targets US Nuns," *National Catholic Reporter* (December 26, 2012), http://ncronline.org/news/women-religious/new-inquisition-vatican-targets-us-nuns, and "Bishops Investigating US Nuns Have Poor Records on Sex Abuse Cases," *National Catholic Reporter* (January 5, 2013), http://ncronline.org/news/women-religious/bishops-investigating-us-nuns-have-poor-records-sex-abuse-cases. Calls to the office of the Apostolic Visitation are answered with an automatic message that "the Apostolic Visitation has been completed and the office has closed." As this book goes to press in January 2013, the convent to which Sr. Kieran Foley, publicity assistant of the Visitation, belongs reports that she is out of town, "for how long we're not sure," and a response from Andrew Walther, spokesman for the K of C, to inquiries about the financing of the Visitation has yet to arrive.

33. Erik Eckholm, "One Man Guides the Fight against Gay Marriage," *New York Times* (October 9, 2012), http://www.nytimes.com/2012/10/10/us/politics/frank-schubert-mastermind-in-the-fight-against-gay-marriage.html and Laurie Goodstein, "Knights of Columbus Donate Millions to Anti-Gay Marriage Effort, Report Says," *New York Times* (October 18, 2012), http://thecaucus.blogs.nytimes.com/2012/10/18/knights-of-columbus-donate-millions-to-anti-gay-marriage-effort-report-says/?pagewanted=print. See also David Gibson, "Chicago Cardinal Leads New Fight against Gay Marriage," *Religious News Service* (January 2, 2013), http://www.religionnews.com/2013/01/02/chicago-cardinal-leads-new-fight-against-gay-marriage/.

34. One of the few investigations of this phenomenon is by James Davison Hunter, *To Change the World: The Irony, Tragedy, and Possibility of Christianity in the Late Modern World* (New York: Oxford University Press, 2010), 81–96.

35. In Our Lady of the Miraculous Medal parish in Montebello, near East Los Angeles, the K of C conducts an annual "Tootsie Roll" drive. According to the weekly church bulletin, "all the contributions benefit people with Intellectual Disabilities. This statewide fund-raising drive will aid programs like education in residential care homes, the Special Olympics, on the job training, and summer camps for people of all ages, regardless of race, creed, or color. Help the Knights help our brothers and sisters. The Tootsie Roll is free. Your contribution is priceless."

36. See Daniel Henninger, "A Lesson in Conservative Optimism," *Wall Street Journal* (December 7, 2012) and Joseph E. Persico, *Casey: The Lives and Secrets of William J. Casey, From the OSS to the CIA* (New York: Penguin, 1991).

37. http://www.alsmithfoundation.org/thedinneer.html. See also the coverage of Massachusetts State Representative Eugene O'Flaherty, a well-known figure in K of C circles, and his campaign against extending the statute of limitations on the sex abuse of children: Milton J. Valencia, "Child Abuse Bill to Go Before Mass. House," *Boston Globe* (March 21, 2012) and various articles in the same paper by Kevin Cullen.

38. See "Earthly Concerns," *Economist* (August 18, 2012), John L. AllenJr., "The Church's Deep Pockets, the Butler Did It, and Myths about Atheism," *National Catholic Reporter* (August 17, 2012), Jeff Sharlet, *The Family: The Secret Fundamentalism at the Heart of American Power* (New York: Harper, 2008), and David Yamane, *The Catholic Church in State Politics: Negotiating Prophetic Demands and Political Realities* (London: Rowman & Littlefield, 2005). Published as a novel in 1977, *True Confessions* premiered as a film in 1981, scripted by Dunne and his wife Joan Didion.

39. See "Chicago Archdiocese: Key Findings of Defenbaugh Due Diligence Report," *Origins* 35 (2006), 695–699.

40. David Crary, "US Study Shows Drop in Child Abuse," *Associated Press* (February 2, 2010). The article summarizes the fourth installment of the National Incidence of Child Abuse and Neglect study. The research compared data collected in 1993 with data from 2005–6, http://www.acf.hhs.gov/programs/opre/research/project/national-incidence-study-of-child-abuse-and-neglect-nis-4-2004-2009.

41. The conclusion that child sexual abuse has declined is based on the convergence of evidence from multiple data sets. This is the thrust of the argument made by the psychologist Thomas Plante, interview, Santa Clara University, October 4, 2011. Some of the data derived from organizational self-reporting, like that provided by the bishops, may be less trustworthy than other sources, such as FBI reports, and even this information may underestimate the absolute level of abuse, given a tendency for victims to under-report. This is the perspective endorsed by Bishops Accountability. Nevertheless, the over-time data all point downward. See Thomas G. Plante (who is a long-time consultant for dioceses) and Kathleen L. McChesney, eds., *Sexual Abuse in the Catholic Church: A Decade of Crisis, 2002–2012* (Santa Barbara: Praeger, 2011) and Eric Goode, "Researchers See Decline in Child Sex Abuse Rate," *New York Times* (June 29, 2012). David Gibson, "Ten Years after Catholic Sex Abuse Reforms, What's Changed?" *Religious News Service* (June 6, 2012), argues that while controls put in place by bishops in the United States have been effective, "progress in other countries is halting." In 2012, Yale University commissioned a conference of scholars in the humanities to comment on sexual abuse in Catholicism. Their preliminary observations, published on the blog sponsored by the Social Science Research Council entitled "Immanent Frame," exhibit a borderline intelligibility; see Kathryn Lofton, "Sex Abuse and the Study of Religion," July 6, 2012, http://blogs.ssrc.org/tif/2012/07/06/sex-abuse-and-the-study-of-religion/.

42. Robert Marquand, "Pope Benedict XVI's 30-Year Campaign to Reassert Conservative Catholicism," *Christian Science Monitor* (August 6, 2010), http://www.csmonitor.com/World/Europe/2010/0806/Pope-Benedict-XVI-s-30-year-campaign-to-reassert-conservative-Catholicism.

43. See Christine Schenk, CSJ, "On the 'Crime' of Ordaining Women," *In the Vineyard* [VOTF online newsletter] 10 (Fall 2010), http://www.votf.org/vineyard/index.html.

44. Deborah Becker, "BC [Boston College] Board Member Resigns amid Allegations of Failed Priest Abuse Oversight," Station WBUR, National Public Radio Boston affiliate, May 23, 2012, http://www.wbur.org/2012/04/19/bc-board-member.

45. Peggy Noonan, "How to Save the Catholic Church: The Vatican Badly Needs New Blood—and a Woman's Touch," *Wall Street Journal* (April 17, 2010).

46. From a talk given at a meeting of the American Catholic Council, Detroit, June 11, 2011.

47. For example, apart from the question of sexual orientation, it is still common to stress the claim that sexual abuse by priests accounts for only a small number of such cases nationwide. This is true, but of course the population of priests is small. The preliminary task—not an easy one, you can't just look it up—is to compare the incidence of abuse in relative terms, across occupations. Neither celibacy nor sexual orientation can be the only factor, since homosexuality tends to be comparatively prevalent in some professions where celibacy is not the norm and where, moreover, child abuse is not known to be widespread. The lack of serious research in the area is remarkable. The possibility of interaction effects between sexual orientation, celibacy, and sexual abuse almost never comes up, though speculation about selective recruitment and toxic opportunities comes close. I am grateful to Jason Berry (personal communications, January 7 and January 8, 2013) for pressing me on this cluster of issues. See Rachel Aviv, "The Science of Sex Abuse," *New Yorker* (January 14, 2013), 36–45, and Colm Tóibín, "Among the Flutterers," *London Review of Books* (August 19, 2010), http://www.lrb.co.uk/v32/n16/colm-toibin/among-the-flutterers.

48. Harriet Ryan and Victoria Kim, "Judge Orders Archdiocese to Restore Names in Abuse Files," *Los Angeles Times* (January 7, 2013) and "Names in Church Sex Abuser Records Should Be Public, Judge Rules," *Los Angeles Times* (January 7, 2013), http://latimesblogs.latimes.com/lanow/2013/01/names-catholic-church-sex-abuse-records-public-judge-ruling.html. See also Laurie Goodstein, "Sexual Abuse Files Cast Shadow on Los Angeles Cardinal," *New York Times* (January 22, 2013), http://www.nytimes.com/2013/01/23/us/mahony-shielded-abusive-priests-documents-show.html and Harriet Ryan, Ashley Powers, and Victoria Kim, "Church Sex Abuse Files Unlikely to Lead to Charges, Experts Say," *Los Angeles Times* (January 22, 2013), http://www.latimes.com/news/local/la-me-church-files-20130123%2C0%2C3180168.story.

49. Contributions from trial lawyers have been estimated to make up about 70 percent of SNAP's budget. Interview with Joelle Casteix, southwest regional director for SNAP, October 21, 2009. When I mentioned this estimate to David Clohessy, he responded that while the figure might approach that range in California, the national percentage doesn't come close. Clohessy reckons the national figure to be somewhere between 15 and 20 percent. Not to put too fine a point on it: getting things straight in such matters is difficult. Efforts to discredit actors by pointing out who is a paid consultant, how much a trial lawyer makes from a case, and so on are routine. By the same token, however, full disclosure about possible conflicts of interest is rare. "Mental reservation" is ubiquitous. The working supposition is that no one is disinterested; everyone has an agenda or is somehow compromised.

50. Laurie Goodstein and Erick Eckholm, "Church Battles Efforts to Ease Sex Abuse Suits," *New York Times* (June 14, 2012).

51. This is the conviction behind the work of Bishop Accountability. Directed by Terry McKiernan and Anne Barrett Doyle, the organization is dedicated to uncovering evidence documenting cases of sexual abuse and their cover-up in the Catholic church. A central premise is that the pertinent files held by the vast majority of dioceses have not been examined thoroughly by competent investigators. The imperative is to expose information so damaging that it is shredded or kept hidden, archived out of sight. Interview with Doyle, January 12, 2013.

52. Compare Katharine Q. Seelye, "Private Pain, Played Out on Public Stage: Abused by a Priest, a Performer Grapples with the Consequences," *New York Times* (January 13, 2013).

CHAPTER NINE VOICE OF THE FAITHFUL AND THE STRUGGLE FOR CATHOLIC PLURALISM

1. Euclides da Cunha, *Os Sertões* [Rebellion in the Backlands], trans. Samuel Putnam (Chicago: University of Chicago Press, 1955), 119 [original published in 1902].

2. David O'Brien, interview, March 11, 2010.

3. Soon after, Baier went on to found Survivors First, out of which grew BishopsAccountability.org, a website devoted to archiving documents about sexual abuse mentioned in the previous chapter. His early business career is described in an interview given to the Harvard Business School, where he graduated in 1994: http://www.hbs.edu/entrepreneurs/pdf/paulbaier.pdf.

4. James Post, interview, February 2, 2010.

5. Investigative Staff of the *Boston Globe, Betrayal: The Crisis in the Catholic Church* (Boston: Little, Brown, 2003).

6. William A. Donohue, "Voice of the Faithful Is Toast?" www.catholic.org, July 15, 2009; don't miss Donohue, "Spanish Harlem Welcomes an Irishman," in *Catholics in New York: Society, Culture, and Politics, 1808–1946*, ed. Terry Golway, 176–178 (New York: Fordham University Press and Museum of the City of New York, 2008).

7. The argument that VOTF succeeded in "opening up a discursive space" runs through Tricia Colleen Bruce, *Faithful Revolution: How Voice of the Faithful Is Changing the Church* (New York: Oxford University Press, 2011).

8. "A Chance for Rebirth," [editorial] *Baltimore Sun* (March 4, 2010).

9. Radio interview, Patt Morrison show, KPCC, May 14, 2010. See also Gregory Boyle, *Tattoos on the Heart: The Power of Boundless Compassion* (New York: Free Press, 2010). Homeboy Industries has since recuperated some of its losses. Megan O'Neil, "Homeboy with a Heart," *Glendale News Press* (February 8, 2011).

10. See for example "Catholic Schools: An Endangered Species—Empty Seats and Rising Costs Taking Their Toll," *Directions, Quarterly Report for Catholic Grantmakers*, FADICA, Washington, DC (Summer 2010).

11. Laurie Goodstein, "Milwaukee Archdiocese Seeks Chapter 11," *New York Times* (January 4, 2011).

12. See Marc Levinson, *The Great A&P and the Struggle for Small Business in America* (New York: Hill and Wang, 2012).

13. The syndrome sounds a lot like ODD—oppositional defiant disorder—a condition so prevalent among school-age children that it has its own diagnostic rubric in medical encyclopedias. Lenin, nothing if not a stern disciplinarian, called it "infantile leftism."

14. Baier, Harvard Business School interview, 2002, see note 3.

15. Some VOTF leaders understood the drawbacks of expressive hyperventilation from the beginning. See David J. O'Brien, "Change the Church?" *America* (August 13, 2012). The article reprints a talk O'Brien gave ten years earlier at VOTF's founding conference.

16. See Rebecca Kolins Givan et al., eds., *The Diffusion of Social Movements: Actors, Mechanisms, and Political Effects* (Cambridge: Cambridge University Press, 2010). Scalability has also been a challenge for the Roundtable, despite a greater commonality of experience and expectations among its members than is the case with adherents of VOTF.

17. Compare Neal Carne, Raj Andrew Ghoshal, and Venes Ribas, "A Social Movement Generation: Cohort and Period Trends in Protest Attendance and Petition Signing," *American Sociological Review* 76 (February 2011), 125–151.

18. For a detailed account of the infighting, see Bruce, *Faithful Revolution*. See also John D. Skrentny, "Policy-Elite Perceptions and Social Movement Success," *American Journal of Sociology* 111 (May 2006), 1762–1815.

19. Interview with John Ryan, November 23, 2009. The comedy is not confined to VOTF. The Leadership Roundtable, covered in the next chapter, has had to work through moments of its own. At one of the first Roundtable get-togethers, a young Wall Street executive suggested to a breakout group of prelates and other dignitaries that Catholicism might be envisioned as part of the leisure-time industry; he went on to suggest that Cornell University's School of Hotel Administration could provide a fresh perspective on the church's management difficulties. The recommendation generated little follow-up except silence and a change of subject.

20. Interview with William Casey, February 26, 2010.

21. Elizabeth Bowen, "On Jane Austen," in *Novelists on Novelists*, ed. Louis Kronenberg (Garden City, NY: Doubleday Anchor, 1962), 11. The reference is to Henry Crawford, one of Austen's characters in *Mansfield Park*.

22. For a more sanguine reading, see Betzaluz Gutierrez, Jennifer Howard-Grenville, and Maureen A. Scully, "The Faithful Rise Up: Split Identification and an Unlikely Change Effort," *Academy of Management Journal* 53 (August 2010), 673–699.

23. Interview, Jim Post, February 3, 2010.

24. See John P. Beal, "Something There Is that Doesn't Love a Law: Canon Law and Its Discontents," in *The Crisis of Authority in Catholic Modernity*, ed. Michael J. Lacey and Francis Oakley, 135–160 (New York: Oxford University Press, 2011).

25. John Myers, "A Voice Not Rooted in the Church," *Catholic Advocate* (October 11, 2002). Myers (who insists on being addressed as "Your Grace") went on to argue that "altering Church teaching on sexual morality, and defiance of the apostolic authority that has guided the Church since its founding 2,000 years ago by Our Lord Jesus Christ, have all found a place in the ranks of Voice of the Faithful."

26. Chuck Colbert, "Voice of the Faithful Members Profiled: Survey Shows Reform Group's High Level of Commitment to Church," *National Catholic Reporter* (March 10, 2006), http://natcath.org/NCR_Online/archives2/2006a/031006/031006j.php and William D'Antonio and Anthony Pogorelc, *Voices of the Faithful: Loyal Catholics Striving for Change* (New York: Crossroad, 2007).

27. Mark Chaves and James C. Cavendish, "More Evidence on U.S. Catholic Church Attendance," *Journal for the Scientific Study of Religion* 33 (December 1994), 376–381.

28. See John P. Dolan, ed., *The Essential Erasmus* (New York: Mentor-Omega, 1964).

29. Nancy T. Ammerman, "Whose Voice? Surveying the Membership of Voice of the Faithful," *Boston College Magazine* (Winter 2008).

30. William D'Antonio et al., *American Catholics Today* (Lanham, MD: Rowman & Littlefield, 2007).

31. Compare Larry Bartels, "Occupy's Impact beyond the Beltway," January 18, 2012, http://billmoyers.com/2012/01/18/has-the-occupy-movement-altered-public-opinion, and Andrew Kohut, "Don't Mind the Gap," *New York Times* (January 26, 2012).

32. See Alexander A. Schuessler, *A Logic of Expressive Choice* (Princeton: Princeton University Press, 2000).

33. Brian S. Krueger, "A Comparison of Conventional and Internet Political Mobilization," *American Politics Research* 34 (November 2006), 759–776.

34. Gladwell, "Small Change," *New Yorker* (October 4, 2010). See also Sidney Tarrow, "Dynamics of Diffusion: Mechanisms, Institutions, and Scale Shift," in *The Diffusion of Social Movements*, ed. Rebecca Collins Givan et al., 204–219 (Cambridge: Cambridge University Press, 2010) and Maxwell T. Boycoff, *Contemporary Sociology* 41 (June 2012), 486–487: review of Jennifer Earl and Katrina Kimport, *Digitally Enabled Social Change: Activism in the Internet Age* (Cambridge, MA: MIT Press, 2011).

35. David R. Swartz, *Moral Minority: The Evangelical Left in an Age of Conservatism* (Philadelphia: University of Pennsylvania Press, 2012) tells a similar story. Compare Christopher A. Ball, "The Fringe Effect: Civil Society Organizations and the Evolution of Media Discourse about Islam since the September 11th Attacks," *American Sociological Review* 77 (December 2012), 855–879.

36. Interview with Casey, February 26, 2010.

CHAPTER TEN THE LEADERSHIP ROUNDTABLE AND THE LONG MARCH THROUGH THE INSTITUTIONS

1. Wilbert T. ("Uncle Robbie") Robinson [manager, Brooklyn Dodgers], *Inside Baseball* (Plymouth, NH: Draper-Maynard, n.d. [1914–1919?]), 1.

2. Michael Novak, "Awakening from Nihilism: The Templeton Prize Address," *First Things* (August–September 1994), http://www.firstthings.com/article/2007/01/awakening-from-nihilismthe-templeton-prize-address-17.

3. James Finn, ed., *Private Virtue and Public Policy: Catholic Thought and National Life* (New Brunswick, NJ: Transaction, 1990).

4. The 1998 document had been foreshadowed by a "Letter to the Bishops of the Catholic Church on Some Aspects of the Church Understood as Communion," issued in 1992 by the Congregation for the Doctrine of the Faith, under Ratzinger's leadership. See Kilian McDonnell, "The Ratzinger/Kasper Debate: The Universal Church and Local Churches," *Theological Studies* 63 (June 2002), 227–250.

5. From a talk given at the annual meeting of the Leadership Roundtable, Wharton School, University of Pennsylvania, July 9, 2004.

6. See Gerard Mannion et al., eds., *Readings in Church Authority* (London: Ashgate, 2003), 201–206.

7. See Kenneth A. Briggs, *Double Crossed: Uncovering the Catholic Church's Betrayal of American Nuns* (New York: Doubleday, 2006).

8. Laurie Goodstein and Stephanie Strom, "Embezzlement Is Found in Many Catholic Dioceses," *New York Times* (January 5, 2007) and Alison Leigh Cowan, "37-Month Sentence for Priest Who Defrauded Parish," *New York Times* (December 5, 2007).

9. Roberto Suro, "American Religion and the Old and New Immigration," *Religion and American Culture* 22 (Winter 2012), 18.

10. Katarina Schuth, *Priestly Ministry in Multiple Parishes* (Collegeville, MN: Liturgical Press, 2006). The actual figure is probably closer to 25–30 percent. The computational discrepancy

reflects the problematic nature of "parishes." Many are "missions" in remote, thinly populated areas and hence not technically parishes. I am grateful to Mark Mogilka for pointing this out. The estimates of parishes without their own pastor are high in either case. The priest-to-parish ratio might improve, of course, by lowering the denominator, that is, by closing down or consolidating parishes. The average size of parishes has grown. See Mark M. Gray, Mary L. Gautier, and Melissa A. Cidade, *The Changing Face of U.S. Catholic Parishes* (Washington, DC: Center for Applied Research in the Apostolate, 2011) and Zoe Ryan, "The Megaparish: More Boom Than Bane," *National Catholic Reporter* (May 24, 2011).

11. David DeLambo, *Lay Parish Ministers: A Study of Emerging Leadership* (New York: National Pastoral Life Center, 2005).

12. See Thomas J. Tierney, "The Leadership Deficit," *Stanford Social Innovation Review* 4 (Summer 2006), 26–35. The talent crunch among laity willing to work for the church was evidently worse in the 1930s, when the acerbic Evelyn Waugh penned this commentary: "I have often observed that the servants of the religious are, as a class, of abnormally low mentality. I do not know why this should be—whether it is that good people in their charity give jobs to those whom no one else will employ, or whether, being poor, they get them cheap, or whether they welcome inefficient service as a mortification, or whether unremitting association of people with superior virtue eventually drives sane servants off their heads." From Evelyn Waugh, "Ninety-Two Days," in *Waugh Abroad: Collected Travel Writing* (New York: Everyman's Travel Writing, 2003), 446.

13. Evan B. Alderfer and Herman E. Michl, *Economics of American Industry*, 2nd ed. (New York: McGraw-Hill, 1950) is a fine period piece documenting the postwar boom.

14. See "Spotlight Catholic Schools," January 26, 2009, http://www.catholichistory.net/Spotlights/SpotlightSchools.htm, and Donald W. Wuerl [archbishop of Washington, DC], "How to Save Catholic Schools," *America* (December 22, 2008).

15. Boisi, concluding remarks to Roundtable meeting, "A Blueprint for Responsibility: Responding to Crises with Collaborative Solutions," University of Pennsylvania Wharton School, Philadelphia, June 25, 2010.

16. The sentiments of obligation expressed in the Roundtable's evolving response resemble some of the ramifications of "grieving" described by Peter Steinfels, "Further Adrift: The American Church's Crisis of Attrition," *Commonweal* (October 22, 2010).

17. From an invocation to the 2007 meeting of the Roundtable, spoken by Dale Melczek, bishop of Gary, Indiana.

18. Vincent's conversations with major leaguers are compiled in the three-volume "Baseball Oral History Project." See volume 2: Fay Vincent, *We Would Have Played for Nothing: Baseball Stars of the 1950s and 1960s Talk about the Game They Loved* (New York: Simon & Schuster, 2008).

19. Robinson, *Inside Baseball*, 1.

20. Albert O. Hirschman, *Journeys Toward Progress: Studies in Economic Policy Making in Latin America* (Boulder, CO: Westview Press, 1993).

21. See Jimmy Breslin, *The Church that Forgot Christ* (New York: Free Press, 2004).

22. To set this in perspective: Domino's Pizza tycoon Tom Monaghan has put roughly 400 million dollars into Ave Maria University, the school he launched near Naples, Florida. David Gibson, "In a World of Its Own," *Tablet* (July 1, 2006). By 2010 the Roundtable staff had expanded, and the Washington headquarters had ten full-time employees.

23. The most amply documented is the Catholic Community Foundation of St. Paul-Minneapolis, the largest operation of its kind in the country. See Tom Gallagher, "Giving Money Away: A Catholic Model," *National Catholic Reporter* (December 31, 2009), http://ncronline.org/news/accountability/giving-money-away-catholic-model. Foundations and endowments at the diocesan levels have been around, in unknown numbers, since at least the 1930s. After spending over $11 million responding to charges of child abuse and consolidating many of its schools, the Philadelphia archdiocese set up "Faith in the Future Foundation" to manage its secondary and special-education system as "the first independently run Catholic school system in the country"; see Kristen Linker and Chris Caselenuevo, "Philly Catholic High Schools To Be Managed By a Private Foundation," *Philadelphia Inquirer* (August 22, 2012).

24. Shawn Francis Peters, *The Catonsville Nine: A Story of Faith and Resistance in the Vietnam Era* (New York: Oxford University Press, 2012).

25. http://www.mountdesalesacademy.org.

26. The conjunction of authority concentrated at the top and administrative decentralization has prompted organizational analysts to characterize Catholicism as a "flat hierarchy." See Allen Grossman and Christina Darwall, "The Roman Catholic Diocese of San Jose," Harvard Business School Case Studies 9-303-059, April 17, 2002.

27. See Charles E. Zech, *Why Catholics Don't Give... and What Can Be Done about It*, rev. ed. (Huntington, IN: Our Sunday Visitor Press, 2006). Capital markets are not completely absent in the philanthropic world, as the growth of "patient capital"—investments in social projects with the potential to generate returns—indicates. See Dayo Olopade, "Gatekeepers," *American Prospect* 21 (October 2010), 6–9. In Catholic circles the largest operation for managing socially sensitive capital is Christian Brothers Investment Services. CBIS began extending its work beyond the Christian Brothers order itself, inviting Catholic organizations in general to join, in the mid-1980s.

28. Michael Winerip, "Catholic School Teachers Wrestle with Faith and Obedience in Negotiating Contract," *New York Times* (September 4, 2011).

29. For more upbeat assessments, see Marti R. Jewell and David A. Ramey, *The Changing Face of Church: Emerging Models of Parish Leadership* (Chicago: Loyola Press, 2010).

30. Terence MacSwiney, the mayor of Cork during the fight against British rule in the early 1920s, voiced an extreme instance of the latter tendency. In the course of the hunger strike that eventually killed him, MacSwiney proclaimed that what counted was "not how much pain we can inflict, but how much suffering we can endure." There are various wordings of the statement, but the message is always the same.

31. Marshall W. Meyer and Lynne B. Zucker, *Permanently Failing Organizations* (Newbury Park, CA: Sage, 1989), 47.

32. The suggestion for exit interviews was later promoted by William J. Byron, SJ, "Who's Conducting the Interview?" *Catholic Herald* (September 1, 2010). Byron, in line with Bossidy, also stressed the importance of communicating "the good news cheerfully and effectively."

33. Larry Bossidy and Ram Charan, *Confronting Reality: Doing What Matters to Get Things Right* (New York: Crown Business, 2004), 46–47.

34. Robinson, *Inside Baseball*, 2.

35. Patrick McCloskey, "Making the Grade in Memphis," *Stats* [George Mason University] (November 10, 2009), http://www.jubileeschools.org/documents/Making%20the%20grade%20in%20Memphis.pdf.

36. Fred Gluck's overview of the "turnaround situation" in the church parallels Bossidy's analysis. Gluck, "Crisis Management in the Church," *America* (December 1, 2003), http://americamagazine.org/issue/462/article/crisis-management-church. For an outline of solutions in the Roundtable spirit, see Gluck, "Can the Church Learn from Wal-Mart?" *America* (May 17, 2004), http://americamagazine.org/issue/485/article/can-church-learn-wal-mart.

37. Thomas J. Healey, "A Church Transparent: What Catholic Leaders Have Learned from the World of Business," *America* (September 8, 2008), http://americamagazine.org/issue/666/article/church-transparent and Healey and John Eriksen, "The Pastor's Toolbox: How Your Parish Can Get Down to Business," *America* (April 12, 2010), http://americamagazine.org/issue/733/article/pastors-toolbox.

38. See Robert J. Egan and Sara Butler, "Women and the Priesthood," *Commonweal* (July 18, 2008), 8–10 and Phyllis Zagano, "Catholic Women Deacons," *America* (February 17, 2003), http://americamagazine.org/issue/422/article/catholic-women-deacons.

39. Lisa Miller, "A Woman's Place Is in the Church," *Newsweek* (April 2, 2010), http://magazine-directory.com/Newsweek.htm. Miller, who became religion editor in 2006, published related articles around the same time in *Newsweek*, including "The Trouble with Celibacy" (April 6, 2010) and "The Bad Shepherd: Why Pope Benedict XVI May Not Be Able to Heal His Church" (March 25, 2010).

40. Frederick W. Gluck, "God's Line Manager," *Financial Times* (May 5, 2005).

41. See Donald Cozzens, *Sacred Silence: Denial and Crisis in the Church* (Collegeville, MN: Liturgical Press, 2002).

42. Compare Melissa J. Wilde et al., "Religious Economy or Organizational Field? Predicting Bishops' Votes at the Second Vatican Council," *American Sociological Review* 75 (August 2010), 586–606.

43. See however David DeLambo, "In Search of Pastoral Excellence," *c.*2007 http://emergingmodels.org/files/2012/05/In-Search-of-Pastoral-Excellence.pdf.

44. See Bernard Hamilton, "Priestly Functions," *Times Literary Supplement* (September 23, 2011): review of Gary Macy, *The Hidden History of Women's Ordination: Female Clergy in the Medieval West* (Oxford: Oxford University Press, 2011) and interview with Gary Macy, "Get the Facts in Order: A History of Women's Leadership," *U.S. Catholic Historian* 78 (January 2013), 18–22. The National Catholic Reporter has taken pains to publicize the unorthodox (for most Catholics) history of women presbyters in the early years of the church; see NCR staff, "Early Women Leaders," *National Catholic Reporter* (January 04–17, 2013), http://ncronline.org/print/news/theology/heads-house-churches-presbyters and Gary Macy, "The Meaning of Ordination and How Women Were Gradually Excluded," *National Catholic Reporter* (January 18–31, 2013), http://ncronline.org/print/news/women-religious/meaning-ordination-and-how-women-were-gradually-excluded

45. Quoted by Michael O'Malley, "Vatican Sets Off Controversy with Church Law Revisions that Lists Ordaining Women with Pedophilia, Other Offenses," *Cleveland Plain Dealer* (July 23, 2010), http://www.cleveland.com/religion/index.ssf/2010/07/vatican_sets_off_controversy_w.html.

CHAPTER ELEVEN FUTURECHURCH AND THE FOG OF REFORM

1. Felipe Fernández-Armesto, *Pathfinders: A Global History of Exploration* (New York: W. W. Norton, 2006), 313.

2. David G. Schultenover, ed., *Vatican II: Did Anything Happen?* (New York: Continuum, 2007), with essays by John W. O'Malley and others.

3. Gumbleton is a retired auxiliary bishop of Detroit and long-time peace activist. His request to stay on in his parish after reaching the mandatory retirement age of seventy-five was denied.

4. See John A. Coleman, SJ, *The Evolution of Dutch Catholicism, 1958–1974* (Berkeley: University of California Press, 1978).

5. Kolpack found work in January 2010 at a local hospice agency. The man hired in August 2009 to replace her at St. Thomas quit the following December. Mike Sweitzer-Beckman, "Terminated: A Visit with a Fired Church Worker," *National Catholic Reporter* (December 16, 2010), http://ncronline.org/blogs/terminated-visit-fired-church-worker.

6. See Laura R. Barraclough, *Making the San Fernando Valley: Rural Landscapes, Urban Development, and White Privilege* (Athens: University of Georgia Press, 2011) and Barbara M. Kelly, *Expanding the American Dream: Building and Rebuilding Levittown* (Albany: State University of New York Press, 1993).

7. The question came from George Bouchey, who maintains a slightly quirky, extremely useful listserve/network referencing news about things Catholic: georgebouchey@comcast.net.

8. About 2,000 attended the conference in Detroit.

9. The lobbying, to extend statute of limitations for cases of sex abuse, eventually failed. Paul Vitello, "For 5th Year, Child Abuse Bill Dies in Legislature," *New York Times* (June 2, 2010).

10. As can Mother Angelica, née Rita Antoinette Rizzo, who holds forth on pre–Vatican II Catholicism in reruns on the Eternal Word Television Network. Except where noted otherwise, all quotes from Schenk are from an interview conducted by the author on November 16, 2010.

11. On her reasons for leaving the Medical Mission Sisters, Schenk reports that "I kept getting depressed and I wasn't so sure about the celibacy thing, so I left. About five years later, I found out that I was horribly hypothyroid, and that cured the depression once I figured it out." The Sisters of Saint Joseph welcomed her in after she confessed "that my whole life I seem to end up getting into these causes that can be edgy, and if that was a problem, we had better talk about it." Tom Roberts, "From the Data, a Map to the Future Church," *National Catholic Reporter* (July 10, 2009). Roberts concludes with the observation that "Apparently they were then and continue to be just fine with 'edgy.' 'They have been terrific from the beginning,' (Schenk) said."

12. For a a short history, see Michael O'Malley, "Lakewood-Based FutureChurch Leads Effort to Press Catholic Church to Allow Married Priests," *Cleveland Plain Dealer* (January 22, 2010), http://www.cleveland.com/religion/index.ssf/2010/01/catholic_church_pressed_to_all.html. Jason Berry details Schenk's crusade against parish closings in *Render unto Rome: The Secret Life of Money in the Catholic Church* (New York: Crown, 2011), 203ff.

13. Trevison died in 2010 at the age of eighty five. Grant Segall, "Rev. Louis J. Trevison Led Resurrection Catholic and FutureChurch," *Cleveland Plain Dealer* (March 19, 2012), http://www.cleveland.com/obituaries/index.ssf/2010/03/rev_louis_j_trivison_led_resur.html.

14. Schenk neglects to mention that many Catholic parishes, unlike most Protestant congregations, are tied to parochial schools and the attendant funding burden. Still, the

number of parish schools has been declining since the 1960s. About half neither sponsor nor support a Catholic elementary school. I am grateful to Melissa Cidade of the Center for Applied Research in the Apostolate (CARA) at Georgetown University for bringing this to my attention.

15. See Michael O'Malley, "Cleveland Catholic Bishop Richard Lennon: A Profile," *Cleveland Plain Dealer* (December 5, 2010).

16. Threatened with closing, the members of a Cleveland parish, St. Peter's, incorporated their own community; their pastor went with them. Michael O'Malley, "The Rev. Robert Marrone, Priest Who Leads Breakaway Cleveland Catholic Congregation, Suspended from 'Priestly Ministry,'" *Cleveland Plain Dealer* (May 30, 2012), http://www.cleveland.com/metro/index.ssf/2012/05/the_rev_robert_marrone_priest.html.

17. Early in 2012, the Vatican overruled Lennon, deciding that thirteen of the fifty parishes shut down or merged should remain open. Brian Roewe, "Cleveland Parishes File Motions in Rome Demanding Their Churches Reopen," *National Catholic Reporter* (March 30, 2012), http://ncronline.org/blogs/ncr-today/cleveland-parishes-file-motions-rome-demanding-their-churches-reopen.

18. This is the Bishops' Synod in Rome in the fall of 2008, where Schenk succeeded in getting about thirty bishops to look over various petitions formulated by FutureChurch. See John Allen Jr., "Synod: Interview with Chris Schenk of 'FutureChurch,'" *National Catholic Reporter* (October 14, 2008), http://ncronline.org/news/synod-interview-chris-schenk-futurechurch.

19. Personal communication, Schenk to McDonough, November 2, 2010.

20. Joseph A. Komonchak, "The American Contribution to Dignitatis Humanae: The Role of John Courtney Murray, SJ," *U.S. Catholic Historian* 24 (Winter 2006), 1–20.

21. See Phyllis Zagano, "Inching Toward a Yes?" *The Tablet* (January 9, 2010).

22. Nicholas D. Kristof, "Tussling Over Jesus," *New York Times* (January 27, 2011). See also John Allen Jr., "Inductions on Money, Religious Freedom, and Polarization," *National Catholic Reporter* (January 28, 2011), http://ncronline.org/blogs/all-things-catholic/inductions-money-religious-freedom-and-polarization.

23. Phyllis Zagano, "It's Time: The Case for Women Deacons," *Commonweal* (December 10, 2012), http://commonwealmagazine.org/it%E2%80%99s-time. See also "Questions from a Ewe: Why Can or Can't Women Be Priests?" blog, January 12, 2013, http://questionsfromaewe.blogspot.com/2013/01/why-can-or-cant-women-be-priests.html?utm_source=feedburner&utm_medium=email&utm_campaign=Feed%3A+QuestionsFromAEwe+%28Questions+from+a+Ewe%29.

PART FIVE

1. W. S. Di Piero, commenting on the television series "The Wire," in "Who Shot Snot?" *Threepenny Review* (Spring 2011), 26–27.

2. Compare for example Larry Gordon, "Lavish New Church, Meeting Center to Serve USC Catholics," *Los Angeles Times* (December 9, 2012) and Lisa Wangsness, "Archdiocese of Boston Unveils Details of First Wave of Parish Reorganization," *Boston Globe* (January 10, 2013), who mentions that "today, fewer than 20 percent of baptized Catholics in the archdiocese attend Mass, down from 70 percent several decades ago." See also Sharon Otterman, "Catholic Schools Await More Closing Bells," *New York Times* (January 14, 2013).

3. See Thomas Reese, "The Hidden Exodus: Catholics Becoming Protestants," *National Catholic Reporter* (April 18, 2011) and Phil Zuckerman, *Faith No More: Why People Reject Religion* (New York: Oxford University Press, 2012).

4. See the untitled essay by Frank Butler in *Being Catholic Now: Prominent Americans Talk about Change in the Church and the Quest for Meaning, ed.* Kerry Kennedy, 87–92 (New York: Crown, 2008).

5. James Martin, SJ, "Bless Me Father," *America* (May 21, 2007).

6. The line of interpretation is inspired by Ann Swidler, "Culture in Action: Symbols and Strategies," *American Sociological Review* 51 (April 1986), 273–286.

7. Richard Deeg and Mary A. O'Sullivan, "The Political Economy of Global Finance Capital," *World Politics* 61 (October 2009), 759.

8. Compare Kelly Moore et al., "Science and Neoliberal Globalization," *Theory and Society* 40 (September 2011), 505–532.

9. James B. Stewart, "University Endowments Face a Hard Landing," *New York Times* (October 12, 2012) and Andrew Martin, "College Endowment Returns Fall Steeply," *New York Times* (October 25, 2012).

CHAPTER TWELVE TWO STEPS FORWARD...

1. Italo Calvino, "The Novel as Spectacle," in *The Uses of Literature*, trans. Patrick Creagh (San Diego, CA: Harcourt Brace, 1986), 191–192.

2. See Melanie M. Morey and John J. Piderit, SJ, *Catholic Higher Education: A Culture in Crisis* (New York: Oxford University Press, 2006).

3. Alexandra Horowitz, "Walk Like a Fish," *New York Times* (December 15, 2012).

4. Margaret O'Brien Steinfels, who retired from *Commonweal* at the end of 2002 after serving as editor of the magazine from 1988, is codirector with her husband Peter Steinfels of Fordham University's Center on Religion and Culture. On retiring, she declared that she had "noticed that my imagination has become a bit stunted," and that "something different is required." Gill Donovan, "Margaret Steinfels to Retire as Editor of Commonweal," *National Catholic Reporter* (November 22, 2002).

5. Lawrence S. Ritter and Mark Rucker, *The Babe: A Life in Pictures* (New York: Ticknor & Fields, 1988), 107.

6. See David Gibson, "The Cardinal's Sins," *New York Magazine* (January 28, 2007).

7. Donald Strong, *Roman Art* (New York: Penguin, 1976), 96.

8. See D. J. Waldie, *Holy Land: A Suburban Memoir* (New York: St. Martin's, 1996), Waldie, "The Darkness beneath Huell Howser," *Zocalo Public Square* online newsletter, http://www.zocalopublicsquare.org/2012/12/03/the-darkness-beneath-huell-howser/ideas/nexus/?utm_source=Waldie%20on%20Huell%20Hower%2C%20Gaming%20UFD%20%28Cancer%2C%20Gaming%29&utm_campaign=10%2F26%2F12&utm_medium=email, and Becky M. Nicolaides, *My Blue Heaven: Life and Politics in the Working Class Suburbs of Los Angeles, 1920–1965* (Chicago: University of Chicago Press, 2002).

9. Perpetua left a "memoir" written before her death in the arena that endures as a feminist text as well as a pious document. "The Passion," the historian Peter Thonemann writes, "shows us a confused young mother, facing the end of her mortal life, afraid of the dark, tormented with worry for her baby, finding hope and strength in the depths of her unconscious mind."

See Thonemann, "A Mother's Dreams," *Times Literary Supplement* (September 14, 2012) and Carolinne White, ed., *Lives of Roman Christian Women* (London: Penguin, 2010).

10. Compare Colm Tóibín, *Sign of the Cross: Travels in Catholic Europe* (London: Picador, 2001), Robert A. Scott, *Miracle Cures: Saints, Pilgrimage, and the Healing Powers of Belief* (Berkeley: University of California Press, 2011), William A. Christian Jr., *Divine Presence in Spain and Western Europe, 1500–1960: Visions, Religious Images, and Photographs* (Budapest: Central European Press, 2012), Lizette Alvarez, "400 Years Later, Still Revered in Cuba (and Miami)," *New York Times* (September 9, 2012), Samuel G. Freedman, "Amid the Ashes, A Statue of Mary Stands as a Symbol of Survival," *New York Times* (November 16, 2012), and Scott Draper and Joseph A. Baker, "Angelic Belief as American Folk Religion," *Sociological Forum* 26 (September 2011), 623–643.

11. Samuel G. Freedman tells the story of Fabian Cervantes, an immigrant expert in church repair: "Pews Tirelessly Restored, and an Immigrant Redeemed," *New York Times* (December 14, 2012).

12. John Crudele, "Goldman's Merger Chief: Geoffrey T. Boisi, Masterminding the Megadeals," *New York Times* (November 3, 1985). See also Bryan Burrough and John Helyar, *Barbarians at the Gate: The Fall of RJR Nabisco* (London: Jonathan Cape, 1990) and Lisa Endlich, *Goldman Sachs: The Culture of Success* (New York: Alfred A. Knopf, 1999).

13. Henry M. Paulson Jr., *On the Brink: Inside the Race to Stop the Collapse of the Global Financial System* (New York: Business Plus, 2010), 12. Like Boisi, Syron completed his undergraduate studies at Boston College. And Boisi, like Mitt Romney, with whom he is close, majored in English literature as an undergrad.

14. See Kurt Eichenwald, "A Leading Deal Maker Quits Goldman Sachs," *New York Times* (November 27, 1991) and William D. Cohan, *Money and Power: How Goldman Sachs Came to Rule the World* (New York: Doubleday, 2011), 299–300.

15. Laura M. Holson, "Chase, the Eager Acquirer, To Buy Investment Boutique," *New York Times* (March 24, 2000) and Holson, "Return of the Native: Chase's Investment Banking Hopes Ride on a Goldman Exile," *New York Times* (June 29, 2000).

16. Phyllis Berman and Lea Goldman, "Catholics in Crisis," *Forbes Magazine* (September 9, 2005) and MacMillan, "A Business Plan for the Catholic Church," *Business Week* (September 30, 2008).

17. Except where noted otherwise, the statements by Boisi in this chapter are excerpted from an interview conducted on March 21, 2011.

18. See the interview with Dubik written up by David Gibson as "Onward, Christian Soldier," *Faith and Leadership* (April 17, 2009), http://faithandleadership.com/people-news/writers/david-gibson.

19. The summer sessions are part of a larger "Pastoral Leadership Development Program" funded by the Lilly Endowment, with seed money from Tom Healey, treasurer of the Roundtable and a close friend of Boisi from his Goldman Sachs days. The program is coordinated by Fr. Paul Holmes of Seton Hall. Dubik's main contribution, a virtual mentoring community for priests called CatholicPastors.org, is detailed in the next chapter. See also the minutes of the 2009 Roundtable at the Wharton School, entitled "Clarity, Candor, and Conviction: Effective Communication for a Global Church" (Philadelphia, 2009) available at http://www.theleadershiproundtable.org/tlr/documents/proceedings2009.pdf.

20. Bob Wells, "Leadership 360: Priests and Lay Leaders Are Benefitting from a New Assessment Tool Customized for the Catholic Church," *Faith and Leadership* (August 16, 2011).

21. Almost all of the funding for the National Federation of Priests' Councils comes from the bishops.

22. Geschke points out that Dubik used Adobe software to communicate with his generals and other senior officers during his assignment in Iraq, where he did not want them to come in for meetings by traveling on roads if they could avoid the danger.

23. James M. Frabutt, "Standards for Excellence Implementation in the Diocese of Gary," University of Notre Dame, June 2010 at http://www.theleadershiproundtable.org/sfx/documents/GaryCaseStudy.pdf.

24. Two methodological issues arise here. One concerns the low absolute numbers; serious multivariate analysis is impossible with only eleven respondents. Second, however, a high nonresponse rate does not necessarily translate into high nonresponse *bias*, at least for point estimates of the value of single variables. Responses to surveys have been dropping for decades, in some cases reaching single digit rates. The surmise of experts is that nonrespondents need not differ significantly from respondents; see James Wagner, "A Comparison of Alternative Indicators for the Risk of Nonresponse Bias," *Public Opinion Quarterly* 76 (Fall 2012), 555–575, and the literature cited therein. Nevertheless, none of this overcomes the commonsensical feeling that very high nonresponse rates "privilege the voices and experiences of the wired, the articulate, and the highly motivated." Scott Keeter, "Survey Research, Its New Frontiers, and Democracy," *Public Opinion Quarterly* 76 (Fall 2012), 606.

25. Rubin and Jacob Weinberg, *In an Uncertain World: Tough Choices from Wall Street to Washington* (New York: Random House, 2003), 316.

26. Since the 1990s, much of Wall Street has moved uptown, with investment companies arrayed along Park Avenue, north of Grand Central Station. See Karen Ho, *Liquidated: An Ethnography of Wall Street* (Durham, NC: Duke University Press, 2009).

27. Thomas J. Curry, "The Best and Worst of Times," *America* (November 20, 2006).

28. See Samuel G. Freedman, "Lessons from Catholic Schools for Public Educators," *New York Times* (April 30, 2010) and *Preserving a Critical National Asset: America's Disadvantaged Students and the Crisis in Faith-Based Urban Schools* (Washington, DC: Domestic Policy Council, 2008), http://www2.ed.gov/admins/comm/choice/faithbased/report.pdf.

29. See Jeff Parrott, "Inexcusable Absence: Catholic Schools Recruit Hispanic Students," *U.S. Catholic* (February 2011) and Thomas M. Suhy, "Sustaining the Heart: Attracting Latino Families to Inner-City Catholic Schools," *Catholic Education* 15 (March 2012), 270–294.

30. The reference is to the Third Plenary Council of Baltimore, held in 1884, where the American bishops mandated the creation of the Catholic parochial school system and the issuance of the Baltimore Catechism, drilled into Catholic school children until Vatican II.

31. "Catholic Action" traces its origins to the Italy of the 1860s. Before Vatican II, the movement encouraged "the organized work of the laity performed under the direction or mandate of a bishop in the fields of dogma, morals, liturgy, education, and charity"; Pope Pius XI designated it in 1927 as "the participation of the laity in the apostolate of the hierarchy." Since Vatican II ecclesiastical rhetoric has given greater recognition to the responsibility of the laity. Compare Jay P. Corrin, *Catholic Intellectuals and the Challenge of the Democracy* (Notre Dame, IN: University

of Notre Dame Press, 2002) and "Joan Schlosser: Lay Apostle," illustrated by Lloyd Ostendorg, *Treasure Chest of Fun & Fact: Catholics in Action* (November 6, 1952).

32. Interview with Mark Mogilka, director of stewardship and pastoral services, diocese of Green Bay, May 10, 2011.

33. Personal communication, Mogilka, May 16, 2011. When he talks about "prying loose the schools," Mogilka means variations on separate incorporation, "already happening in many areas of the country, though the bishop plays a key role in the corporations."

34. The political viability of converting Catholic to charter schools, while retaining their religious identity, is doubtful on constitutional grounds; see Charles J. Russo and Gerald M. Cattaro, "Faith-Based Charter Schools: An Idea Whose Time Is Unlikely to Come," *Religion and Education* 36 (Spring 2009), 72–93.

35. Andy Smarick, "Can Catholic Schools Be Saved?" *National Affairs* 7 (Spring, 2011), http://www.nationalaffairs.com/publications/detail/can-catholic-schools-be-saved.

36. Compare Stephanie Saul, "Public Money Finds Back Door to Private Schools," *New York Times* (May 21, 2012) and Stephanie Banchero and Jennifer Levitz, "Vouchers Breathe New Life into Shrinking Catholic Schools," *Wall Street Journal* (June 14, 2012).

37. See Jenny Anderson, "A Catholic School Retools for a Wealthier Market," *New York Times* (August 19, 2012) and Erik P. Goldschmidt and Mary E. Walsh, "Sustaining Urban Catholic Elementary Schools: An Examination of Governance Models and Funding Strategies," Lynch School of Education, Boston College, 2011, http://www.bc.edu/content/dam/files/schools/lsoe/pdf/Roche_Center/Sustaining_Urban_Catholic_Elementary_%20Schools.pdf.

38. Michael Birnbaum, "Head of Washington's Catholic Schools to Lead Boston College Center," *Washington Post* (March 11, 2010). Quotes are from a phone interview with Weitzel-O'Neill, September 7, 2012.

39. See Editorial Board, "Who Will Rescue the D.C. Voucher Program This Time?" *Washington Post* (April 10, 2012). The *Post* supported the program, which got a mixed though basically positive review from the federal government; see *Evaluation of the DC Opportunity Scholarship Program* (Washington, DC: Institute of Education Sciences, National Center for Education Evaluation and Regional Assistance, 2010), http://ies.ed.gov/ncee/pubs/20104018/pdf/20104018.pdf. The report found "no conclusive evidence that the OSP affected student achievement" in reading and math tests scores even though it "significantly improved students' chances of graduating from high school" and "raised parents', but not students', ratings of school safety and satisfaction."

40. Interestingly, data collected by CARA suggest that what parents want in Catholic schools is "quality religious education," slightly ahead of a "safe environment" and "quality academic instruction"—in other words, religious identity. School leaders (evidently, principals and other top staff) on the other hand rank "discipline and order" higher than "quality religious education." Another intriguing difference between parents and administrators is that the latter are strong on providing a "welcoming environment for non-Catholics," parents significantly less so. Center for Applied Research in the Apostolate, *Primary Trends, Challenges and Outlook: A Special Report on U.S. Catholic Elementary Schools, 2000–2005* (Washington, DC: CARA at Georgetown, 2006), 4. See also Michael Birnbaum, "Former D.C. Catholic Schools Seeking Identity as Charter Schools," *Washington Post* (January 28, 2010). The idea for charter schools seems to have multiple origins. The reference to their Catholic inspiration probably reflects the boost that the idea

got from research directed by the sociologist James Coleman indicating that students in Catholic high schools tend to outperform their peers; see Coleman, Thomas Hoffer, and Sally Kilgore, *High School Achievement: Public, Catholic, and Private Schools Compared* (New York: Basic Books, 1982).

41. See Lyndsey Layton, "Michelle Rhee, the Education Celebrity Who Rocketed from Obscurity to Oprah," *Washington Post* (January 12, 2013), http://www.washingtonpost.com/local/education/michelle-rhee-the-education-celebrity-who-rocketed-from-obscurity-to-oprah/2013/01/12/eed4e3d8-5a8c-11e2-9fa9-5fbdc9530eb9.

42. The document is available online at http://www.catholicschoolstandards.org/. See also Lorraine A. Ozar, "National Standards and Benchmarks," *Momentum* [journal of the National Catholic Education Association] 43 (February–March 2012), 10–13. Ozar, the director of the Center for Catholic School Effectiveness at Loyola University, Chicago, headed the task force and drafted the statement with Weitzel-O'Neill.

43. See Adam Liptak, "Supreme Court Allows Tax Credit for Religious Tuition," *New York Times* (April 4, 2011) for an account of state-level litigation scenarios. The closeness of the five to four ruling was typical of such decisions. In this instance, conservative justices prevailed over liberals in turning back objections to permitting tax credits for donations to private "student tuition organizations" in Arizona.

44. For an analysis that is sympathetic to the general Catholic perspective on vouchers and charters from a neoconservative standpoint, see Chester E. Finn Jr., *Troublemaker: A Personal History of School Reform since Sputnik* (Princeton: Princeton University Press, 2008). Compare Diane Ravitch, "In Mitt Romney's Schoolroom," *New York Review of Books* (July 12, 2012) and Nicholas D. Kristof, "Students Over Unions," *New York Times* (September 12, 2012). The Supreme Court came down closely (five to four) in favor of vouchers in Zelman v. Simmons-Harris (2002), but challenges to that decision remain possible because of restrictions on aid to "sectarian schools" built into state constitutions. See Kern Alexander, "Public Financing of Religious Schools: James B. Blaine and Justice Clarence Thomas' 'Bigotry Thesis,'" *Forum on Public Policy* 2 (2006), 736–758; "'They Drew a Circle that Shut Me In': The Free Exercise Implications of Zelman v. Simons-Harris," *Harvard Law Review* 117 (January 2004), 919–950; and Thomas E. Buckley, "A Mandate for Anti-Catholicism: The Blaine Amendment," *America* (September 27, 2004).

CHAPTER THIRTEEN IN THE LABYRINTH

1. Jorge Luis Borges, "The Circular Ruins," *The Garden of Forking Paths, Collected Fictions*, trans. Andrew Hurley (New York: Penguin, 1998), 97–100.

2. Timothy Dolan, who succeeded Edward Egan as the archbishop of New York, was elected president of the US conference of bishops in November 2010. See Michael Sean Winters, "America's Top Catholic," *New Republic* (November 26, 2010).

3. Charles D. Ellis, *The Partnership: The Making of Goldman Sachs* (New York: Penguin, 2008), 280.

4. See Carl Koch, "Servant Leadership: Can the Bishops Learn from Southwest Airlines?" *America* (July 5–12, 2004).

5. Lisa Endlich, *Goldman Sachs: The Culture of Success* (New York: Alfred A. Knopf, 1999), 81.

6. Ibid., 82–83.

7. At this point matters get complicated. Talk switches from "consumer" to "shareholder value," and establishing what "doing the right thing" means becomes difficult. See William D. Cohan, "When Romney Ran Bain Capital, His Word Was Not His Bond," *Wall Street Journal* (January 13, 2012) and Nell Minow, "Why CEO Pay Spun Out of Control," *New Republic* (February 8, 2012). Minow makes the case that "the roots of elevated CEO salaries lie in the mergers and acquisitions and leveraged-buyout frenzy of the 1980s, plus the dot.com explosion of the 1990s..."

8. However, Kathleen McChesney, long a member of the Roundtable board, played an important role in developing diocesan review procedures when she headed the bishops' commission on sexual abuse in the early 2000s, before joining the Roundtable.

9. See Francis Cardinal George, OMI, *The Difference God Makes: A Catholic Vision of Faith, Communion, and Culture* (New York: Crossroad, 2009), 155ff. For a similar argument from a sociological perspective, see Melissa Wilde et al., "Religious Economy or Organizational Field? Predicting Bishops' Votes at the Second Vatican Council," *American Sociological Review* 75 (August 2010), 586–606.

10. An abbreviated history can be found in http://ecommerce.hostip.info/pages/4/Adobe-Systems-Inc-EARLY-HISTORY-WARNOCK-GESCHKE.html.

11. Much of the history is related in an interview given on August 17, 2009 by Geschke as part of the "famous startup" series; http://startuphistory.ru/post/show/other_people_in. The story is also covered from a slightly different angle in the announcement of the 2010 Marconi award, given to Geschke and Warnock: http://www.marconisociety.org/fellows.html. Geschke pointed out that the wives of the executives who attended the "show and tell" loved the new machines and software because they could see how the equipment would make secretarial work easier.

12. Geschke, talk on "My Life as an Engineer," Santa Clara University, April 19, 2011.

13. The number refers to the global total of bishops and pastors. The most recent figure is slightly higher—31,389—reported for 2011 at http://www.catholic-hierarchy.org/bishop/la.html. The total number of bishops, who must visit Rome every five years, is about 4,800. John Thavis, "The Numbers Game: Stats Give Picture of Pope John Paul's Pontificate," *Catholic News Service* (May 5, 2006).

14. When Geschke gave a talk later that year, at a regional meeting of the Roundtable outside of San Francisco, he presented many of the same criticisms, making clear that he was speaking "not as a representative of the Roundtable but as a lifelong committed Catholic in his mid-seventies."

15. Geschke rounded out his criticism of the church's stance on sexuality with an observation on economic policy and social issues generally: "The vast majority of neoconservatives may call themselves Christians (or Catholics) but they are not followers of Jesus Christ." For the Fed, see Binyamin Appelbaum, "A Bold Dissenter at the Fed, Hoping His Hopes Are Wrong," *New York Times* (January 8, 2013).

16. Unless noted otherwise, all quotations are excerpted from a phone interview with Dubik conducted on May 27, 2011.

17. Dubik was not recruited to the Roundtable. While still in the military, he called up Boisi and volunteered his services.

18. Dubik begins every day with an hour of meditation. See the interview he gave on "Managing the Asset of Time" to the magazine *Faith and Leadership*, n.d. [early 2011?], http://www.faithandleadership.com/multimedia/james-dubik-managing-the-asset-time.

19. According to tax returns filed for 2009, the Roundtable received just under $200,000 for consulting services; almost all the rest of its income, about $770,000, was contributed by donors.

20. The genesis of CatholicPastors.org is laid out in detail in the discussion by Dubik with Lt. Col. Nate Allen and Rev. Kevin Kennedy of "virtual communities of practice," pp. 57–73 in the report of the 2009 annual meeting of the Roundtable. The report, entitled "Clarity, Candor, and Conviction: Effective Communication for a Global Church," is available online; see Chapter Twelve, note 18.

21. It is worth comparing Dubik's calm regarding the pace of change in the American church with his tough assessment of government policy as it relates to the use of decisive military force. See Dubik, "A National Strategic Learning Disability?" *Army Magazine* (September 2011).

22. December 20, 2011.

23. In 2010 the Roundtable began to sponsor regional meetings that also respond to the demand for customization.

24. See Sarika Bansal, "The Power of Failure," *New York Times* (November 28, 2012), opinionator blog, http://opinionator.blogs.nytimes.com/2012/11/28/the-power-of-failure-2/?pagewanted=print.

25. Since the terms are indistinguishable when spoken, "sell-anthropy" is easily confused with "celanthropy"—philanthropy promoted by celebrities, like Bono and Angelina Jolie. See Matthew Bishop and Michael Green, *Philanthrocapitalism: How the Rich Can Save the World* (New York: Bloomsbury, 2008), 194–213.

26. Sharon Otterman and Kate Taylor, "Bookkeeper Accused of Stealing $1 Million from Archdiocese," *New York Times* (January 30, 2012), Joseph Tanfani, "Worker Accused of Stealing $1 million from Archdiocese over Six Years," *Philadelphia Inquirer* (January 28, 2012), and Joseph A. Slobodzian, "Former Philly Archdiocese CFO Gizzard Sentenced for Embezzling $906,000," *Philadelphia Inquirer* (August 25, 2012).

27. By the end of 2011, CatholicPastors.org was getting few takers. The Roundtable then took out ads in Catholic magazines and newspapers and by mid-2012, with Fr. Frank Donio in charge, several hundred pastors had signed up. Evaluating the program has faced the same problem that the Standards for Excellence initiative ran into: the response rate for assessing its reception has run around 10 percent.

28. For a brief account of Bennett's career through the 1990s, see "Legends in the Law: A Conversation with Robert S. Bennett," *Bar Report* (October–November 1995), http://www.dcbar.org/for_lawyers/resources/legends_in_the_law/bennett.cfm.

29. See Joseph Berger, "At Brooklyn Prep, Paterno Learned Latin and Bravado," *New York Times* (January 24, 2012).

30. Quotes are taken from an interview conducted in the offices of Hogan Lovells US LLP on March 22, 2011. Bennett spent much of his career as a partner at Skadden, Arps, Slate, Meager, & Flom; see Lincoln Kaplan, *Skadden: Power, Money, and the Rise of a Legal Empire* (New York: Farrar, Straus, and Giroux, 1993). Bennett treats his involvement with the lay review board in chapter seventeen of *In the Ring: The Trials of a Washington Lawyer* (New York: Three Rivers/Crown, 2008), 306–323. As for the reminiscences of Brooklyn in pre-sixties times, see Thomas Oliphant, *Praying for Gil Hodges: A Memoir of the 1955 World Series and One Family's Love of*

the Brooklyn Dodgers (New York: Thomas Dunne/St. Martin's, 2005)—this is one of Bennett's favorite books—and Elliott Willensky, *When Brooklyn Was the World, 1920–1957* (New York: Harmony, 1986). A semiofficial version is by Joseph Coen, Patrick McNamara, and Peter Vaccari, *Diocese of Immigrants: The Brooklyn Catholic Experience, 1853-2003* (Strasbourg: Editions du Singe/Diocese of Brooklyn, 2004).

31. William J. Bennett, President George H. W. Bush's "drug czar" and former chief of the National Endowment for the Humanities, is Robert Bennett's younger brother.

32. Bennett, *In the Ring*, 148ff.

33. Ideas behind the Catholic Investment Partnership began to come up for discussion between the bishops and the Roundtable in the aftermath of the 2008 financial crisis.

34. Sister Mary Ann Walsh, the director of media relations for the United States Conference of Catholic Bishops, argues that "the government gets huge help from the Catholic Church, to the tune of about $23 billion a year. That is what the government does not have to pay for students because Catholic schools educate about two million US students annually." Sister Mary Ann Walsh, "Catholic Schools Give America More Than Chump Change," *Huffington Post* (August 23, 2012), http://www.huffingtonpost.com/sister-mary-ann-walsh/catholic-schools-give-america-more-than-chump-change_b_1823100.html.

35. The edge in academic achievement that showed up for Catholic schools when comparisons with their public peers were first made in the 1980s, specifically among at-risk students, seems to have grown smaller since then. The reasons include rising tuition costs (which have made more Catholic schools relatively elitist), reforms in some of the public schools themselves, and a continued downward slope in contributions from Catholics, relative to what Protestants and others usually give. See Maureen T. Hallinan and Warren N. Kubitschek, "School Sector, School Poverty, and the Catholic School Advantage," *Catholic Education* 14 (December 2010), 143–172; Patricia Weitzel-O'Neill and Aubrey Scheopner Torres, "Catholic Schools as Schools of Academic Excellence," *Catholic Education* 15 (September 2011), 72–86; and Scott Davies, "Are There Catholic Schools Effects in Ontario, Canada?" *European Sociological Review* 28 (December 2012), 1–13.

36. See Diane Ravitch, "How, and How Not, to Improve the Schools," *New York Review of Books* (March 22, 2012) and Richard Rothstein and Mark Santow, "The Cost of Living Apart," *American Prospect* (September–October 2012).

37. Contrast Michelle Dillon, "Jürgen Habermas and the Post-Secular Appropriation of Religion," in *The Post-Secular in Question*, ed. Philip S. Gorski et al., 249–278 (New York: New York University Press, 2012).

CONCLUSION

1. Péter Nádas, *Parallel Stories: A Novel*, trans. Imre Goldstein (New York: Farrar, Straus, and Giroux, 2012), 47.

2. For an interpretation focusing on the dissemination of Catholic values rather than numbers, see Michelle Boorstein, "Fewer Priests This Easter, But More People Learning Jesuit Ideals," *Washington Post* (April 23, 2011).

3. "Catholics Share Bishops' Concerns about Religious Liberty, but Catholic Voters Back Obama on Social Issues," *Pew Forum on Religion & Public Life* (August 1, 2012), http://www.pewforum.org/Politics-and-Elections/Catholics-Share-Bishops-Concerns-about-Religious-Liberty.aspx#leaders.

4. See Thomas R. Rochon, *Culture Moves: Ideas, Activism, and Changing Values* (Princeton: Princeton University Press, 1996).

5. Besides Call to Action, a few web-reliant organizations (Faithfulamerica.org, for example, and Catholics in Alliance for the Common Good) have pressed forward since the mid-2000s with public policy agendas in opposition to the increasingly conservative platform promoted by the United States Conference of Catholic Bishops.

6. See the discussion of "public regardingness" by Edward C. Banfield and James Q. Wilson, *City Politics* (Cambridge: Harvard University Press, 1963), 41–44.

7. From a talk given at the American Catholic Council, June 11, 2011. Awareness and consciousness raising, rather than the expectation of a quick victory, were the stated rationales behind SNAP's appeal to the International Criminal Court to level charges against the Vatican of crimes against humanity: Jason Walsh, "Why the ICC Likely Won't Charge Pope Over Catholic Church Sex Abuses," *Christian Science Monitor* (September 15, 2011).

8. Nicolas P. Cafardi, "The Abuse Crisis Resurfaces in Philadelphia," *Commonweal* (March 3, 2011); Ana Maria Catanzaro, "The Fog of Scandal," *Commonweal* (May 12, 2011); Bob Smietana, "Take It to the Board: How Effective Are Lay Review Boards in Preventing Sex Abuse?" *U.S. Catholic* 77 (June 2012), 12–17; and Joshua J. McElwee, "Kansas City Bishop's Guilty Verdict Raises National Questions," *National Catholic Reporter* (September 11, 2012).

9. An indicator of no-holds-barred deterioration is the series of events that began to unfold early in 2012. SNAP was ordered to hand over its emails and files of documents at the request of lawyers working for the Kansas City diocese, and David Clohessy was required to give a deposition. See Glenn E. Rice, "SNAP Says It Will Continue Working with Victims," *Kansas City Star* (January 4, 2012). The St. Louis archdiocese adopted a similar strategy; see "Bishops Target Victims' Advocacy Group in St. Louis, Kansas City," *St. Louis Post-Dispatch* (January 5, 2012). The struggle all but bankrupted SNAP; see Joshua J. McElwee, "SNAP Leaders Deposition Made Public," *National Catholic Reporter* (March 2, 2012). For a comparable denouement in Germany, see Mary Beth Warner and Kristen Allen, "Blame Traded after Failed Church Abuse Probe," *Spiegel Online* (January 10, 2013), http://www.spiegel.de/international/germany/blame-traded-after-investigation-into-catholic-church-sex-abuse-fails-a-876790-druck.html.

10. Laurie Goodstein, "Defying Canon and Civil Laws, Diocese Failed to Stop Priest," *New York Times* (September 7, 2012).

11. Michael Burleigh, *Earthly Powers: The Clash of Religion and Politics in Europe, From the French Revolution to the Great War* (New York: Harper Perennial, 2007), 163–174 passim.

12. See Emilio J. Castilla and Stephan Benard, "The Paradox of Meritocracy in Organizations," *Administrative Science Quarterly* 55 (December 2010), 543–576.

13. See John P. Diggins, *Up From Communism: Conservative Odysseys in American Intellectual History* (New York: Harper & Row, 1975), 274ff. People acquainted with the Roundtable often note the similarity between its "way of proceeding" and the Jesuit manner. Many members of the Roundtable are familiar with Ignatian spirituality. The connection would be worth pursuing. For example: The emphasis on staying in formation, the preference for action (in Latin, *age quod agis*, "get on with what you're doing") over theoretical disputation, the simultaneous devotion to hierarchy and agility (the preference for shaping leaders and dealing with the top people), and belief in the utility of sticking with a set of theological precepts as long as they are sanctioned by

church authorities (in the final paragraphs of his *Spiritual Exercises*, Ignatius suggests that one school of theology is pretty much as good as another as long as loyalty to the mission of Rome is shown). See Peter McDonough, *Men Astutely Trained: A History of the Jesuits in the American Century* (New York: Free Press, 1992).

14. Laurie Goodstein, "In Three Countries, Challenging the Vatican on Female Priests," *New York Times* (July 22, 2011).

15. Peter J. Leithart, "Rick Santorum and Secular Natural Law," *First Things* blog (February 24, 2012), http://www.firstthings.com/onthesquare/2012/02/rick-santorum-and-secular-natural-law.

16. This logic reached its zenith in the writings of an anti-Enlightenment aristocrat, compiled by Jack Lively, ed., *Works of Joseph de Maistre* (New York: Macmillan, 1965). For a recent statement in a similar vein, see Antonio Gaspari, "Cardinal Piacenza on Women Priests, Celibacy and the Power of Rome," *Zenit* (September 18–19, 2011), http://www.zenit.org/article-33466?l=english. See also Lisa Miller, "Feminism's Final Frontier? Religion," *Washington Post* (March 8, 2012).

17. Ross Douthat, "Can Liberal Christianity Be Saved?" *New York Times* (July 14, 2012).

18. See Bjørn Thomassen, "Notes toward an Anthropology of Political Revolutions," *Comparative Studies in Society and History* 54 (July 2012), especially 698ff.

19. Compare Daniel C. Dennett, *Breaking the Spell: Religion as a Natural Phenomenon* (New York: Penguin, 2006), 97–246.

20. Compare T. M. Luhrmann, *When God Talks Back: Understanding the American Evangelical Relationship with God* (New York: Alfred A. Knopf, 2012).

21. Zadie Smith, *Changing My Mind* (New York: Penguin, 2009), 74. See the notion set forth by Brendan Gill that "emotionally, we are all six years old." *Here at the New Yorker* (New York: Da Capo, 1997).

22. Graham Greene, *The Lost Childhood and Other Essays* (London: Eyre & Spottiswoode, 1951), 19. See also Edmund Burke, *A Philosophical Enquiry into the Sublime and the Beautiful and Other Pre-Revolutionary Writings*, ed. David Womersley (New York: Penguin, 2003), Robert W. Fogel, *The Fourth Great Awakening and the Future of Egalitarianism* (Chicago: University of Chicago Press, 2000), Mary Lefkowitz, *Greek Gods, Human Lives: What We Can Learn from Myths* (New Haven: Yale University Press, 2003), Geoffrey O'Brien, *The Phantom Empire* (New York: W. W. Norton, 1993), and Judith Shulevitch, "The Power of the Mustard Seed: Why Strict Churches are Strong," *Slate* (May 12, 2005), http://www.slate.com/articles/life/faith-based/2005/05/the_power_of_the_mustard_seed.single.html.

23. Rodney Stark and Roger Finke, *Acts of Faith: Explaining the Human Side of Religion* (Berkeley: University of California Press, 2000).

24. Compare the articles in the sesquicentennial issue of *C21 Resources*, a periodical published by Boston College's Church in the 21st Century Center (Fall 2012) and Joseph H. Fichter, SJ, *The Sociology of Good Works* (Chicago: Loyola University Press, 1993).

25. See for example Susan Jacoby, "The Blessings of Atheism," *New York Times* (January 5, 2013), Robert H. Frank, *The Darwin Economy: Liberty, Competition, and the Common Good* (Princeton: Princeton University Press, 2011), and Czeslaw Milosz, "Catholicism," *New Republic* (March 16, 1982), http://www.tnr.com/print/book/review/catholicism.

26. Susan P. Mattern, *Rome and the Enemy: Imperial Strategy in the Principate* (Berkeley: University of California Press, 1999).

27. See Philip S. Gorski and Ates Altinordu, "After Secularization?" *Annual Review of Sociology* 34 (2008), 58ff.

28. Laurie Goodstein, "Christian Right Fails to Sway Voters on Issues," *New York Times* (November 9, 2012).

29. Compare Stefan Timmermans and Steven Epstein, "A World of Standards but not a Standard World: Toward a Sociology of Standards and Standardization," *Annual Review of Sociology* 36 (2010), 69–89, and Jane Jacobs, *The Death and Life of Great American Cities* (New York: Vintage, 1961).

30. For good discussions of the "performance builds trust" fallacy, see Ezra Suleiman, *Dismantling Democratic States* (Princeton: Princeton University Press, 2003) and several of the essays in Theodore K. Rabb and Ezra N. Suleiman, eds., *The Making and Unmaking of Democracy: Lessons from History and World Politics* (New York: Routledge, 2003).

31. See John Torpey, "Religion and Secularization in the United States and Western Europe," in *The Post-Secular in Question*, ed. Philip S. Gorki et al., 279–306.

32. Much of Murray's thinking about consensus grew out of the Cold War politics of his time. See Jonathan P. Herzog, *The Spiritual-Industrial Complex: America's Religious Battle against Communism in the Early Cold War* (New York: Oxford University Press, 2011) and Jason W. Stevens, *God-Fearing and Free: A Spiritual History of America's Cold War* (Cambridge: Harvard University Press, 2010). It is probably no coincidence that Murray found his voice at about the same time that the Supreme Court, through decisions outlawing Bible-reading and prayer in public schools, was "de-Protestantizing" the "moral establishment" of American political culture. See David Sehat, *The Myth of American Religious Freedom* (New York: Oxford University Press, 2011).

33. For a study of the rhetorical strategy deployed by neoconservatives, see Mark A. Smith, *The Right Talk: How Conservatives Transformed the Great Society into the Economic Society* (Princeton: Princeton University Press, 2007). For a perceptive assessment of the strategic mobilization of idealism alongside moneyed interests in the pursuit of "durable advantage," see Steven M. Teles, *The Rise of the Conservative Legal Movement: The Battle for the Control of Law* (Princeton: Princeton University Press, 2008), especially 265ff. Compare Rick Perlstein, *Before the Storm: Barry Goldwater and the Unmaking of the American Consensus* (New York: Hill and Wang, 2001), especially 6–95, and Donald T. Critchlow and Nancy MacLean, *Debating the American Conservative Movement* (Lanham, MD: Rowman & Littlefield, 2009).

34. For an overview from within neoconservative ranks, see Weigel, "End of the Bernardin Era."

35. Ivan Krastev, "Paradoxes of the New Authoritarianism," *Journal of Democracy* 22 (April 2011), 13.

36. D. Michael Lindsay, "Evangelicals in the Power Elite: Elite Cohesion Advancing a Movement," *American Sociological Review* 73 (February 2008), 60–82.

37. Rosabeth Moss Kanter, *Confidence: How Winning Streaks and Losing Streaks Begin and End* (New York: Three Rivers, 2004).

38. See Peter A. Hall, "*Historical Institutionalism in Rationalist and Sociological Perspective,*" in *Explaining Institutional Change*, ed. James Mahoney and Kathleen Thelen (Cambridge: Cambridge University, 2010), especially 218, where Hall remarks that "institutions can change as a consequence of processes of 'defection' in which actors gradually stop adhering to the practices

formerly constitutive of an institution, whether seriatim or in groups, without any formal agreement to do so. Although it may be an exaggeration to claim... that 'shirkers are the motor of history,' there is little doubt that processes such as these are important elements in many instances of institutional change."

39. For a demographic overview that emphasizes the "softening involvement in religious organizations" as a kind of surrogate secularization, see Mark Chaves, *American Religion: Contemporary Trends* (Princeton: Princeton University Press, 2011).

40. Timothy Matovina, "American Religion and the Old and New Immigration," *Religion and American Culture* 22 (Winter 2012), 7–14, and Matovina, *Latino Catholicism: Transformation in America's Largest Church* (Princeton: Princeton University Press, 2012).

41. Vegard Skirbekk, Erick Kaufman, and Anne Goujon, "Secularism, Fundamentalism, or Catholicism? The Religious Composition of the United States to 2043," *Journal for the Scientific Study of Religion* 49 (June 2010), 293–310; Shawn F. Dorius and Glenn Firebaugh, "Trends in Gender Global Inequality," *Social Forces* 88 (July 2010), 1941–1968; Dennis Hodgson, review of Eric Kaufman, *Shall the Religious Inherit the Earth? Demography and Politics in the Twenty-First Century* (London: Profile Books, 2011), in *Population and Development Review* 37 (December 2011), 793–795; and J. D. Long-García, "Hispanics in the Pews, Not on the Altar," *U.S. Catholic* (August 2011).

42. For contrasting views, see David L. Leal, "Religion and the Political and Civic Lives of Latinos," in *Religion and Democracy in the United States: Danger or Opportunity?* ed. Alan Wolfe and Ira Katznelson, 308–352 (New York/Princeton: Russell Sage Foundation and Princeton University Press, 2010) and Michael Sean Winters, "The First Pilgrims," *New Republic* (April 12, 2012). See also Archbishop José Gomez, "Immigration and the 'Next America,'" address delivered at the Napa Institute, July 28, 2011, available at http://www.zenit.org/article-33462?l=english, Catherine E. Wilson, *The Politics of Latino Faith: Religion, Identity, and Urban Community* (New York: New York University Press, 2008), and Jane Junn, Tali Mendelberg, and Erica Czaja, "Race and the Group Bases of Public Opinion," in *New Directions in Public Opinion*, ed. Adam J. Berinsky, 119–138 (New York: Routledge, 2012). For the demographics, see Susan Saulny, "U.S. Birthrate Dips as Hispanic Pregnancies Fall," *New York Times* (December 31, 2012); for the changes in attitudes, see Celinda Lake, Michael Adams, and David Mermin, "New Voters, New Values," *American Prospect* 24 (January–February 2013), 38–43.

CONJECTURE

1. Tacitus, *The Annals of Imperial Rome*, trans. Michael Grant (London: Penguin, 1989), 150.

2. See Garry Wills, "The Council We Are Still Living," *National Catholic Reporter* (October 4, 2002), http://natcath.org/NCR_Online/archives2/2002d/100402/100402a.htm.

3. See Stephanie Coontz, *The Way We Never Were: American Families and the Nostalgia Trap* (New York: Basic Books, 1992) and Patrick H. McNamara, *A Catholic Cold War: Edmund A. Walsh, SJ, and the Politics of American Anticommunism* (New York: Fordham University Press, 2005).

4. Catholics Come Home, a campaign founded by the layman Tom Peterson and endorsed by many bishops, has been working since the early 2000s to bring back defectors.

5. For a more hopeful view, see Clare Malone, "Holy Rollers," *American Prospect* 23 (September–October 2012), 7–11. Compare Kathleen M. Blee, *Democracy in the Making: How Activist Groups Form* (New York: Oxford University Press, 2012).

6. Though far from all, as the common history of the diaspora and the persistence of Yiddish as a lingua franca indicate. I am indebted to discussions with Alan Greenberg on this point.

7. Compare Karen Barkey, *Empire of Difference: The Ottomans in Comparative Perspective* (Cambridge: Cambridge University Press, 2008) and John Darwin, *The Empire Project: The Rise and Fall of the British World-System, 1830–1970* (Cambridge: Cambridge University Press, 2009). I am grateful to Kiren Aziz Chaudhry for guidance about Ottoman history.

8. Giancarlo Casale, *The Ottoman Age of Exploration* (New York: Oxford University Press, 2010).

9. See Christine M. Philliou, *Biography of an Empire: Governing Ottomans in an Age of Revolution* (Berkeley: University of California Press, 2011) and Halil Inalcik, *The Ottoman Empire: The Classical Age, 1300–1600* (New York: Praeger, 1973).

10. Kemal H. Karat, *The Politicization of Islam: Reconstructing Identity, State, Faith and Community in the Late Ottoman State* (New York: Oxford University Press, 2001).

11. A major difference is that the Ottomans lost much of their population and territory, especially during the nineteenth century, because they were defeated in a succession of wars, whereas the number of Catholics worldwide has been growing. The closest approximation the church has to population loss is the erosion of clerical control over ministries.

12. Erik Jan Zurcher, *Political Opposition in the Early Turkish Republic: The Progressive Republican Party, 1924–1925* (Leiden: E. J. Brill, 1991).

13. See Erik Jan Zürcher, *The Young Turk Legacy and Nation Building: From the Ottoman Empire to Atatürk's Turkey* (London: I. B. Taurus, 2010), especially 55–150, and Handan Nezir Akmese, *The Birth of Modern Turkey: The Ottoman Military and the March to World War I* (London: I. B. Taurus, 2005). Compare Dexter Filkins, "Letter from Turkey: The Deep State," *New Yorker* (March 12, 2012) and Ellen Kay Trimberger, *Revolution from Above: Military Bureaucrats and Development in Japan, Turkey, Egypt, and Peru* (New Brunswick, NJ: Transaction, 1978).

14. Compare Bernardo Sorj, "Transgressive Individualism and Public Institutions: The Democratization of Oligarchic Culture in Latin America," working paper 7, November 2012, Edelstein Center for Social Research, www.centroedelstein.org.bra/english, and Hugh Eakin, "Will Saudi Arabia Ever Change?" *New York Review of Books* (January 10, 2013), 37–39, http://www.nybooks.com/articles/archives/2013/jan/10/will-saudi-arabia-ever-change/?pagination=false&printpage=true.

15. See David Brion Davis, *In the Image of God: Religion, Moral Values, and Our Heritage of Slavery* (New Haven: Yale University Press, 2001).

16. David Brion Davis, *Inhuman Bondage: The Rise and Fall of Slavery in the New World* (New York: Oxford University Press, 2006), Michael O'Brien, *The Idea of the American South, 1920–1941* (Baltimore: Johns Hopkins University Press, 1979), and Alexander Tsesis, *For Liberty and Equality: The Life and Times of the Declaration of Independence* (New York: Oxford University Press, 2012). An example closer to home is the rejection of the church's historic anti-Semitism, promulgated at Vatican II; see John Connelly, *From Enemy to Brother: The Revolution in Catholic Teaching on the Jews* (Cambridge: Harvard University Press, 2012), Connelly, "Nazi Racism and

the Church," *Commonweal* (February 24, 2012), and more generally John T. NoonanJr., *A Church That Can and Cannot Change: The Development of Catholic Moral Teaching* (Notre Dame, IN: University of Notre Dame Press, 2005).

17. John Pierce, supervisor of the Bell Labs team that built the first transistor, quoted by John Gartner, *The Idea Factory* (New York: Penguin, 2012), 204.

18. Compare Conrad Hacker and Brian J. Grim, *The Global Religious Landscape* (Washington, DC: Pew Forum on Religion AND Public Life, December 2012), http://www.pewforum.org/global-religious-landscape.aspx.

19. Compare Fritz Stern, *The Failure of Illiberalism: Essays on the Political Culture of Modern Germany* (New York: Alfred A. Knopf, 1971) and Arno Mayer, *The Persistence of the Old Regime: Europe to the Great War* (New York: Pantheon, 1981).

20. See Michael Novak, *The Catholic Ethic and the Spirit of Capitalism* (New York: Free Press, 1993) and Carl Anderson, *Beyond a House Divided: The Moral Consensus Ignored by Washington, Wall Street, and the Media* (New York: Doubleday Image, 2010).

21. A good example of such coalition building is the coordination between Pennsylvania's tax credit legislation and the creation of the Faith in the Future Foundation by the archdiocese to manage the church's high school in Philadelphia under lay supervision. See Jeremy Roebuck, "Philadelphia Archdiocese School Manager Sets Growth Goal," *Philadelphia Inquirer* (September 13, 2012).

22. For a fresh look at the latter heritage, see Nicholas P. Miller, *The Religious Roots of the First Amendment: Dissenting Protestants and the Separation of Church and State* (New York: Oxford University Press, 2012). One of the most thorough treatments of the school crisis generally, by Greg J. Duncan and Richard J. Murnane, eds., *Whither Opportunity? Rising Inequality, Schools, and Children's Life Chances* (New York: Russell Sage Foundation, 2011), has a chapter on charter schools but no discussion of vouchers or tax credits.

23. See Robert A. Dahl, *How Democratic Is the American Constitution?* 2nd ed. (New Haven: Yale University Press, 2003) and Sanford Levinson, *Framed: America's Fifty-One Constitutions and the Crisis of Government* (New York: Oxford University Press, 2012). For a glimpse at contending views based on a myriad of constitutional principles and meat-and-potato considerations, see the letters to the editor entitled "Can the Catholic Schools Be Saved?" *New York Times* (January 13, 2013), http://www.nytimes.com/2013/01/14/opinion/can-the-catholic-schools-be-saved.html.

24. Patrik Johnsson, "Judge Blocks Gov. Bobby Jindal's Signature School Voucher Program," *Christian Science Monitor* (December 1, 2012) and Motoko Rich, "Enrollment in Charter Schools Is Increasing," *New York Times* (November 14, 2012). See also Evan Halper, "Reforming California: Easier Said than Done," *Los Angeles Times* (November 25, 2012) and Thomas J. Healey, John Eriksen, and B.J. Cassin, "All Hands on Desks: A Call for Catholic Mobilization to Finance Our Schools," *America* (February 4, 2013).

25. The travails of the European Union are a case in point. See Neil Walker, Jo Shaw, and Stephen Tierney, eds., *Europe's Constitutional Mosaic* (Oxford: Hart, 2011).

26. Matt Flegenheimer, "Gifts for Dolan at First Sunday Mass since News of Elevation," *New York Times* (January 8, 2012), Laurie Goodstein, "A Comedian and a Cardinal Open Up on Spirituality," *New York Times* (September 15, 2012), and Nicole Santa Cruz, "Orange County

Catholics Welcome New Bishop, Kevin W. Vann," *Los Angeles Times* (December 11, 2012). The salt-of-the-earth shtick is well established. See John Cardinal O'Connor and Edward I. Koch, *His Eminence and Hizzoner: A Candid Exchange* (New York: William Morrow, 1989).

27. See David Brion Davis, "The Universal Attractions of Slavery," *New York Review of Books* (December 17, 2009), Davis, "Honor Thy Honor," *New York Review of Books* (October 27, 2011), and the exchange between Davis and Barbara L. Solow, "The British & the Slave Trade," *New York Review of Books* (January 12, 2012).

28. Henninger, "Obama's Ruinous Course," *Wall Street Journal* (December 5, 2012).

29. See Matt Flegenheimer, "'Carlin Street' Resisted by his Old Church. Was It Something He Said?" *New York Times* (October 25, 2011) and James Heffernan, "Woolf's Reading of Joyce's *Ulysses*, 1918–1920," Modernism Lab at Yale University, 2010, http://modernism.research.yale.edu/wiki/index.php?title=Woolf%27s_Reading_of_Joyce%27s_Ulysses,_1918-1920&printable=yes.

30 The reference is to Roy Bourgeois, the Maryknoll advocate for women's ordination. In November 2012, "disobedience and preaching against the teaching of the Catholic Church about women's ordination led to his excommunication, dismissal, and laicization." Joshua L. McElwee, "Maryknoll: Vatican Has Dismissed Roy Bourgeois from Order," *National Catholic Reporter* (November 19, 2012). See also the editorial beginning "The Call to the Priesthood is a Gift from God," *National Catholic Reporter* (December 3, 2012).

INDEX